The Green Pharmacy

anti-ageing

prescriptions

The Green Pharmacy

anti-ageing prescriptions

Herbs, foods & natural formulas to keep you young

DR JAMES A. DUKE

with MICHAEL CASTLEMAN

RODALE

This edition first published in the UK in 2005 by
Rodale International Ltd
7–10 Chandos Street
London W1G 9AD
www.rodalestore.co.uk

Cover design by Button One to One
Cover photograph from Photodisc
Interior design by Emma Ashby

Printed and bound by Rotolito Lombarda S.p.A

A CIP record for this book is available from the British Library
ISBN 1–57954–975–6
ISBN 978–1–57954–975–6

1 3 5 7 9 8 6 4 2

To all those who respect ecology more than economics;

To all those who would forego a factory for a forest;

And to all those who prefer the holy green in the hollow
to the hollow green of the dollar.

RODALE

WE INSPIRE AND ENABLE PEOPLE TO IMPROVE
THEIR LIVES AND THE WORLD AROUND THEM

Notice

This book is intended as a reference volume only, not as a medical manual. The information given here is designed to help you make informed decisions about your health. It is not intended as a substitute for any treatment that may have been prescribed by your doctor. If you suspect that you have a medical problem, we urge you to seek competent medical help.

You should consult your doctor or a practitioner with expertise in herbs before treating yourself with herbs or combining them with any medications. Women who are pregnant or who are considering becoming pregnant should not use herbs or other medications without seeking the approval of their doctors.

Beginning on page 515, you will find safe use guidelines for supplements, herbs, and essential oils recommended in this book that will help you use these remedies safely and wisely.

Mention of specific companies, organisations, or authorities in this book does not imply endorsement by the publisher, nor does mention of specific companies, organisations, or authorities in the book imply that they endorse the book.

Internet addresses and telephone numbers given in this book were accurate at the time this book went to press.

A Note on Doses and Tinctures

All suggested doses in this book are for an average adult, unless a specific condition is stated. For baby doses it is vital that you consult a professional practitioner.

Doses

1 teaspoon = 5 ml = 80 drops
0.5 teaspoon = 2.5 ml
1 cup = 240 ml = 8 fl oz

3–7 years = quarter adult dose
7–12 years = half adult dose
Children 12 years or more can be treated as adults as long as they are over 44.5 kg (7 stone/98 lb)

Tinctures

Tinctures vary in strength from 1:1 to 1:5, but 1:2 and 1:3 are the most common.
1:1 tinctures are the strongest, being the same strength as liquid extract.
The tincture doses given refer to 1:2 or 1:3 strength.

Background Information

Please note that the suggested doses given are Dr Duke's own recommendation or in the case of 'the usual' herbal recommendation, the suggested dose in the United Kingdom. In 1995 the European Union spent the equivalent of £4 billion on plant-based pharmaceuticals. This has prompted the preparation of the Directive on Traditional Herbal Medicine Products to regulate over-the-counter herbal products. The first draft of this directive was published in 2002. Discussions involved the Medicines Control Agency (MCA), the European Herbal Practitioners Association (EHPA) and the British Herbal Medicine Association (BHMA). Several bodies are working together on the directive. They can be found as follows:

The Department of Health (DoH), who have formed the DoH Herbal Medicines Regulatory Working Group: *www.doh.gov.uk/herbalmedicinerwg/index.htm*
The Prince of Wales's Foundation for Integrated Health (POWFIH): *www.fihealth.org*
The European Herbal Practitioners Association (EHPA): *www.euroherb.com*
The Medicines Control Agency (MCA): *www.mca.gov.uk*

Acknowledgements

I extend my gratitude to those who helped create the Green Farmacy Garden, my very own Garden of Youth: my wife, Peggy; landscaper John Snitzer and biologist Kerrie Kyde; and the inspiration of YinYang Yuan, Andrea Ottesen.

I thank Michael Castleman, who helped turn my thoughts into poetic prose, and my daughter, Celia Duke Larsen, for providing the gardening tips that appear throughout the book. I'm also grateful to everyone at Rodale Inc., past and present, who in some way contributed to the conception, development, and promotion of this book: Hugh O'Neill, Ed Claflin, Tammerly Booth, Susan Berg, Darlene Schneck, Christina Gaugler, Lynn Gano, Karen Neely, Carol Gilmore, Dorothy West, Cathy Strouse, Karen Arbegast, Denyse Corelli, Laura Herzog Kaplus, Cindy Ratzlaff, Mary Lengle, Tom Mulderick, and Peter Igoe.

Thanks also to my behind-the-scenes electronic right-hand women, Judi DuCellier and Mary Jo Bogenschutz-Godwin, and to those who helped build the second-best phytochemical database upon which I drew consistently: Stephen Beckstrom-Sternberg, Ed Bird, Leigh Broadhurst, Jimmie Mowder, and Allan Stoner.

Last and most, thanks to all those workers and volunteers who have shared in the pleasures and pains of the Green Farmacy Garden, including Alex, Ellen, and Holly, and the great gang of Abigail, Edwin, Nelson, Otto, Rigo, and Santos.

Contents

Part Three

Fighting the Enemies That Age You

INTRODUCTION

Growing Younger *in the* Garden *of* Youth

Welcome! In the pages that follow, you're going to discover what you can do to slow the ageing process and preserve your youthful vigour and vitality. Much of what I suggest comes from my experience in studying and using medicinal plants. So often we blame Nature for making us older, when in fact she offers a marvellous bounty of herbs and foods that help us stay young.

This book was inspired by my Green Farmacy Garden, which I fancy as my very own Garden of Youth. It's 740 square metres (8,000 square feet) of herbs organised into 80 plots, each plot devoted to a specific condition that becomes more common with age – or that just makes you feel old before your time. I refer to my garden so often that you'll probably know every bit of it by the time you're finished reading.

I've been working with medicinal plants in some capacity for the better part of my 72 years. To season my mostly plant-based diet, I use herbs. To protect myself from disease, I use herbs. To extend my life span – and to fill those extra years with vibrant health – I use herbs.

I do take conventional pharmaceuticals now and then. Not too often, though. Herbs are the medicines that I prefer, and they're pretty much the only ones that I need. Of course, everyone is different; I can't promise that what works for me will work for you. But I think you'll discover that herbs offer a great deal to those of us who want to protect our youth and forestall the ravages of the ageing process.

While I've written quite a few books in my lifetime, this one may be the most personal. It's not only rooted in medicinal plants but also firmly grounded in my Garden of Youth, my sanctuary on this earth. Working the soil and tending my plants provide me with plenty of exercise. They help me to mellow out when I feel stressed. They put me in touch with nature and the healing spirit of her plants. As you can see, all the elements of a long, healthy, happy life take me back to my garden, the Garden of Youth.

So come with me. Walk down the hillside to my garden and dig your toes into the rich, warm earth. Inhale the sweet fragrances, absorb the vibrant colours, experience the textures. Together we'll work the soil, sow seeds, weed, water, and spread compost. Together we'll watch the herbs grow. Together we'll discover their secrets for keeping us healthy and young.

Before we venture into the Garden of Youth, I hope that you'll indulge my inner poet by allowing me to share this tribute to my backyard muse:

I come to the Garden alone
While the dew is still on the primrose.
And the air I share, as I tarry there,
Health and perfume drift to my nose.
And I drink to thee in my herbal tea;
There's therapy in this greenery.
And the peace I share as I ponder there
A peace not everyone knows.

I hope that you'll enjoy my Garden of Youth and embrace its health-preserving, life-affirming medicinal plants. Through them, nature will reveal its secrets of lasting, vital youth.

How to Use This Book

If you have a particular health concern that you'd like to address, you may wish to turn directly to the relevant chapters. That's fine. But I would encourage you to go back and read through the introductory chapters (part 1) when you have a chance. They tell you a bit more about me and my Garden of Youth. They'll also introduce you to my SEVENTY anti-ageing principles and my Healthy Sevens eating plan, which I feel are important components of a health-promoting, youth-preserving lifestyle. Both are mentioned throughout the book.

Some conditions that I discuss in part 2 are mentioned in part 3 as well. That's because part 2 focuses on preventive measures, while part 3 deals with treatments. Sometimes the same herbs and foods that protect against a particular ailment also help to heal it. So you may notice some overlap between the two sections of the book.

As you flip through the pages, you'll come across a special feature called Dr Duke's Anti-Ageing Elixirs. These recipes are made from unique combinations of the healing ingredients (herbs and foods) recommended for specific conditions. Many of the recipes are for teas, but some are for soups, salads, smoothies – even shampoo. I've tried to keep them simple so that everyone can take advantage of their potent anti-ageing potential.

One final note: much of the information presented in the pages that follow is based on my own experience studying and sampling healing herbs and foods. I cannot guarantee that you'll get the same results from the medicinal plants that I suggest. Experiment to see what works for you. If you have persistent symptoms, or if you're already taking a prescription medication, I strongly recommend that you consult your doctor before you begin using medicinal herbs.

PART ONE

Bountiful Benefits *from the* Garden *of* Youth

CHAPTER 1

Cultivating *the* Promise *of* Lifelong Youth

At the ripe young age of 72, after a career as a botanist with the United States Department of Agriculture (USDA) – much of it spent as chief of the Medicinal Plant Resources Laboratory – I have finally created my very own fountain of youth. Not a fountain, really, but a garden.

Originally, as I planned it, I called it the Green Farmacy Garden after a book I'd written, *The Green Pharmacy*. At the time, the play on words – *farmacy* – seemed fitting. My garden is a farm, actually a 2.4-hectare (6-acre) farmette on a sunny hillside bordering a tree-lined brook in rural Fulton, Maryland. It's also a pharmacy, consisting of 80 plots of medicinal plants arranged along four stone-walled terraces.

In the process of writing this book, I began to envision my garden as a Garden of Youth. The name applies for two reasons: working in the garden helps keep me young, and the herbs growing there help to prevent or treat many conditions associated with ageing.

In many ways, gardening itself helps slow – and sometimes even reverse – the ageing process. It's good exercise, building strength, flexibility, and stamina. It's relaxing. It's an antidepressant. It provides plenty of fresh air (plants release oxygen) and sunshine (but be careful not to get too much). And it involves communion with nature and my favourite plants, the medicinal herbs, which I've found to always be good for the spirit.

Born to Garden

Being a botanist, I've gardened almost my entire life. I inherited the interest and gift from my grandmother and mother back in Alabama, where I was born, and in North Carolina, where I spent most of my youth.

Just as it takes many years of adulthood to appreciate the gift of youth, it has taken me quite a few years, almost 30, to develop my Garden of Youth. That's longer than my wife, Peggy, and I have lived anywhere else. We bought our farm in 1972 from a man who kept sheep and cattle on the property. We inherited a sturdy barn, where he kept his livestock, and a very well fertilized hillside, where he grazed them.

Thirty years later, we're still enjoying the benefits of that natural fertilizer. I grow some of the tallest feverfews (for preventing migraines), mulleins (for soothing coughs and sore throats), and valerians (for easing insomnia) that I have ever seen. The sheep and cattle had badly damaged the forest half of the property. Thankfully, it bounced back and is thriving.

Visions of a Vineyard

When Peggy and I bought our farm, my work for the USDA focused on isolating cancer-fighting compounds from plants around the world. Our botanists collected plants for analysis by the chemists at the National Cancer Institute. We collected and they analysed thousands of plants – in fact, 10 per cent of the plants on earth. It was a huge job, and it took me around the world several times.

I loved the travel; I still do. But while I was at home, I got a notion to grow grapes organically and make my own juices, like my grandparents did back in Alabama. So I christened the farm the Herbal Vineyard and planted my vines. Unfortunately, I failed miserably at my attempt to grow grapes organically, despite planting them side by side with aromatic herbs – mostly mints, which help repel insects. (Mints also aid digestion, which is why after-dinner mints are so popular.)

Unfortunately, I chose to use the newfangled grape hybrids. They were pesticide dependent and quickly succumbed to the diseases that often attack high-tech plants in a low-tech environment. So I gave up on grapes and dropped the name Herbal Vineyard.

But now that I've reinvented the place as the Garden of Youth, I think I'll try some heirloom grapes – the kind my grandmother grew with no pesticides at all – and low-maintenance grapes that retain their natural pest repellents. I'll also grow varieties such as 'Concord', 'fox', and 'Niagara' – which, by the way, contain compounds that may work like the erectile dysfunction drug sildenafil (Viagra).

To me, few things in life are more refreshing and rejuvenating than spending a crisp autumn day eating grapes right off the vine, taking in all of their antioxidants that may help prevent heart disease, cancer, Alzheimer's disease, cataracts, and other ailments of ageing. The experts say that red wine is the way to go, but the research I've reviewed suggests that red grapes and grape juice are as effective, or nearly so.

Planting for All Seasons

After I gave up on grapes, I began referring to the forested area of my farm as Phenology Valley. Phenology is the study of the timing of plant and animal life. I've always been partial to flowers. Different flowers bloom in every season, obeying their own natural timing, or phenology.

Over the years, I've planted things all around our property – on the hillside, in the woodland, down by the bog, by the brook, and out by the barn. That way, something is flowering every month of the year. In October, there's witch hazel, a marvellous astringent that soothes haemorrhoids and helps treat the skin and mouth inflammations that plague old folks like me if we don't take our herbs. It's followed a few months later by the winter-blooming Christmas rose, an age-old folk remedy for ageing kidneys, head colds, and even menstrual problems. And, of course, there are lots of spring, summer, and fall flowers.

Most exciting to me are the flowers that herald the return of spring, especially the crocuses, which help stimulate digestion. They usually emerge in early February and they're quickly followed by the march of spring wildflowers – many medicinal, some edible, and all making oxygen.

During the farm's Phenology Valley years, I took particular pleasure in the differences between the plants on the north-facing slope and those on the south-facing slope. The warmer, sunnier south-facing slope brought forth its flowers and fruits about 2 weeks earlier than the cooler, shadier north-facing slope.

Over the years, I established a fern-lined path along each side of the spring-fed brook that runs through our property. Even most herbalists don't consider ferns medicinal, but several of the plants are. Native Americans used rattlesnake fern to treat tuberculosis and Christmas fern for fever, indigestion, and muscle and joint aches and pains.

The brook has never run dry in our nearly three decades of living here. So for a time, I went crazy for ferns: cinnamon ferns, ostrich ferns, royal ferns, and shield ferns, among others. In fact, I had so many I toyed with the idea of changing Phenology Valley to Fern-ology Valley, like the Fern Valley at the USDA's National Arboretum in Washington, D.C.

A New View of the Valley

Then a good friend and avid gardener, Andrea Ottesen, brought me my first yinyanghuo, a shade-tolerant herb that did very well on the north side of Phenology Valley. Andrea started something with that plant. I thought that *yinyanghuo* meant male/female herb, but a Chinese colleague corrected me. It actually means 'horny goat weed'. The plant is reputed to have aphrodisiac powers.

Aphrodisiacs have always been an interest of mine, both botanically and personally. I found myself planting quite a few species and varieties of yingyanghuo, and I now have quite a collection.

I'm still undecided about yinyanghuo's sex-stimulating action. One Japanese colleague of mine swears by it. But he may be susceptible to the placebo effect (that is, he thinks the herb works, so it does). I keep trying to persuade my colleagues in the chemical industry to analyse yinyanghuo's ability to inhibit the activity of a form of the compound phosphodiesterase-5. This is what the erectile dysfunction drug Viagra does. I suspect yinyanghuo may have a similar effect.

Yinyanghuo got me thinking about the yin and yang of Chinese philosophy and herbal medicine. I don't claim to be an expert, but as I understand it, the Chinese believe that the oneness of the universe is divided into two opposite but complementary forces: yin and yang. Yin is female and cool, the shady side of my valley. Yang is male and warm, the sunny side. Inspired by the proliferation of my horny goat weed and by my travels to China, where I obtained some of the ginseng that grows in the woodland above the brook, I began referring to the woodland behind my garden as YinYang Valley.

The name naturally led me to a greater appreciation of the yin and yang of various herbs. For example, one beautiful spring day, I found two plants – a wild yam and a sarsaparilla, the former presumably yin, the latter yang – growing intertwined in a forest near my home. Wild yam vine is the original source of the steroids used in the first birth control pills. Sarsaparilla contains sarsapogenin, which can be converted into testosterone.

I went for a big shovel, dug up both plants at once, and planted them back home. Later, I added more plants, so I now have wild yam vine and sarsaparilla growing on either side of an arched trellis at the entrance to the woodland below the Garden of Youth. Having the two plants intertwined on the trellis in symbolic union of yin and yang, male and female, seems fitting for YinYang Valley and for the Garden of Youth. After all, sex is a great activity for staying young at heart.

Laying the Foundation

When I retired in 1995, I figured that I should take my USDA Medicinal Plant Laboratory back home with me, at least spiritually. I'd gardened my farm for years, introducing many medicinal herbs, but I'd never been all that organised about it. With more time on my hands, I began dreaming of a big garden filled with all the medicinal herbs that I could grow in rural Maryland.

But I hesitated because for several years, I'd been deeply involved in a medicinal herb garden in the Peruvian Amazon – the ReNuPeru garden, maintained by the Amazon Center for Environmental Education and Research (ACEER). This nonprofit organisation runs workshops on rainforest plant conservation, and I teach some on medicinal rainforest plants.

Botanically, the Amazon is an amazing place – the most diverse, least understood forest on earth. ACEER has strung hanging walkways among the trees, allowing groups of visitors to examine the rainforest close-up. The experience is intense, not just because of the challenges of surviving in the Amazon but also because of the profusion of life there.

In Maryland, I have about six woody plant species per hectare (2.47 acres). ACEER's ReNuPeru garden has 300 species per hectare. Perhaps, I thought, I should put my energy into my work in the Amazon and let go of my dream of a big herb garden at home.

Eventually, I realised that I couldn't keep commuting to the Amazon forever, as much as I enjoy my work there. So I decided to start my own medicinal garden right here, on my farm.

I asked landscapers John Snitzer and his wife, Kerrie Kyde, to help me design and build my garden. It turned out to be a much bigger project than any of us had imagined. Just planning the garden took several months. Clearing the brush from the hillside and laying out the beds took several more months. Then we spent the better part of a year pulling up stumps and rocks, rough-grading the terraces with a couple of tractors, and building the walls, which took 26 tons of stone from a nearby quarry.

When the heavy lifting was done, we had four rock-walled terrace beds 3 m x 60 m (10 ft x 200 ft) long – 743 square metres (8,000 sq ft) in all – plus a gazebo and a lovely rock-bordered pond cut into the sunny yang hillside above the tree-lined brook at the bottom of YinYang Valley. We worked for the better part of another year making the beds organic, which involved hand-pulling established weeds, covering the beds with black plastic sheeting to absorb sunlight to heat-kill weed seeds, and repeated tilling.

Finally, in 1998, my garden was complete. John and Kerrie presented me with a big dedication stone engraved with these words: 'Green Farmacy Garden, Jim and Peggy Duke, Established 1998.' It's also decorated with an etching of one of my favourite herbs, the evening primrose, from a drawing by my wife, Peggy, an artist with a true gift for botanical illustration. The stone now sits at the head of my garden, just a short stroll down the path from my back deck.

Smaller stones pepper the four terraces, each stone inscribed with the name of a condition that nearby herbs can prevent or treat. I love the stones. They're informative and elegant, and they lend an aura of permanence to my garden that tickles me.

Some herbs benefit several conditions. Garlic, for example, is a potent antibiotic that also reduces cholesterol and blood pressure and helps prevent and treat heart disease. I plant garlic and other multipurpose herbs in the appropriate bed for every condition they help. It feels right, and it ensures that I always have on hand lots of garlic, which I love. My cholesterol and blood pressure are fine, and I attribute my good fortune to the 'four Gs': genes, gardening (which I consider exercise), garlic, and greens.

Growing in the Garden of Youth

My garden contains plants for conditions that can occur at any time of life, from infancy to old age. But most of the plots are devoted to ailments that most commonly affect older folks.

In the top terrace are herbs for Alzheimer's disease, prostate enlargement, dizziness, hyperthyroidism, menopause, osteoporosis, glaucoma, and ulcers. The second terrace contains herbs for cancer prevention and treatment, heartburn, heart disease, high blood pressure, diabetes, obesity, depression, fibromyalgia, and insomnia.

Terrace number three has herbs for a number of ailments, including allergies, arthritis, gout, asthma, bronchitis, bursitis and tendinitis, urinary tract infection, irritable bowel syndrome, colitis, laryngitis, sinus infection, vaginitis, yeast infection, constipation, diarrhoea, indigestion, and gallstones. In the fourth terrace, I grow herbs for burns, cuts and bruises, ear problems, fever, colds and flu, and herpes, as well as herbs that stimulate the immune system.

Below the fourth terrace is the pond, which accommodates a few aquatic medicinals. Water lotus, for example, is used by the Chinese to promote circulation and strengthen vitality against the infirmities of old age.

Beyond the pond is the path that leads through the yin-yang trellis into the woodland and bog. I've deliberately kept these areas wild, because that's the nature of bogs and woods. Plus, they provide a contrast with the more orderly terrace plots, which strikes me as poetically fitting in a yin-yang sort of way.

The woodland is where I grow my prized ginsengs. Every time I visit them (often to replace the pointed stakes the deer have knocked down), I feel younger. What a lucky old young man I am to have my hope and inspiration, my medicine chest and fountain of youth, all so conveniently located just a stone's throw from my home.

Reclaiming Youth through Nature

Most clear, warm days between April and October, I spend several hours outdoors pottering in my Garden of Youth and walking around the farm. I often walk two or three laps through YinYang Valley – and sometimes as many as seven – to see how all my friends, the plants, are doing. Over the years, I've blazed a network of trails so that one complete spin around the valley is just a tad over a mile.

I don't have to tell you that walking briskly is one of the best things that you can do to stay young at heart and youthful in body, mind, and soul. Moderate exercise like walking helps relieve stress, elevate mood, and improve sleep. It also helps prevent and treat arthritis, heart disease, diabetes, obesity, several types of cancer, and many other conditions.

Most folks have to walk close to automobile exhausts and far from nature. I consider myself lucky to live in a semirural area, far from cars and close to nature, in what I consider my temple – my garden and woods. I breathe the oxygen that my plant friends release and visit the animals that share my green temple.

When our children were young, we had a dog and too many other pets. Then the kids grew up, and the pets gradually disappeared. But we still have plenty of animals on the property: chipmunks chewing on everything from apples to yew berries, goldfinches munching on milk thistle seed, squirrels squirrelling away acorns and any other nuts they can find, terrapins feasting on mushrooms that would be poisonous to us humans, orioles gleaning bugs high in the tulip poplars (my dominant and biggest trees).

Unfortunately, there are also plenty of groundhogs tearing up my plantain and ever-pesky deer looking to make a meal of just about everything I plant. The deer love to eat my echinacea, the immune system stimulant that helps treat all manner of infectious diseases, and my ginseng, the herb revered by Asians as a youth promoter and life extender.

I tried to chase away the deer with all of the old home remedies, including soap and urine. None of them worked. The best thing I've found to protect my echinacea and ginseng is to surround the plants with a loose fence of sharp, pointed sticks. Before the deer can chomp on the plants, they get poked. Works pretty well – not perfectly, but pretty well.

Understand, I don't hate these animals. Eating gardens is how they survive. It's all part of nature's grand plan. Of course, if the deer and groundhogs have been particularly destructive, I get upset. But before the stress makes me feel like a grumpy old man, I remind myself that these animals actually help make the Garden of Youth even more medicinal.

You see, the healing compounds in most plants taste bitter, in part to ward off pests, which generally dislike things that taste bitter. So the deer tend to nibble on my least bitter herbs, the ones that aren't the most potent. The deer ignore the really bitter plants, which pack the most medicinal punch. So in a way, they're doing me a favour, pruning my

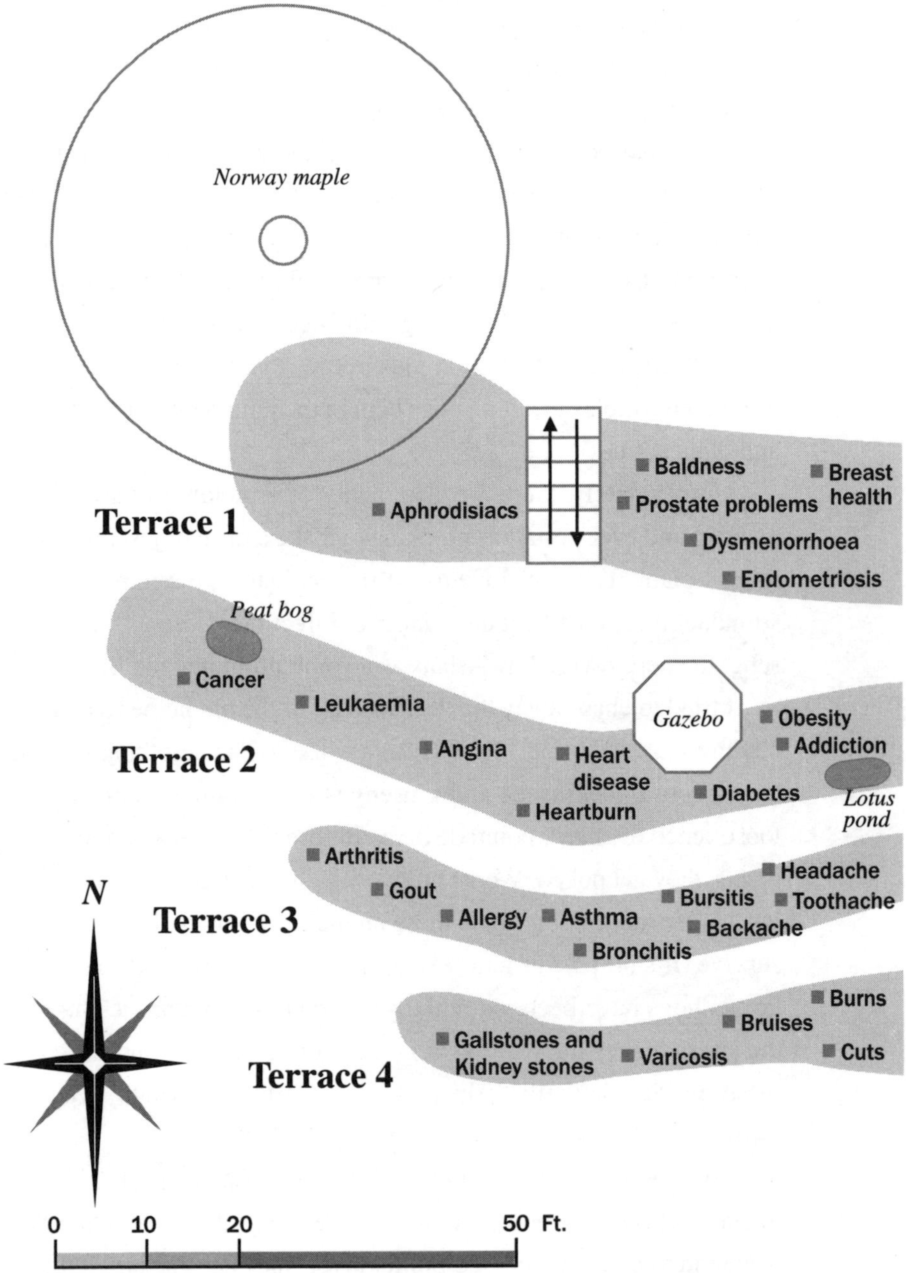
Norway maple
Terrace 1
Aphrodisiacs
Baldness
Prostate problems
Breast health
Dysmenorrhoea
Endometriosis
Peat bog
Cancer
Leukaemia
Terrace 2
Angina
Heart disease
Heartburn
Gazebo
Obesity
Addiction
Diabetes
Lotus pond
Arthritis
Gout
Terrace 3
Allergy
Asthma
Bronchitis
Bursitis
Backache
Headache
Toothache
N
Terrace 4
Gallstones and Kidney stones
Varicosis
Bruises
Burns
Cuts
0 10 20 50 Ft.

The Garden of Youth: A Bird's-Eye View

It took 3 years to design and build my Green Farmacy Garden, a.k.a. the Garden of Youth. I must say that I'm quite proud of the results. The garden covers some 743 square metres (8,000 square feet) and contains 80 plots of medicinal plants, each plot designated for a specific condition. I'm continually adding plants, as I learn more about their disease-fighting and age-defying properties. In fact, my garden keeps me busy for several hours a day during growing season, from spring through autumn.

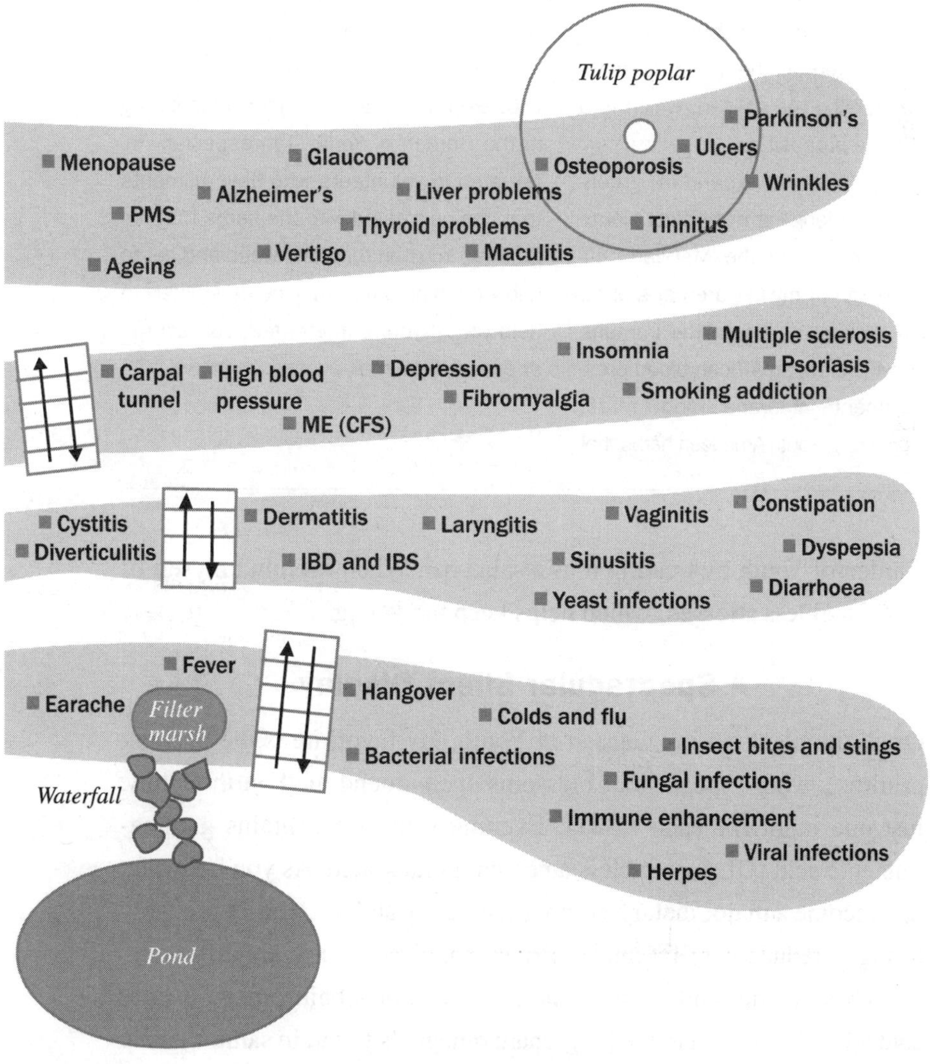

Making Gardening a Community Effort

I should mention that the Garden of Youth is not open to the general public. But I occasionally conduct half-day and daylong lecture tours by reservation for groups of up to 20 people. I don't like to do too many tours – travelling and lecturing already keep me pretty busy – so I set the price high enough to discourage all but the most herbally committed. All the money goes towards maintaining the garden, which is a very expensive proposition.

Eventually, I hope to expand my greenhouse to grow a long list of tropical plants not naturally suited to the Maryland climate. At the top of my list are cat's claw, which can be used to boost the immune system; devil's claw, an African blood pressure treatment; guarana and maté, caffeine-containing South American herbs that keep us from dozing; mukul, an Indian herb that lowers cholesterol; pygeum, an African herb that helps treat prostate enlargement; and yohimbe, a West African tree whose bark helps treat impotence, like a natural form of Viagra. If you would like to help add these plants to the Garden of Youth, please contact me at JimDuke@cpcug.org or JimDuke@allherb.com.

If you live in the greater Washington, D.C. area, you might consider volunteering in the Garden of Youth. I'm especially interested in volunteers who have ailments that can be treated with the herbs that I'm growing. You can tend and weed and get to know the plants that may be most likely to help you. If you're interested, contact me at one of the e-mail addresses above.

Garden of Youth by treating it as a salad bar. When I remind myself of this, I feel less stressed, which helps keep me young.

A Spectacular Silent Display

Of all the plants in my Garden of Youth, my favourite is the evening primrose, whose spectacular blossoms open around the Fourth of July, just one night for each flower. Evening primrose contains gamma-linolenic acid (GLA), which is an essential fatty acid. As you know, fat has become a major dietary no-no. Like Peggy and me, you're probably trying to reduce your fat intake. But essential fatty acids are different.

These compounds, which include the short-chain omega-3 fatty acids (they're related to the long-chain omega-3s found in salmon), help prevent the internal blood clots that trigger heart attacks. They also give the immune system a gentle boost. And there's some evidence that they help treat premenstrual syndrome, menstrual cramps, rheumatoid arthritis, and gout.

Evening primrose is not the only plant source of essential fatty acids, nor even the best. Borage oil and black currant oil contain more. But neither of these plants blooms with as much splendour as the charismatic evening primrose.

Just before dusk, none of the flowers is open. All you see are the unopened bud, the four green sepals (collectively called the calyx) that house the flower, and the four stigmas, yellow structures resembling the antennae of snails that stick out the top of the bud. At dusk, the sepals begin to move. Then suddenly, they flick out perpendicular to the flower stem, revealing the rounded bulge of the flower's dainty, butter yellow petals. The petals tremble as they emerge from their tight cocoon and splay out a good 2.5 cm (2 inches) across, radiant in the last light of day. Their unfolding takes about a minute, sometimes less.

Each flower opens for only one night. By morning, it starts withering and eventually dies. So it has only a few hours to send its pollen to fertilize other flowers. The pollen sits in clumps on long filaments that extend from the centre of the flowers. It's sticky and densely packed, so it can be picked up and transported by passing hawk moths.

The moths arrive just after dusk and hover over the flowers like miniature helicopters. There may be dozens, even hundreds, of flowers per plant. The moths want the nectar deep inside the flowers. As they dive in to drink, they emerge covered with pollen, then flit off to other flowers, fertilizing them.

For more than 20 years, I've found the blooming of the evening primrose breathtaking. As the years pass, my appreciation just keeps growing. I feel that I've become soul-bonded to the evening primrose, spiritually connected in the way that my shaman friend says he's connected to the plants of the Amazon.

CHAPTER 2

SEVENTY Secrets *for* Growing Youthful

Here I am, 72 – an age that seemed ancient when I was a boy. How times have changed. Nowadays, experts say that seventysomething isn't old. A person has to be at least 80 to be considered elderly. So the older I get, the older 'old' is. I like that.

Of course, being 72, I know I'm no longer a young whippersnapper. For example, sometimes I have trouble remembering things. That's normal. To compensate, I come up with little tricks to help jog my memory.

One of my favourite memory devices occurred to me shortly after my 70th birthday. Appropriately enough, it's the acronym SEVENTY, in which each letter stands for a key principle of a healthy, youth-promoting lifestyle.

- **S**ensible diet
- **E**xercise
- **V**itamins and other supplements
- **E**scaping stress
- **N**o-no's
- **T**ouch
- **Y**ou

I'm fortunate in that I'm able to apply many of these principles to my own lifestyle through my Garden of Youth. For example, my diet features many of the fruits, vegetables, and, of course, herbs that grow in the garden. And my exercise programme consists largely of digging around in the garden, plus frequent walks around YinYang Valley.

Even though you may not have a Garden of Youth in your own backyard, you can certainly incorporate the SEVENTY principles into your lifestyle. So let's take a look at each of these principles and how they help keep you young, no matter what your age.

S Is for Sensible Diet

Eating healthfully is so important that I've devoted an entire chapter to it (see chapter 3). I'm not suggesting that the other elements of SEVENTY are less important. On the contrary, every one of them is crucial to good health, well-being, and lifelong youth.

But had I stuffed all of the information on diet and nutrition into this chapter, it would have grown unwieldy, and the other topics would have got lost. So I decided to be flexible. After all, flexibility helps keep us young at any age.

I will tell you that I favour a near-vegetarian diet consisting primarily of plant-based foods, with just a few servings of meat a week. Based on all the research I've done, I'm convinced that this sort of diet provides the best mix of disease-fighting, anti-ageing nutrients. I've even come up with an eating plan that I call the Healthy Sevens, because it recommends that you eat seven kinds of food per day from each of a variety of plant-based food categories, including herbs and spices. I'll give you all the details in the next chapter.

E Is for Exercise

Next to a nutritious diet, frequent (ideally, daily) moderate exercise is probably the most important factor in slowing down the ageing process and living a long, youthful life. I consider myself an active person; I've been gardening and hiking for years. But I know that the older I get, the more valuable exercise becomes in keeping me healthy and young.

Sometimes when I'm writing or doing other desk work, I get so involved in the task at hand that I forget to stand up and move around. So I've placed an alarm clock by my computer and set it to ring about once an hour, reminding me that it's time for an exercise break. I get up, stretch for a few minutes, then walk around the garden or ride my stationary bike for about 10 minutes.

You probably already know that exercise is important to good health. It becomes even more important as you grow older. Unfortunately, as we age, we tend to be less and less active. We say things like, 'I'm too old for that now.' But the research is very clear: it's not the passage of years that brings on most of the infirmities of ageing. It's how we live our lives.

If you're sedentary or if you work out only occasionally, you're likely to be looking at chronic health problems and an early grave. I'm not exaggerating. Just consider all that exercise can do for you. Exercise:

- *Supports weight loss and weight maintenance*
- *Reduces your risk of cardiovascular disease, including high blood pressure, high cholesterol, heart disease, and stroke*
- *Helps prevent several types of cancer, including breast and colon cancers*
- *Makes you less prone to back problems*
- *Minimises the pain and stiffness of osteoarthritis*
- *Lowers your risk of diabetes*
- *Helps protect against osteoporosis*
- *Sharpens mental function, especially memory and*

reasoning ability
- *Helps fight depression and anxiety*
- *Enhances your immune system, which fends off all manner of illness*
- *Improves your quality of sleep*
- *Boosts libido and sexual function*
- *Increases self-confidence and feelings of well-being*

Think about this list for a moment. Every item in it is an issue for older people. That's why you ought to exercise. And you're never too old to start.

In one study, Harvard researchers worked with a group of 85-year-old residents at a Boston nursing home, none of whom had exercised in decades. The study participants were enrolled in a class that involved walking and weight lifting – nothing too strenuous, just enough to get their muscles moving and their blood pumping. It didn't take long for them to show gains in strength, stamina, and flexibility. Several people who had been using walkers were able to get rid of them.

If you haven't exercised in a while, I suggest striving for 7 minutes of physical activity up to seven times a day to start. Do different things, such as stretching, walking, and weight lifting (cans of food make good hand weights). Gradually work up to 45 minutes of continuous physical activity a day. If you notice any soreness, you're doing too much too soon. Slow down, but don't let the soreness stop you. Keep exercising every day.

Once you're working out regularly, the quality of your sleep should improve rather quickly. The other benefits take longer to develop. But within about 6 months, controlling your weight will seem easier. You'll have a greater sense of vitality and self-confidence, too.

What about aerobic exercise, the kind that makes you breathe faster and your heart pump harder? Personally, I think it has been oversold. You really don't need to join a gym and spend an hour on a stairclimber or in a cardio kickboxing class to reap the health benefits of exercise. If your goal is to stay young, a brisk walk every day is good enough.

If you work in an urban area, chances are that you're close to a park.

Use it. Go walking on your coffee break instead of running to the break room for a doughnut and coffee. In the long run, you'll add years to your life and life – and youth – to your years. Besides, you'll get out of that stressful office environment for a few precious minutes.

For myself, I prefer walking all around my farm. In bad weather, I stay inside and ride my stationary bike. I keep a pair of 8-pound dumbbells by my bike, so I can lift while I'm pedalling if I want to. And I'm constantly digging around in my Garden of Youth.

Most fitness experts don't say much about gardening, but it's really great exercise. It builds stamina, strength, and flexibility, the three components of overall fitness. Walking back and forth, toting tools, dragging the garden hose, hauling rubbish – all of these develop stamina. Likewise, the carrying and lifting increase strength, while the bending and squatting improve flexibility. Yes, gardening can provide quite a workout. Whenever I spend an hour or two toiling in my Garden of Youth, I feel younger.

Even if you don't have as much land as I do, you can take advantage of the benefits of gardening. Container gardening – growing plants in pots or window boxes, for example – can provide similar benefits. It also brings more fresh, youth-enhancing oxygen into your environment and enhances your outlook on life.

V Is for Vitamins and Other Supplements

Since very few of us get all of the nutrients we need from even a carefully planned diet, I suggest taking a daily multivitamin/mineral formula. Odds are that you're running a little low on one or more of the nutrients supplied by a good supplement.

For years, holistic and nutrition-minded physicians have said that taking a multivitamin should be as automatic as brushing your teeth. Mainstream medicine used to challenge this advice, saying that supplements do little more than create expensive urine. (This is a reference to the fact that the body excretes any amount of a nutrient that it can't use.) Fortunately, most mainstream doctors have come around to the view that supplements are helpful, even if you don't have a deficiency disease such as scurvy or beriberi. The big turnaround came in the early 1990s, when research showed that vitamin E could reduce heart attack risk by about 40 per cent. That impressed a lot of doctors.

The older you get, the more likely you are to be deficient in one or more of the essential nutrients. Even if you're only mildly deficient, you pay a hefty price in terms of premature ageing and increased risk of illness. For example, researchers at Johns Hopkins University in Baltimore gave 96 older people either an off-the-shelf multivitamin or a placebo (a fake pill). The study participants were also instructed to keep a health diary. Over the next year, the supplement takers recorded half as many 'sick days' as the placebo takers. What's more, blood tests showed that compared with the placebo group, the supplement group had enhanced immune function.

E Is for Escaping Stress

Give yourself a much-deserved break from undue pressures. There are many ways to do this. I like to take walks, spend time with my family and friends, play my guitar, and potter around in my Garden of Youth. You might prefer to meditate, listen to music, play with a pet, read poetry, or commune with the higher being of your choice.

However you choose to do it, make stress management a regular part of your life. It rejuvenates your body, mind, and spirit. It gives you a calming, youth-promoting perspective on life. It encourages you to make time for recreation, relaxation, and relationships. When you're feeling old, tired, and out of kilter, stress-management techniques can restore a sense of youth, energy, and balance.

N Is for No-No's

As you incorporate into your life all of the things that you can do to stay happy, healthy, and young for your years, don't forget to avoid the evils that are lying in wait to make you feel and look older than you are.

CIGARETTES. Avoid tobacco entirely. I say this as an ex-smoker who sucked down three packs a day for years. Back then, who knew? Soon after I learned how dangerous smoking is, I quit cold turkey. Today, there's absolutely no excuse for smoking – or for being around second-hand smoke, for that matter. Quitting is probably the single best thing that you can do to stay healthy and young.

And I'm not just talking about reducing your risk of lung cancer. Smoking increases your chances of developing heart disease and many other illnesses, as well as facial wrinkles that add years to your appearance. After I quit, my crow's-feet seemed to get smaller.

ALCOHOL. Limit yourself to one alcoholic drink a day if you're a woman, two if you're a man. (A drink is defined as 350 ml/12 fl oz of regular beer, 150 ml/5 fl oz of wine, or a cocktail made with 45 ml/1½ fl oz of spirits.) Compared with men, women carry a greater proportion of body tissue as fat, which doesn't metabolise alcohol as well as lean muscle. So more alcohol stays in their blood, and drink for drink, women feel the effects faster.

A little alcohol helps prevent heart disease by raising levels of good cholesterol (high-density lipoproteins, or HDLs). But consume too much, and you're courting trouble. Drinking excessively is associated with cirrhosis, sex problems, and an increased risk of several types of cancer, not to mention car crashes and other accidents. So be smart. Stay healthy and young by drinking only in moderation.

FAT AND CAFFEINE. Speaking of moderation, limit your consumption of dietary fat (especially red meat and dairy products) and caffeine. How much is too much? That's controversial, but personally, I'd suggest eating no more than five servings of meat a week. When my wife, Peggy, is here, I have four or five servings a week; when she's away, I cut back to one or two. I'd limit ice cream to a few scoops a week.

As for caffeine, I'd recommend drinking no more than three cups of coffee a day. This reduces your chances of caffeine jitters, a stressor that can wreak havoc on your body.

PESTICIDES. Avoid synthetic pesticide residues if possible. They cause damage at the cellular level, which means that they're a factor in the ageing process.

You can either grow your own food or buy organic if you can afford it. My daughter buys organic produce, and I tremble when I see what she pays for it. I confess that I don't buy organic, but I grow a good deal of my own vegetables. I've made it to the age of 72, so I figure I'm doing all right.

GENETICALLY ENGINEERED FOODS. These are my newest no-no's. The latest research shows that genetically engineered foods kill monarch butterflies. That makes me very nervous about what they're doing to us humans. I can't help thinking that the monarch butterfly is the proverbial canary in the coal mine when it comes to gene-altered foods, a harbinger of potential disaster to come. In Europe, they're passing laws against gene-altered foods. They might have the right idea.

SUN EXPOSURE. During the summer months, try to spend no more than 15 minutes a day in direct midday sun. I figure it's safe to get up to an hour of sun exposure early or late in the day, or anytime during the winter months. More than that, and you may be more likely to develop wrinkles, making you look old before your time, or even skin cancer.

NEGATIVE THINKING. Negative thinking can drag you down into anxiety and depression. That hurts your immune system, which, in turn, hurts your chances of ageing youthfully. Personally, I find that a nice walk around my YinYang Valley is a powerful antidote to any upsetting or unsettling thoughts. Nature has always been my temple of comfort.

PHARMACEUTICALS. Avoid medications if you can find safe herbal alternatives that are as effective or almost as effective. I'm mighty glad that herbal remedies have become more popular in recent years, as a growing number of doctors recommend echinacea for preventing colds, ginger for relieving travel sickness and morning sickness, and ginkgo for sharpening memory and treating Alzheimer's. But we still have a long way to go. Most doctors still view herbs as a last resort, to be tried only after pharmaceuticals haven't worked. That's backward. The best way to treat ailments and protect your health is to use herbs first and leave pharmaceuticals as your last resort.

Why? Mainly because drugs are dangerous. Most of us, even most doctors, don't know just how dangerous they can be. Drug companies know, but they're not talking.

Fortunately, a few studies published in prestigious medical journals such as the *Journal of the American Medical Association* reveal the shocking truth. One study found that pharmaceutical side effects kill 140,000 Americans a year and cost more than $136 billion annually. These numbers don't account for suicides and addictions, just side effects of prescribed medications in hospital patients. A subsequent study concluded that drug side effects kill 106,000 Americans a year and seriously injure 2.2 million more, making pharmaceutical side effects the nation's fifth leading cause of death.

By comparison, based on the statistics I've seen, medicinal herbs kill fewer than 50 people a year. Many of these deaths can be attributed to college kids foolishly taking Chinese ephedra (ma huang) as an intoxicant, not knowing that in very high doses – much higher than any responsible herbalist would recommend – this herb can cause potentially fatal heart problems.

To put the number of herb-related deaths in perspective, consider that about 100 people a year die from serious allergic reactions (anaphylactic reactions) to peanuts, shrimp, and other foods. That's twice the number of people who die from using medicinal herbs.

So pharmaceuticals kill more than 100,000 people a year, while herbs kill 50 at most. Yet open your newspaper or turn on your TV, and you'll see some pious 'expert' warning that herbs are dangerous. Now I believe that herbs must be used carefully by well-informed consumers, which is why I've written so much about them. But when you compare herbs and drugs head-to-head, it's very clear which one poses the real danger.

The other thing you often hear is that herbs are unresearched and unproven, while pharmaceuticals must be thoroughly tested for safety and effectiveness before they're put on the market. Yes, the FDA requires preapproval drug testing, but the process has more holes in it than ripe Swiss cheese.

In a 1990 report, the United States General Accounting Office, which is the investigative arm of Congress, took a hard look at the Food and Drug Administration (FDA) drug-approval process. The report revealed that after new medications are put on the market, more than half (51.5 per cent) turn out to cause serious side effects that were not known about at the time they were approved.

In other words, when you take pharmaceuticals, especially newly approved ones, you're playing Russian roulette. And which drugs are the most heavily advertised? Which ones are pushed on doctors, who, in turn, push them on you? The newest ones, whose side effects are least understood. Maybe that's part of the reason that Americans now make an estimated 425 million visits a year to alternative medicine practitioners, more than they make to all US primary-care doctors (386 million).

One of the main themes of this book is that when strong evidence supports the substitution of a medicinal herb for a pharmaceutical, you should choose the herb. That way, you reduce your likelihood of experiencing life-threatening, age-inducing side effects. Personally, I've not taken a prescription medication in more than 2 years, knock on wood.

In fact, for nearly a decade, I've bet my prostate gland that saw palmetto would provide as much relief from benign prostate enlargement as the first pharmaceutical approved to treat the condition – finasteride, sold under the brand name Proscar. Since then, several studies have shown that saw palmetto is indeed as effective as finasteride. And guess what? Saw palmetto has fewer side effects. It's the side effects that usually age us and too often kill us.

So take herbs first, and make pharmaceuticals your last resort. And tell your doctor that you're doing it. If enough people mention it to enough doctors often enough, maybe mainstream medicine will get its priorities straight.

I have reason to be optimistic that this day will come. Not long ago, I gave a presentation to the St. Louis Herb Society that was hosted by a woman whose husband is a respected allopathic (mainstream) doctor. But he's open to herbal remedies. He even keeps a copy of my book *The Green Pharmacy* in his office, along with other herb references. He hopes this might encourage his patients to openly discuss herbal therapy with him.

This is important, because doctors need to know when their patients are using herbs. Certain herbs can interact with pharmaceuticals – sometimes beneficially, sometimes harmfully.

T Is for Touch

To borrow a line from a phone company ad, reach out and touch someone – the people around you and the world around you. Look for love, which is rejuvenating. Avoid hatred, which, like all stresses, is ageing.

If you have a spouse, strive to maintain and nurture the intimacy of your relationship. Enjoy each other's company. Make love regularly. Make each other laugh. Strive for playfulness together.

If you don't have a spouse, cultivate close personal relationships. Connections to others are the spring from which the fountain of youth flows.

When I say relationships, I don't mean ties to just people. A loving relationship with a pet is very good for health, longevity, and youthfulness. Over the years, my family has had horses, goats, rabbits, cats, chickens, and a solitary mutt. Now I have the birds in the trees and the wildlife that calls my place home.

Connections to nature – for example, to vegetables you grow or flowers you tend – are also rejuvenating. Plant a garden. Call it what I call mine, the Garden of Youth. I don't mind if you use the name.

And always stay connected to your dreams, whatever they may be. Dream of the future, of what you hope to see and do and feel. Dream of the past, of friends and lovers long gone. Relationships don't end as long as you cherish them.

Y Is for You

Pamper yourself once in a while. If it means every so often breaking the rules you live by and bending your budget, that's all right. You deserve it. Get a massage or a manicure. Plan a weekend getaway at a bed-and-breakfast. Enjoy an occasional indulgence or two, as long as you do so in moderation.

Or try something new and different that surprises you and maybe your spouse and friends. Learn a new language. Take up ballroom dancing or scuba diving or rock climbing. Follow your curiosity.

Youth is a time of experimentation. As long as you're experimenting, growing, and challenging yourself, you're staying young.

CHAPTER 3

The Healthy Sevens: Foods *that* Fight Ageing

Getting older is supposed to make us wiser. At 72, I've certainly had my share of life experiences. I've been a husband (twice), father, grandfather, researcher, ecotour leader, lecturer, bureaucrat, beachcomber, country musician, jazz musician, gardener, teacher, world traveller, and writer. I don't know whether all this experience has given me much wisdom. But I can impart at least one bit of indisputable sagacity: green plants are where it's at.

Directly or indirectly, green plants generate probably 99 per cent of the earth's oxygen through a process called photosynthesis and contribute about 99 per cent of its food supply. (Some fungi and bacteria make their own food supply for energy, but they do it by recycling the products of photosynthetic plants.) Green plants also scrub pollution from the air. Without them, we – and the entire animal kingdom – could not exist.

Think about this the next time you look out your window. Every green plant you see is taking carbon dioxide from the atmosphere and transforming it into sugar (carbohydrates, for energy) and oxygen. These substances keep us humans alive. All of us are deeply indebted to our plant friends for our food, our oxygen, and 50 per cent of the world's medicines. But too few of us realise it.

Step into the Phyto-Pharmacy

Ironically, as scientists have learned over the past 15 or so years, the oxygen from green plants that's so vital to our existence also has the potential to harm us. In our bodies, some of it turns into renegade particles called free radicals, which can attack our tissues, our cells, and even our DNA. Most experts on ageing now agree that the damage produced by free radicals, called oxidative damage, is *the* major driving force in the ageing process. It's also the underlying cause of most of the diseases associated with ageing, including heart disease, stroke, and cancer – the top three causes of death.

Of course, green plants supply the oxygen that ultimately forms free radicals. But the plants themselves have little to do with generating those toxic bad boys. Most free radicals result from smoking and from eating a high-fat diet, one with lots of meat, dairy products, and junk foods. But we can easily protect our bodies from much of the oxidative damage caused by free radicals. We just need to eat more plant-derived foods.

Plant foods supply an array of vitamins, minerals, and phytochemicals – many of which are antioxidants. The antioxidant nutrients safeguard plants against the very oxygen that they produce. In us humans, these nutrients prevent and even reverse oxidative damage by neutralising free radicals.

Among the known antioxidants are vitamin C, vitamin E, and the mineral selenium; the carotenoids, including beta-carotene; the anthocyanidins, pigments that give plums, grapes, blueberries, cranberries, blackberries, and other dark fruits their colour; and coenzyme Q_{10}. The more plant foods you eat, the more antioxidants you get, and the healthier – and younger – you become.

Why Foods Are Better Than Supplements

Now you may be thinking, 'I don't have to eat so many plant foods, because I take an antioxidant supplement.' Well, I'm all for taking supplements, because as I mention in chapter 2, they're a good, cheap form of nutritional insurance. But supplements are no substitute for plant foods, and they can't undo the damage caused by an unhealthy diet.

To begin with, supplements can't match the fibre content of plants, and fibre is crucial to health, longevity, and youthfulness. What's more, supplements – even the ones that seem to contain every vitamin and mineral under the sun – don't come close to supplying the array of nutrients available in plant foods.

Take vitamin A, for example. Most supplements contain A, plus beta-carotene and possibly one or two other carotenoids that are converted to A in the body. (Lycopene has become popular because research shows that it's especially good for preventing prostate cancer.) By comparison, plants contain some 600 carotenoids, which you won't find in any one supplement – or in any one food, for that matter. The best way to get a good mix of all 600 is to build your diet around a variety of plant foods.

Besides, there's something to be said for the way nature packages nutrients in plant foods. The nutrients are in balance with one another, so you get them in the amounts that are most usable and safe – amounts that your body and genes are accustomed to.

The Oldest Diet Keeps Us Young

When you consider the abundance of nutrients found in plant foods, it makes sense that in study after study, vegetarians (who eat a plant-based diet) come out healthiest. I must confess that I am not a strict vegetarian. Nor do I believe that strict vegetarianism is necessary for good health and youthfulness. I follow what many nutritionists describe as a near-vegetarian diet. That means that I have meat a few times a week. Mostly, though, I eat plant foods, a wide variety of them to get the broadest possible mix of nutrients.

Another name for this sort of plant-based, near-vegetarian diet is Palaeolithic because it involves eating the way our hunter-gatherer ancestors did. Now I want to be clear that I'm not advocating a return to cave dwelling. Life was very tough in those days, and few people made it past 40 because of starvation and infectious diseases. But as far as diet is concerned, that of our ancestors was healthier than ours is today.

Looking back about a million years, the typical diet consisted of fruits, leaves, roots, nuts, seeds, fish and shellfish, and maybe an occasional grub, with a little honey and a periodic occasional gorging on meat when the hunters brought home a large game animal. History books and Hollywood movies have focused on the hunters (males) of Palaeolithic times, but in reality, the gatherers (females) supplied most of the food back then. Hunting was an iffy proposition with just spears, and bows and arrows didn't improve the odds all that much. Often, days or weeks passed before the hunters made a major kill. And when they did, they had only a few days to eat it. There was no refrigeration, so meat spoiled quickly.

Meat was not only less plentiful in those days, it was just plain different. The meat we eat has been bred for fattiness over generations because the fat is what makes it tender and juicy. By comparison, Palaeolithic meat was tough and lean. Eating it was less harmful (meaning that it produced fewer free radicals) because it contained so much less fat.

But that's not the only reason why a Palaeolithic diet is healthier for us humans. On a more basic level, it's just better suited to our biology. The human species has not experienced any significant evolutionary changes in some 100,000 years. But post-Palaeolithic agriculture has existed for only 8,000 to 10,000 years, and our food supply has evolved much faster than we have. This means that our bodies haven't had a chance to adjust to the 'new' foods that agriculture has made available to us – notably refined grains, dairy products, meat from domesticated animals, sweets, and ultraprocessed, nutritionally useless junk foods.

What we feed our bodies today is pretty far removed from what they're designed to handle. From a genetic point of view, our bodies have trouble coping with refined grains, dairy products, fatty meats, sweets, and fatty junk foods. No wonder they are overwhelming our systems. The very processed foods that so-called intelligent man developed in an effort to outsmart Mother Nature are the very foods responsible for much of the chronic illness prevalent today.

In the Western world, starvation is no longer an issue for most people, and water purification, sewage disposal, and medical advances have eliminated most of the infectious diseases that decimated our Palaeolithic ancestors. But we're dying of diseases that our ancestors never could have imagined, in part because they ate a diet that protected them.

That's why I'm such a strong advocate of the Palaeolithic diet – low-fat, plant-based, and near-vegetarian. If we learn to eat more like our ancestors did, we'll greatly reduce our risk of heart disease, cancer, diabetes, and many of the other noninfectious diseases that are responsible for most deaths today.

Why Fresh Is Best

Here's something else to consider about the Palaeolithic diet: everything that our ancestors ate was fresh. I'm all for fresh foods, too, and I recommend using them as often as possible.

Food processing and preservation are fairly recent innovations. Although they've had some benefits – namely, safer, cheaper foods and a more consistently available food supply – they've also enabled the development of products that too often provide nothing but empty calories.

Processing removes fibre, vitamins, minerals, and other beneficial phytochemicals from foods, replacing them with sugar, salt, preservatives, artificial flavours, and often extra fat. In effect, processing means removing the preventive medicines and replacing them with free radicals, which are nothing more than slow-acting poisons. That's why I prefer fresh whole foods – whole grains, whole fruits, whole veggies, whole beans, whole spices, and whole herbs – over processed foods.

Another advantage of eating fresh foods is that you avoid synthetic preservatives, genetically engineered foods, and animal-plant cross-species hybrids, all of which are unfamiliar to human genes. It may be months, years, even decades before we realise how these high-tech foods can harm us. I suspect that healthwise, their batting averages will be about the same as those of synthetic pharmaceuticals. (As I mention in chapter 2, more than half of all medications are found to have serious side effects *after* they've been approved.)

That's why I prefer to build my meals around whole, minimally processed foods. I suggest that you do the same.

A Closer Look at the Healthy Sevens

The National Cancer Institute (NCI) in the USA has launched its own campaign to persuade Americans to eat at least five servings of fruits and vegetables a day. It's called the Strive for Five programme, and it's based on a tremendous amount of research showing that the more plant foods you eat, the less likely you are to develop cancer. Most Americans don't get even five servings a day, so the Strive for Five programme makes sense. It's a step towards the Palaeolithic diet.

But Strive for Five can be confusing. Should you eat five fruits and five vegetables, for a total of 10 servings a day? Or can you mix and match fruits and veggies for a total of 5 servings a day? The NCI advocates a total of five 100 g (3½ oz) servings, which unfortunately doesn't go far enough. This isn't just my opinion. Many nutritionists as well as many health organisations now recommend getting 8 to 10 servings of fruits and vegetables a day.

So I've come up with my own programme, which I call the Healthy Sevens. It recommends a daily diet consisting of seven fruits and seven vegetables, plus seven beans, seven whole grains, seven nuts and seeds, seven herbs and spices, and seven glasses of water.

I haven't included meats or dairy products because they're not plant foods. You're free to eat them if you wish; I eat them myself. My only advice is to keep your portions small – by dicing chicken into a vegetable medley, for example.

Why seven of everything? Well, I came up with the programme around the time of my 70th birthday, so seven seemed like a good number, one that would be easy to remember.

Keep in mind that I'm recommending seven *kinds* of foods from each category, not seven servings. I'm more concerned with variety than with quantity. It seems to me that the greater variety of plant foods you eat, the more likely you are to consume the broadest possible range of nutrients. The NCI and I agree on this basic point.

That said, here's my advice for getting your Healthy Sevens each and every day.

SEVEN FRUITS. To meet my fruit quota every day, I like to eat fruit salad and fruit cocktail. That way, I'm getting a variety of fruits, each in a small portion. I also drink fruit juices that I blend myself; they count towards my Healthy Sevens, too.

Of course, getting all those fruits is easier in summer than in winter, when fresh produce isn't as plentiful. But you can do it if you include dried fruits such as prunes, raisins, currants, figs, and dried blueberries, cranberries, and apricots. That's seven right there.

SEVEN VEGETABLES. I get my seven veggies in essentially three ways: salads, soups, and juices. If you tend to eat the same vegetables over and over again, here's your chance to branch out and try some new ones. For example, when I make a salad, I may mix together an assortment of leafy greens such as chicory, cress, endive, lamb's lettuce, rocket, sorrel, and spinach. That's seven varieties of greens, some of which I grow in my Garden of Youth. And I haven't even touched on the several types of lettuce now available in most supermarkets.

Personally, I avoid iceberg lettuce, which doesn't have much going for it beyond its fibre and water content. The most nutritious greens are the dark, leafy ones, such as broccoli, chard, spinach, kale, chicory, dandelion, and mustard. These greens tend to have a bitter taste, which reminds me of the 'bitter herbs' mentioned in the Bible. The Bible promotes bitter herbs for religious reasons, and now scientific research suggests these plant foods may be the most healthful as well. I guess there's something to be said for that old-time religion.

Like salads, soups provide a wonderful opportunity to expand your vegetable repertoire. Depending on their ingredients, they can be exceptionally healthful, supplying an abundance of antioxidants and other nutrients.

Even if you don't like a particular vegetable raw or cooked, you might enjoy it in a soup. I know people who dislike cauliflower or spinach but will eat cauliflower soup or spinach minced into minestrone.

In addition to eating lots of vegetable-rich salads and soups, I drink plenty of vegetable juice. It's available ready-made but I like to concoct my own. All it takes is a home juicer or blender.

Juices are no substitute for whole vegetables, however. Whole veggies supply fibre, which is important in its own right. But if you eat a near-vegetarian diet, you almost certainly get enough fibre. By removing the bulky fibre with a juicer, you concentrate some of the vegetables' other nutrients in the juice, especially the antioxidants that are so vital to health and youthfulness.

Like soups, juices are a great way to consume vegetables that you don't otherwise like. You may not mind them in juices, especially when they're blended with other veggies that you enjoy.

SEVEN BEANS. Beans don't get much respect. Many people don't even consider them vegetables, although that's what they are. Worse, they've earned a rather unsavoury (yet deserved) reputation for their connection to flatulence.

But beans are a marvellous food for good health and lasting youth. I believe that a good mixed-bean soup – spiced up with chilli pepper, cumin, garlic, ginger, onions, savory, and turmeric – can help prevent many of today's major killer diseases, saving more lives than pharmaceuticals can cure.

At our house, we usually have a big pot of bean soup in the fridge. Then when we want a quick, wholesome meal or snack, we just scoop some soup into a pot and reheat it. It may feature one kind of pulse, such as split peas, lentils, black beans, broad beans, navy beans, haricot beans, or butter beans. Or it may be a mixed-bean soup, with a handful of each of the aforementioned pulses, plus others.

Besides soups, I recommend bean salads containing garlic and onions. Bean sprouts are great, too.

SEVEN WHOLE GRAINS. I'm sure you're familiar with wholemeal bread. But whole wheat is just one of many whole grains that you can eat to stay healthy and young. Personally, I enjoy barley, buckwheat, corn, millet, oats, quinoa, rice, rye, and spelt. These and other whole grains are typically baked into breads or used as ingredients in cereals. Many also make tasty additions to soups.

In an ongoing study of a large group of middle-aged (to me, they're quite young) women in Iowa, researchers have found that as whole grain consumption increases, so does overall health and longevity. I should mention, though, that some people have trouble digesting the gluten in grains. If you have this condition, called coeliac disease, you'll need to avoid many grains.

SEVEN NUTS AND SEEDS. The more I read, the more I realise that nuts were an integral part of the Palaeolithic diet. Nuts have developed a less-than-stellar reputation because they're high in fat. But it's mostly vegetable fat, which is a great deal less harmful than the saturated fat found in meats and dairy products. If you eat a near-vegetarian diet, nuts will do you more good than harm.

It takes just three Brazil nuts to provide a healthy dose (200 micrograms) of the superb antioxidant selenium. If consumed regularly, that's enough selenium to significantly reduce your chances of developing several types of cancer, including those of the colon, lung, and prostate (at least according to certain studies). Almonds are one of the best sources of vitamin E. And other nuts are equally nutritious.

Seeds are great for health and longevity, too. I often munch on pumpkin and sunflower seeds. And I add caraway, celery, coriander, dill, fennel, flax, poppy, and sesame seeds to many dishes.

Seeds are rich in vitamin E and other nutrients. I'm convinced that some compounds in pumpkin seeds can help relieve prostate symptoms in young old guys like me. And I credit celery seeds with helping to keep me free of gout attacks for 5 years now.

SEVEN HERBS AND SPICES. Being a herbalist, I use lots of herbs and spices (which, technically, are also herbs). Today, these plants are added to foods to perk up the taste. But long ago, when our ancestors were shifting from a Palaeolithic diet to agriculture, they weren't interested in flavour enhancement, though that was a nice side benefit. Rather, they relied on herbs and spices to preserve foods, especially meats.

The aromatic oils that give herbs and spices their distinctive flavours are also potent antioxidants. They help retard meat spoilage, thanks to their antibacterial, antifungal, and antiviral properties. They afford us the same protection.

Outside in my Garden of Youth, I'm growing probably 70 species of herbs that can be brewed into tea, which is one tasty way to tap into their nutrients. Among my favourite herbs are the mints, all richly endowed with youth-preserving antioxidants. You can brew a tea using just one kind of mint, but I like to mix several herbs together. I grab a few leaves of this and that, choosing from bee balm, dittany, horehound, hyssop, lemon balm, marjoram, oregano, peppermint, rosemary, sage, savory, self-heal, spearmint, and thyme, and throw them in a teapot.

You've probably read newspaper accounts of studies showing that one or another of these herbs is 'best' because it contains the most antioxidants. Both rosemary and oregano have been awarded this distinction by various research teams. But it obscures a more important point: all of these herbs are rich in antioxidant nutrients. Use any of them. Use all of them. Just use them, as long as you're not allergic to them.

Another way to use herbs and spices is in cooking. There's no great distinction between culinary herbs and spices – only that the herbs are usually leafy, while the spices tend to be woody. Some of my favourite herbs for cooking include basil, celery, chives, dill, fennel, fenugreek, garlic, marjoram, onion, oregano, parsley, rosemary, sage, savory, tarragon, and thyme. Among the spices, I especially like allspice, bay leaf, black pepper, cardamom, cinnamon, cloves, ginger, nutmeg, paprika, saffron, turmeric, and vanilla.

SEVEN GLASSES OF WATER. To round out the Healthy Sevens programme, I recommend drinking seven 240 ml (8 fl oz) glasses of water a day. Water is the forgotten nutrient, yet our bodies are mostly H_2O. And even minor dehydration can cause problems such as confusion and loss of strength, stamina, and coordination. I sip water throughout the day. I also get fluids in the form of juices, soups, and teas. Do the same, and you might feel better – more energetic and alive.

CHAPTER 4

Getting *the* Most *from the* Youth-Preserving Herbs

In my Garden of Youth, I'm growing 253 species of herbs. I hope to grow more than 300 soon.

Because I'm an avid gardener, and because gardening provides an abundance of health benefits, I always encourage those who can grow their own herbs to do so. At the risk of seeming a little flaky, I believe that growing your own herbs helps you establish a spiritual bond with them. When you plant herbs, water them, weed them, fret over them, harvest them, and either consume them on the spot or prepare them for later use, you connect with them and, I believe, with their nutritional and therapeutic powers.

The problem with growing your own is that you become so attached

Harvesting and Drying Your Herbs

If you grow your own herbs, you need to harvest selectively so you don't kill your mother plants. Pinch off only aerial shoots, taking care not to tear other shoots or the main stem. Sometimes, with herbs such as basil, bay, rosemary, and thyme, your best bet is to cut off just the desired number of leaves. This is as painless to the plant, I think, as haircuts are to us humans.

Feel free to use the shoots, leaves, and flowers fresh, especially if you're adding them to food. Fresh culinary herbs and spices always taste best. I often take herbs straight from the Garden of Youth to the dish I'm cooking, the salad I'm tossing, or the tea I'm brewing.

For medicinal purposes, shoots, leaves, and flowers are typically dried. Drying is important; it can be done in the sun or the shade. I actually prefer the shade. It takes longer, but it preserves more of a herb's aroma.

You can also dry herbs in a paper bag. Just don't stuff your bag too full. You want air to get in there. Be sure to write the collection date on the outside. I always make a run through my herb garden with paper bags just before the last killing frost, gathering herbs for my winter medicines, soups, and teas.

Check your brown-bagged herbs after about a week. If they're not clearly drying (they should become papery and crumbly), spread them out on newspapers or on clean wood or screening in a dry, dark area. That way, they can dry before mildew attacks.

How you dry your herbs depends a great deal on the climate and weather conditions in your area. If it's arid, herbs may dry too rapidly, especially in direct sunlight. If it's humid or foggy, you may have to use heat, baking your herbs in an oven to remove the moisture.

I am often asked whether microwave

to the beauty of your garden that you're reluctant to harvest anything, even when you need to. When my grandchildren are visiting and they're sick with colds, I ought to uproot some of my echinacea and use it to stimulate my immune system. But I often have trouble sacrificing the plants, which are known for their beautiful daisylike flowers. So usually I opt for a commercial preparation, while continuing to commune with my living echinacea plants.

You don't even need a garden to grow your own herbs. Your kitchen window sill can support small pots of them. Aloe vera thrives in pots and ovens are suitable for drying herbs. I think they do an okay job, though in my experience they tend to leave the herbs less aromatic. Experiment for yourself and decide whether microwaving provides the results you want.

Once you've dried your herbs, you can leave them in paper bags or stuff them into opaque plastic bags or place them in dark glass jars with lids. You want to protect them from light, which robs them of their potency. The same is true of heat and oxygen. So store your herbs in a cool place, such as a cellar or a cupboard that's far from any heat source. And keep your herb containers as full as possible to prevent air from circulating inside. In fact, as you use up your herbs, I'd suggest transferring them to smaller containers.

If you're using seeds from your herb plants, your best bet is to collect them during their season of ripening. Some seeds are harvested in their moist, or 'milk', stage; others, after they've hardened. It varies from plant to plant. In general, seeds destined to be consumed as food are best collected before they've hardened, while those intended for planting should harden before they're harvested.

Hardened seeds require minimal processing, but those collected in the milk stage must be handled with care to prevent contamination and decomposition. They may also require drying, like most leaves; you can use the same techniques described above.

As for herb roots, they're best gathered in spring or fall. The moister the root, the more drying it will require. Bark may be harvested in spring, especially if the compounds you seek are in living bark, in which sugars rise with the sap. (The sugars' movement indicates that the bark's cells are alive.) Living bark may need to be dried, while dead bark is often so dry that it can be used as is.

is a good herb to keep in the kitchen, since most household burns happen there. Other herbs that do well on window sills include rosemary, basil, parsley, savory, sage, thyme, and chives. The key is to keep them well-watered. Potted plants dry out, especially if the pots get direct sun – in which case, they need to be watered every day. (For information on processing your home-grown herbs, see 'Harvesting and Drying Your Herbs' above.)

The next best thing to growing your own herbs is to buy from someone who does. Try to find a local grower and buy direct from the farm. Every major metropolitan centre that I've visited has at least a few commercial herb growers in the area. Most of them concentrate on the culinary herbs, which is just fine. Culinary herbs are medicinal, with rich supplies of the antioxidant nutrients that help keep you young.

But these days, with the herbal renaissance in full swing, many commercial herb growers have taken to raising non-culinary plants. Often these growers have greenhouses, so they can cultivate herbs not well-suited to the local climate. They can also help you with information on processing the herbs they sell or on growing your own if that's what you choose to do.

Making Your Own Medicines

Whether you buy your herbs or raise them yourself, you'll most likely prepare them as teas, tinctures, or capsules when you're taking them for medicinal purposes.

Teas come in two forms: infusions and decoctions. Which one you make depends on which parts of a herb you're using.

If the medicinal parts are the flowers, leaves, or fleshy roots, then an infusion is usually the way to go. To make an infusion, you steep the dried, usually powdered (or at least crushed) herb in freshly boiled water for 10 to 20 minutes. In most cases, you use ½ to 2 teaspoons of dried herb per cup of water, or double that amount of fresh herb. Though to be perfectly honest, I've never in my 72 years measured when making my teas. When the time is up, discard the plant material and allow the infusion to cool before drinking it. I prefer mine warm but not too hot. I also enjoy them iced in the summer.

For medicinal barks and woody roots, decoctions work best. To make a decoction, you simmer the dried or fresh chopped herb in boiling water for 10 to 20 minutes. The amounts are the same as for an infusion: ½ to 2 teaspoons of dried herb, or double that amount of fresh, per cup of water. Strain out the plant material and let the decoction cool before drinking it.

Preparing teas by infusion or decoction is quick and easy. But dried herbs are bulky; they take up a good deal of shelf space and don't travel all that well. They also lose their potency fairly quickly. Usually, when I want to make a refreshing tea or add some herbs to my cooking, I just grab some of the organic herbs that I've nurtured myself, out in my Garden of Youth.

Compared with dried herbs, tinctures are less bulky and retain their potency much longer. Preparing them takes much longer, too. Most people buy them ready-made in health food stores.

Tinctures are herbal extracts made with alcohol or, in some cases, glycerin or vinegar. If you want to try making your own, place 30–60 g (an ounce or two) of dried, crushed herb in a jar and add twice the amount of alcohol necessary to cover the herb. (I use the cheapest vodka I can buy.) Close the jar and let it sit in a cool, dark spot for a week or two, shaking the brew every couple of days. When it's done steeping, transfer the tincture to a dropper bottle. Tinctures are often taken by the dropperful.

Few people make their own capsules, but you can if you wish. Most companies that sell herbs by mail also offer empty capsules. Just pull open a capsule, fill it with dried, powdered herb, and close it.

Which Form Works Best?

You may be wondering whether one of these herbal preparations – teas, tinctures, or capsules – is better than the others. My advice is to take whatever works best for you. Personally, I use all three.

I favour tinctures when I'm dealing with herbs whose medicinal properties depend largely on their aromatic constituents. Generally, I don't have much faith in naturally pungent herbs that have been deodorised. I know that deodorised garlic is heavily promoted and that it has even been shown in some studies to have the same benefits as whole garlic. But for my money, the volatile aromatic compounds account for most of a herb's medicinal effects. When the smell goes, so do some of the benefits.

While I have hundreds of herbs in my own backyard, I sometimes use commercial preparations instead of or in addition to my own. For example, I grow garlic, echinacea, ginkgo, goldenseal, and ginseng, but

I rarely harvest the plants. Oh, I'll whip up an experimental mixture now and then, but for the most part, I rely on ready-made products simply because they're more convenient.

I take my garlic in capsules, though I also buy whole cloves in the supermarket and use them in abundance in food – raw, juiced, or cooked, fresh or dried. During flu season, I sometimes take echinacea in both capsule and tincture forms, knowing that capsules contain more of some active ingredients while tinctures contain more of others. For ginkgo, I prefer concentrated extracts. For goldenseal, I use capsules or tinctures.

When I buy commercial herbal preparations, I look for standardised

Build Your Own Herb Library

In parts 2 and 3 of this book, I present a variety of herbs and herb formulas that can help you fight age-related diseases and stay young in body and mind. I've selected these herbs based on my own research and experience. If you want to learn more about them, you many want to do some research of your own. I suggest checking out the herb references in your local library or investing in one or two books for your home.

One essential reference is Germany's Commission E Monographs. In German pharmacies, herbal products are sold right alongside conventional medications. Herbs account for about 30 per cent of Germany's nonprescription drug sales, and they're routinely recommended by pharmacists and prescribed by doctors (especially general practitioners). In fact, German pharmacists and doctors are required to study herbal medicine as part of their professional training.

In 1978, the German government established Commission E, a panel of physicians, pharmacists, pharmacologists, toxicologists, epidemiologists, and other professionals familiar with the vast body of historical and scientific literature pertaining to herbs and medicinal plants. The panel's mission is to pass judgement on the safety and effectiveness of various herbs as treatments for human health complaints. To date, Commission E has reviewed more than 300 herbs and has published a report (or monograph) on each herb's therapeutic dosage, benefits, and side effects.

English translations of the Commission E Monographs are available on the Internet from a number of outlets specialising in herbal products.

products. These contain herbs that have been specially bred and grown or processed to contain certain amounts of some of their medicinal compounds. Dose control – that is, knowing how much of the active ingredients you're getting – can be a problem with herbs. Many factors can affect herbal potency: plant genetics, growing conditions, time of harvest, and length of storage.

A decade ago, I wasn't too keen on standardisation. But then I became aware of the horrendous variations in the concentrations of medicinal compounds in individual herbs – variations of tenfold, hundredfold, and sometimes even thousandfold from one plant to another. As a result, I'm now convinced that standardisation is well worth the cost and effort.

Standardised products don't completely eliminate dose-control problems. But among herbal medicines, they provide the best dose control by far – much better than you'd get from herbs that may have spent 2 years at the bottom of a bin in a health food store.

Something else to keep in mind: while every variety of herb contains literally thousands of biologically active compounds, only one or two of these compounds are subject to standardisation. Fortunately, they tend to be the most important, based on existing scientific research.

A Herbal Buying Guide

So now you're in the health food store, scanning shelves of herbal products in search of good standardised extracts. And you're wondering which brand should you buy.

At this point, I must reveal that since I retired some years ago, I've been serving as a consultant to Nature's Herbs, a wholly owned subsidiary of Twinlab. I'm a senior science advisor, helping the company to select the best herbs and the best extraction processes so that it can produce the best products. I took the job because I've always admired the company and its commitment to manufacturing quality herbal supplements. So I endorse Nature's Herbs.

Of course, if you think my affiliation taints my endorsement, feel free to ignore it and go with some other company. Other brands that I trust include Bioforce, Eclectic, Enzymatic Therapy, HerbPharm, Indena, Klinge, Lichtwer, Madaus, Nature's Way, PhytoPharmica, Quanterra, Scotia, Schwabe, and Solaray.

While some of the manufacturers are American, others are European, including Indena (Italy), Klinge (Germany), Madaus (Germany), Schwabe (Germany), and Scotia (United Kingdom). Many of these firms have been in business a long time, in part because herbal medicine is more mainstream in Europe than in the United States. What's more, they were pioneers in developing standardised extracts, which they sell wholesale to many American herb companies.

When you're out shopping for herbal products, don't hesitate to ask questions. Many health food shop assistants are fairly well-informed about herbs. Also, be sure to read product labels carefully. If a label lists only a herb's common name and you're not familiar with it, don't buy the product. Look for a standard common name as well as the botanical nomenclature, which identifies a herb by its genus and species.

Labels reveal other valuable information about the quality of herbal products. My advice is to consider the following when making your selection.

STANDARDISATION. As I mentioned earlier, I prefer standardised extracts over other herbal preparations because they indicate that I'm getting a specific amount of one or more of a herb's medicinal compounds. If a product is standardised, its label should say so. The label should also indicate which of a herb's active ingredients have been used for standardisation. A well-researched product will declare that it contains a certain per centage of a herb's main medicinal compound.

For example, St. John's wort has for years been standardised to contain 0.3 per cent hypericin. Now some scientists are recommending standardisation of hyperforin. Of course, each active ingredient has its advocates. I don't know which is more important, but if I were given a choice, I'd choose a product that contains both.

INGREDIENTS. Some herbal products have ingredients other than the herbs themselves. Tinctures, for example, are made with alcohol or glycerin. Tablets may contain all sorts of filler substances. Does the product you're considering have extra ingredients? If so, how does it look? It should be clean, with no obvious extraneous materials.

DOSAGE. A product's dosage can serve as a good indicator of its quality. Sometimes a dose of one brand is two to three times the dose of another brand. In this case, more is not necessarily better!

Beware the Hazardous Herbs

While I prefer herbs to pharmaceuticals in part because herbs are safer, I'm not suggesting that all herbs are harmless. In fact, some can be quite deadly. Fortunately, they're rarely, if ever, sold in stores that carry well-labelled, commercially marketed herbal preparations. But they're listed here anyway – just in case. None of these herbs should be taken internally, though some are safe for external use (arnica, for example).

- Arnica (*Arnica montana*)
- Belladonna (*Atropa belladonna*)
- Bittersweet (*Solanum dulcamara*)
- Bryony (*Bryonia dioica*)
- Chaparral (*Larrea tridentata*)
- Comfrey (*Symphytum officinale*)
- European pennyroyal (*Mentha pulegium*)
- False hellebore (*Veratrum viride*)
- Foxglove (*Digitalis purpurea*)
- Henbane (*Hyoscyamus niger*)
- Indian snakeroot (*Rauwolfia serpentina*)
- Ipecac (*Cephaelis ipecacuanha*)
- Jimsonweed (*Datura stramonium*)
- Lily of the valley (*Convallaria majalis*)
- Male fern (*Dryopteris filix-mas*)
- Mandrake (*Mandragora officinarum*)
- Mayapple (*Podophyllum peltatum*)
- Mistletoe (*Viscum album*)
- Pasqueflower (*Anemone pulsatilla*)
- Pennyroyal (*Hedeoma pulegioides*)
- Pheasant's eye (*Adonis vernalis*)
- Pokeberry (*Phytolacca americana*)
- Squill (*Urginea maritima*)
- Yellow jessamine (*Gelsemium sempervirens*)

Other herbs that I wouldn't consider dangerous may still cause side effects. For example, Chinese ephedra (ma huang) can cause heart problems when taken in large doses and should be taken only under a doctor's supervision. Licorice can raise blood pressure. And cascara sagrada, like most laxatives, can be habit-forming. That's why I recommend reading product labels, so you can learn as much as possible about potential side effects and other negative reactions – and hopefully avoid them.

I'm not comfortable recommending dosages, because I'm not a doctor. That's why I generally recommend buying products with dosage instructions on the label and following them to the letter.

EXPIRY DATE. All herbal products lose potency over time. Bulk herbs and teas go first; tinctures and capsules last a bit longer. Ideally, any packaged product that you choose should have an expiry date.

WARNINGS. Check the label for warnings. Any herb might trigger an allergic reaction, and many herbs may cause side effects or may interact with pharmaceuticals. As scientists expand their herb research, more of this critical information is likely to surface and eventually show up on packaged products.

LOT NUMBER. In the rare event of a product recall, you'll need to know the lot number. Make sure one is listed somewhere on the label.

MANUFACTURER INFORMATION. The company should provide its address. Of course, if you experience any unusual or severe side effects, don't call the company – at least not right away. Seek emergency medical care first, and take the herbal product with you. The doctor will likely need some information about it – for example, whether it contains any ingredients that may trigger an allergic reaction.

PRICE. If one brand costs substantially less than all the others, its quality may have been compromised. Keep that in mind when you're making your selection.

PART TWO

Natural Strategies *that* Stop *the* Clock

CHAPTER 5

The Best Herbs *for* Staying Young

Even though I am often called a herbalist, I do not consider herbs to be the bedrock foundation of health and youthfulness. That honour goes to regular exercise and good nutrition. But herbs are important. In fact, I would say that they're essential for living to a ripe old age and feeling young when you get there.

Of course, you could argue that herbs are a component of the bedrock foundation of health and youthfulness because the diet that I advocate is largely plant-based. All herbs are plants, and in a broad sense, all plants are herbs. But most people think of herbs as being different from food plants, so I've tried to preserve that distinction here.

In this chapter, I'm going to focus on a collection of herbs with special 'ingredients' or properties that make them valuable allies in the pursuit of lifelong youthfulness. You'll come across many of them again in later chapters. Each in its own way can help you to feel and look your best, no matter what your chronological age.

Occasionally, people ask me to reveal a 'secret formula' that will help them stay young. The fact is, everyone's formula would be different, depending on genes, health status, and lifestyle. You can create your own simply by selecting the herbs below that most closely match your health needs and concerns. Of course, if you're experiencing persistent symptoms of one sort or another, you should see a doctor for proper diagnosis before starting any herbal regime.

The Top 12 Youth Preservers

I myself have taken lots of different herbs – well over 100 – and experimented with hundreds more. But for the past few years, I've been keeping track of the ones that I use most often, the ones that I view as particularly beneficial to maintaining overall health and enhancing youthful vitality. There are 12 in all.

With the exception of celery seed, I don't take any of the following herbs every day. That would get expensive. But I do use them regularly.

BILBERRY (*VACCINIUM MYRTILLUS*). A close relative of blueberry, bilberry contains special antioxidants called anthocyanosides that help prevent many age-related ailments. But the herb is particularly good for preserving vision and preventing degenerative eye diseases.

I don't have a bearing bilberry bush, so I usually use capsules standardised to contain 40 milligrams of concentrated extract with 25 per cent anthocyanosides. The recommended dose is two capsules twice a day, but I rarely take that much because I eat so many other kinds of berries.

CELERY SEED (*APIUM GRAVEOLENS*). Some studies have shown that eating celery can help lower high blood pressure, which is a concern for everyone over the age of 50. And celery seed has a reputation for preventing gout and other types of arthritis. While there's no good American research to support this benefit, the herb is known to contain more than a dozen anti-inflammatory ingredients, including apigenin, a COX-2-inhibiting compound similar to the pharmaceuticals celecoxib (Celebrex) and rofecoxib (Vioxx). Celery seed extract is the only herb that I take religiously every day, mainly because it's been so effective at protecting me from gout attacks over the past 5 years. The usual dosage is two 500-milligram capsules twice a day, before meals – though I rarely take that much because I eat lots of celery. Therapeutic doses should be taken cautiously by those with kidney disorders – see page 517.

Not all celery seed products are standardised. The one that I have right now is standardised to contain 2.2 per cent volatile oil.

ECHINACEA (*ECHINACEA,* VARIOUS SPECIES). In my opinion, echinacea is one of the best herbal immune-system enhancers. It helps keep germs from setting up shop in my ageing body. I grow my own echinacea, but I rarely dig up my plants. Instead, I take a commercial tincture that's standardised for echinacosides. Just follow the package directions for proper dosage.

EVENING PRIMROSE (*OENOTHERA BIENNIS*). Occasionally, I use evening primrose oil in combination with saw palmetto (more on this herb later) to protect myself from benign prostate enlargement. Some people, including me, collect and eat the seeds. My grandson prefers the flowers. Usually, though, I buy commercial preparations. I take one big 1,300-milligram capsule that's standardised to contain 130 milligrams of gamma-linolenic acid (GLA).

For premenopausal women, evening primrose oil helps prevent PMS and menstrual cramps. I'd recommend one or two capsules a day between periods, increasing to three or four a day during periods.

Evening primrose contains an abundance of GLA, a compound that helps protect against heart disease. If you want to reduce your heart disease risk, experts suggest taking between 1 and 4 grams a day.

GARLIC (*ALLIUM SATIVUM*). Garlic is a veritable wonder herb. It's a potent antimicrobial that helps defeat a wide range of viruses, bacteria, and fungi. I take lots of it when my grandchildren come to visit and they're sick with colds or the flu. Garlic also helps prevent heart disease by lowering blood pressure and cholesterol as well as inhibiting the formation of internal blood clots that trigger heart attack.

I grow garlic in the Garden of Youth, but I rarely harvest it. Instead, I buy whole cloves in the store. I add the herb to vegetable juices. I use lots of it in soups. I chop it fine, mix it with olive oil, and spread the mixture on toast. I roast the bulbs and squeeze out the contents onto toast or savoury biscuits.

Almost daily during flu season, I pop a 400-milligram enteric-coated garlic capsule standardised to contain 3 milligrams of allicin, about the amount you'd get from a clove or two. But I strongly recommend using fresh garlic as long as your spouse and friends can stand it.

GINKGO (*GINKGO BILOBA*). This living relic of the Dinosaur Age is a certifiable, singular fountain of youth. Among ginkgo's many benefits, it improves bloodflow throughout your body, especially in your brain and extremities. In fact, it's one of the best herbs for brain health, with the potential to prevent stroke and Alzheimer's disease. It also protects against heart attack, macular degeneration, tinnitus, and the kind of impotence that's caused by impaired bloodflow into the penis.

If I felt the need to supplement ginkgo, I would take between 60 and 240 milligrams a day of an extract, standardised to contain 24 per cent flavonoid glycosides. To reap the herb's benefits, you have to use a commercial preparation. The bulk leaf has too small concentrations of the medicinal compounds to do much good.

HAWTHORN (*CRATAEGUS MONOGYNA*). Hawthorn is the best herbal heart tonic around. It gently normalises heart function in both congestive heart failure and coronary artery disease. Some days I take two or three 500-milligramme capsules standardised to contain 1.8 milligrams of vitexins, the medicinal compounds in hawthorn. But I don't do this often. My diet is filled with heart-healthy herbs, and I get plenty of exercise, so I'm not all that concerned about heart disease.

HORSE CHESTNUT (*AESCULUS HIPPOCASTANUM*). Horse chestnut helps protect against varicose veins, a concern for all of us as we get older. I recommend taking it as two 485-milligram capsules: one at breakfast, the other at dinner. The capsules that I have on hand are standardised to contain 18 to 22 per cent triterpenoid glycosides. By the way, never take fresh horse chestnut internally – it's poisonous. Commercial preparations, on the other hand, are safe because they have been detoxified – but see the warning on page 519.

MILK THISTLE (*SILYBUM MARIANUM*). Milk thistle is the best herb for safeguarding your liver against cirrhosis and hepatitis. New evidence suggests that the herb may help prevent cancer, type 2 (non-insulin-dependent) diabetes, and syndrome X – all ailments in which age can be a risk factor. (If you're not familiar with syndrome X, it's actually a collection of symptoms characterised by high levels of cholesterol, triglycerides, blood pressure, and blood sugar, plus overweight.)

Even if you don't have these conditions, you may find yourself taking more medications as you get older. These drugs get processed by your liver, which can strain it. Milk thistle helps keep your liver functioning smoothly.

When I'm taking milk thistle for my liver, I prefer capsules – one or two a day, with water, before meals. Each capsule should be standardised to contain 140 milligrams of the herb's active compounds, collectively known as silymarin.

ST. JOHN'S WORT (*HYPERICUM PERFORATUM*). St. John's wort is an effective treatment for mild to moderate depression. Besides causing emotional turmoil, depression impairs immune function and, by extension, aggravates all sorts of health problems that speed the ageing process. Because St. John's wort can lift your spirits, it gives your immune system a chance to rebound.

Personally, I'm prone to a seasonal depression that I call the winter blues. Doctors refer to it as seasonal affective disorder. For some people, it comes on in fall and may not let up until spring. For relief, I use commercial preparations of St. John's wort, standardised to 0.3 per cent hypericin. I suggest following the package directions for proper dosage – but see page 520 before you decide to take it.

SAW PALMETTO (*SERENOA REPENS*). I'm betting my prostate gland that saw palmetto prevents benign prostate enlargement just as effectively as pharmaceuticals. I've been taking the herb on and off for years, especially when I'm away from home and I'm not eating very healthily. But I haven't touched finasteride (Proscar), the primary drug prescribed for prostate enlargement. So far, so good.

My doctor is impressed with my prostate and tells me to keep doing

Make the Most of Your Spice Rack

I am a strong believer in food as preventive medicine. I am also a strong believer in tasty food. With the herbal spices, I'm able to put both principles to practical use.

The herbal spices enhance flavour as they enhance health. Most of them have antioxidant properties. For our ancestors, who lived in the days before refrigeration, this meant they could preserve their food by killing the micro-organisms that cause spoilage. For us, it means we can protect ourselves from the illnesses caused by oxidative damage – notably heart disease, most cancers, and most strokes.

Here's my list of recommended spices. Chances are that you use only a handful of them regularly. I suggest exploring all the others. Your tastebuds will be wowed, and you'll grow healthier to boot.

I use spices straight from the spice rack, as long as they retain their aroma. Freshly ground organic spices may be richer in health-giving phytochemicals. Let your nose be your guide.

- Allspice
- Anise
- Basil
- Bay leaf
- Black cumin
- Black pepper
- Caraway
- Cardamom
- Celery seed
- Chilli pepper (paprika, cayenne, other peppers)
- Chives
- Cinnamon
- Cloves
- Coriander
- Cumin
- Dill
- Fennel
- Fenugreek
- Garlic
- Ginger
- Marjoram
- Mustard
- Nutmeg
- Onion
- Oregano
- Parsley
- Poppy seed
- Rosemary
- Saffron
- Sage
- Savory
- Sesame
- Tarragon
- Thyme
- Turmeric
- Vanilla

what I'm doing. When I take the herb, it's in the form of a 320-milligram soft-gel capsule standardised to contain 85 to 95 per cent fatty acids and biologically active sterols. But, before you start using saw palmetto to treat an enlarged prostate, be sure to see your doctor for diagnosis.

TURMERIC (*CURCUMA LONGA*). Many of us notice more aches and pains as we get older. Often they result from inflammation of joints (arthritis), tendons (tendinitis), bursae (bursitis), or muscles (myositis). Incidentally, all of these condition names end in *-itis* because that means inflammation.

When I'm achy or sore, I bypass nonsteroidal anti-inflammatory drugs (NSAIDs), which can cause serious gastrointestinal distress and bleeding. Instead, I reach for turmeric, which has remarkable anti-inflammatory activity. If I've just hurt myself, I take the herb as a powder in capsules, standardised to contain 95 per cent curcumin (a natural COX-2 inhibitor). Otherwise, I just add the herb to curries and soups.

Staple dishes in Indian cuisine, curries get their characteristic yellow colour from turmeric. I can't specify a dose for the herb – I just pour it on to make curried chicken, curried vegetables, you name it. I even eat curried asparagus.

The Eight Anti-Ageing Elixirs

The herbs that I describe above can keep you healthy and prevent dozens of illnesses. But they're not the whole story. I also favour the fountain-of-youth herbs, my name for what Asians call tonics and a growing number of Western scientists call adaptogens. No matter how you refer to them, these herbs act slowly to enhance overall health and well-being as well as to promote youthfulness and longevity.

Adaptogen/tonic/fountain-of-youth herbs are controversial in the West for several reasons. First, the concept of slow-acting health enhancers is not well-established here. Second, many Asian studies of these herbs, particularly ginseng, are not rigorous by Western standards. And third, several of these herbs have been touted as aphrodisiacs, a claim that always makes Western scientists sceptical – though in my book, a healthier animal tends to be a more amorous animal.

Being a Western-trained botanist myself, I share my colleagues' scepticism, and I feel honour-bound to declare that there isn't much solid science to substantiate the health benefits of the adaptogen/tonic herbs. But there are some good studies, and the more I read, the more I'm persuaded that these herbs do indeed normalise body systems, help the body adapt to stresses, and basically live up to the traditional claims made for them.

Now for a bombshell: I'm convinced that all plants contain adaptogenic/tonic compounds, because plants have to contend with a good deal of stress themselves. The ones listed here may be just a little more potent as youth enhancers than, say, carrots and celery.

ASHWAGANDHA (*WITHANIA SOMNIFERA*). Several African tribes consider ashwagandha an aphrodisiac. The Indian Ayurvedic literature agrees. I'll admit that the scientific research is thin. But in my experience, when this kind of cross-culture agreement exists, it usually has some merit. So I grow ashwagandha in the Aphrodisiac section of my Garden of Youth.

On firmer scientific ground, the herb is a proven tranquillizer and anxiety reducer. There's also some decent evidence that it's an immune system stimulant with antibiotic, anti-inflammatory, antispasmodic, and blood-pressure-reducing properties. In my opinion, that makes ashwagandha an adaptogen/tonic.

The recommended daily dose is two 150- to 300-milligram capsules, standardised to contain 2 to 5 milligrams of withanolides. I haven't heard of any safety problems with ashwagandha, but the literature says that abdominal cramps are possible.

ASTRAGALUS (*ASTRAGALUS MEMBRANACEUS*). As early as 1531, Chinese herbalists were recommending astragalus – also known as huang qi – for fatigue. Asians view the herb as a tonic that's almost as effective as ginseng. Modern research suggests that astragalus stimulates the immune system (though in my opinion, it's not quite as effective as echinacea), counteracts fatigue, treats many infections (including flu), and supports the kidneys.

I grow astragalus, but I don't harvest it. Herbalists recommend taking 3 to 5 millilitres (½ to 1 teaspoon) of tincture three or four times a day, or one 500-milligram capsule twice a day. If I wanted to use astragalus, I'd buy a commercial preparation and follow the package directions for proper dosage. The herb appears to be safe.

GINSENG – ASIAN (*PANAX GINSENG*), AMERICAN (*P. QUINQUEFOLIUS*), SIBERIAN

(*ELEUTHEROCOCCUS SENTICOSUS*). Andrew Weil, M.D., one of the few medical doctors who study herbs as I do, frequently recommends ginseng to people of low vitality who have been weakened by old age or chronic illness. Among the Chinese and Koreans, the herb is especially valued as a tonic for the elderly, because it can improve appetite and digestion, tone skin and muscles, and restore depleted sexual energy.

The Chinese generally recommend limiting your use of ginseng until you get older. That's when the herb's tonic benefits kick in. At 72, I'm almost ready to start taking ginseng regularly. I have four species of the herb growing around my Garden of Youth. Unfortunately, the deer are eating too much of it. Maybe that's why they seem so healthy.

As far as I know, ginseng is safe, even though various references, including my database, mention an array of minor side effects. I suggest buying a commercial preparation and following the package directions for proper dosage.

GOLDENSEAL (*HYDRASTIS CANADENSIS*). Goldenseal is best known for its antibiotic properties. In fact, the herb is often marketed along with echinacea for infections and infectious illnesses. It contains berberine, which qualifies as an adaptogen/tonic largely because it stimulates the immune system. That's one reason why goldenseal is good for infections. The herb helps prevent and treat noninfectious diseases as well.

I have a lot of goldenseal growing down in YinYang Valley. It's in the shade, where it thrives. If you want to try the herb, I suggest buying a commercial preparation from a cultivated crop, because goldenseal is threatened in the wild. Follow the label directions for proper dosage.

GOTU KOLA (*CENTELLA ASIATICA*). After ginseng, gotu kola – also called fo ti tieng – is one of the most widely touted anti-ageing herbs. Its reputation appears to have mythological roots. According to an old Chinese legend, an elderly man, Li Ching Yun, had many wives whom he satisfied with no problem. He drank a great deal of fo ti tieng tea, to which he credited his longevity and virility.

I like this story, regardless of whether it's true. It inspires me to eat a few gotu kola leaves whenever I wander past the plant, which grows best among the rocks lining the pond near my Garden of Youth.

Australians also nibble the leaves, not so much to promote longevity and virility as to prevent and treat arthritis. Since I'm trying to stave off both arthritis and old age, I enjoy my three leaves a day.

Research suggests that gotu kola has anti-inflammatory properties to help relieve an assortment of aches and pains. The herb is also antimicrobial, which makes it useful in treating all manner of infections.

If you can't munch fresh leaves, as I do, the recommended dose is ½ to 2 teaspoons of dried leaf taken as a tea. (To make a tea, use about a cup of freshly boiled water, and allow the herb to steep for 10 to 20 minutes before straining.) You can drink up to three cups of tea a day. Gotu kola appears to be safe, though indigestion and allergic reactions are possible. In addition, the literature warns pregnant women not to use the herb, as it may induce miscarriage.

JIAOGULAN (*GYNOSTEMMA PENTAPHYLLUM*). According to research, this Chinese herb is an adaptogen/tonic. It's also an antioxidant and immune system stimulant that protects the heart and lowers cholesterol and blood pressure. The recommended daily dosage is two or three tablets of standardised extract containing 85 per cent gypenosides. I've not seen any reports of side effects or problems associated with jiaogulan.

LICORICE (*GLYCYRRHIZA GLABRA*). Licorice has an unfortunate reputation. If you take extraordinarily large doses for a year or so, you can develop a hormonal problem called pseudoaldosteronism. This is very rare, but it has dampened enthusiasm for a really useful herb.

Many studies show that licorice treats ulcers as effectively as Tagamet. The herb has potent anti-inflammatory properties, so it's good for arthritis and other aches and pains. It makes a throat-soothing cough remedy when prepared as a tea, by steeping the herb in a cup of water for 10 minutes, then straining. It also protects the liver, stimulates the immune system, and is an antioxidant.

The recommended dose is ½ to 2 teaspoons of powdered root made into tea, up to three times a day; or 1 to 2 millilitres (about ¼ teaspoon) of liquid extract three times a day; or 2 to 5 millilitres (¼ to 1 teaspoon) of tincture three times a day. Liquid extracts and tinctures may be standardised to contain glycyrrhizin.

Some references say that licorice can cause an enormous number of side effects, such as high blood pressure. These side effects are actually associated with pseudoaldosteronism. But as I mentioned before, you'd have to consume an enormous amount of licorice for a very long time to develop pseudoaldosteronism. For the typical user, the risk of side effects is tiny. Still, to be on the safe side, I suggest taking licorice at the recommended dose for up to 6 weeks at most. That way, side effects are unlikely.

SCHISANDRA (*SCHISANDRA CHINENSIS*). You may know this herb by the name Chinese magnolia vine. In Asia, it ranks up there with ginseng and astragalus as a tonic.

There's good research to show that schisandra, like milk thistle, protects the liver from damage caused by drugs and other toxic compounds. The research also suggests that the herb inhibits cell mutations, which means that it might protect against cancer. What's more, it helps strengthen the heart, relieves fatigue, and treats bacterial infections.

Since schisandra is a food, I would not hesitate to take the recommended dose – 1.5 to 6 grams of dried berries a day, or 3 millilitres (about ½ teaspoon) of tincture a day. The herb is considered safe, although some people develop itchy allergic reactions, while others report stomach upset.

The Seven Wonder Weeds

Perhaps you can't afford all those expensive standardised herbs. You can get a boatload of health-enhancing, youth-preserving phytochemicals from the following plants (although, unfortunately, not all of them grow wild in Europe). Once you know how to identify them, you can collect them for free and eat as much of them as you want. Just be sure you know what they look like before you start foraging for them. I'd suggest taking a field class with a knowledgeable herbalist or botanist if one is offered in your area.

Personally, I believe that these seven really are fountains of youth – more so than many other herbs with that reputation. As a bonus, when you're out gathering them, you're communing with nature and getting great exercise all at the same time. If that doesn't promote youth and vitality, I don't know what does.

AMARANTH (*AMARANTHUS,* VARIOUS SPECIES). This standby American weed keeps coming up in abandoned pastures, old farmsteads, and weedy plots. Look for it in rich soil and full sun. As a source of certain minerals, amaranth is near the top of the charts. Do you like spinach? Amaranth is cheaper and just as nutritious (though you may have to make do with spinach). Gather the young leaves and steam them. I often add lemon, vinegar, and hot pepper sauce.

CHICKWEED (*STELLARIA MEDIA*). An annual, chickweed pops up early in rich, abandoned soils. It has lots of vitamin E and oestrogenic isoflavones, which help prevent breast cancer. Gather the young leaves and steam them. Some people, including me, like to add a few raw leaves to their salads.

DANDELION (*TARAXACUM OFFICINALE*). This is probably our best-known and most despised lawn and garden weed. But I love it, and I eat it often. Dandelion is extremely rich in beta-carotene, boron, calcium, iron, lecithin, and potassium. You can add the raw leaves to salads or steam them for a side dish.

LAMB'S-QUARTER (*CHENOPODIUM ALBUM,* FAT HEN). Often found growing close to amaranth or chickweed in the US, this herb tastes a lot like spinach. In fact, I once fooled my wife, Peggy, by serving cooked lamb's-quarter and telling her it was spinach. The weed is a great source of calcium, phosphorus, potassium, and riboflavin, as well as the amino acids alanine, cysteine, glycine, isoleucine, leucine, and lysine. While some folks like their lamb's-quarter steamed, I prefer mine overboiled.

PURSLANE (*PORTULACA OLERACEA*). The most nutritious weed around, purslane is my all-time favourite. It has more potassium than spinach, and it's also a diuretic. Because of these attributes, it's excellent for helping to control high blood pressure, one of the major plagues as we gets older.

In animal studies, purslane lowers blood sugar, suggesting that it might help manage diabetes. And if I were lost in the bush without medicine, I wouldn't hesitate to apply crushed purslane to wounds, because it soothes all manner of stings and bites. It contains an array of vitamins and minerals, including beta-carotene, vitamin C, vitamin E, calcium, magnesium, and potassium. And according to a report in the *New England Journal of Medicine*, 'Purslane is the richest source of [heart-protective] omega-3 fatty acids of any [leafy] vegetable yet examined.' I love it fresh, cooked, or juiced. I also dry it and crumble it into winter soups for added heartiness and nutrition.

RED CLOVER (*TRIFOLIUM PRATENSE*). You find red clover in sunny meadows and pastures. Its flowers are rich in the oestrogenic isoflavones daidzein and genistein, which are said to be good for preventing breast cancer and osteoporosis, two major health concerns among older women. Red clover is also rich in calcium, manganese, and selenium, which is a key cancer-fighting antioxidant. I munch the flower heads, but not everyone likes them. Some people dry the flower heads, turn them into a powder, and add them to soups.

SORREL (*RUMEX ACETOSELLA*). This perennial weed has a tart taste, perhaps too tart for some. I like it raw or cooked. Generally, sorrel grows in acidic soil. I find it in bare spots on sunny old lawns and at the edges of hedgerows but if you can't find it locally you can easily grow some in your home or garden. It's rich in beta-carotene, as well as a cancer-fighting, heart-healthy compound known as emodin.

A Final Thought

Now suppose that you'd like to take every herb mentioned in this chapter every day. You'd probably have to spend a lot less if you grow your own. But what do you spend on pharmaceuticals right now? I'm not just talking about the copayments on your health insurance. I'm talking about the real cost of all the medications you're using. I bet that amount is more than you'd spend on these herbs.

I'd never tell anyone not to take medicines that their doctors have prescribed. My point is that by investing in nature's medicines – these health-enhancing, youth-promoting herbs – you'll probably save a bundle by protecting yourself against many of the diseases that require treatment with high-priced pharmaceuticals. And you'll feel and look better all the way to the bank.

CHAPTER 6

Strong Bones

Dr Duke's Anti-Ageing Elixir

• *Bone-Bracing Bean Broth*

If you've been following all the news reports about osteoporosis, the brittle-bone disease that affects so many postmenopausal women (and a surprisingly large number of elderly men), you've probably noticed a common theme. Everyone – from the medical establishment, to the government, to the media – seems eager to pin blame for the disease on a lack of dietary calcium.

Every time you turn around, some organisation or agency is issuing a study or a press release citing an epidemic of calcium deficiency. They're rallying people to get more of the chalky mineral by guzzling more milk and eating more dairy products, which is music to the ears of the dairy farmers.

Calcium certainly is a factor in bone health because it's the main mineral in bone. But if you delve more deeply into the subject of osteoporosis, you'll discover a few things that my former colleagues at the USDA never quite get around to mentioning.

For example, elderly Asian women are nowhere near as likely to develop osteoporosis as white American women – or Asian-American women, for that matter. Yet on average, Asians consume considerably less calcium (and fewer dairy products) than Americans.

And some years back, when scientists had the opportunity to study the centuries-old skeletons of elderly women dug up from a graveyard in England, they discovered that the bones of these long-dead ladies showed very few signs of disease. Yet during their lifetimes, these women probably were not eating large amounts of dairy products either.

How do the experts account for such findings? Until recently, the best explanation had to do with exercise. Weight-bearing physical activities such as walking, gardening, and dancing – anything that involves supporting your own weight – helps build bone and prevent osteoporosis. Even today, Asians walk more than Americans. And hundreds of years ago, when those elderly women lived in England, everyone walked more than we do now. So far, so good.

But here's the catch: when compared with American women who exercise more than they do, Asian women are *still* less likely to develop osteoporosis. So what's protecting their bones? Quite possibly, it's their near-vegetarian, isoflavone-rich Palaeolithic diet.

Americans eat a lot more meat than Asians do – and a lot more than people did in 18th-century England. How could eating meat lead to bone loss?

Meat is loaded with protein that your body breaks down into amino acids, which circulate in your blood. All those amino acids make your blood more acidic. When your blood becomes acidic, your body neutralises it by adding calcium that's taken from your bones. So the more protein you eat, the more calcium your bones lose.

This is easy to show in human studies. The amount of calcium excreted in the urine increases with the amount of animal protein that people consume. In the standard American diet, the greatest source of protein is meat, followed by dairy products, which, ironically, many women make a point of eating in the possibly mistaken belief that dairy helps prevent osteoporosis.

I'm all for getting the 1,000 to 1,500 milligrams of calcium per day that many experts recommend. But by itself, calcium isn't enough. To keep your bones strong, healthy, and youthful, forgo the milk and cheese and get your calcium the Palaeolithic way – from herbs, vegetables, and grains.

Calcium Without the Cow

You've undoubtedly got the message from one source or another that you should be eating dairy products to strengthen your bones. Did you ever wonder where dairy cows pick up the calcium that they pass along to you? Cows are herbivores. They don't eat meats or dairy foods. Their entire calcium intake comes from dark leafy greens.

If you want to protect yourself against osteoporosis, my advice is to follow the herd and eat those dark leafy greens. Eat lots of them.

Pigweed (*Amaranthus*, various species), one of my favourite weeds, is a great source of calcium; 30 g (1 oz) of dried pigweed leaves supplies 1,500 milligrams of the mineral, the highest daily intake that experts recommend. For myself, I like to boil the leaves and serve them as a side dish. Sometimes I chop them up raw and toss them into salads and soups.

Other calcium-rich greens include lamb's-quarter and stinging nettle, both of which grow in my Garden of Youth. Broccoli, broad beans, brussels sprouts, cabbage, kale, lettuce, spinach, and watercress contain respectable amounts of the mineral, as do licorice, marjoram, red clover shoots, savory, and thyme.

Most of the greens can be boiled and served as a side dish or chopped up raw and added to salads and soups. Cook broad beans as you would any other bean. I use a licorice root stick to stir my herbal teas, and marjoram, savory, and thyme to season foods. And I eat my red clover straight from the garden.

Magnesium and Manganese: The Dynamic Duo

While few experts discourage eating greens, many say that greens are not as rich in calcium as dairy products. That's true. But calcium isn't the be-

Dr Duke's Anti-Ageing Elixir

Bone-Bracing Bean Broth

If you're concerned about osteoporosis, this is the soup for you. It delivers a generous supply of calcium, a mineral that's essential for strong bones, as well as other important nutrients like magnesium and boron.

WHAT YOU NEED

115 g (4 oz) dried black beans
115 g (4 oz) dried black-eyed peas
115 g (4 oz) dried broad beans
115 g (4 oz) dried split peas
Salt
Ground black pepper
Hot-pepper sauce
115 g (4 oz) chopped carrots
115 g (4 oz) chopped tomatoes
455–910 g (1–2 lb) shredded leafy greens (your choice of amaranth, asparagus, broccoli, brussels sprouts, cabbage, kale, lettuce, stinging nettle, pigweed, purslane, sorrel, spinach, and watercress)

WHAT TO DO

Put the dried pulses in a pot and add water to cover. Allow to soak overnight. The next morning, strain the pulses and add fresh water to the pot. Season with the salt, pepper, and hot-pepper sauce. Bring to the boil, then reduce the heat and simmer. As the pulses start to get tender, add the carrots and tomatoes. Add more water to cover. After 20 minutes, add the greens of your choice. Simmer for 5 to 10 minutes more.

---

all and end-all of bone health. You need several other minerals as well, including magnesium and manganese. You'll find both of them in greens.

Women with osteoporosis often have low levels of magnesium. For preserving bone density, the combination of magnesium and calcium is much more effective than calcium alone. If you need more magnesium, you may want to start eating more black-eyed peas, purslane and spinach. All three are good sources of the mineral, as are amaranth, stinging nettle, and sorrel.

More Wisdom *from the* Garden

Whole Grains Are Good for Bone Gains

A major reason for the high rate of osteoporosis in the United States is that Americans eat too much white bread. The milling process that produces white flour strips away nearly three-quarters of the magnesium content of wheat. You'll do your bones a big favour by eating wholemeal breads instead of white. And be sure to start your day with a bowl of whole grain cereal. You can add milk, but half the time, I pour orange juice over mine.

Prepare black-eyed peas as you would any other bean. Boil the greens as a side dish or chop them up and toss them into salads and soups.

For manganese, black tea is one of the best sources. As a bonus, it supplies a decent amount of fluorine, another bone preserver. Black tea is the kind most often sold in tea bag form in grocery stores. Drink a cup or two a day.

You can also get manganese from black-eyed peas, lettuce, red clover, and spinach, as well as from bilberry, buchu, cardamom, catnip, cloves, fennel seed, ginger, and parsley. Fresh bilberries aren't always readily available; you'll have to settle for the extract or substitute blueberries, which also contain manganese. Fresh parsley can be eaten straight from the garden. The rest of the herbs can be prepared as teas.

Vitamins D and K: Supporting Players in Skeletal Health

Minerals aren't the only nutrients essential to bone health. Your skeleton needs support from vitamins – specifically, vitamins D and K.

Vitamin D helps your body absorb all the calcium that you're getting from herbs and food plants. To get your daily dose of D, you don't have to drink vitamin-fortified milk. Your body makes its own supply of the nutrient when your skin is exposed to sunlight. If you garden, as I do, you probably get quite a bit of sunshine. For most people, 20 to 30 minutes a day is enough.

There is one caveat, though: you can't wear sunscreen, since it interferes with your skin's synthesis of vitamin D. So you need to be extra careful not to burn. My advice is to get your dose of sunshine in the early morning or late afternoon, when the sun's rays are least intense.

If your time outdoors is limited to a dash from your car to your house or workplace and back, you may not be getting enough sun for your body to manufacture vitamin D. In fact, vitamin D deficiency is a big problem among older folks, who spend most of their daylight hours inside. If you're indoor-bound for any reason, I'd suggest taking a vitamin D supplement – 400 IU if you're under age 70 and 600 IU if you're older but want to stay young. Except for vitamin-fortified dairy products and fatty saltwater fish such as salmon, few foods contain adequate amounts of vitamin D.

for the Gardener

Parsley

Petroselinum crispum

Parsley is considered a biennial, but sometimes the plants survive for 3 or 4 years if they don't flower or seed (perhaps because of harvesting or nature's intervention). They do best in well-drained, organic loam, the kind of soil that's in my Garden of Youth.

Plant the seeds about 5 mm (¼ in) deep in rows 46–60 mm (18 to 24 in) apart. Then wait patiently: parsley germinates very slowly. To mark the rows, some gardeners recommend mixing parsley with a species that germinates more quickly, such as radish. You can harvest the radishes as you thin the parsley to 15- to 23-cm (6- to 9-in) spacing.

Harvest parsley leaves throughout the summer, cutting the older stems from the outside of the plants and leaving the new growth in the centre. Store the leaves in a dark, dry place.

Note: Never, ever harvest parsley in the wild. Often what looks like parsley is actually hemlock or some other poisonous plant.

As for vitamin K, Dutch studies have shown that supplements of the nutrient stimulate osteoblasts, special cells that create bone. You can get ample amounts of vitamin K from leafy greens – the darker, the better. Kale is a top-notch source. Other good choices include parsley, spinach, green cabbage, watercress, broccoli, brussels sprouts, and lettuce. Eat a variety of these greens, and you'll keep your K in good supply.

Other Nutrients You Need to Know

Among the bone-building herbs and food plants, pulses (soya and other beans) don't get much recognition. But they're important. They're a good source of plant protein, which is less likely than meat protein to contribute to osteoporosis. Plus, they contain phyto-oestrogens, specifically the isoflavones daidzein, genistein, and sometimes glycitein. These help prevent the breakdown of bone.

Phyto-oestrogens are plant compounds that seem to function like the pharmaceutical oestrogen that doctors often prescribe to menopausal and postmenopausal women. Like phyto-oestrogens, pharmaceutical oestrogen protects bones. But it has side effects and may increase your risk of breast cancer.

Don't feel as if you have to get your phyto-oestrogens from soya – though if you enjoy soya foods, by all means eat them. The fact is, all pulses (with the exception of peanuts) contain phyto-oestrogens. These other sources are lower in fat to boot.

I believe that phyto-oestrogens are probably just as good at preserving bone. Yet beans cause few, if any, side effects – perhaps flatulence from eating them. And they've not been associated with breast cancer. In fact, there's considerable evidence that phyto-oestrogens help prevent breast cancer.

Some evidence also shows that omega-3 essential fatty acids can help preserve bone. In the latest studies, the anti-inflammatory properties of omega-3s appear to inhibit the breakdown of bone tissue. The most publicised sources of these 'good fats' are cold-water fish such as salmon. If you're a strict vegetarian, you can still get your omega-3s from purslane, flaxseed oil, and walnut oil.

More Wisdom *from the* Garden

This Ratio Can Make or Break Your Bones

One contributor to osteoporosis that doesn't get much attention is the calcium-to-phosphorus ratio of foods. While calcium builds bone, phosphorus breaks it down. So even if you're getting enough calcium, your bones suffer if you're consuming too much phosphorus.

Compared with most other foods, greens have the best calcium-to-phosphorus ratios – from 2:1 to 4:1. Now you have another good reason to eat herbs and leafy veggies for your bones.

More Ways to Boost Bone Strength

By getting a mix of the aforementioned herbs and foods in your diet on a daily basis, you can help keep your bones strong and resilient for a lifetime. Other lifestyle strategies are important, too. Here's what I recommend, based on my own research.

Take supplements for nutritional support. If you're concerned that you might not be getting enough of the bone-building nutrients through diet alone, you can make up for any shortfall by taking supplements. The recommended daily intakes from foods and supplements combined are 800 milligrams of calcium, 300 milligrams of magnesium, 2 to 5 milligrams of manganese, and 80 micrograms of vitamin K.

Just be careful with supplemental calcium. Some sources of the mineral, such as bonemeal, dolomite, and oyster shell, might be contaminated with lead, a toxic heavy metal. Calcium carbonate is considered the best and safest choice. You can buy a supplement or take over-the-counter antacids like Rolaids or Tums, which are mostly calcium carbonate.

Engage in weight-bearing exercise daily. Bone is a little like muscle: use it or lose it. When you subject it to the controlled stress of exercise, it gets stronger. Weight-bearing activities – those that put weight on your major bones – are best. You can work out for 30 to 60 minutes at a time or squeeze in several shorter periods of activity throughout your day.

Of course, you have many good reasons to exercise. But bone preservation is a big one. I get my daily dose of weight-bearing activity by walking around YinYang Valley and gardening, wielding those heavy watering cans. For those cold and rainy days, I keep a set of dumbbells by my stationary bicycle. Perhaps you'd rather take up dancing or sign up for an aerobics class (though if you're my age, you may want to stick with low-impact or water aerobics). Do whatever you like. Just be sure to get some weight-bearing exercise every day.

Be aware of the bone robbers. A few things can hurt bone and therefore should be avoided. Smoking is a big offender, as cigarettes deplete bone mass. Likewise, caffeine, alcohol, salt, and sugar increase your body's excretion of calcium, so you'd be wise to monitor your consumption of these substances. And watch out for cola soft drinks, which are very high in bone-dissolving phosphorus.

Several classes of prescription drugs pull calcium out of bone. Corticosteroids and thyroid medications are especially problematic. If you're taking either drug, you may want to talk to your doctor about keeping tabs on your bone density.

By the way, if you've been contemplating a trip into outer space, you may want to rethink your travel plans. Weightlessness can trigger osteoporosis. It has been a problem for several astronauts.

CHAPTER 7

Easy Breathing

Dr Duke's Anti-Ageing Elixirs

- *Burning Broncho-Buster Tea*
- *Asthma-Arrest Tea*
- *Better Breathing Brew*

As I recall, this incident happened in the late 1930s, when I was 7 or 8 years old. At the time, my family lived in Durham, North Carolina, a centre of the tobacco industry. I was playing in front of our house when I noticed a lit cigarette butt that someone had discarded. I picked it up and took it to the backyard, where my parents were pottering around our garden.

I proceeded to demonstrate how grown up I was by puffing on the cigarette. My parents were none too pleased. They viewed smoking as a nasty vice – and that was long before it would be linked to lung cancer.

A few years later, despite my parents' exhortations not to smoke, I began sucking on cancer sticks with the gang of boys that I played with. By the time I graduated from high school, I was hooked. I smoked three packs a day in college, and I kept at it for longer than I care to remember.

Then as my kids were growing up, the research that connected smoking to lung cancer became too compelling to ignore. In 1964, the first Surgeon General's report on smoking urged Americans to quit. I knew that the Surgeon General was right, but I kept on puffing until my kids nearly pestered me to death. Finally, in 1970, I quit cold turkey.

Quitting was no fun. It left me hungry and fidgety, in need of something to do with my hands. Munching carrots seemed like the perfect solution. I used to eat them on the way to work, at the office, any time I would normally have reached for a cigarette. In fact, for several years after I stopped smoking, I still got the urge to light up. Instead of giving in, I'd grab a big carrot and nibble on it while strolling through a field or forest, inhaling the fragrances of all the aromatic plants. I couldn't do that as well when I smoked, because I had a less-keen sense of smell.

Substituting carrot sticks for cancer sticks turned out to be one of the best things that I ever did for my health. As studies have since shown, the vitamin A-like carotenoids that give carrots their orange colour are major antioxidants that work together to help prevent lung cancer in ex-smokers.

These days, I no longer feel the urge to smoke. I still munch a lot of carrots, though – in part because I like them, in part because as a former heavy smoker, I'm still at risk for lung cancer.

I don't grow carrots in the Garden of Youth. But maybe I should, since I credit them with saving my lungs. Then again, buying them is cheaper than growing them.

The Basics of Good Respiratory Health

If you smoke, you've probably heard this hundreds of times. But I'm going to say it anyway: do whatever you must to quit. You'll not only live much longer, you'll also look much younger. Smoking is a major cause of skin wrinkling. After you quit, some of those wrinkles will disappear, giving you a more youthful appearance.

While you're at it, stay away from secondhand smoke as much as possible. There's still some controversy over just how harmful it is, but I'm convinced that it's bad enough to be avoided. The same goes for smog, automobile exhaust, and vapours from factories, paints, and anything that gives off chemical fumes.

Beyond kicking the habit and steering clear of secondhand smoke, you can keep your lungs in good shape by engaging in regular aerobic exercise. That's true for youngsters of all ages – 7, 47, or 70. Like the American Lung Association, I advise against doing anything aerobic, especially jogging, near busy highways. All that air pollution harms the lungs.

Of course, I'm fortunate enough to live in a rural area, with my home situated just a few steps from my Garden of Youth, where the green leaves make fresh oxygen and scrub pollutants from the air. Even on days when the air quality tends towards smog, I walk around my garden and the rest of YinYang Valley, making sure I move briskly enough to elevate my respiration and heart rates (the criteria for an aerobic workout).

Along the way, I just might munch on the leaves of some of the garden's edible greens, such as mint, chickweed, dandelion, lamb's-quarter, stinging nettle, purslane, and sorrel. These plants are particularly rich in antioxidants that can help prevent lung damage. I try to eat at least seven kinds of leafy greens every day. I suggest you do the same. (For more on my Healthy Sevens eating plan, see chapter 3.)

We get our share of hard rains here in Maryland, so sometimes my walks around YinYang Valley are washed out. On those days, I keep my lungs healthy and young by riding my stationary bike, which is conveniently located right next to my computer. I also perform yoga-like stretches morning and night. I began doing them some time ago because of back problems, but as I've learned, yoga is also very good for the lungs.

Between getting regular aerobic exercise and reducing your exposure to cigarette smoke and other noxious fumes, you dramatically increase your odds of having healthy lungs for a lifetime. You can do even more to protect yourself against some common respiratory complaints, which can turn quite serious when they affect older folks. Here's what I recommend.

Colds: Make Yourself Virus-Proof

As a grown-up, you're most likely to catch a cold if you have kids or grandkids under the age of 5. Young children are magnets for colds because their immune systems haven't fully matured and because they haven't been sick often enough to build their defences against the 200 known cold-causing viruses. They pass their colds to their parents and grandparents, who can't resist snuggling up to under-the-weather tots. The adults are easy targets for all the virus particles that the kids release.

Cold viruses spread in two ways: through the air and by direct contact. To reduce your odds of playing host to a virus floating on the breeze, increase the ventilation in your home. Of course, you can't leave the windows wide open in the dead of winter, at the height of cold and flu season. But you can open them just a crack for some of the time.

Avoiding direct contact with cold viruses is more of a challenge, simply because of human behaviour. If you're like most people, you touch your face, especially your nose, several times an hour without realising it. When you have a cold and you touch your nose, you get the cold germs on your hands. Then you deposit those germs on the hard objects you come in contact with, such as doorknobs, countertops, and telephones. Anyone who touches those objects after you can pick up your cold virus and transfer it to their own noses. They can also get the virus just by shaking your hand.

How can you break the chain of direct contact? Your mum's advice is still the best: wash your hands frequently with soap and water. That gets rid of the virus before you can deposit it elsewhere.

You can also reduce your susceptibility to cold viruses by keeping your stress levels in check. Emotional stress depresses your immune system, so a virus can easily sneak in and infect you. By relieving stress, you help reinforce your body's immune defences. My own stress-management programme consists of walking and gardening. But you may prefer meditation, visualisation, yoga, or something else that calms your body, mind, and soul.

Of course, there are herbs that may help boost your resistance to colds. For myself, I prefer garlic and echinacea – the former as a

growing younger naturally

Her Sinus Infections Are History

Sinus infections are often mistaken for colds – which makes sense, since their symptoms are so similar. In fact, acute sinus infections often come on the heels of a cold or the flu. Chronic infections usually result from some environmental trigger, such as airborne particles of dust, pollen, or smoke.

One of my colleagues, registered nurse Sue Mustalish, had the opportunity to work with a 42-year-old woman who had a several-year history of chronic sinus infections. She would start a new course of antibiotics (Biaxin) about every 4 to 6 weeks.

Sue advised her new client to make some adjustments in her diet, cutting back on dairy products and refined sugar while drinking more water. Sue also recommended cat's claw, a natural antibiotic and immune system booster, and regular inhalation of the vapours from teas made with eucalyptus, lavender, and thyme. All three herbs have antiseptic and decongestant properties, so they help open the sinuses.

Once she started this regime, Sue's client was able to get through the entire winter without needing antibiotics. After years of suffering, she finally found relief.

flavourful ingredient in many of the foods I eat, the latter as a standardised tincture (a teaspoon or so in juice several times a day) or possibly as capsules. I don't use echinacea year-round, but I may take it daily during cold and flu season.

Sometimes when a nasty cold was making its way through the family, I'd take one of the echinaceas straight from my Garden of Youth and chew the root, swallowing the juice just as the Native Americans of the Great Plains did. Since then, scientists have learned that all parts of the echinacea plant are antiviral and immune-system-boosting. So I don't uproot my echinaceas anymore. Instead, I chew on the flower petals or the rather bitter leaves.

To ward off colds and other viral infections, I also recommend black and green teas, both of which have abundant supplies of antiviral compounds, including tannins. The teas are rich in antioxidants, too. Once you reach a certain age, you can't get too many antioxidants in your diet. These nutrients help prevent many of the major age-related conditions, including heart disease, cancer, and cataracts. Even outside cold season, you may benefit from drinking a few cups of black or green tea a day.

If, despite your best efforts, you still come down with a cold, I recommend eating lots of hot, spicy foods and drinking lots of hot, spicy teas to help you get better. The trouble with colds and most other respiratory ailments is that they usually cause an accumulation of thick mucus in the respiratory tract. The mucus is hard to cough up, so it just sits there inside the bronchial tubes. It makes breathing difficult and triggers coughing.

Long ago, the ancients discovered that fiery spices help break up bronchial mucus, thinning it so it's easier to cough up. That's why when I have a cold or another respiratory complaint, I often drink water spiked with 10 to 20 drops of Tabasco sauce. I also brew up my Burning Broncho-Buster Tea, a mucus-clearing blend of seven heat-packing herbs.

More Wisdom *from the* Garden

A 'Berry' Smart Way to Boost Your Immunity

Tannins are compounds that make foods and herbs tart and astringent. Soluble tannins also have antiviral properties and help fend off colds, flu, and other infectious diseases.

In my Garden of Youth, I grow a variety of tannin-rich herbs, including blackberry, blueberry, chokeberry (also known as aronia), cranberry, elderberry, raspberry, and wineberry (a close relative of raspberry). I'd recommend their fruits not only for the antiviral tannins but even more for the antioxidant anthocyanidins, compounds found in the pigments that give the berries their colour.

Of course, all of these fruits taste great. They're a delicious way to stay healthy and young.

Dr Duke's Anti-Ageing Elixir

Burning Broncho-Buster Tea

When I have a cold or some other respiratory complaint, I brew up this tea. It contains seven hot, spicy herbs that clear out excess mucus and help me breathe more easily.

WHAT YOU NEED

1 small chilli pepper, chopped (wear plastic gloves when handling)

1 clove garlic, chopped

Dash of ground ginger

1 tablespoon pulverized horseradish root

1 teaspoon mustard powder

1 large onion, chopped

Dash of turmeric

WHAT TO DO

In a medium saucepan, add the chilli pepper, garlic, ginger, horseradish, mustard, onion, and turmeric to a few cups of boiling water. Reduce the heat, then simmer for 20 minutes. Strain the tea and allow it to cool slightly before drinking it.

Variation: You can also make a tasty spread from the Burning Broncho-Buster herbs. Just mash them up and make a paste with a little olive oil. You can spread it on bread or crackers.

Flu: Take This Bug Seriously

Many people refer to any bad cold as the flu. Like colds, flu is caused by a respiratory virus. But that's where the similarity ends. Flu is much more severe, and for older folks like me, it's potentially fatal. Every year, thousands of people over 65 die from flu-related pneumonia. You don't want to take the flu lightly.

The best way to reduce your chances of coming down with the flu is to get an annual flu shot. The older you are, the more important this is. You should get a shot every year in the autumn because the virus is always changing and you want protection against the specific strain that the experts predict is likely to hit each winter.

Keep in mind that while a shot can make you less vulnerable to the flu, it doesn't provide absolute protection. This is especially true for older folks like me because our immune systems aren't what they used to be. The good news is that if you receive a shot but develop the flu anyway, it's usually a mild case.

A flu shot takes about 2 weeks to kick in. That's why you should schedule your shot in early November, before the start of flu season.

Most GPs' surgeries offer flu shots every autumn although you will probably have to pay for them if you are not in a high-risk group.

I certainly recommend flu shots, especially for 'old youngsters'. Given the large number of elderly people who die from flu-related pneumonia each year, the shots can be a matter of life or death. To be honest, I've been getting the shot only when I remember, and only when it's convenient. It may come back to haunt me one of these years.

Even after you receive your shot, make every effort to steer clear of people who already have the flu. The virus spreads through the air quite rapidly, much more rapidly than colds. If you can't avoid contact with flu sufferers, you may be able to boost your defences by taking echinacea (as a tincture or in capsules, according to the label directions) and garlic (one to two cloves a day, or the equivalent in capsules). Also, eat lots of spicy foods and drink plenty of my Burning Broncho-Buster Tea (see page 91).

Bronchitis: The Cough That Just Won't Quit

There are two kinds of bronchitis: chronic and acute. The chronic variety is usually a by-product of smoking. If you smoke and you want to avoid chronic bronchitis, you can probably guess my advice. You have to kick the habit – and the sooner, the better.

Acute bronchitis usually shows up at the tail end of a cold. It starts with a dry, hacking cough that just won't quit. Sometimes the cough gets so bad that your chest starts hurting and you really feel old.

If you seem to be getting over a cold and you develop a serious cough as well as a fever, you need to see your doctor right away. You could have pneumonia (more on this condition below).

If you're dealing with run-of-the-mill acute bronchitis, there's not much that your doctor can do. Antibiotics are unlikely to help because they treat bacterial infections, not viruses. On the other hand, my Burning Broncho-Buster Tea (see page 91) may provide some relief. And sucking on boiled sweets can soothe your throat and keep it moist.

Pneumonia: Prompt Treatment Is Key

If you're over 65 and you come down with the flu, you need to be careful that it doesn't turn into pneumonia. At first, you may start to feel better. Your fever breaks, your respiratory symptoms clear up, and your energy returns. But then the fever comes back. In addition, you might develop chest tightness or have some trouble breathing.

My Burning Broncho-Buster Tea (see page 91) may help you feel a little better, but it's no cure. Get yourself to your doctor as soon as you can. Flu-related pneumonia requires prompt professional treatment.

Of course, I'd never give myself entirely to conventional medicine. I'd continue taking echinacea to boost my immune system and garlic to battle both viral and bacterial infections. In fact, garlic is an ideal herbal treatment for flu-related pneumonia because the pneumonia can be viral or bacterial or both.

If I ever ended up in a hospital – whether for pneumonia or some other illness – I'd take plenty of echinacea and garlic for the duration of my stay if the staff permitted me to do so. Yes, hospitals can work wonders, but they're also convenient harbours for a host of supergerms.

Other herbal immune-boosters include astragalus, burdock, ginseng, and goldenseal. I'd recommend buying commercial preparations in a health food store and following the package directions for proper dosage.

Asthma: Grown-Ups Get It, Too

No one in my family has asthma. But a young friend of mine died from it in the prime of life.

Many people consider asthma a childhood condition. Lots of kids have it, but it's actually more common among adults. Just as surprising, many adults with asthma never had it as kids.

I can remember a time when asthma wasn't all that common. These days, more people than ever are wheezing and gasping for breath. The experts argue about the reasons for asthma's rise. Personally, I'm convinced that air pollution, allergies, and chemical exposure have a good deal to do with it.

Allergies, in particular, are a very common asthma trigger. If you have asthma, you should work with an allergist/immunologist to identify your particular allergens, substances that bring on your allergy symptoms. Then you should avoid those substances like the plague.

In the Garden of Youth, on the third terrace, I grow two of the better asthma herbs: Chinese ephedra (ma huang) and tea. I also have potted coffee, tea, and cocoa plants, which I keep in my greenhouse during winter months. One day, I hope to grow guarana, maté, and guayusa as well. All of these plants contain stimulant compounds that can prevent and treat the narrowing of the air passages (bronchoconstriction) that, along with inflammation of those passages, plays a key role in asthma attacks.

Dr Duke's Anti-Ageing Elixir

Asthma-Arrest Tea

I'd wager that in clinical trials, this tea would compare well with conventional asthma medications. That said, if you have asthma, never discontinue your drug treatment unless under the supervision of a doctor.

WHAT YOU NEED

Equal parts of any or all of the following herbs: ground coffee beans, ground cocoa beans, Chinese ephedra (ma huang), guarana, guayusa, maté, and black or green tea

1 cup water

Powdered licorice root, anise, or any natural sweetener (optional)

WHAT TO DO

Blend together the herbs of your choice. Add about as much of the herb blend to freshly boiled water as you would when making a cup of coffee. (You don't want to go overboard, or you may end up with caffeine jitters and insomnia.) Steep for 10 to 20 minutes, then let the tea cool slightly and strain before drinking it. Add the licorice, anise, or other sweetener, if you wish.

Chinese ephedra is currently being scrutinised by the FDA and may ultimately be banned because it has been associated with several deaths. Most of the people died after taking ridiculously high doses of the herb to get intoxicated. Chinese ephedra can cause heart problems when taken in very large amounts. But when used responsibly in the recommended doses to treat asthma, it seldom causes harm – at least in my experience. Nevertheless, if you have asthma – and especially if you're using medication for the condition – you should absolutely check with your doctor before trying Chinese ephedra.

The other herbs mentioned above contain caffeine, which few people realise is a potent bronchodilator. If you feel an asthma attack coming on and you don't have your medicine or inhaler handy, a cup or two of strong coffee just may nip the attack in the bud.

Another way to get a dose of caffeine is with my Asthma-Arrest Tea. It's made with the herbs mentioned above and often spiked with licorice, or anise (which tastes like licorice).

One final thought on the subject of asthma: many people with this respiratory condition give up exercising because they think it's dangerous. On the contrary, they need to exercise to keep their lungs as healthy as possible. Work

Dr Duke's Anti-Ageing Elixir

Better Breathing Brew

All of the ingredients in this tea are rich in cineole, a natural expectorant. Among the best sources of the compound are cardamom, eucalyptus, spearmint, rosemary, ginger, lavender, and nutmeg. You can also try bee balm, peppermint, cinnamon, turmeric, basil, and lemon. Feel free to mix and match the herbs and spices to get the taste that you like best.

For my own version of Better Breathing Brew, I use this recipe.

WHAT YOU NEED

1 handful rosemary leaves
A few peppermint leaves
A few spearmint leaves
Dash of nutmeg
Dash of cinnamon
1 cup water
A natural sweetener (optional)

WHAT TO DO

Combine the herbs. Add a total of 2 teaspoons of the herb blend to the freshly boiled water. Steep for about 10 minutes. Make sure that the tea has cooled before you strain and drink it. Add a sweetener, if you wish.

with your doctor to design a fitness programme that suits you.

Many studies show that yoga can help prevent asthma attacks. If I had asthma, I'd definitely practise yoga every day.

Emphysema: Above All Else, Banish Those Butts

My older brother, Edwin, used to have a cigarette habit. He was more of a social smoker than a chain smoker. Still, he wasn't big on exercise, and he didn't make a point of eating lots of carrots and other produce that could have helped protect his lungs. He wound up with emphysema.

Fortunately, it's a mild case; Edwin is still carrying on at the age of 80. He's luckier than most. Emphysema often causes slow suffocation that makes even mild exertion – like going from sitting to standing – completely exhausting.

The best way to avoid emphysema, of course, is to not smoke. If you already have the disease, you can tote around an oxygen canister to make breathing easier. You can also make some lifestyle adjustments, based on recommendations from ASH (Action on Smoking and Health), which can be found at *www.ash.org.uk.*

When my brother was diagnosed with emphysema, I told him all about the respiratory benefits of hot, spicy foods. I also suggested that he drink my Burning Broncho-Buster Tea (see page 91).

Of course, if you have emphysema, your lungs need all the help they can get. You may also want to try my Better Breathing Brew (see page 95). It's made with herbs that are rich in an expectorant compound called cineole, which may help keep the air passages clear.

CHAPTER 8

Cancer Prevention

Dr Duke's Anti-Ageing Elixir

Colon-Care Tea

So far, my 72-year-old body has had three brushes with cancer. In 1980, I developed a small patch of squamous cell skin cancer, the result of spending so much time in the sun as a globe-trotting botanist. Lucky for me, squamous cell is one of the non-malignant types of skin cancer. It poses no real health threat, provided it's caught early. A surgeon cauterized it, and that was that.

Then in 1990 and 1995, I had a few polyps removed from my colon. Both of my brothers have had the same procedure. Colon polyps are not the same as colon cancer. But they can become cancerous, which is why I had mine taken out. I do everything that I can to protect myself from colon cancer, because my dad and two of his brothers died from it.

These experiences convinced me to create my own personal cancer prevention programme. It's a simple programme, really. But it's based on sound scientific evidence identifying ways to reduce cancer risk. Some of the steps I've already completed; others will be with me for a lifetime. Here they are.

- *I quit smoking.*
- *I'm careful about my alcohol consumption.*
- *I engage in regular exercise.*
- *I watch my weight.*
- *I work on maintaining a positive attitude.*
- *I try to avoid carcinogens.*
- *I eat a Palaeolithic diet.*
- *I take supplements.*
- *I use herbs.*
- *I support my immune system.*
- *I get regular cancer screenings.*

The way I figure, these steps will not only help me avoid cancer but also keep me young and vital. They may do the same for you. Let's look at each one in turn.

Quit Smoking

I gave up cigarettes in 1970. Admittedly, I should have done it sooner. But at least I quit – cold turkey no less, after smoking for 30 years. Believe me: if I can do it, anyone can.

For a while, I did miss the oral gratification of cigarettes. To compensate for it, I began munching on carrot sticks. Not a bad idea, since carrots are rich in cancer-fighting antioxidants.

Be Careful about Your Alcohol Consumption

A little alcohol – the equivalent of one to two drinks a day – can help protect against cardiovascular disease, reducing your risk of heart attack and stroke. But if you exceed that limit, you may increase your chances of developing several kinds of cancer. So if you're going to imbibe, be sensible about it. (Incidentally, a drink is defined as 350 ml (12 fl oz) of regular beer, 150 ml (5 fl oz) of wine, or a cocktail made with 45 ml ($1\frac{1}{2}$ fl oz) of 80-proof distilled spirits.)

Red wine, which is not my favourite in terms of flavour, seems better endowed with cancer-preventive polyphenols than the other libations that I enjoy. Of course, I put so many antioxidant mints in my gin-and-tonic that I can hardly recognise the gin.

Engage in Regular Exercise

Good research has shown that regular physical activity helps prevent several types of cancer, including breast cancer. Frankly, I'm not surprised. Even modest exercise boosts immune function, your body's frontline defence against all kinds of diseases.

I get a good workout just going about my daily business. Between walking around YinYang Valley and working in my Garden of Youth, I log quite a distance every day in good weather. When I can't be outside, I pedal my stationary bike and lift light dumbbells.

Watch Your Weight

Obesity contributes to several types of cancer – not to mention heart disease, stroke, diabetes, and several other health problems that you can do without. Actually, if you exercise regularly and follow a Palaeolithic diet, you'll maintain a healthy weight *and* protect yourself against cancer.

Maintain a Positive Attitude

Research proves it: your attitude affects your immune function. Of course, other things influence your immunity, too. But your attitude is one factor that's reasonably within your control.

Good research has shown that compared with people who are basically happy, those who are chronically depressed get sick more often and more severely, and recover more slowly. They also have higher death rates, including from cancer. It makes sense, since depression impairs the immune system, and an impaired immune system isn't as effective at protecting against cancer.

Lately, there has been a good deal of controversy concerning whether depression and a negative attitude can directly cause cancer. I don't think that negativity by itself causes cancer any more than happiness guarantees protection from the disease. But I do believe that a positive attitude supports cancer prevention and good health in general.

Avoid Carcinogens

Cigarette smoke ranks as one of the top carcinogens, or cancer-causing substances. But constant exposure to pollutants, pesticides, and other toxic chemicals also raises your cancer risk.

This is part of the reason why my place has been pesticide-free since 1972. I use only organic fertilizers in my Garden of Youth. I like to munch on things as I walk through the garden. I don't want to drag them to the sink to wash them, hoping to scrub off all the chemicals.

Eat a Palaeolithic Diet

As I've been saying throughout this book, the diet of our Stone Age ancestors was much healthier than ours today. It consisted primarily of plant foods – fruits and vegetables. Sure, our ancestors ate meat, when they could get it. And it was wild game meat, which is much lower in fat than our red meat.

The Palaeolithic diet was naturally high in fibre and low in fat, especially the saturated fat found in most animal products and processed foods. This is exactly the sort of diet that experts now recommend to reduce cancer risk.

The best proof that I've seen comes from a review conducted by Gladys Block, Ph.D., of the University of California, Berkeley, School of Public Health. Dr Block gathered up all the research correlating diet and cancer risk, more than 150 studies. Every one of them showed that as fruit and vegetable consumption increases, cancer risk decreases. And not just for a few cancers either. These plant foods protect against every form of the disease – lung, breast, colon, prostate, you name it.

What makes fruits and veggies such potent weapons against cancer? Quite simply, they're our best sources of antioxidant nutrients.

Antioxidants help prevent and even reverse the cell damage that sets the stage for cancer, as well as heart disease and other conditions normally associated with ageing. It's complicated, but briefly, here's what happens.

Normal metabolic processes, as well as dietary fat and carcinogens, introduce highly unstable oxygen molecules called free radicals into your bloodstream. Free radicals strive to stabilise themselves by gaining electrons. They do this by snatching electrons from other molecules that they encounter, leaving behind a path of cell damage.

Usually, your body's immune system can repair this cell damage.

More Wisdom *from the* Garden

Fibre: Protector or Poppycock?

Besides being a fabulous source of antioxidants, the plant-based Palaeolithic diet also delivers a generous supply of fibre. In a study that I just recently read about, the more fibre women ate (from cereals, vegetables, and fruits), the less likely they were to develop endometrial cancer. Compared with those who reported the lowest fibre intakes, those who had the highest intakes showed a 46 per cent reduction in endometrial cancer risk.

Many other studies have shown that fibre helps prevent colon and rectal cancers by adding bulk to stools. This helps sweep carcinogens out of your body more swiftly.

Just recently, though, the media latched on to a single study suggesting that a high-fibre diet provides no protection against colon cancer. Personally, I believe this study was off the mark, as do some of my colleagues. The medical establishment simply hasn't bought into the idea that natural strategies like eating a high-fibre diet can reduce colon cancer risk, even though hundreds of studies involving thousands of people have proved otherwise.

Because of my family history of colon cancer, I continue to follow my high-fibre Healthy Sevens eating plan, which is patterned after the Palaeolithic diet. I'd encourage anyone who wants to avoid cancer, especially colon cancer, to do the same. (For more information about the Healthy Sevens, see chapter 3.)

But over time, the free radicals get the upper hand. That's when they start causing health problems.

Antioxidants have a wonderful ability to donate electrons to free radicals, stabilising the renegade molecules without producing additional cell damage. Some of the key antioxidant nutrients are vitamins C and E, the carotenoids (including beta-carotene), and the mineral selenium.

All fruits and vegetables contain generous amounts of antioxidants. Recently, though, researchers at the USDA set out to determine which foods have the highest antioxidant content. They developed a scale to measure oxygen radical absorbance capacity (ORAC) – in layman's terms, the ability of various foods to neutralize free radicals. The higher the ORAC score, the more antioxidant protection a food provides.

'The Best Cancer-Fighting Foods' chart shows how the best antioxidant sources stack up. Unfortunately, the USDA research team excluded several antioxidant-rich foods, including garlic, kiwifruit, pink grapefruit, white grapes, cauliflower, and green tea. I bet that all of these would get pretty high ORAC scores.

Now you can see why the National Cancer Institute in America encourages people to 'strive for five' – get at least five servings of fruits and vegetables a day. The average American gets only about 3½ servings, for a total ORAC score of about 1,200. By meeting the five-servings-a-day mark, we could raise our ORAC scores to at least 1,640.

But according to the USDA researchers, even that isn't good enough. They'd like to see us go even higher, to an ORAC score of 3,000 to 5,000. The only way to accomplish that is to eat lots more than five servings of fruits and vegetables a day. As part of my Healthy Sevens eating plan, I aim for seven different fruits and seven different vegetables every day – and I usually succeed. (For more information on the Healthy Sevens, see chapter 3.)

Of course, many other plant foods that didn't make the USDA's high-ORAC list have been found to help prevent various types of cancer. Here's just a sampling.

TOMATOES. Tomatoes and tomato-based foods are rich in lycopene, a member of the carotenoid family. Harvard researchers have determined that eating just two servings of tomato-based foods a week can reduce a man's chances of developing prostate cancer by about one-third. Eat more tomato-rich foods, and risk drops even more.

But lycopene's benefits don't stop there. According to a team of Italian researchers, tomato-rich foods also help prevent mouth, throat, oesophageal, stomach, rectal, and colon cancers.

You can get lycopene from fresh and canned tomatoes; tomato sauce, puree, paste, and juice; ketchup; and even pizza (just go easy on the high-fat toppings). I put tomatoes in soups, sandwiches, and salads. I also eat cherry tomatoes right off the plant all summer long.

BEANS. Almost all edible beans – not just soyabeans – contain two important compounds: genistein and daidzein. They're best known as being oestrogenic, helping to control hot flushes and other discomforts of menopause. But they're also

The Best Cancer-Fighting Foods

A team of researchers at the USDA has developed a scale to assess the antioxidant content of various plant foods. It's called the ORAC scale, for oxygen radical absorbance capacity.

Basically, the ORAC score reflects a food's ability to neutralize cell-damaging free radicals. The higher the score, the better the cancer protection.

In the chart below, all of the scores are based on a 100-g (about 4 oz) serving. Notice how prunes and raisins rate much higher than their source fruits, plums and red grapes. That's because the latter contain a great deal of water. Dehydrating plums and red grapes to create prunes and raisins concentrates their antioxidants.

FOOD	ORAC SCORE
Prunes	5,770
Raisins	2,830
Blueberries	2,400
Blackberries	2,036
Kale	1,770
Strawberries	1,540
Spinach	1,260
Raspberries	1,220
Brussels sprouts	980
Plums	949
Alfalfa sprouts	930
Broccoli florets	890
Beetroots	840
Oranges	750
Red grapes	739
Red peppers	710
Cherries	670
Onions	450
Corn	400

anti-angiogenic, which means they help prevent the growth of new blood vessels to nourish developing tumours.

Tumours need a blood supply. They use chemical signals to trick your body into growing new blood vessels for them, a process called angiogenesis. Scientists are experimenting with drugs to arrest this process, in effect starving tumours to death before they get big enough to cause problems.

I'm all for the development of anti-angiogenic drugs, because they promise to be more effective and less toxic than the chemotherapy drugs currently in use. But we already have anti-angiogenic foods – namely, beans. By eating more beans, you reduce your risk of cancer.

BRAZIL NUTS. You need just three Brazil nuts to get the 200 micrograms of selenium that studies have shown to have a potent anti-cancer effect. As a bonus, when you eat Brazil nuts, which grow best in the Amazon rainforest, you support the conservation of one of my favourite places on earth. So you're not only protecting your body, you're saving the environment.

Take Supplements

I'm a food man myself. I think that we should get as many nutrients as possible from the whole foods that package together all of nature's bounty. I'm not a big fan of dissecting foods, isolating their major nutritional compounds, concentrating those compounds in a laboratory, and using them as the 'active' ingredients in supplements.

That said, I realise that most people don't get all of the fruits and vegetables that I do. Many don't even meet the five-servings-a-day quota that the National Cancer Institute in America has deemed the minimum for cancer prevention. So if you're not getting as many servings of fruits and veggies as you should, supplements can give you a little extra nutritional support.

The supplements that I'd recommend for cancer prevention are the antioxidants: vitamins C and E, beta-carotene, and the mineral selenium. You might also consider the newly popular grape seed extract, which is generously endowed with polyphenols, resveratrol, and anthocyanosides – all antioxidant compounds.

Use Herbs

Of course, what would my cancer prevention programme be without herbs? Mother Nature has generously endowed a number of her herbal medicines with cancer-fighting properties. Here are a few favourites.

GARLIC (*ALLIUM SATIVUM*). Of all the research examining the relationship between garlic and cancer, this finding made the biggest impression on me: in China, people who ate no garlic were *1,000 times* more likely to develop stomach cancer than those who regularly consumed large quantities of the odoriferous bulb.

Garlic contains diallyl sulphide, a compound that reduces the potency of nitrosamines, which are a major class of carcinogens. The herb also enhances immune function, helping to fend off several types of cancer, including leukaemia and melanoma.

As you already know, garlic is also the major herb for preventing heart disease and stroke. Together, these three ailments – cancer, heart disease, and stroke – are responsible for killing almost two-thirds of us. If this statistic doesn't persuade you to eat more garlic, I don't know what will.

GREEN TEA (*CAMELLIA SINENSIS*). Many studies have identified a powerful correlation between drinking green tea and reducing cancer risk. Green tea is the beverage of choice in Japan. Many people prefer black tea, but the two are made from the leaves of the same plant. They're just fermented differently. Fermentation produces a richer, fuller-bodied flavour and darker colour, but it also removes some of the antioxidants.

Black tea has some antioxidants. But if you want the most cancer protection per cup, drink green tea. These days, even supermarkets carry green tea in tea bag form. To buy the loose herb, you'll need to go to a health food shop or Asian market. Use a teaspoon or two of herb per cup of freshly boiled water. Steep for 10 minutes, then strain. Studies have found that about 95 per cent of the herb's antioxidants pass into the water within 10 minutes.

Plenty of cancer-prevention experts now encourage people to drink three to four cups of green tea a day. Seems like good advice to me.

LICORICE (*GLYCYRRHIZA GLABRA*). Licorice belongs in the diet of anyone who's predisposed to cancer. The herb is a powerful immune system booster. Most of the research to date has focused on the ability of licorice to treat viral infections. But I'm convinced that the same mechanism, immune stimulation, can also protect against cancer.

I grow licorice in my Garden of Youth. To make a tea, use 1 to 2 teaspoons of powdered root per cup of freshly boiled water. Steep for 10 minutes, then strain.

TURMERIC (*CURCUMA LONGA*). Turmeric is the spice that gives curry blends their yellow colour. It contains curcumin, a compound that has become pretty well known for its anti-inflammatory action.

Curcumin helps relieve joint pain in people with osteoarthritis and sports injuries. It works because it's a natural COX-2 inhibitor. Right now, pharmaceutical COX-2s are the hottest trend in mainstream medicine. Two drugs in particular, celecoxib (Celebrex) and rofecoxib (Vioxx), are being hyped for joint pain because they're just as effective as their predecessors, the nonsteroidal anti-inflammatory drugs, but they cause fewer gastrointestinal problems. Personally, if I had arthritis, I'd try the curcumin in turmeric first, only switching to drugs if the herb didn't provide sufficient relief.

So how does all this relate to cancer? Well, it turns out that COX-2 inhibitors help prevent the growth of new blood vessels to nourish tumours. Like beans, they're anti-angiogenic. COX-2s also discourage the uncontrolled cell division typical of cancer. Celebrex and Vioxx are starting to be promoted for the prevention of colon cancer, but I'd be happier trying the natural COX-2 compounds in turmeric.

I've calculated how much turmeric I'd have to eat to get the 10 milligrams of curcumin per kilogram of body weight that researchers consider cancer-preventive. I weigh about 90 kg, just over 14 stone, so I'd need about 60 g (2 oz) of the herb. I like turmeric, and I cook with it. But that amount a day is a bit much even for me. So if I wanted to use the herb to reduce my cancer risk, I'd buy a commercial extract containing concentrated curcumin and take it according to the package directions. (Incidentally, the piperine in black pepper improves the absorption of curcumin, so you may want to take the two together.)

By the way, you can get COX-2-inhibiting compounds from other good herbs, including barberry, feverfew, ginger, green tea, holy basil, Japanese knotweed, oregano, rosemary, sage, skullcap, and thyme. You can use some of these in cooking, or make them as teas – 1 to 2 teaspoons of herb per cup of freshly boiled water, steeped for 10 minutes, then strained.

Of the herbal COX-2 inhibitors, rosemary is particularly attractive as a cancer preventer. In addition to its COX-2-inhibiting compounds, the herb contains about 20 different antioxidants.

WILLOW BARK (*SALIX,* VARIOUS SPECIES). This herb contains salicin, a compound that's a chemical precursor to aspirin. You can use willow bark tea as a herbal pain reliever. You can also use it to prevent heart attack, because like aspirin, willow bark is a blood thinner (anticoagulant). In other words, it makes blood less likely to form the internal blood clots that lead to heart attacks and most strokes.

This same anticoagulant effect helps prevent cancer, or more precisely, the spread of cancer (called metastasis). In addition, regular use of low-dose aspirin has been shown to reduce the risk of digestive tract cancers, especially those of the colon and rectum. I suspect that willow bark would have the same benefit. So would wintergreen and meadowsweet, two other herbs that contain salicin.

To make a tea from willow bark or wintergreen, simmer 1 to 2 tea-

Dr Duke's Anti-Ageing Elixir

Colon-Care Tea

If pharmaceutical companies can push their synthetic COX-2 inhibitors as colon cancer preventives, then this tea – with its COX-2-inhibiting ingredients – should provide the same benefit.

WHAT YOU NEED

1–2 teaspoons green tea
1 cup water
Any or all of the following herbs: camomile, clove, ginger, holy basil, lavender, marjoram, oregano, rosemary, sage, turmeric

WHAT TO DO

Add the green tea to the freshly boiled water. Mix in a dash each of the COX-2-inhibiting herbs of your choice. Steep for 10 minutes, then strain. Make sure that the tea has cooled before drinking.

spoons of the herb in a cup of boiling water for 10 to 20 minutes. With meadowsweet, you don't need to simmer. Just steep 1 to 2 teaspoons of herb per cup of freshly boiled water for 10 minutes. For all three teas, strain out the herb before drinking.

LEMON (*CITRUS LIMON*). If you drink herbal teas to lower your cancer risk, don't forget to add lemon. The peel, fruit, and juice of this tangy fruit contain limonene, a compound that's a potent cancer preventive.

In one study, a group of laboratory animals was injected with a chemical that causes lung cancer. Some of the animals were also given a single 25-milligram dose of limonene. Compared with the animals that didn't receive the compound, those that did developed 78 per cent fewer tumours. Other research suggests that limonene can help prevent breast cancer.

Lemon is not the best source of limonene. Oddly enough, that distinction goes to caraway seed. Other good sources of the compound include cardamom, celery, fennel, lime, orange, spearmint, tangerine, and thyme. Use these as ingredients in foods or as teas.

Support Your Immune System

Many of the measures mentioned above in some way enhance your immune function, so you're less likely to develop cancer. If you want to boost your body's defences even more, apply the strategies presented in chapter 14.

Get Regular Cancer Screenings

Screening doesn't actually prevent cancer, but it offers the next best thing: early detection. This means a better chance of successful treatment and less opportunity for the cancer to spread, or metastasize.

Because of my family history, I get tested for colon cancer more frequently than the average person. In fact, I'm about due for another colonoscopy. If you are in doubt, consult your doctor or contact Cancer Research UK or Macmillan Cancer relief for guidlines.

Of course, women should do monthly breast self-examinations and take up their options for routine mammograms.

CHAPTER 9

Great Digestion

Dr Duke's Anti-Ageing Elixirs

* *Herbal Stomach Settler*
* *Outsmart-Ulcer Tea*

When I'm at home, I rarely have problems with constipation. That's because I eat a high-fibre diet, drink lots of juices and herbal teas, and engage in a good deal of exercise. On the road, it's another story. Sometimes I have to go without my fruits and vegetables, fluids, and physical activity. Then I might get stopped up.

This first happened when I was in the army. The mess hall served few fruits and vegetables, so I found myself eating meat and potatoes, much to my chagrin. Years later, when I was doing botanical research in Panama, I had a few days out in the bush when I lived off canned meat, white rice, and fried bread. That also gummed up the works, so to speak.

Now when I travel, I make a conscious effort to guard against constipation. For breakfast, I often partake of bran cereal. It's probably the safest, cheapest, and easiest way to keep myself regular. Adding fruit to my cereal gives me an extra dose of fibre. Some of my favourite fruits are raisins because they travel well and have plenty of fibre (not to mention antioxidant anthocyanidins that help keep older folks young). A bowl of raisin bran in the morning, and I feel good the rest of the day.

Like raisins, prunes travel well and are rich in fibre and anthocyanidins. They're great for preventing and relieving constipation. I like to drink prune juice as often as I can on the road. I munch on carrot and celery sticks, too.

By keeping my fibre intake up, I not only avoid getting constipated but also reduce my risk of other digestive complaints. The fact is, as we get older, our digestive systems become a lot more temperamental. One reason is that the muscles lining our digestive tracts, especially our in-

More Wisdom *from the* Garden

You Can Have Your Meat and Eat It, Too

The key to preventing constipation is to eat a high-fibre diet – one that features plenty of fruits, vegetables, pulses and whole grains. All that fibre adds bulk to stools, which helps keep your colon in shape and allows things to pass more easily.

Of course, you may have an avowed carnivore in your family, someone for whom a meal just isn't complete unless it contains meat. If that's the case, a little culinary creativity can satisfy his tastebuds while sneaking in a serving or two of plant foods.

In my family, my grandkids love charcoal-grilled steak. I make it for them, but instead of serving a big slab of beef, I dice it into small bits and make a stew that's loaded with carrots, potatoes, and healthy spices. Likewise, if the kids want McDonald's, I take them. But I skip the Quarter Pounders and order them regular hamburgers, which have proportionately less meat and more ketchup (with its antioxidant lycopene) and mustard (with its isothiocyanates).

I figure that if I can use what they like to cajole them into eating more vegetables, they'll be better off in the long run. And I'm not just talking about avoiding constipation. I'm talking about reducing the risk of the major killers: heart disease, cancer, and stroke.

testines, grow weaker. Another is that our stomachs slow their production of acid, which can cause stomach pain and impair the absorption of certain nutrients. Then there's the whole issue of prescription drugs: older folks are more likely to be using them, yet they're known to take a serious toll on the gut.

If you want to ward off all manner of digestive ailments, my advice is to eat plenty of fibre, drink plenty of fluids, and get plenty of exercise. More than anything else, this trio of lifestyle strategies can keep your digestive system running efficiently and trouble-free.

If you're concerned about a particular digestive problem, you may want to try some of the herbal remedies and other natural measures recommended below.

Constipation: the Right Foods and Herbs Can Keep You Going

Do you remember my SEVENTY principles for growing youthful? As I explained in chapter 2, the S in SEVENTY stands for sensible diet, while the first E stands for exercise. These two principles are the foundation of healthy digestion. Apply them to your own lifestyle, and you may not need herbs to keep yourself regular.

You already know that a nutritious, fibre-rich diet makes for a healthy colon. But you may wonder how exercise fits in. Simple: when your arms and legs are moving, other things are moving as well.

That said, if you're prone to constipation and you find yourself buying lots of laxatives from the drugstore, then you probably need more than diet and exercise. For you, herbs may come in handy.

In my Garden of Youth, I have an entire plot devoted to constipation. It's populated with aloe, buckthorn, fenugreek, flax, psyllium, rhubarb, and senna.

Of these, my favourites for healthy digestion are fenugreek, flax, and psyllium. These herbs are amphoteric, the herbal equivalent of ambidextrous. They help prevent and treat a pair of polar-opposite digestive distresses: constipation and diarrhoea.

If it seems impossible that the same herbs could be effective for both not going and going too often, get ready for the magic of the Garden of Youth. Fenugreek, flax, and psyllium are all rich in a special fibre called mucilage that soaks up water like a sponge. When exposed to liquid in the gut, these herbs absorb water and expand to many times their original size. Taking up all that fluid helps prevent and relieve diarrhoea. And by expanding, the herbs add bulk to stools, which helps prevent and relieve constipation.

The extra bulk also softens the stool, so it passes more comfortably with less straining. That's what makes these herbs good for preventing haemorrhoids, too.

Personally, I don't need commercial preparations, because I grow my own psyllium in my Garden of Youth. Well, it's not true psyllium (*Plantago ovata*) but a close relative, a local weed called plantain (*Plantago major*). I strip the husk from the plant and use the mucilage-rich seed for my homemade almost-psyllium. It works just as well. But if you can't grow psyllium yourself (and most of us don't have the right climate), you can easily get hold of it at health food shops.

Flaxseed is another of the mucilage-rich herbs, and the one that's most popular in Europe. Commission E, the expert panel that evaluates the safety and effectiveness of herbs for the German government, has approved the use of 1 to 3 tablespoons of whole or crushed flaxseed two or three times a day for persistent constipation. In my opinion, that's a bit conservative. I'd take a little more, mixed into juice.

Every now and then, you hear a scary story about flaxseed containing cyanide. It does, but in such small amounts that I don't think you need to worry about taking a few tablespoons of the herb a few times a day. But if you are concerned, you can always use psyllium or fenugreek instead.

Like the other mucilage-rich herbs growing in my Garden of Youth, fenugreek is good for both constipation and diarrhoea. The nice thing about fenugreek is that it has an unusual but pleasant taste, like bitter maple syrup. I take fenugreek as a tea – 1 to 2 teaspoons of seed steeped in a cup of boiled water for 10 minutes. Others prefer to take capsules, which are sold in health food stores, or to grow sprouts and eat them.

More Wisdom *from the* Garden

That Morning Cup Helps Mobilize Your Gut

Many people count on coffee to jump-start their days. But that's not the only way it gets things moving. It's also a gentle laxative. In fact, if you skip your morning java jolt, you may find yourself dealing with a bout of constipation.

I've started throwing a few seeds into my juice blends.

There are other herbal laxatives, including cascara sagrada, senna, buckthorn, and aloe. All of them work. In fact, they're the active ingredients in a number of over-the-counter products. Senna, in particular, is found in many commercial laxatives; you'll read more about this herb in chapter 29.

As much as I value herbal medicines, I don't really recommend these herbal laxatives. Prevention is the way to go, as it were. So stick with a high-fibre diet. Get plenty of exercise. And if you need a little help, take psyllium, flax, or fenugreek. Blend them into your juices, and you'll never know the difference – but your colon will.

Incidentally, these preventive strategies do more than spare you the discomforts of irregularity. They also reduce your odds of developing a common age-related digestive condition called diverticulitis. (For more information on diverticulitis, see chapter 32.)

Diarrhoea: Cut Your Risk of the Runs

Sometimes diarrhoea strikes for no apparent reason. But most times you have a pretty good idea of what's behind it.

Perhaps you've been bingeing on junk food while struggling to meet a deadline; the combination of food and stress can bring on diarrhoea. Or maybe you're lactose intolerant and you've eaten some dairy products; food sensitivities are another common trigger.

Certain medications can cause diarrhoea, as can large doses of vitamin C. Then there's traveller's diarrhoea, the notorious health hazard that results from bacteria picked up on trips to exotic locales like the Peruvian outback.

If you're badgered by frequent bouts of the runs, you may want to take a look at your eating habits and stress levels. You'll do your gut a world of good by laying off junk food and controlling stress. I like to unwind by working in my garden and taking walks around YinYang Valley. You might prefer to exercise, meditate, or listen to music (which I do as well – my favourites are bluegrass, flamenco, country, pop, and light classical) or a relaxation tape. All of these are good stress-reducers.

You may also want to cut back on dairy products. Many adults, especially older adults, are mildly lactose intolerant. You can eat some dairy without problems, but if you eat a lot, things start to get loose.

Likewise, don't go overboard on vitamin C supplements. How much is too much? That varies from person to person. Doses of up to 2,000 mg a day seem to not cause problems. But if you take more, you may end up with the runs.

When you're travelling, your best bet is to stick with 'safe' beverages like bottled water and hot drinks made with boiled water – tea, for example. And forgo the ice: while your cola may be harmless, the water used to make the ice could harbour bacteria.

If you get diarrhoea anyway, no matter what the cause, the most important thing that you can do is to keep drinking fluids. You may not feel like it, but do it anyway. You have to replace all of the fluids that you're losing out the other end.

Just be sure to steer clear of coffee and alcohol. For many people, coffee acts as a laxative, which you don't need when you have diarrhoea. And alcohol irritates the digestive tract, something else you want to avoid when you're running like a fountain.

Diarrhoea also depletes electrolytes – that is, sodium and potassium. If you run really low on these minerals, you can develop muscle weakness and in extreme cases even heart failure. So you need to replace them. Munching on some salty pretzels helps replenish sodium, while eating bananas boosts your supply of potassium. This mineral is even more plentiful in some of the greens growing in my Garden of Youth,

More Wisdom *from the* Garden

This Tropical Fruit Stops Diarrhoea Fast

Bananas are a classic diarrhoea remedy, and not just because of their potassium content. They're soothing to your digestive tract, and they help bind stools.

In fact, bananas are one ingredient in the so-called BRATT diet, which many doctors recommend to relieve diarrhoea. Besides bananas, the diet consists of rice, stewed apple, tea, and toast (hence the name BRATT). I'd also recommend plain apples for their pectin. Or you could find an apple spread for your toast.

Just be sure to steer clear of fatty foods and junk foods until you're feeling better.

especially purslane and lamb's-quarter.

I've already mentioned that psyllium, flax, and fenugreek help relieve both constipation and diarrhoea, the latter by absorbing excess fluids in the gut. Herbs rich in astringent tannins can also help soothe your digestive tract and relieve diarrhoea. Perhaps the best herb for this purpose is black tea, but many others are beneficial when brewed as teas. My favourites are blackberry leaf and raspberry leaf. Both grow in my garden, and I also have wild blackberries on my property.

If you're dealing with traveller's diarrhoea, you may want to try a few other herbs as well. One is echinacea, an immune system stimulant that can help your body fight infection. I recommend taking capsules according to the package directions or 1 to 2 teaspoons of tincture three times a day, mixed into juice or bottled water.

Another helpful herb is goldenseal, which contains the antibiotic berberine. I've seen several studies showing that goldenseal is an effective treatment for diarrhoea caused by all sorts of nasty bacteria, including *E. coli*, shigella, and salmonella.

Unfortunately, goldenseal is close to becoming an endangered species. Other herbs with berberine may be equally effective. Among the best sources are barberry (*Berberis vulgaris*) and Oregon grape (*Mahonia aquifolium*). To make a tea from either herb, add ½ teaspoon of dried root or bark to a cup of boiling water and simmer for 10 to 20 minutes. Strain out the herb and make sure the tea has cooled before drinking it.

If you can't find barberry or Oregon grape, or if you simply prefer goldenseal, I suggest taking 1 to 2 teaspoons of tincture three times a day. Once you start feeling better, you may want to eat lots of garlic, which is also a powerful antibiotic. It works against the same bacteria as goldenseal.

Speaking of bacteria . . . you may be aware that your intestines are populated by millions of beneficial (probiotic) bacteria that support good digestion. Diarrhoea depletes their numbers, which can slow your recovery time.

Nutrition experts often recommend rebalancing your intestinal ecology after a bout of diarrhoea by taking *Lactobacillus acidophilus* or *L. bulgaricus*. You can get these good bacteria by eating yogurt. But not just any yogurt: the phrase 'contains live cultures' should appear on its label. You can also get these beneficial bugs in powder form, as a supplement. Follow the package directions for proper dosage.

Indigestion: Don't Let Dinner Come Back to Haunt You

In the US, back in 1990, the FDA gave me a bad case of indigestion by ruling that peppermint was ineffective as a treatment for stomach upset. How the FDA reached its conclusion is way beyond me.

Peppermint has been used to prevent and treat indigestion since ancient times. The Romans had a practice of munching on mint leaves after banquets. In the Middle Ages, mint liqueurs were served as a stomach-soothing after-dinner drink. These days, we have after-dinner mints.

The research that I've seen is very clear. Peppermint is antibacterial, fending off any bad bugs that you might pick up from food. It promotes gastric secretions, so you digest food more efficiently. It's antispasmodic, helping to prevent and relieve abdominal cramps. And it's carminative, meaning that it settles the stomach and prevents gas. If that's not a top-notch formula for protecting against indigestion, I don't know what is.

The FDA made the wrong call on peppermint. After a big meal, I often slip down into the Garden of Youth, pick a few leaves from my peppermint plants, and munch them, enjoying their distinctive taste and appreciating all the good they're doing in my gut. (They sweeten bad breath as well.)

Many other herbs help prevent indigestion. One of my favourites is ginger. Ever wonder why Chinese restaurants always list ginger fish and ginger shrimp on their menus? The recipes date back thousands of years in China's history, to when fish and seafood weren't always fresh and, as a result, often caused indigestion – or worse. Ancient Chinese cooks discovered that if they flavoured their fish with ginger, it was less likely to cause stomach upset. Ginger has been the spice of choice for fish ever since.

Ginger has the same benefits as peppermint. Ginger ale (originally ginger beer) is an age-old folk remedy for stomach problems. Growing up, I always envied the neighbouring kids whose mothers gave them ginger ale for their tummy aches. Mine was more likely to give me castor oil.

Dr Duke's Anti-Ageing Elixir

Herbal Stomach Settler

The carminative herbs contain compounds that can soothe the stomach and prevent gas. They're ideal for preventing and treating indigestion.

WHAT YOU NEED

Any combination of the following herbs (use fresh or powdered leaf or bruised seed): anise, cardamom, camomile, cilantro, cinnamon, coriander, ginger, lavender, lemon balm, licorice, peppermint, red pepper, and spearmint

240 ml (8 fl oz) water

WHAT TO DO

Combine the herbs of your choice to taste. Steep 1 to 2 teaspoons of the plant material in the freshly boiled water for 10 minutes. Strain. Make sure that the tea has cooled slightly before drinking it.

In fact, many herbs are natural stomach soothers: anise, cardamom, camomile, cinnamon, coriander, lavender, lemon balm, licorice, and spearmint. All of these grow in my Garden of Youth. Cinnamon is my wife Peggy's favourite indigestion remedy. Our plant is potted. It stays outdoors in the summertime, but I have to bring it inside before the first frost, along with our cardamom plant. Both are tropical, so they would not survive our Maryland winters.

Even chilli peppers can help soothe your stomach. This may come as a surprise, since most people believe that chilli peppers actually cause indigestion. Not so. Cultures all over the world, from Mexico to India, use chilli peppers to relieve stomach upset. I've never seen any research linking these spices to indigestion, but I have experienced their stomach-comforting, indigestion-preventing benefits many times. If you want to try chilli pepper for yourself, just carefully add it to your food.

Heartburn: Herbal Teas Douse the Fire

I wish that I could forget my experiences with heartburn. But I can't. The pain is all too memorable.

Television commercials touting remedies for this condition refer to it either as heartburn or as acid indigestion. If it gets really bad, doctors call it GERD, for gastro-oesophogeal reflux disease. But you'll never have to experience GERD, or even heartburn for that matter, if you know how to prevent it. I learned how, and nowadays, I rarely get that uncomfortable burning sensation beneath my breastbone.

Heartburn has nothing to do with your heart. It actually involves your stomach and oesophagus, the tube that carries food from your throat down to your stomach. At the end of the oesophagus where it meets your stomach is a ring of muscle known as the lower oesophageal sphincter. The sphincter opens to let food pass through, then closes to keep stomach acid from washing up (or refluxing) into your oesophagus. In heartburn, the sphincter doesn't stay shut when it should. So the acid refluxes and burns your oesophagus, causing pain in your chest and throat.

Those in the know say that you can reduce your odds of developing heartburn by avoiding alcohol, coffee, chocolate, citrus fruits, tomatoes, garlic, onions, and peppermint. All of these tend to relax the lower oesophageal sphincter. For myself, I think I'd almost rather have heartburn than do without tomatoes, garlic, onions, and peppermint. Besides, none of these foods has ever given me problems.

Frankly, I can't believe that the experts, whoever they are, blame peppermint for causing heartburn. As far as I'm concerned, peppermint ranks as one of the best herbs for preventing and treating the condition. That's why it's planted in the Heartburn plot of my Garden of Youth. Spearmint, camomile, and licorice also grow there.

You can make a tea from peppermint, spearmint, or camomile by steeping about 2 teaspoons of dried mint leaves or camomile flowers in a cup of hot water for 10 minutes. With licorice root, just simmer a few teaspoons in a cup of boiling water for 10 minutes. Whichever tea you brew, be sure that it has cooled slightly before you strain and drink it.

My Heartburn plot also contains several other traditional, and effective, heartburn relievers: anise, dill, fennel, and, in pots, cardamom and cinnamon. You can make a tea from any of these herbs the same as you would from camomile.

But sipping herbal tea isn't the only way to protect yourself from heartburn pain. These lifestyle strategies can help, too.

Give up cigarettes. Smokers are more likely than nonsmokers to experience heartburn.

Watch your weight. Those extra pounds press down on your stomach, and that pressure can open your lower oesophageal sphincter. That's why women who are pregnant often report problems with heartburn.

Loosen your belt a notch or two. Anything that presses on your abdomen can contribute to heartburn, including a too tight belt or waistband.

Eat small meals. If you stuff yourself with food, it causes your stomach to stretch. So your lower oesophageal sphincter is more likely to open.

Always chew thoroughly. When you inhale your food rather than taking time to chew it, your lower oesophageal sphincter has to open wide to let those big chunks through. If it opens too wide, it may not close completely.

Relax at mealtime. Many people, myself included, have noticed that their heartburn is stress-related. It's most likely to affect me when I'm on the run and gobbling my meals. Stress increases the production of

growing younger naturally

Camomile Came to His Rescue

My good friend Francisco J. Morón, M.D., Ph.D., is a professor of pharmacology at the Medical University of Havana in Cuba. While he does some work with plant-derived medicines, his focus is primarily on conventional pharmaceuticals. But he credits a very traditional herbal digestive aid with helping his father-in-law, who developed serious gastrointestinal problems several years ago. Here is their story.

'When my father-in-law was 70 years old, he was diagnosed with several gastrointestinal ailments: a duodenal ulcer, stomach inflammation (gastritis), and chronic heartburn (gastro-oesophageal reflux). His doctor treated him with the standard pharmaceutical medications, including antacids and ranitidine (Zantac). This made perfect sense to me. But my father-in-law said he experienced little or no relief.

'After a while, my mother-in-law grew tired of his complaints. She told me that she wanted to give him camomile tea. I discouraged her, insisting that there was no way a herbal remedy could outperform the more potent pharmaceuticals he was already taking. But my mother-in-law insisted on giving him camomile. I couldn't stop her.

'From his first cup, my father-in-law said the camomile tea made him feel better. It wasn't long before he reported substantial pain relief. I found it hard to believe, but intriguing.

'Eventually, my wife (who is my research partner) and I tested several camomile extracts on the small intestines of guinea pigs. We found that the herb produced a greater spasmolytic effect (relief from spasms, which cause cramping) than the pharmaceuticals papaverine and atropine.

'It would be premature to conclude that camomile's spasmolytic effect explains my father-in-law's positive response. But in his case, a traditional herbal remedy worked better than pharmaceutical drugs.'

stomach acid, and the more acid you are producing, the more likely it is to find its way into your oesophagus.

Stomach Acid Deficiency: More Common with Age

All those television commercials for heartburn remedies create the impression that excess stomach acid is an epidemic health problem. The ads must be pretty persuasive, because people, especially older folks, spend a small fortune on antacids every year.

Based on the research that I've seen, I suspect that the real problem is not too much stomach acid but too little. One study showed that more than half of the population aged 60 or more has low stomach acidity. This condition is responsible for incomplete digestion as well as nutritional deficiencies.

To correct low stomach acidity, naturopaths often prescribe supplemental stomach acids such as glutamic acid hydrochloride, betaine, and pepsin hydrochloride. They're fine if you need them. I prefer more traditional remedies: apple cider vinegar and lemon juice (both very acidic), pineapple (with its digestive enzyme bromelain), and bitter herbs, also known as aromatic digestive tonics or aromatic bitters.

Most people are unfamiliar with digestive bitters. Those who do know about them generally consider them a quaint relic of a bygone era. But the fact is, bitter herbs support good digestion.

When a bitter substance hits your tastebuds at the base of your tongue, stimuli travel to triggering cells in your cerebral cortex. These cells send signals to your salivary glands, which increase their production of saliva. The signals also reach your stomach, where they promote the secretion of the hormone gastrin. Gastrin, in turn, stimulates the release of hydrochloric acid by your gastric glands.

The seven bitter herbs that I think do the most good are aloe, dandelion, gentian, quassia, quinine, rhubarb, and wormwood. I recommend taking a drop or two of the concentrated herbal essence in water, as needed. You can also buy the tincture form and use it according to the label directions.

Ulcers: Cabbage Can Keep You Pain-Free

The medical community has certainly changed its tune on ulcers. Doctors used to instruct their patients with ulcers to avoid hot, spicy foods

Dr Duke's Anti-Ageing Elixir

Outsmart-Ulcer Tea

Each of the four herbs in this tasty tea contain potent anti-ulcer compounds. Together, they can help keep you ulcer-free.

WHAT YOU NEED

1 teaspoon powdered licorice root
1 teaspoon ground ginger
1 teaspoon oregano
1 easpoon goldenseal
4 cups water

WHAT TO DO

In a small saucepan, add the licorice, ginger, oregano, and goldenseal to the freshly boiled water. Allow to steep for 10 minutes before straining. I'd suggest drinking a cup of tea at a time, spreading the 4 cups over the course of the day.

Variation: You can substitute barberry or Oregon grape for goldenseal, which is on the verge of becoming endangered.

and to take antacids. Now they know that most ulcers are caused not by diet but by bacteria – specifically, the bacteria known as *Helicobacter pylori.*

This finding validates the herbal tradition of treating ulcers with chilli pepper and other hot spices. As research has shown, these sultry seasonings are loaded with antibacterial compounds.

While you're turning up the heat in your meals, you may want to make sure that you're eating plenty of plant foods. The antimicrobial compounds in plant foods help control *H. pylori*. This may explain why ulcers are less common in traditional cultures, where diets are largely plant-based.

Perhaps the best plant food for treating an existing ulcer is cabbage. Naturopaths often recommend drinking raw cabbage juice. My advice is to eat boiled cabbage that's made with celery and potatoes and seasoned with ginger, chilli pepper and black pepper. All of these ingredients contain anti-ulcer compounds.

Among the herbs used for treating ulcers, licorice is the best, in my opinion. Several studies have shown that licorice heals ulcers as effectively as pharmaceuticals, often even curing them. Other herbs that are rich in anti-ulcer compounds include ginger, oregano, and goldenseal. You can make a tasty tea from a blend of all four. (See my Outsmart-Ulcer Tea.)

Several other herbs and foods have some anti-ulcer value, though they're not as potent as the ones mentioned above. These include bananas, cabbages, camomile, gentian, garlic, meadowsweet, milk thistle, onions, pineapple, and pumpkin.

Inflammatory Bowel Disease: First, Identify the Offenders

Inflammatory bowel disease (IBD) is an umbrella term for two similar but distinct conditions: ulcerative colitis and Crohn's disease. Both cause abdominal pain (sometimes severe) and bloody diarrhoea. Both involve open sores along your lower digestive tract. The difference is that in colitis, the sores develop in your colon, while in Crohn's, they develop in your colon and small intestine.

Michael Murray, N.D., a naturopath from Seattle whom I respect, observes that many people with IBD often have underlying food sensitivities that contribute to the condition. He recommends following an elimination diet, under medical supervision, to weed out the offending foods. This seems like good advice to me. I know that if I had IBD, I'd try an elimination diet.

I'd also take lots of herbs that soothe the digestive tract. My top recommendations for IBD are peppermint and ginger, followed by camomile and fennel. To make a tea from any of these herbs, simply steep 1 to 2 teaspoons of dried herb in a cup of freshly boiled water for 10 minutes. Then strain before drinking. If you wish, you can combine any or all of these herbs in proportions that suit your tastebuds.

Another herb that may be effective for IBD is asafoetida. You may not have heard of this Middle Eastern garlic-scented spice before. I first encountered it in Iran many years ago. Since then, I've seen a few studies suggesting that asafoetida can help treat bowel and digestive problems. I still don't have an asafoetida plant in the Garden of Youth, but I have a plot reserved for one if I can ever lay my hands on it.

One other herb worth considering is cat's claw, also known as *uña de gato*. This Amazonian vine is revered in Peruvian folk medicine for inflammatory conditions. It hasn't been researched very well, but the studies that I've seen support its anti-inflammatory properties and its

for the Gardener

Fennel

Foeniculum vulgare

A hardy perennial, fennel is easily started from seeds. Plants can reach 2 metres (6 feet) with minimal care, as long as they're weeded early on. They tolerate all kinds of soil, though they prefer well-drained loam or black, sandy soil. They thrive in full sun or partial shade.

If you want to grow your fennel from seed, you need to get started in spring. Select fully ripe yet green seeds and let them dry in the shade, to prevent excess moisture from accumulating. Since fennel doesn't transplant well, sow the seeds right where you want them, at a depth of about 5 mm (¼ in). They may germinate in 1 to 2 weeks. If you must move your plants, dig deeply so that you don't disturb the taproot.

If your fennel is as potent as mine, bruising it as you harvest it will fill the garden with a delightful aroma. When the seeds have ripened – usually between August and October in my neck of the woods – strip them from the plants, pat away any excess moisture, and store them in a cool, dry place.

safety as a remedy. I've also heard anecdotal reports that cat's claw helps relieve IBD symptoms. Some herbalists that I respect recommend it as well. If I had IBD, I might try cat's claw. If you're interested, you can buy capsules in a health food shop and take them according to the label directions.

Irritable Bowel Syndrome: Eat Well to Rein In Symptoms

Irritable bowel syndrome, or IBS, really isn't a disease. Rather, it is a collection of annoying abdominal symptoms: cramps, bloating, flatulence, and diarrhoea or constipation. Some people develop more diarrhoea; others, more constipation. Either way, if you have IBS, you feel as though something is wrong with your digestive tract.

Stress can contribute to IBS, and IBS can make you feel tense. You get caught in a vicious circle: stress, then IBS, then more stress, then worse IBS. To reduce the frequency and severity of your symptoms, I recommend a relaxation programme. My personal 'programme' consists of digging around in my Garden of Youth and taking long walks. You may prefer meditation, yoga, or some other form of exercise.

A low-fat diet can help control IBS symptoms because fatty foods are hard to digest. Other foods and substances have been linked to IBS as well. I'd recommend limiting your consumption of alcohol, caffeine, the artificial sweetener sorbitol, and – if you're lactose intolerant – milk and dairy products.

If you've been diagnosed with IBS, you need to monitor not just what you're eating but how much. In general, people with IBS feel better on five or six small, snacklike meals than on three big ones. These mini-meals are spread evenly throughout the day.

You may also get some relief by taking certain herbs. Marshmallow, peppermint, and turmeric all have compounds that can calm and soothe an irritable bowel. All three herbs are sold as commercial preparations; buy one and use it according to the label directions.

Coeliac Disease: When Grains Turn Disagreeable

Coeliac disease is characterised by an inability to digest gluten, a protein that's found in most of the grains consumed by us humans. The gluten in wheat, for example, works with yeast to give bread the ability to rise.

In those with coeliac disease, gluten irritates the small intestine, which leads to the deterioration of the fingerlike villi that absorb nutrients into the bloodstream. The only way to deal with coeliac disease is to avoid everything that contains gluten, especially wheat (including durum and triticale), rye, barley, and oats (though some people can eat oats in moderation). This may seem difficult at first, but with a little experience – and lots of label reading – you can eat well without gluten.

Keep in mind, too, that some grains are okay even on a gluten-free diet. These include amaranth, corn (usually), millet, quinoa, and rice.

CHAPTER 10

Youthful Energy

Dr Duke's Anti-Ageing Elixirs

- *Amazing Energizer Tea*
- *Stimulating Sipper*

Got that tired, run-down feeling? It could be a symptom of some underlying health problem, such as Addison's disease, adrenal gland dysfunction, chronic fatigue syndrome/ME, fibromyalgia, hypoglycaemia, hypothyroidism, multiple chemical sensitivities, myasthenia gravis, sleep deprivation, or stress.

Then again, it could be nothing more than that tired, run-down feeling – what I call TRF.

In general, if fatigue persists for more than 2 weeks, you should see your doctor for a thorough check-up. You want to rule out anything serious. If your doctor can't find anything diagnosable, that's good news. The bad news is that you'll still have TRF, which can leave you dragging. And your doctor won't be able to offer much relief.

As far as I'm concerned, the best remedy for fatigue – and the foundation for youth-preserving energy and vitality – is my SEVENTY programme. As explained in chapter 2, each letter in SEVENTY stands for a specific lifestyle strategy.

- **S***ensible diet*
- **E***xercise*
- **V***itamins and other supplements*
- **E***scaping stress*
- **N***o-no's*
- **T***ouch*
- **Y***ou (as in your commitment to these strategies)*

The SEVENTY programme is both preventive and curative, though as you've probably figured out, I prefer preventing disease to treating it. Apply the SEVENTY principles in your life, and you reduce your chances of getting ill. That means you're less likely to experience fatigue and more likely to feel vital and alive.

A Morning Routine for All-Day Vigour

That said, even people committed to the SEVENTY programme can experience TRF as they become older. They realise that their get-up-and-go is starting to flag. I've noticed that myself, even though I'm a mere 72 years young and a long way from old age.

In my Garden of Youth, I'm growing quite a few herbs that can help prevent and treat TRF. Actually, I think that just having the garden – tending it, walking through it, smelling its many aromas, munching its many edible leaves – helps recharge my batteries. Maybe that's why I no longer need a cup of coffee first thing in the morning. Not that I have anything against drinking coffee in moderation. It's just that I've found other ways to marshal my energy at the start of the day.

Today, for example, I rolled out of bed around 5.30 a.m. I proceeded to fill a big glass with water and gather my standardised herbal extracts.

My herbal regimen varies from one day to the next, depending on what I feel I need. I always take two capsules of celery seed to stop my gout from flaring up. Then I may add some, or perhaps all, of the following: one capsule of bilberry (for good vision and general antioxidant benefits), one capsule of evening primrose oil (for protection against cardiovascular disease and inflammatory conditions, including prostatitis), one capsule of ginkgo (for a sharp mind), one capsule of horse chestnut (for improved blood circulation), one capsule of milk thistle (for a healthy liver), and one capsule of saw palmetto (for managing an enlarged prostate).

After taking my herbs, I walked outside and watered the top two terraces of the Garden of Youth. (I save the lower two terraces for dusk.) I also watered all of the potted plants in my greenhouse and under my Norway maple, including a 2.4-m (8-ft) banana plant.

Spending time in my garden thoroughly invigorates me. I feel a vitality borne of inner peace and purpose, not of caffeine, which is what used to get me going in the morning.

As a botanist, I have the highest respect for coffee, our favourite stimulant. My point is that I prefer to have my life – not a herb or a drug – create my vitality.

Once I've been up and around for a while, then I enjoy my cup of coffee, usually around 7 a.m. At that hour, enough time has passed that I don't have to worry about certain compounds in the coffee, called phenolics, interfering with the herbs that I would have taken earlier.

I don't drink as much coffee as I used to. But when I have to accomplish something on a deadline, like this book, I find that coffee helps me channel my energy in a productive way.

A Potent Energizer – But Handle with Care

Of course, coffee is just one of an array of herbal stimulants. These herbs vary greatly in the degree of stimulation that they provide. In fact, some can be overstimulating.

The most intense stimulation comes from what I refer to as the frantic herbs. These include illegal drugs such as cocaine, which has caused so much addiction in the United States, and khat, a similarly addictive herb that's grown in Yemen and other countries of the Middle East. Actually, I grew coca plants, which are the primary source of cocaine, for 20 years – for research purposes only, of course – while I was working for the USDA. My advice is to steer clear of cocaine and khat.

Another frantic herb, Chinese ephedra (ma huang), can boost your energy if it's used properly. This herb is still legal, though the FDA has threatened to restrict it because it has been linked to several deaths from heart attack. In most of these cases, people had taken enormous doses of the herb in order to experience an amphetamine-like high.

I'd hate to see Chinese ephedra banned because of a handful of unfortunate incidents. When used responsibly in the recommended doses, the herb is a valuable treatment for TRF. It also helps control asthma by opening the bronchial tubes. And it can play an important role in medically supervised weight-loss programmes because it boosts the basal metabolic rate, the speed at which the body burns calories.

If you want to try Chinese ephedra to boost your energy and vitality, I urge you to consult a herbalist or a doctor of Chinese medicine. You don't want to take too much.

I have a couple of Chinese ephedra plants in my Garden of Youth. Unfortunately, they're not good role models for energy and vitality. For reasons that I can't fathom, they're not doing too well. Maybe I don't provide the proper stimulation.

Caffeine Provides a Satisfying Kick

One rung down the stimulant ladder, we have all of the herbs that contain caffeine: cocoa, coffee, guarana, guayusa, kola, maté, and tea. Of this group, only tea grows in my Garden of Youth. I also have potted cocoa, coffee, kola, and tea plants, which I keep in my greenhouse during the winter months. I hope to add the other plants someday.

I get my caffeine from tea, coffee, and cocoa. I think the virtues of moderate caffeine consumption – the equivalent of a cup or two of brewed coffee a day – are under-recognised and the hazards of overuse exaggerated.

Caffeine is more than a pick-me-up. It keeps the bronchial passages open for easy breathing. It sharpens concentration and memory, which tend to decline with age. When taken with aspirin, it improves pain relief – a bonus for those of us plagued by stiffness and soreness. It raises the basal metabolic rate to support weight loss and maintenance, another big concern for older folks. In my book, all of these benefits add up to enhanced vitality.

If you're worried about caffeine giving you insomnia or jitters, you needn't be, as long as you limit your consumption to the morning and afternoon hours, and you drink only as much as you're used to. As for all the headlines linking caffeine to various cancers, none of the studies has panned out. In fact, coffee contains cancer-preventive compounds.

I usually drink three caffeinated beverages a day – two in the morning and one after lunch (but almost never any after dinner). Sometimes I have my coffee straight. Occasionally, I mix it with cocoa. And sometimes I brew up what I call my Amazing Energizer Tea.

Dr Duke's Anti-Ageing Elixir

Amazing Energizer Tea

This is my brew of choice whenever I need a dose of energy-boosting caffeine but I'd rather not drink coffee.

WHAT YOU NEED

Any combination of the following herbs: black or green tea, guarana, guayusa, kola, and maté

1 cup water

WHAT TO DO

Add 1 to 2 teaspoons of the herb or herb blend to the freshly boiled water. Steep for 5 to 10 minutes, then strain. Make sure the tea has cooled slightly before drinking it.

Sometimes a Little Lift Is All You Need

Next on the stimulant ladder, we have the herbs that contain pleasantly aromatic volatile stimulants such as carveol, carvone, chlorogenic acid, cineole, cinnamaldehyde, menthol, piperine, and verbenalin. Carveol is found in caraway, celery, cumin, dill, parsley, peppermint, and spearmint; carvone, in caraway, dill, and spearmint; chlorogenic acid, in sunflower seeds and coffee; cinnamaldehyde, in cinnamon; menthol, in the mints; piperine, in black pepper; and verbenalin, in verbena and dogwood.

For ongoing vitality, my personal favourite is cineole. A gentle stimulant, cineole can still boost energy, improve physical performance, and prevent insomnia. If I'm feeling a tad sluggish but I don't want the big boost of caffeine,

I'll munch some cineole-rich herbs straight from my Garden of Youth or add some to a herbal tea.

Besides providing gentle stimulation, cineole seems to improve mental function. In laboratory experiments, it enhances rats' abilities to navigate mazes, whether the cineole is inhaled, ingested, or applied topically. Maybe it can help you get through life's maze a bit more easily. Cineole is also an expectorant, so it comes in handy when you have a cold or a sinus infection and you want to cough up gunk.

If I've already had enough coffee for the day, or if I want a stimulant that's a little gentler than caffeine, I'll brew up my Stimulating Sipper (see page 132). I don't have a fixed recipe, but the tea usually includes some combination of bee balm, cardamom, eucalyptus, ginger, peppermint, rosemary, and spearmint. All of these herbs are rich in cineole, and all seem to thrive in my Garden of Youth.

Your Best Cineole Sources

A number of herbs contain rich supplies of cineole, a mild stimulant. If you'd like to try cineole to boost your energy levels, any of the following herbs may help.

HERB	MAX. CINEOLE (PPM)
Cardamom	56,000
Eucalyptus	29,750
Spearmint	9,375
Rosemary	8,125
Sweet annie	6,600
Ginger	5,000
Nutmeg	3,520
Lavender	3,435
Bee balm	2,735
Peppermint	1,390
Yarrow	960
Cinnamon	800
Basil	776
Turmeric	720
Lemon leaf	700
Hyssop	610
Tarragon	500
Lemon verbena	450
Fennel	300

Tonics Make You Feel Better All Over

The gentlest of the herbal stimulants are the adaptogen/tonics, which stimulate the immune system along with the rest of the body. I could make a case that all herbs have some adaptogen/tonic qualities. But three of the most potent are astragalus, ginseng, and schisandra.

Dr Duke's Anti-Ageing Elixir

Stimulating Sipper

This beverage is rich in cineole, a gentle stimulant that seems to enhance physical and mental performance.

WHAT YOU NEED

Any combination of the following herbs: bee balm, cardamom, eucalyptus, ginger, peppermint, rosemary, and spearmint

A natural sweetener

WHAT TO DO

Combine the herbs of your choice to taste. (My favourite blend is eucalyptus, peppermint, rosemary and spearmint, with just a little cardamom floating on top.) Put a few tablespoons of your herb blend into a pot of freshly boiled water. Steep for 10 minutes, then strain. Add a sweetener, if you wish. Refrigerate any leftover tea for later use.

ASTRAGALUS (*ASTRALAGUS MEMBRANACEUS*). Also known as huang qi, astragalus has been used for centuries by the Chinese to boost energy and vitality. Several studies of the herb have convinced me that it's an immune system stimulant as well. In fact, it appears to be almost as effective as echinacea.

Astragalus helps counteract TRF. And because the herb enhances immunity, it helps treat all manner of infections, which can deplete your energy. But the herb's effects are subtle, very subtle, so don't expect a coffee buzz.

I've never seen any evidence of safety concerns with astragalus, though allergic reactions are possible. Most herbalists recommend taking 3 to 5 ml (½ to 1 teaspoon) of tincture three or four times a day, or two 400-ml capsules three times a day. If I wanted to use astragalus, I'd buy a commercial preparation and follow the dosage directions on the label.

GINSENG – ASIAN (*PANAX GINSENG*), AMERICAN (*P. QUINQUEFOLIUS*), SIBERIAN (*ELEUTHEROCOCCUS SENTICOSUS*). You probably already know that Asians revere ginseng as the king of the adaptogen/tonics, especially for those of us who want to stay energetic, vital, and young. The herb contains compounds called ginsenosides that stimulate the central nervous system, but not as potently as caffeine.

Ginseng also stimulates appetite, which can be important as you get older. Loss of appetite is a common problem later in life, and if you don't eat, you can forget about energy and vitality.

Some research suggests that ginseng can increase sexual energy, too. Studies have shown that the herb makes rats randier. Personally, I've never noticed any sexual effects.

Many traditional uses of ginseng relate to the enhancement of adrenal gland function, which makes sense since sluggish adrenal glands are a major factor in TRF. The existing research basically supports such uses, showing that ginseng extracts correct adrenal insufficiency. They also boost thyroid and pituitary function. Both of these glands help regulate energy and vitality.

The medical literature mentions quite a few minor side effects for ginseng, so I suppose they're possible. Personally, in several decades of studying and using the herb, I've yet to have anyone tell me of a bad experience with it. I suggest buying a commercial preparation and following the package directions for proper dosage.

SCHISANDRA (*SCHISANDRA CHINENSIS*). Also known as Chinese magnolia

More Wisdom *from the* Garden

A Sweet Solution for Easing Fatigue

For boosting energy, one of my favourite herbs is licorice. It contains glycyrrhizin, a compound that stimulates the adrenal glands and prolongs the action of the adrenal hormones. These hormones play a major role in regulating metabolism.

You don't want to take too much licorice, because it can overstimulate your adrenals. But in the recommended doses, it's quite an effective energizer. I recommend taking the herb as a tea. Steep 1 to 2 teaspoons of powdered licorice root in a cup of freshly boiled water for 10 minutes, then strain. You can drink as many as three cups a day for up to 6 weeks.

Because licorice has a sweet taste, you can also use it to flavour tea made from ginseng or schisandra, both of which are mild stimulants. Simply stir the tea with a licorice root stick (not the licorice sweets, which typically contain little to none of the actual herb).

vine, schisandra is not all that common in the West. But Asians consider it just about as tonic as astragalus and ginseng. It helps strengthen the heart and appears to combat bacterial infections, which probably accounts for its effectiveness in treating TRF.

The recommended dose of schisandra is 5 ml three times a day or a decoction of 5 g of crushed berries, simmered in 100 ml of water for 30 minutes and then left to cool. Divide the cooled liquid into 3 glasses and drink over 24 hours. While the herb is considered safe, it could trigger allergic reactions in some people. There have also been scattered reports of mild stomach upset.

Is Your Thyroid Making You Tired?

While you can use herbs to enhance your energy and vitality, remember that many health problems, some of them quite serious, can leave you feeling fatigued. If your TRF doesn't subside in a few weeks and you still feel sluggish, consider seeing your doctor.

One of the leading causes of TRF is an underactive thyroid gland, a condition called hypothyroidism. The thyroid plays a key role in regulating metabolism. If the gland is underactive, you don't burn enough calories to fulfil your body's energy requirements.

Doctors usually treat hypothyroidism with replacement thyroid hormone. Take what your doctor prescribes, but for extra support, you may want to consider certain plant foods with thyroid-stimulating compounds. Personally, I've eaten self-heal greens and bugleweed tubers, spiced with basil, oregano, rosemary, and spearmint. All of these contain rosmarinic acid, a compound that may raise levels of thyroid hormone when they're low. It has already been shown to reduce hormone levels when they're high.

While the studies of rosmarinic acid have been controversial, the herbs themselves are relatively safe. I don't see any harm in trying them. If you prefer, you can blend them together to make a tea.

CHAPTER 11

Sharp Eyesight

Dr Duke's Anti-Ageing Elixirs

- *Macula-Saving Salad*
- *Cataract-Combating Tonic*

Without my glasses, I don't see quite as well as I used to, I'm sorry to say. Despite reassurances from my ophthalmologist at my last annual visit, I'm convinced that some of my past sins have contributed to the deterioration of my vision. After all, I smoked for 30 years, and I've spent countless hours outdoors without sunglasses, exposing my eyes to the sun's ultraviolet rays. On top of that, several of my aunts and uncles have had cataracts, so I'm probably at risk, too.

Yet other than the fact that I need to wear glasses, my eyes are in surprisingly good shape, considering that I haven't always taken good care of them. What has protected them? Based on the research that I've read, I give credit to my Garden of Youth and all the fruits, veggies, beans, and herbs that I've consumed.

As I explain in chapter 3, plant foods have the highest concentrations of antioxidant nutrients. And a diet rich in antioxidants is key to preventing two of the most common and most insidious age-related vision problems: cataracts and macular degeneration.

Eating lots of plant foods isn't the only way to protect your eyes, of course. The following lifestyle strategies can also help.

- *Stop smoking and steer clear of secondhand smoke.*
- *Limit your exposure to eye-irritating air pollutants.*
- *Consume alcohol only in moderation.*
- *Avoid steroid drugs if at all possible.*
- *Wear sunglasses in bright sunlight.*

Regular exercise is good for your eyes, too. In fact, when I ride my stationary bike, I often give my eyes a workout at the same time: rolling them, shifting them from side to side, looking up and down.

Feast Your Eyes on the Free-Radical Fighters

Of all these protective measures, eating foods rich in antioxidants is probably the best way to preserve your vision. Antioxidants prevent the cell damage caused by highly reactive oxygen molecules called free radicals.

Colleagues of mine at the USDA once described free radicals as molecular pickpockets. Antioxidants – among them vitamin C, vitamin E, and the carotenoids (including beta-carotene, lutein, lycopene, and zeaxanthin) – circulate in your bloodstream, in effect handcuffing the pickpockets before they can snatch anything vital from the cellular machinery. As it turns out, your eyes are especially sensitive to free radicals, so they benefit quite a bit from antioxidant nutrients.

For a long time, only nutritional medicine experts and botanist/herbalists like yours truly believed that antioxidants could shield the eyes from damage and deterioration. But now some mainstream ophthalmologists are climbing on the bandwagon. One whom I admire is Robert Abel Jr., M.D., clinical professor of ophthalmology at Thomas Jefferson University in Philadelphia and author of *The Eye Care Revolution.* Like most ophthalmologists, Dr Abel performs a lot of cataract procedures – some 500 a year. But he figures that he treats four times as many people without surgery, primarily through nutritional approaches such as antioxidant supplementation.

Cataracts and Macular Degeneration: the Best Prescription is Prevention

Dr Abel's 500 cataract operations are just a fraction of the 500,000 performed annually in the United States. Cataracts affect millions of people worldwide.

A cataract is a cloudy spot on the part of your eye called the lens. Normally, the lens should be clear to let in light. When a cataract develops, it dims your vision and increases glare.

Cataracts are often associated with diseases that affect the eyes (notably diabetes) and with the long-term use of certain medications (such as corticosteroids). They also seem more common in people who've had years of excessive exposure to ultraviolet radiation, the same kind of sunlight that causes sunburn.

More Wisdom *from the* Garden

The Way to Healthy Eyes May Be through Your Stomach

According to Robert Abel Jr., M.D., clinical professor of ophthalmology at Thomas Jefferson University in Philadelphia and author of *The Eye Care Revolution*, poor digestion may contribute to cataracts and macular degeneration. If you don't digest well, his theory goes, your body can't use all of the antioxidants that you eat. Makes sense to me.

One common cause of poor digestion is low stomach acidity, which affects more than half of all people aged 60 and over. To correct this condition, Dr Abel recommends taking hydrochloric acid supplements as well as eating lots of papaya and pineapple. These foods contain enzymes that support good digestion. He also suggests taking several herbs that soothe inflammation in the gut, including garlic, ginger, and licorice.

If cataracts have a bright side, it's that they're treatable. The same can't be said for macular degeneration. In fact, this condition is the leading cause of blindness in the elderly.

Macular degeneration involves deterioration of the macula, the central area of the nerve-rich retina. The macula allows you to see colour and fine detail. If it deteriorates, objects at the center of your field of vision appear wavy and go from colour to black and white. As the condition progresses, you may end up viewing the world from the corners of your eyes.

Age-related macular degeneration (known as AMD) is the most common cause of sight loss in people over 60 all over the world, but it never leads to complete sight loss since peripheral vision remains intact.

There are two kinds of macular degeneration: wet and dry. The dry type is much more common, accounting for 90 per cent of all cases. In dry macular degeneration, tiny deposits called drusen accumulate in your retina. The drusen are believed to consist of waste products that build up because of a lack of antioxidants.

Wet macular degeneration, which accounts for the other 10 per cent of cases, occurs when blood vessels underneath your retina begin to increase in number. This process destroys your macula and causes rapid vision loss, usually within 2 to 3 years.

A small number of people with wet macular degeneration may benefit from surgery to stop leakage from the multiplying blood vessels, thus slowing vision loss. Personally, I'd rather do what I can to protect myself from any form of the disease. That's why I make certain to get plenty of antioxidants in my diet.

Build Your Defences with Carrots and Company

Both macular degeneration and cataracts result from free-radical damage. Both conditions can be prevented, or at least delayed, by eating lots of antioxidant-rich foods.

As proof of the protective power of antioxidants, consider the findings of the ongoing Harvard Nurses' Health Study, which has been tracking the health status and lifestyles of 120,000 female nurses since

1972. As part of the study, researchers compared the diets of women who had undergone cataract surgery with the diets of women who hadn't. The researchers determined that the more vitamin C and carotenoids that the nurses consumed from foods, the less likely they were to need surgery. In fact, the women with the highest intakes of these antioxidant nutrients had 40 per cent less chance of developing cataracts than the women with the lowest intakes. The single most protective food was spinach.

Similar findings have been documented for macular degeneration. In particular, research has shown that vegetarians are substantially less likely to develop the disease than meat eaters. That's because a vegetarian diet is so much richer in plant foods, which contain many more antioxidants.

In my Garden of Youth, I grow a number of antioxidant-rich plants. It's such a pleasure to stroll through the garden's terraces and pick fresh fixings for a vision-preserving dish: a handful of purslane, one of the best sources of vitamin C, vitamin E, and carotenoids; some peppers, with their ample supplies of vitamin C; and a few cherry tomatoes, loaded with the carotenoid lycopene. A quick steaming, and I will have a dish that both pleases my palate and protects my eyes.

Now you may be wondering, what about carrots? After all, carrots have a long-standing reputation of being good for the eyes. And they do contain impressive amounts of vitamin A and certain carotenoids, including beta-carotene, lutein, lycopene, and zeaxanthin.

Dr Duke's Anti-Ageing Elixir

Macula-Saving Salad

Treat your macula to this delicious mix of greens and veggies. It's rich in lutein, a carotenoid that helps prevent macular degeneration. It's also easy to make.

WHAT YOU NEED

Any combination of the following greens: broccoli, collards, kale, mustard greens, rocket, spinach, and turnip greens

Carrots, diced

Tomatoes, sliced

WHAT TO DO

In a large bowl, toss together the greens of your choice. Add as much of the carrots and tomatoes as you wish.

Dr Duke's Anti-Ageing Elixir

Cataract-Combating Tonic

Since I don't have a bearing bilberry bush, I use blueberries in this recipe, which supplies an abundance of eye-friendly anthocyanosides.

WHAT YOU NEED

1 cup blueberries
1 handful catnip
1 handful rosemary
1 handful lemon balm
2 cups water
1 small piece of fresh ginger
A little turmeric

WHAT TO DO

In a blender, process the blueberries to a drinkable consistency. Set aside.

Put the catnip, rosemary, and lemon balm in a saucepan and add the water. Bring to the boil. Add the ginger and turmeric. Steep for 20 minutes, then strain.

Combine the tea with the blueberry juice. Drink a few cups every day, refrigerating any left over for later use.

Variation: You can substitute any dark-coloured fruit for the blueberry and any edible or culinary mint for the catnip, rosemary, or lemon balm.

Personally, I think carrots are great, and I munch them often. But tomatoes and leafy greens are also well-endowed with carotenoids, especially lutein and zeaxanthin, two that are strongly recommended for macular health.

Regrettably, I don't have every single one the lutein-rich plants in my Garden of Youth. But I do have the numero uno lutein source: rhubarb. Other top-notch sources include broccoli, collards, kale, mustard greens, rocket, spinach, and turnip greens.

Even though lutein isn't all that well-represented in my garden, the rest of the carotenoid family is. I grow gotu kola, nasturtium, purslane, sorrel, spinach, and watercress – all of which contain impressive amounts of various carotenoids.

I also grow several kinds of mint, all of which are packed with antioxidants. These herbs can help protect your eyes against cataracts and macular degeneration. Perhaps you'd enjoy a cup of mint tea with your steamed purslane, peppers, and tomatoes. Or you might prefer catnip tea. It's easy to remember: catnip for cataracts. In fact, the names of two cataract-fighting compounds, nepetin and nepetrin, come from the botanical name for catnip *(Nepeta cataria).*

Berries Are Very Beneficial, Too

While I'm on the subject of antioxidants, I mustn't forget to mention the potent anthocyanosides, which are found in dark-coloured fruits. The most frequently cited source is the bilberry, though it's far from the only source. Other fruits rich in anthocyanosides include blackberries, black cherries, blackcurrants, blueberries, boysenberries, cherries, cranberries, grapes, plums, prunes, raisins, redcurrants, red grapes, red raspberries, and wineberries (a close relative of raspberries). Generally, the darker the fruit, the more anthocyanosides it contains.

Right now, I have only about half of these plants in my Garden of Youth. One of these days, I expect I'll get around to adding the others. Growing season has already ended for the blackberries, blueberries, cherries, and currants. But just last night, I put some garden-fresh

More Wisdom *from the* Garden

Supplements Can Fortify Your Eyes' Defences

In most studies, food sources of antioxidants seem to work better than supplements in protecting against cataracts and macular degeneration. Nevertheless, supplements can help.

When researchers assessed the use of vitamin C supplements among a group of female nurses participating in the Harvard Nurses' Health Study, they found that the women who developed cataracts were least likely to be taking supplements. By comparison, the women who had been taking vitamin C for more than a few years were much more likely to be cataract-free.

In addition, an article in the journal *Ophthalmology* concluded that a daily multivitamin can reduce cataract risk by one-third, while a daily vitamin E supplement can cut risk by about one-half. I wouldn't be surprised if the same supplementation regime helped prevent macular degeneration as well.

I like to think of supplemental antioxidants as a little extra insurance for your eyes. That's invaluable when your vision is at stake.

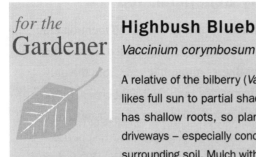

for the
Gardener

Highbush Blueberry

Vaccinium corymbosum

A relative of the bilberry (*Vaccinium myrtillus*), highbush blueberry likes full sun to partial shade and rich, acidic, evenly moist soil. It has shallow roots, so plant it away from paths, sidewalks, and driveways – especially concrete ones, which raise the alkalinity of surrounding soil. Mulch with pine needles, peat moss, or shredded oak.

Avoid pruning blueberry bushes until after the third year, since the fruits grow near the tips of branches that are at least 2 years old. After that, remove any weak and diseased branches as well as any branches that are more than 5 years old. Prune them all the way back to the main stem.

red raspberries into my lemonade.

I also get impressive amounts of anthocyanosides when I eat black beans, which are among my favourites. As a bonus, they – and most other beans – contain ample supplies of genistein, a phyto-oestrogen (or plant oestrogen) that has the ability to slow and even stop the development of new blood vessels. Genistein may help prevent wet macular degeneration and diabetic retinopathy, both of which result from abnormal blood vessel growth in the eyes. So if you want to safeguard your vision, eating a bowl of bean soup a few times a week might help.

Glaucoma: Catch This Vision Villain Early

Cataracts and macular degeneration aren't the only diseases to threaten ageing eyes. Glaucoma affects some millions of older people, though half of them don't even know they have it.

That's because the most common form of the disease, called open-angle glaucoma, begins very slowly, with an imperceptible loss of peripheral vision (unlike macular degeneration, which involves the loss of central vision). You may not notice any problem until your eyes have suffered permanent damage. In fact, glaucoma is among the world's leading causes of blindness, reinforcing its reputation as 'the silent thief of sight'.

Glaucoma occurs when the fluid that circulates through your eye (called the aqueous humour) can't drain away as it's supposed to. Normally, it flows through a tiny structure (the drainage angle) into a tube, then from the tube into your bloodstream. But sometimes the drainage angle or the tube below it gets blocked, causing the fluid to back up. This increases pressure inside your eye, eventually destroying your optic nerve and stealing away peripheral vision.

While the vision loss associated with glaucoma can't be reversed, the disease itself can be stopped or at least slowed, provided it's caught early enough. That's why experts advise adults to get tested for glaucoma – every 2 to 3 years after the age of 40, then every 1 to 2 years after the age of 60. (The changes associated with open-angle glaucoma usually begin after 60.) The screening itself is quick and painless.

The Glaucoma plot in my Garden of Youth has just one plant, a South American native called jaborandi by the Tupi Indians. The word *jaborandi* means 'that which makes you slobber'. It describes the plant perfectly. Jaborandi contains a compound called pilocarpine that increases the flow of saliva up to tenfold.

The extracted form of pilocarpine happens to be the drug of choice for treating glaucoma. It's often prescribed as eyedrops. I'll bet that the deer around YinYang Valley have good eyesight. They've almost defoliated my jaborandi.

Other plants that may help prevent or treat glaucoma include bilberry, oregano, and pansy. I grow all three, though not in the Glaucoma plot because they're not all that potent against the disease. They're certainly worth taking for their many other health benefits. If they help your eyes in the process, so much the better.

CHAPTER 12

Good Hearing

Dr Duke's Anti-Ageing Elixir
• *Old-Fashioned Ear Easer*

My wife, Peggy, seems to have worse hearing than I do. It's not just my mumbling. Quite often, when the television is On, she misses what is clearly audible to me. She asks me what was said, and I tell her. Then I remind her that much of what's on TV isn't worth hearing anyhow.

Most hearing problems don't respond well to treatment. So prevention is not just the best way to go, it's quite possibly the only way to go.

Like all of our senses, our hearing does decline somewhat as we get older. But a great deal of what's often referred to as natural or age-related hearing loss is neither natural nor age-related. In fact, it has two primary causes: noise and cardiovascular disease. And both of these, to a great extent, are within our control.

Surround Yourself in Peace and Quiet

All loud sounds – whether from car alarms or drills or police sirens or some other source – slowly and imperceptibly chip away at your sense of hearing. So does all loud music, not just rock.

The journey to hearing impairment is a one-way ride. Each time you're exposed to noise, it damages the microscopic hairs in your inner ear that transmit sound to the auditory nerve. Once injured, the hairs never recover, and they cannot be repaired with current medical technology.

I can't undo the damage that has resulted from years of assaulting my ears with loud noise. But I can preserve the hearing that I have left by putting a stop to noise exposure. And I can teach my kids and grandkids (at least those who want to learn) about the ravages of noise, so they can protect their own ears from abuse.

For all of us, the basic rule is the same: avoid loud noise whenever possible. If you see a fire engine or ambulance approaching with siren wailing, always cover your ears until it's long gone. The same goes if you find yourself around aeroplanes, motorboats, trains with blowing horns – anything that produces deafening sounds.

There's no shame in protecting your ears. More and more people are doing it, now that they're learning about the potentially harmful effects of loud noise on hearing.

Just how loud is too loud? Sound volume is measured in decibels (dB). Normal conversation registers about 60 dB; restaurant chatter, 70 to 80; vacuum cleaners, 80; motorcycles, 90; drills, 100; rock concerts, 100 to 130; and gunfire, 140. According to the experts, prolonged exposure to any sound that exceeds about 80 dB can damage your hearing. So if you're around anything that seems louder than your vacuum cleaner, cover your ears.

Even better, if you know in advance that you're probably going to be exposed to loud noise, you can protect your hearing by wearing earplugs. Inexpensive foam or wax earplugs are available at your local chemist.

I worry about my grandkids' hearing. Their lives are much noisier than mine was at that age. Have you seen some of the toys being made for kids these days? The battery-powered ones often contain microchips that make a real racket. I'd advise not buying them for your children or grandchildren. They're bad for youngsters' ears, not to mention not much good for your own.

Personal computers can also make a racket if they're equipped a certain way. You might be familiar with one of the special attachments that's marketed for video games, a sound effects device called Sound Blaster. The name says a lot: this gadget is way too loud.

If the youngsters in your family like to listen to their rock music on their personal stereos, they're really putting their ears at risk. Headphones and heavy metal are a combination that can lead to hearing loss. No wonder one group goes by the name Def Leppard.

I know that young people like to tell older folks to lighten up when they say, 'Turn that music down!' But I bet that my hearing aged 72 is as good as or better than the hearing of a lot of college kids. In a study at the University of Tennessee, audiologists gave hearing tests to 1,000 freshmen. An astonishing 60 per cent of the students showed hearing impairment typical of people three times their age. It's not just because of the rock music. It's because of all the things that are making our world louder and noisier than ever.

Take Care of Your Heart – And Your Hearing

The fact that noise is hard on hearing should come as no surprise. But this might: cardiovascular disease can take a toll on your ears, too.

You already know that cardiovascular disease is the underlying cause of heart attacks and most strokes, as well as some forms of impotence. It involves the narrowing of arteries throughout your body, including the tiny arterioles that supply blood to your inner ears. When these arterioles get smaller, it can set the stage for hearing impairment.

You can safeguard your ears against hearing loss in the same way that you protect your heart and brain from problems: follow a near-vegetarian Palaeolithic diet, exercise regularly, manage stress – and if you smoke, quit. These are the principles of my youth-promoting SEVENTY programme, outlined in chapter 2.

You may also want to consider taking ginkgo, a herb known for improving bloodflow throughout the body, including circulation to the inner ear. In fact, ginkgo is recommended by naturopaths for two hard-to-treat hearing problems associated with ageing: chronic ringing in the ears (tinnitus) and cochlear deafness. Most naturopaths recommend taking 40 milligrams of ginkgo extract three times a day. If I had a hearing problem, I'd try it.

Besides cardiovascular disease and noise exposure, certain common ailments can affect your hearing, especially as you get older. Most are highly treatable and easily preventable. Keep them in check, and your ears will continue to serve you well.

Excess Earwax: Unclog with Olive Oil

If you've ever had a buildup of earwax, you know that it can affect your hearing. You're more likely to have problems as you get older and the consistency of the wax begins to change.

Believe it or not, earwax serves a very important purpose. This yellowish to brownish gloop lines your ear canal to protect it, especially from water. The wax is supposed to stay soft, so the old stuff can wash out and the new stuff can slide into place. But it tends to dry out and harden with age, causing a buildup that can block your ear canal. Quite often this leads to partial hearing loss. You may experience pain, too.

Usually, you can get rid of excess earwax on your own, using simple self-care measures. One thing you *don't* want to do is try digging out the wax with cotton swabs. They tend to push the wax further into your ear canal, making matters worse.

A much better treatment option is olive oil. When you're getting ready to go to bed, simply heat some oil until it's warm – never hot. Then use a dropper to put a few drops in your affected ear. The oil softens the wax and helps restore your body's natural wax-removal process.

If you wish, you can follow your olive-oil treatment with gentle irrigation of your ear the next morning. All you need is warm water and a bulb syringe, which you can buy in almost any pharmacy.

If the wax plug doesn't come out right away, be patient. Keep using the olive oil and rinsing your ear canal with warm water. The earwax will eventually come out.

Now Hear This: Nothing Smaller Than Your Elbow!

As a grown-up, you should know better than to stick things in your ears that don't belong there. But in case it does happen, never try to remove a foreign object by poking in your ear with a hair grip, needle, matchstick, or cotton swab. Most likely, all you'll do is push the object further inside.

Instead, try tilting your head towards the side of the affected ear and shaking it. If the object doesn't budge, try floating it out by adding a few drops of warm water or vegetable oil with a dropper. If that doesn't work, get yourself to a doctor as soon as possible.

Ear Infections: Antibiotics Aren't the Answer

Excess earwax isn't the only cause of ear pain. Perhaps the worst pain comes from middle-ear infections, what doctors call otitis media. This condition can affect anyone at any age. But it's most common in young children who have colds. A cold causes congestion that narrows or blocks the tube responsible for draining fluid from the middle ear. The fluid backs up and gets infected.

You may wonder why – in a book intended for grown-ups who want to stay young – I'm covering a condition that primarily strikes youngsters. First, adults do get ear infections, though not nearly as often as kids. Second, the conventional way of treating ear infections could have long-term repercussions for all of us.

Infectious disease specialists from the Centers for Disease Control and Prevention in the US and from leading universities agree that doctors in general are too quick to prescribe antibiotics for ear infections and other infectious conditions. This practice helps breed antibiotic-resistant bacteria, which are a public health hazard for everyone, especially the elderly, whose immune systems have lost some firepower.

In America alone, children receive almost one-quarter of the 145 million antibiotic prescriptions handed out annually. I'd guess that a good number of these prescriptions are for ear infections. The reason so many doctors recommend antibiotics – and so many parents request them – is the belief that childhood ear infections can lead to hearing impairment and even deafness.

While this can happen, my research suggests that it's pretty rare. It's not even an issue for kids who get only one or two ear infections a year. And as researchers in the Netherlands found, infections in children over the age of 2 often begin clearing up on their own within 48 hours, making antibiotics unnecessary.

In fact, in most cases of ear infection, antibiotics aren't only unnecessary, they're completely ineffective. Why? Because the drugs treat only bacterial infections. As many as 9 in 10 ear infections are caused by viruses, and they simply don't respond to antibiotics.

Even the *Journal of the American Medical Association* has questioned the use of antibiotics as the first-choice treatment for ear infections. In a published meta-analysis – that is, a statistical compilation of several previous studies – the results were clear and compelling: the standard practice of prescribing 10 days of antibiotic therapy for acute otitis media is ill-advised and perhaps even dangerous.

Doctors in the Netherlands have developed a new protocol for treating kids' ear infections. Instead of prescribing antibiotics, they tell parents to monitor their children for a few days, using pararcetamol to relieve pain. If their infections don't clear up, the kids get antibiotics on their second visit. Interestingly, only about 5 per cent of the youngsters need antibiotic treatment.

While I'm not a medical doctor, this protocol makes sense to me – for kids as well as grown-ups who develop ear infections. By reducing our antibiotic use, we prevent the development of antibiotic-resistant bacteria.

The only caveat: if you're treating your child's or grandchild's ear pain, be sure to use *only* pararcetamol, not aspirin or willow bark (the herbal equivalent of aspirin). In youngsters with viral infections, such as the colds that lead to most middle-ear infections, aspirin can cause a rare but potentially fatal illness called Reye's syndrome.

Certain herbs can also help treat ear infections. Echinacea, for example, stimulates your body's immune system to fight off viruses as well as bacteria. For an ear infection, I'd suggest taking a teaspoon or so of echinacea tincture every few hours, in juice. Or you can buy standardised capsules and take them according to the label directions.

You can also try putting calendula or mullein tincture or oil directly in your affected ear, as long as you're sure that your eardrum isn't damaged. I don't know of any studies that show clear benefits from using these herbs. But I do know several respected herbalists who advocate this treatment approach.

Both calendula and mullein have anti-inflammatory properties. Mullein is also antibacterial. To make an oil from either herb, place a

Dr Duke's Anti-Ageing Elixir

Old-Fashioned Ear Easer

In folk medicine, earaches are often treated with warm, herbed vegetable oil. I'd sooner try that than expose myself – or my children or grandchildren – to an unnecessary round of antibiotics. Here's a good recipe featuring garlic, a natural antibiotic and immune system stimulant. It's adapted from *Herbal Antibiotics: Natural Alternatives for Treating Drug-Resistant Bacteria*, by herbalist Stephen H. Buhner.

WHAT YOU NEED

120 ml (4 fl oz) vegetable oil (almond, avocado, rapeseed, evening primrose, flaxseed, or olive)

5 cloves garlic, crushed

20 drops eucalyptus oil

15 drops grapefruit seed extract

WHAT TO DO

In a small saucepan, combine the vegetable oil and the garlic. Cook on the stove, until the garlic aroma is strong. Strain out the garlic and add the eucalyptus oil and grapefruit seed extract. Mix well.

When the oil has cooled, use a dropper to apply a few drops in the painful ear. Store the rest in an amber bottle, away from light and heat. You can repeat the treatment up to three times a day. (The oil should not be used by anyone whose eardrums have been damaged.)

handful of chopped plant material into a jar. Add enough olive oil to cover. Put a lid on the jar and store it in a warm place for at least 3 days (some herbalists recommend 2 weeks).

To use the oil, first strain out the plant material, then place a few drops into the affected ear with a dropper. Repeat the treatments up to three times a day. Store any remaining oil away from light and heat for up to 3 months.

Incidentally, if you ever intend to treat a youngster with an oral herbal remedy – such as echinacea, for an ear infection – you need to adjust the dosage. I follow this simple rule: divide the child's age on his next birthday by 24, then use that fraction of a typical adult dose. Suppose the child is 6 years old. Divide 6 by 24, and you get 0.25, or ¼. That means you'd give the child a quarter of the typical adult dose.

Swimmer's Ear: What to Do When You're Waterlogged

Like otitis media, swimmer's ear is a painful, infectious condition. One key difference: swimmer's ear affects your outer ear rather than the middle. It occurs when the outer structures are repeatedly exposed to water, which washes away too much earwax and leaves the ear tissue vulnerable to germs.

I had more than my share of swimmer's ear as a teenager, when I'd spend entire days swimming around the muddy lakes of the Carolinas. I haven't had a bout in more than 50 years, but to this day I can remember how much the infection hurt.

You can reduce your chances of getting swimmer's ear by wearing earplugs when you swim and even when you bathe. When you get out of the water, dry your ears thoroughly, but not with cotton swabs, which can further traumatise already-irritated ear canals and contribute to infection. Instead, twist the end of a disposable facial tissue and use that to gently dab your outer ears. Follow up by putting a few drops of a mild acid solution into your ears. The usual recommendation is for equal parts white vinegar (acetic acid) and rubbing (isopropyl) alcohol.

If, despite your best efforts, you find yourself nursing a case of swimmer's ear, white vinegar can still help fight the infection. Using a dropper, put a few drops in the affected ear several times a day.

For adults with swimmer's ear, I recommend using willow bark, which has the same active ingredient as aspirin. (In fact, you can just take aspirin if you prefer.) Make a tea from the herb by adding 1 to 2 teaspoons of powdered bark to a cup of boiling water. Simmer for 10 minutes, then strain. I suggest drinking up to two cups a day.

Aeroplane Ear: Don't Get Grounded by Pain

'Aeroplane ear' is the name for the intense earache that strikes many an unfortunate airline passenger, including my wife, Peggy. Doctors refer to the condition as barotitis. It results from a rapid change in air (barometric) pressure within a plane's cabin, usually while the plane is landing.

Normally, the pressure inside your ears is the same as the pressure outside. If the pressure outside changes rapidly – as it can during a plane's landing – the difference can stress your eardrums, producing pain. The pain can linger for up to a few days, and it may be accompanied by hearing impairment.

Most people can avoid or alleviate aeroplane ears by swallowing, yawning, or chewing gum. If that doesn't work, or if you're travelling with a cold, you may want to take an over-the-counter decongestant. Or you can choose a herbal alternative. The caffeine in coffee, tea, and kola has decongestant properties, as does the ephedrine in Chinese ephedra (ma huang).

There is some anxiety about Chinese ephedra because several people have died after taking the herb, often in extraordinarily large doses. I'm hoping that it won't be pulled off the market.

CHAPTER 13

Healthy Heart

Dr Duke's Anti-Ageing Elixir
• Heart-Smart Soup

Here's a sobering statistic: we Americans are more likely to die from cardiovascular disease than from any other condition, including cancer. While cancer claims about 23 per cent of the US population each year, cardiovascular disease kills almost double that number and the same is true in many other Western societies.

Still, we don't seem as concerned as we should be about our cardiovascular health. (*Cardio-* means heart; *-vascular* refers to blood vessels.) We may take steps to keep our blood pressure or cholesterol in check if our doctors tell us to. But most of us don't know that trouble is brewing until we experience a catastrophic event like a heart attack or stroke.

By now you've probably figured out that I view prevention as the best 'treatment' for most health problems. This is especially true for cardiovascular disease.

Consider heart disease, a form of cardiovascular disease that affects millions of people worldwide each year. To treat it governments and individuals spend billions of dollars – billions which, if used to fund preventitive programmes, would make us all a great deal better off.

These sentiments are not just the ravings of an admittedly opinionated author. Even the National Institutes of Health (NIH) in the United States agrees. In a 1994 report, the NIH declared: 'For health-care reform truly to succeed at reducing costs and increasing access, disease prevention must be the ultimate focus of the primary health-care system, rather than disease treatment.'

You Don't Want This Plaque on Your Artery Walls

The chances are that you already have a good idea of what brings on cardiovascular disease. But a brief review is in order.

The main cause is *atherosclerosis*, popularly known as hardening of the arteries. Actually, the arteries don't harden. They narrow because of a buildup of fatty, cholesterol-rich gunk that forms deposits called plaques.

By themselves, plaques are bad enough. But if one happens to break open, its contents could spill out, possibly obstructing a section of artery that's already narrowed by other plaques. If an artery becomes completely blocked, blood can't reach your cells as it's supposed to, and some tissue dies. When this happens in your heart, it's a heart attack. In your brain, it's a stroke.

While some strokes occur because of bleeding in the brain (these are described as haemorrhagic), most, about three-quarters, result from blocked arteries (these are called ischemic, which means loss of bloodflow). In fact, ischemic strokes are so similar to heart attacks that experts have begun referring to them as brain attacks.

What Puts You at Risk?

Heart attacks and strokes are just two of many serious health problems that arise from cardiovascular disease. It also causes angina, chest pain that occurs during rest or mild exertion; congestive heart failure, a tired heart that can't pump well enough to circulate blood properly;

arrhythmia, a persistent problem with the heart 'skipping' beats; intermittent claudication, leg pain that results from minor exertion; and transient ischemic attacks (TIAs), mini-strokes that last from a moment to a few minutes and then resolve on their own.

Even impotence has been linked to cardiovascular disease. According to experts at the National Institutes of Health, 'Atherosclerosis of the penile artery is the primary cause of impotence in nearly half of the men over age 50 who have erectile dysfunction.'

Because all of these conditions are manifestations of the same basic problem, atherosclerosis, they have essentially the same basic risk factors, too. These include a family history of cardiovascular disease, a high-fat diet, lack of exercise, smoking, chronic stress, obesity, diabetes, high blood pressure and high cholesterol.

Of course, you can't change your family history. But you can take steps to rein in those other risk factors. Here are some suggestions. (For specific information on weight control, diabetes, high blood pressure, and high cholesterol, refer to the respective chapters later in this book.)

The Way to a Healthy Heart Is through the Stomach

In America and the United Kingdom, heart disease was rare before the 20th century. Then the standard diet began to change from one fairly low in fat to one with a much higher fat content.

Yes, our hardworking 19th-century ancestors ate high-fat sausage and bacon, but not as much as we'd like to think. Plus, they didn't have the fatty junk foods and fast foods that we do – everything from Mars Bars to pepperoni pizzas to Big Macs. In countries around the world with native diets similar to the plant-based Palaeolithic diet, heart disease is much less of a problem.

The Palaeolithic diet is the way to go for two reasons. First, it's low in the types of fat that contribute to atherosclerosis. Second, because the diet consists primarily of fruits, vegetables, pulses, and whole grains, it's rich in antioxidants and phytochemicals. These nutrients are important because they can prevent, or at least delay, atherosclerosis.

To some extent, they even treat the disease.

My Healthy Sevens eating plan closely follows the Palaeolithic principles and may help protect against heart disease. To learn more about it, see chapter 3.

Regardless of whether you make the Healthy Sevens part of your lifestyle, you can benefit simply by eating more of the following plant foods. All contain substances that are good for your heart.

CHICORY. First thing every summer morning, the pasture out beyond YinYang Valley turns blue, as all of the chicory flowers open up. By afternoon, they close again.

Chicory is the best source of inulin, a compound that helps prevent and treat congestive heart failure. It also helps lower cholesterol and appears to slow the progression of atherosclerosis.

What's more, Egyptian researchers have discovered that chicory can slow a rapid heartbeat. Certain compounds in the root have a mild heart-stimulating effect similar to digitalis, but the amounts of the compounds are low enough to be safe.

Roasting doesn't destroy the inulin in chicory root, which is noteworthy because several commercial coffee alternatives contain roasted chicory root. Chicory is also consumed as a salad.

OLIVE OIL. Among the plants on my wish list for the Garden of Youth is an olive tree. The more I read about olive oil, the more I believe that the olive tree belongs in the plot devoted to heart disease.

Consumed daily, olive oil provides significant protection against heart disease. It's rich in monounsaturated fat. In general, too much fat is bad for your heart and arteries, but the monounsaturated kind is one exception to the rule. It plays a major role in the Mediterranean diet, and in Mediterranean populations, heart attacks are rare.

PULSES. Many Americans know the schoolyard rhyme that begins with this line: 'Beans, beans, they're good for your heart …' Well, beans *are* good for your heart, for reasons other than the one cited in the playground ditty.

Most varieties are rich in a B vitamin called folate. This nutrient helps lower levels of homocysteine, a substance in your body that's a

Dr Duke's Anti-Ageing Elixir

Heart-Smart Soup

This recipe produces a mixed-bean soup that tastes great and helps prevent cardiovascular disease.

WHAT YOU NEED

455 g (1 lb) dried lentils
455 g (1 lb) dried black-eyed peas
230 g (8 oz) dried split peas
230 g (8 oz) dried pinto beans
230 g (8 oz) dried butter beans
230 g (8 oz) dried chopped onions
2 carrots, chopped
2 cloves garlic, crushed
1 finger-length piece fresh ginger, grated
Curry powder
Turmeric
Ground cayenne pepper

WHAT TO DO

In a soup pot, combine the lentils, black-eyed peas, split peas, pinto beans, and butter beans. Add enough water to double the height of the beans in the pot. Soak overnight.

The next day, strain out the beans, then put them back in the pot with fresh water. Bring the beans to a gentle boil, then reduce the heat and simmer until tender. Add more water if necessary. Then add the onions, carrots, garlic, and ginger. Season to taste with the curry powder, turmeric, and cayenne pepper. Simmer until the vegetables are tender.

---

risk factor for cardiovascular disease.

In addition, they contain a compound called genistein that reduces cholesterol and helps prevent atherosclerosis. Soyabeans have developed a reputation for being the best source of genistein, but heart-healthy amounts are found in almost all edible pulses. In fact, my colleague Peter Kaufman, Ph.D., professor emeritus of biology and chemical engineering at the University of Michigan in Ann Arbor, has shown that split peas contain almost twice as much genistein as soya beans. Pea soup, anyone?

PURSLANE. One of my favourite weeds in the Garden of Youth is purslane. It volunteered for service in the garden, but when it appeared, I was delighted. I've just let it do its thing ever since.

Purslane is a juicy mass of medicinal food and, relatively speaking, one of the most heart-healthy plants that I grow. It's very well-endowed with antioxidant nutrients. It's the best leafy source of omega-3 fatty acids, another of the 'good fats' (like the monounsaturated fat in olive oil). It's also one of the best vegetable sources of magnesium. I've seen estimates that more than two-thirds of us don't get enough magnesium, which is a real problem. A shortage of this mineral contributes to cardiovascular disease by raising blood pressure and triggering heart-rhythm disturbances.

Purslane is a forager's treasure in the summer. I periodically harvest a pound or so of luscious tender stems and leaves for steaming. They can also be dried, pickled, or canned for use in the winter. Drying is done slowly, out of direct sunlight, just as for other culinary herbs. I like to crumple dried purslane into winter bean soups. The herb is almost as good a thickener as okra.

More Wisdom *from the* Garden

Vitamin E Offers Extra Protection

A potent antioxidant, vitamin E helps prevent heart attack. Studies by Harvard researchers have shown that a diet rich in the nutrient, daily supplementation (100 to 400 IU), or both can reduce heart attack risk by about 40 per cent in men and about 25 per cent in women.

Most multivitamins contain vitamin E, as do most antioxidant formulas. But if you're like me, you want to know which foods have the best supplies. Vegetable oils rank first, followed by nuts, then whole grains and poppy and sesame seeds. Among fruits and vegetables, the top sources include peppers, tomatoes, currants, blueberries, peaches and plums (and prunes).

SPINACH. The leafy green that Popeye made famous is among the best plant sources of folate. According to University of Washington researchers, 13,500 to 50,000 deaths from cardiovascular disease could be prevented every year if everyone took folic acid (the supplement form of folate) every day. All you need is 200 micrograms a day. You can get more than that from 170 g (6 oz) of spinach (or lentils, pinto beans, butter beans, black-eyed peas, or sunflower seeds) or a cup or two of spinach soup. What a pleasant way to stave off stroke and heart attack!

Of course, spinach and pulses aren't the only great sources of folate. Others include parsley, cabbage, asparagus, broccoli, brussels sprouts, endive, okra, avocado, peanuts, sunflower seeds, and orange juice.

Work Your Body's Most Important Muscle

Eating healthfully and exercising regularly are the dynamic duo of heart health. Exercise is important, and not just because it conditions your heart. It also has a direct impact on other risk factors for heart disease.

Exercise lowers your blood pressure and improves your cholesterol profile by reducing LDL cholesterol (the bad kind) and raising HDL (the good kind). It helps you control your weight, cutting your risk for obesity and diabetes. It alleviates stress. And if you're trying to quit smoking, it quells your cravings for cigarettes.

By incorporating a minimal amount of physical activity into your daily routine, you slash your odds of all kinds of cardiovascular disease, including heart disease. As a bonus, you protect yourself against gallstones and certain types of cancer (especially breast cancer). You also enhance your immune system function, so you're less vulnerable to just about every other ailment imaginable.

You don't need to get yourself all tuckered out to reap the benefits of regular physical activity. Nor must you complete your entire workout at once. Just be sure to accumulate 30 to 45 minutes of moderate exercise every day.

I find that the most pleasant way to fulfil my daily exercise requirement is to take walks. I put in a few miles a day, hiking around YinYang Valley and pottering in my Garden of Youth. No matter where you live, you can go walking. If the weather is uncooperative, head to the nearest shopping mall for a few brisk laps indoors.

I also ride my stationary bike. You may prefer bicycling outdoors or dancing or swimming or playing golf (which is walking, punctuated by frustration). Just do something that gets you moving. Even sex counts!

More Wisdom *from the* Garden

The Truth about Alcohol and Heart Health

Overindulgence in alcohol is a major national health problem. But a little alcohol – one drink a day for women, one to two for men – can help prevent cardiovascular disease. (A drink is defined as 350 ml (12 fl oz) of regular beer, 150 ml (5 fl oz) of wine, or a cocktail made with 45 ml (1½ fl oz) of 80-proof distilled spirits.)

Some 30 long-term studies have shown that moderate alcohol consumption reduces the risk of heart attack by 25 to 40 per cent. People who have a drink or two a day experience fewer cardiovascular problems than both excessive drinkers and teetotallers.

Alcohol helps keep your heart healthy by raising levels of HDL cholesterol, the good kind. Red wine has an additional benefit: it's rich in anthocyanosides and other antioxidant compounds that help prevent atherosclerosis.

No doubt you're familiar with the French paradox, the phenomenon that allows the French to enjoy an abundance of high-fat pâtés and cheeses without raising their risk of cardiovascular disease, which is considerably lower than ours. Their reduced risk is attributed, at least in part, to the fact that they drink alcohol. And their alcohol of choice is red wine.

If you don't drink, don't feel that you have to start. You can get many of the heart-protective benefits of red wine by drinking red or purple grape juice or eating dark-coloured fruits. All of these are rich in anthocyanosides.

Another option is green tea, a good source of polyphenols and other important antioxidant compounds. You may want to make it your beverage of choice, especially if you're a teetotaller.

People and Pets Are Powerful Preventives

I love a story told by heart disease researcher Dean Ornish, M.D., about a group of genetically similar laboratory rabbits. All of them ate the same food and got the same amount of exercise. But for some reason, the rabbits in the lower cages had 60 per cent fewer heart attacks than those in the upper cages.

The researchers were baffled – until they realised that the laboratory technician wasn't tall enough to reach the upper cages. So while all the rabbits got fed, only the ones in the lower cages got petted.

Moral of the story: a little love is a life preserver. Like the rabbits, we humans are a social species. We need contact with other people and with other beings, especially pets.

Many studies have proven that the more social connections you have, the less likely you are to develop cardiovascular disease. And if you experience a heart attack or stroke, the more social connections you have, the more likely you are to survive and recover.

Break Your Tobacco Habit

This should go without saying, but I'll mention it anyway: smoking is absolute hell on your arteries. Cigarettes, cigars, pipes – all of them accelerate atherosclerosis. So don't smoke. And if you are a smoker, stop *now*.

The good news is that once you give up smoking, your risk of cardiovascular disease will begin declining right away. Your risk of lung cancer will remain elevated for a number of years, but it will eventually start to drop, too.

Keep Stress in Check

Stress and anger increase your heart rate and raise your blood pressure. If you make a point to 'stop and smell the roses' as often as possible – or to break away from a harried Type A lifestyle altogether – you can lower your risk of heart attack substantially. By learning to control your temper, you'll reduce your risk even further. You'll also cut your chances of a stroke by half.

I handle my stress by working in my Garden of Youth, walking around YinYang Valley, making love, and staying in touch with my friends. You may wish to meditate, play with a pet, or volunteer to help those less fortunate. Any activity that refocuses attention from your own problems to the world around you can reduce your stress levels.

If you tend to lose your temper often or easily, you can do yourself a world of good by finding ways to rein in your anger. Studies show that emotion-driven outbursts send blood pressure soaring and significantly increase your risk of heart attack or stroke. Instead of venting your anger on the spot, walk away from a tense situation. Then do what you can to relax. Count to 10, practise deep breathing, meditate, even call a friend – whatever helps you unwind and regain control.

Herbal Remedies Improve Your Risk Profile

A number of herbs can help prevent heart disease and other forms of cardiovascular disease. Some can also help manage certain cardiovascular risk factors. Here's what works and why.

HAWTHORN (*CRATAEGUS MONOGYNA*). In nature, hawthorn is the closest thing to a herb specifically created to protect against cardiovascular disease. Its compound can help prevent and treat just about all heart-related conditions: angina, arrhythmia, atherosclerosis, congestive heart failure, coronary artery disease, high blood pressure, and high cholesterol.

Hawthorn works in a number of ways. It gently but significantly

for the Gardener

Hawthorn

Crataegus monogyna

My hawthorn tree still has some edible fruits. I like to make smoothies out of them. I also enjoy nibbling on the fresh, new leaves. Both the fruits and the leaves are good for the heart, and I hope to keep mine ticking quite a bit longer.

I've tried coaxing some of my hawthorn seeds into germinating, without success. Unless you're extremely patient, I suggest investing in a well-established hawthorn tree from a nursery. Plant it in an ample hole in a sunny, well-drained location.

conditions your heart to beat more efficiently and pump a greater volume of blood. It improves the supply of blood and oxygen to your heart by opening up your coronary arteries and improving your heart's metabolism. It lowers cholesterol and normalises heart rhythm, so you experience fewer episodes of arrhythmia. In Europe, hawthorn preparations are widely used to treat mild to moderate angina.

Commission E, which evaluates the safety and effectiveness of herbal medicines for the German government, says that hawthorn has no known risks or hazardous interactions with other drugs. Nevertheless, if you've been diagnosed with a cardiovascular condition, you should use hawthorn only with medical supervision. The commission suggests taking 160 to 900 milligrams a day of a standardised extract.

I like to think of hawthorn as a preventive 'farmaceutical'. When used as a treatment, it's not a quick fix. If you're taking it for angina, for example, you may not notice any significant reduction in chest pain for up to 8 weeks.

GARLIC (*ALLIUM SATIVUM*). A clove of garlic a day can save you from heart attack and stroke. It's true: in various studies, a daily dose of 800 milligrams of garlic powder (standardised to 1.3 per cent allicin content) – that's the equivalent of about one clove – reduced cholesterol levels by an average of 12 per cent, which cut heart attack risk by 24 per cent.

Garlic ranks right up there with hawthorn as a cardiovascular herb. It helps prevent atherosclerosis, high blood pressure, and high cholesterol, delivering a triple whammy that no pharmaceutical can match. Garlic is also a potent antioxidant. In one study, taking garlic supplements every day for a few months 'caused a statistically significant reduction of [atherosclerotic plaques] that averaged about 50 per cent.' Other members of the garlic family – including shallots, chives, onions, and leeks – bestow similar benefits.

But with garlic, as with all things, moderation is key. Consuming more than five cloves a day may cause flatulence, gastric distress, and heartburn. And taking garlic in combination with anticoagulant drugs may thin your blood too much.

GINGER (*ZINGIBER OFFICINALE*). Like garlic, ginger prevents cardiovascular disease in several ways. It reduces cholesterol. It makes the blood less likely to clot. It increases the strength of heart muscle tissue. And it reduces blood sugar – a plus for people with diabetes, who are at very high risk for cardiovascular disease.

In the cardiology clinic of one Israeli hospital, the doctors now advise all of their patients to take ½ teaspoon of ground ginger a day. Makes sense to me. So does drinking ginger tea. To make a tea, add 1 to 2 teaspoons of fresh grated ginger to 1 cup of freshly boiled water and steep for 10 minutes. Strain the tea before drinking it. I'd also suggest using ginger as a spice in cooking whenever the spirit moves you.

EVENING PRIMROSE (*OENOTHERA BIENNIS*). The oil of the evening primrose contains a fair amount of gamma-linolenic acid (GLA). This compound reduces blood pressure and prevents the blood clots that trigger heart attack and ischemic stroke. Borage and currant oils are even richer sources of GLA.

You see all sorts of dosage recommendations for evening primrose oil, with most experts suggesting 1 to 4 grams a day. Stay towards the low end of the range if you don't have significant risk factors for cardiovascular disease. If you do, you may want to aim for the high end.

If you're at high risk for a heart attack or you've already had one, you might want to combine your evening primrose oil with fish oil. Together, they provide even more heart protection.

SALICYLATE-CONTAINING HERBS. Perhaps you've heard that taking ½ to 1 standard aspirin tablet a day can help protect against heart attack. Aspirin helps by making your blood less likely to form the clots responsible for triggering heart attacks as well as ischemic strokes.

But you don't have to take little white pills to get aspirin's active compounds, called salicylates. You'll also find them in willow bark, meadowsweet (queen of the meadow), chilli pepper, and wintergreen.

In my Garden of Youth, I have three willows, a couple of meadowsweets, and almost too many chilli peppers – all bearing prolifically. I'm not suggesting that you go gnaw on a willow branch. I just want you to be aware that herbal alternatives to aspirin are available for your use.

More Wisdom *from the* Garden

Fruits Supply Natural Aspirin

Several vividly coloured fruits are rich in salicylates, the same compounds that give aspirin its heart-protecting power. The best sources include grapes (and raisins), plums (and prunes), raspberries, red and black currants, apricots, and dates.

I've seen estimates that vegetarians get up to 10 times more natural salicylates than people who eat meat at least once a day. That's another reason why a Palaeolithic diet can be so good for your heart.

Likewise, if you need to avoid aspirin, you'll want to steer clear of the salicylate-containing herbs as well.

The Aspirin Advantage

If you've had a heart attack, or if you're at high risk for one, you should seriously consider taking an aspirin a day, whether in pill or herb form. Experts in the US estimate that regular aspirin consumption could prevent as many as 600,000 heart attacks a year, including 200,000 fatalities. It could also avert 25,000 stroke deaths and 24,000 deaths from colorectal cancer every year, according to the latest research.

If you're already using pharmaceutical aspirin as a preventive, you need to be careful not to overdo it. Taking too much can corrode your stomach. In fact, aspirin and other nonsteroidal anti-inflammatory drugs (NSAIDs) cause about 20,000 deaths a year from gastrointestinal bleeding. (Herbal aspirin can irritate the stomach, too, but usually not to the degree of its pharmaceutical counterpart.)

While aspirin helps protect against ischemic stroke – the kind caused by a blocked artery in the brain – it can make you slightly more vulnerable to haemorrhagic stroke. The expert consensus is that aspirin's overall benefits for preventing heart attack and ischemic stroke outweigh its risk for triggering haemorrhagic stroke. Still, you should check with your doctor before making aspirin part of your heart-healthy lifestyle.

CHAPTER 14

Super Immunity

Dr Duke's Anti-Ageing Elixirs

- *Spicy Sinus Saver*
- *Chinese Immune Brew*
- *Antiviral Vitali-Tea*

'She loves me, she loves me not …' These words seem to run through my mind whenever I'm tending the echinaceas that grow in my Garden of Youth. They are beautiful – tall plants with striking pinkish purple, daisylike flowers that invite plucking, perhaps with a few rounds of the traditional verse.

Echinacea – also known as coneflower, for the cone-shaped structure that anchors the pink-to-purple 'petals' – is my top-choice herbal immune-system booster. Too bad most people never get to see the plant in bloom. They buy their echinacea in juice, in capsule, or in tincture form at the health food store.

When my grandkids are visiting, you'll find me loading up on echinacea and other herbs that reinforce my ageing immune system. That way, the youngsters' germs can't knock me down. (Children under the age of 5 are the primary carriers of cold viruses and other infectious illnesses.)

Stimulating the immune system is still a rather foreign concept in conventional medicine. Doctors focus on killing germs and attacking the bad guys, often weakening the patient in the process. But in other healing disciplines, notably Chinese medicine, practitioners focus on strengthening the body. They help the good guys so that the bad guys can't invade in the first place.

In my opinion, aiding the good guys – experts call it enhancing host resistance – is the way to go. I think it's a crying shame that echinacea and other immune-system-boosting herbs aren't more widely used. Instead, doctors keep writing prescriptions for antibiotics, which gradually breed stronger, more virulent germs that require stronger, and always more expensive, antibiotics.

Generally speaking, pharmaceuticals have just one active ingredient with which to fend off an infectious invader. That's like going into battle with one bullet in your rifle. What's great about herbs is that each one contains many, even hundreds, of biologically active compounds, some in dose ranges that might provide real benefit to us humans. Herbs give your body an entire arsenal from which to select the weapons it needs.

Can your body actually make choices like this? Yes, through a process called homeostasis. Your body knows what it needs and takes it when it can. In most cases, I'd rather give my body the many active compounds in a herb than the single active ingredient in a drug.

A Lifestyle for Optimum Immune Function

Before I delve into the herbs known as immune system stimulants, I should mention that all plants contain some immune-enhancing compounds – like polysaccharides, vitamins, and minerals. Not that celery or pineapple is going to give you as much immune support as echinacea or ashwagandha. Still, every little bit helps.

If you adopt the near-vegetarian Palaeolithic diet that I've been advocating throughout this book, you'll get a lot of little immune-stimulating hits. For example, vitamin C, vitamin E, and the big carotenoid family all have some immune-strengthening properties. You don't get these nutrients from roast beef, cheese, or sweets. You get them from plant foods. (My Healthy Sevens eating plan is built around plant foods. To learn more about it, see chapter 3.)

Besides eating healthily, remember to exercise regularly. Moderate physical activity helps bolster your disease defences. Deep relaxation, adequate sleep, a strong network of friends, a good love life, and anything that keeps you from getting depressed also boost immunity.

On the other hand, certain things can inhibit immune function. They include smoking, excessive alcohol consumption (more than one to two drinks a day), severe stress, and exposure to pesticides and other toxic chemicals. Do what you can to control or eliminate these risk factors in your life.

Herbs That Strengthen Your Defences

Now the immune system is very complicated. It's made up of several different types of white blood cells; lots of antibodies, immunoglobulins, interferons, interleukins, and other immune modifiers; plus the lymph system, thymus gland, tonsils, appendix, liver, and bone marrow, among other body parts.

Experts can split hairs about which herb does what to which component of the immune system. For most people, it just doesn't matter. Here's what *does* matter: research has shown that immune-boosting herbs exert a general enhancing effect on the entire immune system.

While I wholeheartedly support the use of these herbs, I also advise moderation. That's because several studies have found that large doses of immune stimulants may, ironically, depress the immune system. So don't overdo it.

One additional word of caution: if you keep getting ill despite taking immune-boosting herbs, see your doctor. You may have a health problem that requires professional treatment.

Now for the herbs (in alphabetical order):

ASHWAGANDHA (*WITHANIA SOMNIFERA*). In several intriguing laboratory trials, researchers gave mice substances known to suppress the immune system. Some of the rodents also received ashwagandha, an Ayurvedic herb that's considered tonic – that is, strengthening. The mice that ingested the herb experienced very little decline in immune function.

Other studies have revealed that mice given ashwagandha are better able to fend off several types of bacterial infection, including pseudomonas, salmonella, and staphylococcus. In addition, the herb triggers significant increases in bone marrow activity, boosting the production of red blood cells. These cells carry oxygen around your body, another aspect of ashwagandha's role as a strengthener.

The recommended daily dose is two 150- to 300-milligram capsules, standardised to contain 2 to 5 milligrams of withanolides or 2.5 mls of tincture once or twice a day. I haven't heard of any safety problems with ashwagandha, though the literature says that abdominal cramps are possible.

ASTRAGALUS (*ASTRAGALUS MEMBRANACEUS*). Also known as huang qi, astragalus is one of the premier immune-system boosters in traditional Chinese medicine. Practitioners prescribe the herb to treat colds, flu, bronchitis, sinus infections, and other infectious ailments. They also recommend it for people whose immune systems have been suppressed by chronic illnesses such as AIDS.

These uses are supported by modern research. Various studies have shown astragalus to be an immune stimulant that's effective against a variety of bacteria, including salmonella and staphylococcus. The herb also has anti-tumour action, preventing metastasis in 80 per cent of mice with cancer in one laboratory trial. (*Metastasis* is the spread of cancer cells from one part of the body to another.) And according to research, astragalus stimulates T-cell activity and improves immune function in cancer patients.

Astragalus appears to be safe. I grow it, but I've yet to harvest it. I just leave it in the ground. If I wanted to use it, I'd buy a commercial preparation and follow the label directions. Generally, herbalists recommend taking 3 to 5 millilitres (½ to 1 teaspoon) of tincture three or four times a day, or one 500-milligram capsule twice a day.

BONESET (*EUPATORIUM PERFOLIATUM*). I was never that big a fan of boneset until two things happened: the plant showed up in my Garden of Youth, and I learned that it has some immune-stimulating properties, besides being a pain reliever and fever reducer. These findings pretty much confirm the traditional herbalists' view that boneset helps treat colds, flu, and other ailments that produce fever and achiness.

In one study, boneset stimulated white blood cells to devour bacteria even better than echinacea. According to Stephen H. Buhner, author of the excellent book *Herbal Antibiotics: Natural Alternatives for Treating Drug-Resistant Bacteria,* 'Increasing numbers of herbalists report that boneset is a reliable and effective immunostimulant, especially for infections that just won't go away.'

Buhner suggests making a boneset tea by adding 1 teaspoon of the herb to 1 cup of freshly boiled water. Steep for 10 minutes, then strain. Drink four cups of the tea a day.

CAT'S CLAW (*UNCARIA TOMENTOSA*). Also known by its Spanish name, *uña de gato*, this vine climbs trees in the Amazon with the help of sharp hooks that resemble ... well, you know. Research determined that cat's claw extracts greatly enhance production of interleukin-1 and interleukin-6, two important components of the immune system. This suggests that the herb has strong immune-boosting properties.

While scientists are still debating which compounds in cat's claw act as immune system stimulants, the latest studies show that the whole plant extract works better than any individual constituent. This gives me a chance to say, 'I told you so', because, as I said before, I always favour an arsenal of multiple herbal compounds over the bullet of an isolated active ingredient.

If you want to try cat's claw, you can buy a commercial preparation in a health food shop. Follow the label instructions for proper dosage.

ECHINACEA (*ECHINACEA,* VARIOUS SPECIES). I've already mentioned that echinacea is my numero uno herb for immune enhancement. In studies, echinacea has been found to contain compounds that are pain-relieving, flu-fighting, wound-healing, anti-inflammatory, antibacterial, expectorant, and generally immune-stimulating.

In one laboratory trial, mice were given a lethal dose of candida, the fungus that causes vaginal yeast infections. Some also received echinacea, which boosts the body's ability to fight candida. The mice that got the herb survived, while the other mice died.

Another study tested echinacea as a treatment for women with yeast infections. Among those who used a standard pharmaceutical antifungal preparation, 61 per cent experienced a recurrence of their infections. But among those who used the pharmaceutical plus echinacea, the rate of recurrence dropped to just 16 per cent.

Meanwhile, a separate study involving 180 people with colds found that treatment with a large dose of echinacea led to a speedier recovery than treatment with either a low dose of the herb or a placebo (a fake pill).

Now I should mention that there has been some scientific backlash against echinacea. Recent reports in the *Journal of the American Medical Association* and the *New England Journal of Medicine* contend that the herb doesn't prevent colds and flu after all. Researchers generally acknowledge that echinacea helps treat colds and flu, but they're disputing whether it acts as a preventive.

Frankly, I don't buy the criticism. I don't understand how a herb could stimulate the immune system only when you're ill, not beforehand. Seems to me that if immune boosters are effective – and I'm convinced that they are – then they should work preventively as well as therapeutically.

There's also controversy about which of the three primary species of echinacea – *E. purpurea, E. angustifolia,* and *E. pallida* – works best. On this issue, I'll go with the opinion of Paul Bergner, editor of the excellent newsletter *Medical Herbalism.* He believes that a mix of all three echinaceas is better than any one of the species alone.

Many studies have found that echinacea causes no side effects, except for a temporarily numb tongue, which is harmless. But herbalists generally advise against using echinacea every day as an immune-system-boosting tonic. Most authorities whom I respect seem to agree that the herb should be taken only when you're already sick or when you're going to be in a situation that puts you at risk of infection.

Commission E, the expert panel that evaluates the safety and effectiveness of herbal medicines for the German government, recommends that echinacea be used to treat only minor infectious ailments – for example, colds, flu, bronchitis, and urinary tract infections. In the commission's opinion, the herb isn't appropriate for more serious conditions such as HIV infection, multiple sclerosis, tuberculosis, and autoimmune disorders. The reason is that echinacea's immune-stimulating activity isn't all that well understood.

Personally, I would feel comfortable taking the herb for any of these conditions, with the exception of the autoimmune disorders (such as

for the Gardener

Echinacea

Echinacea purpurea, E. angustifolia

In order to germinate, echinacea seeds require moist, cold stratification. The easiest way to do this is to sow the seeds 5 mm (¼ in) deep in flats that are 10 to 15 cm (4 to 6 in) deep. To speed the process, move the flats to a sunny windowsill (or into a greenhouse if you have one) in late winter to early spring.

Once the seedlings are well-established, transplant *E. purpurea* so that they're 30 to 60 cm (12 to 24 in) apart and *E. angustifolia* so that they're 15 to 30 cm (6 to 12 in) apart. Both species prefer full sun, though they'll tolerate partial shade. If you're planning to use your echinacea for medicinal purposes, planting them in humus-rich, moist but well-drained soil will encourage good root production.

Harvest the roots at the end of their second year of growth. Wait until the plants have gone dormant – as indicated by their shrivelled brown leaves – before prying them up with a pitchfork. Wash the roots well and let them drip-dry overnight. Then process them into a tincture right away.

While echinacea's roots are considered most potent medicinally, its flowers and leaves can be harvested and prepared as an immune-boosting tea. Sometimes I nibble on the petals as I wander through my Garden of Youth.

lupus, rheumatoid arthritis, and scleroderma). As their name suggests, these diseases result from an overactive immune system. Taking an immune stimulant could make matters worse.

ELDERBERRY (*SAMBUCUS,* VARIOUS SPECIES). Elderberry is an age-old antiviral herb. Recent research determined that an elderberry preparation can help treat flu. One reason is that the herb is an immune booster. Another is that it contains several antiviral phytochemicals.

Chances are that we'll be hearing a lot more about elderberry in the future, as more studies get published. If I had the flu or another viral infection, I'd look for a commercial preparation – many health food shops carry them – and take it according to the label directions.

GARLIC (*ALLIUM SATIVUM*). Most folks know garlic as a natural antibiotic that also helps prevent heart disease by lowering cholesterol and blood pressure and by preventing the internal blood clots that trigger heart attack. But the herb has potent immune-enhancing properties, too.

In fact, garlic contains several immune-boosting compounds, including alpha-linolenic acid, beta-carotene, chlorogenic acid, ferulic acid, inulin, phosphorus, and zinc. What's more, its antibiotic compound alliin also has some immune-stimulating action. Specifically, it prompts white blood cells to devour more pathogens.

In one study involving old guys like me, taking 600 milligrams of garlic powder a day for 3 months improved the ability of white blood cells to combat infection by *Escherichia coli* bacteria, the ones that usually cause urinary tract infection. In a separate study, AIDS patients who consumed 5 to 10 grams of garlic every day for 12 weeks more than quintupled the activity of natural killer cells, another component of the immune system.

Unlike echinacea, garlic can be taken every day, as long as you and those around you can deal with garlic breath. Why is one herbal immune stimulant okay for daily use, while the other isn't? Frankly, I don't know. But that's what the experts whom I've consulted say. Personally, I take garlic almost every day, usually as an ingredient in soups.

GINSENG – ASIAN (*PANAX GINSENG*), AMERICAN (*P. QUINQUEFOLIUS*), SIBERIAN (*ELEUTHEROCOCCUS SENTICOSUS*). Herbal medicine uses primarily these three types of ginseng. They are different plants, but they contain rather

Dr Duke's Anti-Ageing Elixir

Spicy Sinus Saver

I recommend this concoction for all manner of upper respiratory and sinus infections. It's basically a garlic-and-onion soup, heavily laden with sinus-clearing hot spices.

WHAT YOU NEED

A few onions, chopped
Several cloves garlic, chopped
A few mushrooms, such as reishi or shiitake, sliced
Ground ginger
Horseradish
Mustard seed
Cayenne pepper

WHAT TO DO

Combine the onions, garlic, and mushrooms in a medium-size pot. Add water to cover. Bring to the boil. Season to taste with the ginger, horseradish, mustard seed, and cayenne pepper. Reduce the heat to low, cover, and simmer for 10 minutes, or until the vegetables are tender.

similar compounds. Skilled Asian practitioners tend to use Asian and American ginsengs for different purposes, but in the West, the herbs are often used interchangeably.

The ginsengs are best known as adaptogen/tonics, meaning that they exert a subtle but significant health-enhancing effect on the entire body. One way in which they achieve this effect is by stimulating the immune system.

I have all three ginseng species growing in my Garden of Youth, down in the shady woodland by the creek. I also have dwarf ginseng (*Panax trifolius*), which has never become a commercial species, though it was used for medicinal purposes by Native Americans.

If you want to try ginseng, I'd suggest buying a commercial extract and using it according to the label directions.

HONEYSUCKLE (*LONICERA JAPONICA*). Honeysuckle contains known virucides (virus-destroying compounds). It's a major antiviral and immune-stimulating herb in traditional Chinese medicine.

I'm a believer. When I feel a head cold or the flu coming on, and echinacea and garlic have failed to protect me, I bring in the herbal reinforcements – honeysuckle and forsythia, a classic Chinese virucidal combination. I mix them with European lemon balm, which has antiviral and antioxidant properties. (It also tastes much better than honeysuckle and forsythia.) This blend, prepared as a hot tea, is especially nice just before bed. (For instructions on making the tea, see my Chinese Immune Brew.)

JIAOGULAN (*GYNOSTEMMA PENTAPHYLLUM*). This herb has no English name. The Chinese call it *xiancao*, which means 'herb of immortality'. That's a bit of an overstatement. But jiaogulan is an antioxidant and immune system stimulant, which no doubt helped to solidify its reputation as a tonic and anti-ageing herb.

The recommended daily dosage of the herb is two or three tablets of standardised extract containing 85 per cent gypenosides. I don't know of any reports of side effects or other problems.

LICORICE (*GLYCYRRHIZA GLABRA*). I'm trying to grow licorice in quite a few places in my garden because it has many uses. I have plants in the plots for asthma, bacterial infection, bursitis, cancer, depression, fungal infection, heartburn, hepatitis, herpes, HIV, menopause, psoriasis, and ulcers, to name but a few.

How can one herb help so many conditions? Because it's an immune booster. Chinese herbalists agree. They consider licorice 'the great harmoniser', and they include it in the multiherb formulas that are used to treat an enormous number of health problems.

Modern research also agrees. Licorice tea helps treat many different kinds of viral infection by inhibiting a number of processes involved in viral replication. The herb also has some anti-tumour activity, probably

Dr Duke's Anti-Ageing **Elixir**

Chinese Immune Brew

Tastewise, this tea won't appeal to everyone. But it's loaded with antiviral, immune-stimulating ingredients.

WHAT YOU NEED

About 1 litre (2 pints) water
½ handful honeysuckle
½ handful forsythia
2 handfuls lemon balm
½ handful raspberry leaves
115 g (4 oz) blackberries
15 g (½ oz) wild cherry bark (optional)

WHAT TO DO

In a large saucepan, bring the water to the boil. Throw in the honeysuckle, forsythia, lemon balm, raspberry leaves, and blackberries. Add the wild cherry bark for extra flavour (if using). Remove from the heat and steep for 10 to 20 minutes, then strain. I drink up to three cups a day, refrigerating any left over for later use.

because of its immune-enhancing properties.

What's more, certain compounds in licorice called saponins help to make the phytochemicals in other herbs more available and usable for the body. This characteristic probably accounts for licorice's reputation as a harmoniser. It also helps explain why licorice shows up as an ingredient in so many Chinese herbal formulas.

When I want to use licorice, I prefer to steep a licorice stick in a cup of tea, as a sweetener. For a more standardised dosage, you may want to buy a commercial preparation and take it according to the label directions.

LIGUSTRUM (GLOSSY PRIVET, *LIGUSTRUM LUCIDUM*). Among the many immune-boosting compounds found in herbs is one called oleanolic acid. And ligustrum has the most, according to an authoritative report that analysed the oleanolic acid content of 215 herbs.

Traditional Chinese medicine practitioners recommend ligustrum for a number of health concerns, including backache, constipation, prematurely grey hair, tinnitus, and vertigo. It's also considered a tonic, in part because of its immune-enhancing powers.

In one study, 152 cancer patients were given either ligustrum extract or a placebo. Those who were taking the extract showed significantly better immune function. Compared with the placebo group, more people in the extract group experienced improvement. Ligustrum also seems to reduce the suppression of white blood cells that occurs during chemotherapy.

More Wisdom *from the* Garden

For an Extra Immune Boost, Try These Herbal Helpers

Since I'm discussing immune stimulants, I mustn't forget to mention two of my favourite herbs: turmeric and ginger. They're not heavy-hitting immune boosters, but both give the immune system a gentle tweak, thanks to the gingerol and curcumin they contain.

Experts familiar with ligustrum recommend taking 4 to 15 grams a day or 5 ml of tincture three times a day. If I wanted to use it, I'd first consult a practitioner of traditional Chinese medicine.

MUSHROOMS. Several species of mushroom – including shiitake (*Lentinus edodes*), reishi (*Ganoderma lucidum*), and maitake (*Grifola frondosa*) – are considered immune system stimulants. They contain compounds called polysaccharides that are similar to those found in other immune-boosting plants, such as astragalus and echinacea. These compounds increase the ability of white blood cells to devour germs.

Shiitake mushrooms also contain lentinan, a substance with known antitumour activity. Lentinan has been reported to increase the survival rate and length of life among women with various types of cancer. Japanese doctors often advise cancer patients to use lentinan in conjunction with chemotherapy.

In Asia, all three species of mushroom are traditional ingredients in soups and teas. Elsewhere, they're available in a growing number of health food shops and supermarkets. If you can find them, use them in cooking, just as you would other mushrooms. They are quite tasty. After reviewing the research, I'm tempted to start cooking with them myself.

Chinese doctors also freeze-dry the mushrooms and turn them into a powder, so they can be sold in capsule form. If you'd prefer the capsules, ask a Chinese medicine practitioner about them.

Dr Duke's Anti-Aging Elixir

Antiviral Vitali-Tea

I brew this tea when I feel a cold coming on or when I know there's a bug going around. It's loaded with proven antiviral immune-boosters.

WHAT YOU NEED

30 g (1 oz) echinacea flowers

15 g (½ oz) each of any or all of the following herbs: ashwagandha, astragalus, forsythia, garlic, ginger, honeysuckle, licorice, reishi, Siberian ginseng, and turmeric

1 litre (2 pints) water

WHAT TO DO

In a large saucepan, add the echinacea and your choice of the rest of the herbs to the freshly boiled water. Steep for 10 to 20 minutes. Strain. Drink up to three cups a day, refrigerating what is left for later use.

CHAPTER 15

Pain-Free Joints

Dr Duke's Anti-Ageing Elixirs

- *Joint Juice*
- *Gout Chaser*

Arthritis runs in my family. My two brothers and I have gout, which is one of the approximately 100 ailments that can cause joint pain. My mother had what I assume was osteoarthritis, complicated by a stroke. During the last decade of her life, her right arm got stiff and eventually locked permanently. The same thing happened to her left arm.

My mother passed away in 1995. At her graveside memorial service, my brother Edwin, who's 8 years older than I, could hardly get up from his folding chair. Besides gout, he has severe osteoarthritis in his knees. We had to help him stand.

I owe Edwin my thanks. His arthritic knees put the fear of God into me. Since my mother's funeral, I've been walking more often, riding my stationary bike more regularly, and doing 25 to 100 deep knee bends just about every day. (Because of a bout of arthritis brought on by Lyme disease, I've also been doing leg raises with light weights around my ankles, on the advice of my orthopaedist.) I fully believe that low-impact, full-range-of-motion exercise is both preventive and curative for osteoarthritis.

So far, I don't have any trouble sitting down and standing up. But I do have some early-morning stiffness, which tells me that osteoarthritis is softly knocking at my door.

The Many Faces of Arthritis

It is estimated that one person in every six has some form of chronic joint inflammation, or arthritis. That number is expected to increase in the coming decades.

Of the more than 100 ailments that can cause joint pain, the most common is osteoarthritis, also known as degenerative joint disease. It's the condition that most people mean when they say 'arthritis'.

Osteoarthritis affects millions of people, mostly women over the age of 45. Its main symptom is morning stiffness and pain in the affected joints, with diminishing discomfort as the day progresses. Other symptoms include stiffness that occurs after periods of rest and pain that worsens with strenuous use of the affected joints.

After osteoarthritis, the second most common source of joint pain is rheumatoid arthritis. It too affects millions of people, three-quarters of them women.

Rheumatoid arthritis causes pain, swelling, warmth, tenderness, and often purplish discoloration of the affected joints. Symptoms tend to come and go – flare-ups followed by periods of feeling all right. The pain is often severe, and the joints can become deformed. Within 10 years of diagnosis, half the people with rheumatoid arthritis develop some sort of disability.

Gout is also a form of arthritis. It causes inflammation and often intense pain in one or more joints, most commonly the big toe. For reasons that remain unclear, the vast majority (some 95 per cent) of those affected are men over the age of 30.

Some types of arthritis are brought on by infection – for example, gonorrhoea, staphylococcal infections, tuberculosis, and Lyme disease.

In my case, the culprit was Lyme disease, which is quite a problem in Maryland, where I live.

Lyme is spread by deer ticks. Where you have deer, you have deer ticks. We have so many deer in our area that they've become pests. They think my Garden of Youth is their breakfast, lunch, and dinner. I'm always struggling to keep them – and the ticks they carry – at bay. (Lyme disease is also carried by mice, which may be even harder to control.)

In chapter 28, I'll talk more about treatments for the various forms of arthritis. In this chapter, the focus is on prevention. To avoid contracting the infectious forms of arthritis, you have to prevent the infection. Avoiding the noninfectious types – osteoarthritis, rheumatoid arthritis, and gout – requires a different set of strategies.

Osteoarthritis: Nothing Natural about It

Most doctors say that we can't do much to protect ourselves against osteoarthritis. In fact, many believe that everyday wear and tear almost inevitably brings on the disease as we get older.

Well, I don't believe that osteoarthritis is a fact of life. And, apparently, the *Journal of the American Medical Association* is coming around to my point of view. A 1999 journal article put it this way: 'Osteoarthritis is not an inevitable part of the aging process. Obesity, joint injury, and genetics are all thought to contribute to the cartilage breakdown and other factors that lead to its development and progression.'

Here's how I'd go about keeping my joints safe from osteoarthritis.

Maintain a healthy weight. The more extra pounds you carry, the more stress you place on your major joints, particularly your hips, knees, and ankles. In one study, people who were overweight were twice as likely as people of normal weight to develop osteoarthritis. In another study, researchers at the Boston University School of Medicine identified 598 elderly people who did not have osteoarthritis of the knee, then tracked the group for 10 years. For every 4½ kilograms (10 pounds) the participants gained during that decade, their risk of osteoarthritis jumped 40 per cent.

Get plenty of moderate, low-impact exercise. The American

Council on Exercise suggests activities that not only get your heart rate up near the aerobic range but also move your major joints through their full range of motion. Consider brisk walking with your arms swinging, or swimming. Other good activities include gardening, yoga, tai chi, and dancing. They're less aerobic, but they give your joints a good workout.

Besides keeping your joints flexible, exercise helps you control your weight, which is important in preventing osteoarthritis. Just be sure that your workout is moderate and low-impact. High-impact activities that pound your joints actually increase your risk of osteoarthritis.

Fill up on fruits and vegetables. Throughout this book, I've been harping on about the importance of antioxidant nutrients – notably vitamin C, vitamin E, and the carotenoids (including beta-carotene). These nutrients help prevent the cell damage linked to many age-related conditions, including heart disease and cancer. Guess what? Antioxidants also help protect against osteoarthritis.

At Boston University, Timothy McAlindon, M.D., surveyed the eating habits of 640 older adults, then tracked the group's knee health over a 10-year period. Diet didn't seem to have any effect on whether or not people developed osteoarthritis. But those who had the highest intakes of vitamin C, vitamin E, and beta-carotene also had the mildest cases of the disease.

More Wisdom *from the* Garden

For Joint Health, Berries Can't Be Beat

Berries get their colour from anthocyanosides, pigments that are potent antioxidants. They also help stabilise cartilage, so they are great for preventing osteoarthritis.

To increase your intake of anthocyanosides, eat more deeply coloured berries – cherries, blueberries, elderberries, raspberries, blackberries, and bilberries. Or blend together any combination of these berries, then add ½ to 1 teaspoon each of ginger, turmeric, and oregano. Enjoy this juice with a couple of stalks of celery.

Vitamin C was the most beneficial, which is not surprising, since research shows that low levels of the nutrient accelerate cartilage loss in the joints. Foods rich in vitamin C include cabbage, broccoli, spinach, peppers, cauliflower, citrus fruits, and strawberries.

Make pineapple a fruit of choice. Pineapple is rich in bromelain, a compound that may prevent and alleviate inflammation. Naturopaths often prescribe bromelain supplements to treat osteoarthritis, but I prefer to get mine straight from the source.

If you want to protect your joints, be sure to eat lots of pineapple. And if you can get papaya without spending too much, try that, too. Papaya contains papain and chymopapain, two enzymes that are similar to bromelain. I eat lots of papaya when I'm in Peru.

Be cautious about foods in the nightshade family. Many years ago, Rutgers University horticulturist Norman Childers claimed that he had cured his own osteoarthritis by eliminating dairy foods as well as plant foods in the nightshade family – tomatoes, potatoes, aubergine, peppers, and chilli peppers. His theory was that some people are genetically prone to joint pain when they consume the solanum alkaloids found in nightshades.

The Arthritis Foundation and most doctors in the United States give Childers' approach absolutely no credence. Personally, I think there may be something to it. In my years of lecturing, many people have told me that they experienced relief from joint pain after avoiding dairy products and nightshades for at least 6 months.

The Childers diet doesn't work for everyone, but I'm persuaded that it works for some. You may want to try it as a preventive measure.

Extra Protection for Your Joints

Making a few changes in your eating habits and lifestyle can help keep your joints mobile and pain-free. So can taking certain nutritional supplements and herbs. Here's a handful that may do your joints some good.

ANTIOXIDANTS. I always prefer getting my nutrients by eating a wide variety of foods, especially fruits, vegetables, pulses and grains. But a multivitamin/mineral supplement is a good idea for general health. And if you have osteoarthritis in your family, antioxidant supplements may provide extra protection for your joints.

I can't cite any specific research on this. But a few studies have found that antioxidant supplements help treat osteoarthritis, so it seems reasonable to think that they help prevent the condition, too. Alan Gaby, M.D., professor at Bastyr University, the naturopathic medical school near Seattle, suggests a daily antioxidant regime consisting of 1,000 to 2,000 milligrams of vitamin C, 400 to 800 IU of vitamin E, and 100 to 200 micrograms of the mineral selenium.

VITAMIN D. Dr McAlindon conducted another study in which he linked low levels of vitamin D to the development of osteoarthritis. Vitamin D helps keep the cartilage in joints from breaking down. Foods rich in the nutrient include D-fortified dairy products and fatty saltwater fish such as salmon, halibut, sea bass, tuna, cod, and herring.

Your skin can manufacture its own vitamin D when exposed to the sun. So remember these words to live by: exercise outdoors on a sunny day, and you might keep arthritis at bay. Just be careful not to overdo it. In order for your skin to manufacture vitamin D, you can't wear sunscreen. But too much sun can cause unprotected skin to age prematurely. I suggest going outside in the morning or late afternoon. During the midday hours in summer and in a hot climate, limit your sun exposure to 20 minutes.

GLUCOSAMINE. For treating osteoarthritis, glucosamine is the supplement of choice these days. In several studies, about half of those who tried it reported benefits from it. The nutrient works by helping to repair damaged cartilage.

But why wait until you have morning stiffness to start repairing your cartilage? If you have osteoarthritis in your family, or if you're noticing the first signs of symptoms, there's no harm in taking glucosamine. Personally, I've never heard of the supplements causing harm, though some of the scientific literature mentions possible side effects such as stomach upset, heartburn, and diarrhoea. Follow the recommended dosage on the package. Glucosamine is available in health food shops and many pharmacies.

Some people combine glucosamine with chondroitin, another safe supplement, which helps draw fluid into cartilage. It's the fluid that gives cartilage its shock-absorbing ability. You may want to try chondroitin as well. Follow the recommended dosage on the package.

GINGER (*ZINGIBER OFFICINALE*). Ginger is an age-old treatment for inflammation, particularly in Ayurvedic medicine. No wonder: the herb contains 24 distinct anti-inflammatory compounds. One study that I've reviewed shows that large doses of ginger (of the order of 4,000 milligrams a day) help treat both osteoarthritis and rheumatoid arthritis, with no side effects. I see no reason why the herb wouldn't help prevent these conditions as well.

Personally, I love ginger. I drink ginger tea often, and I use the herb in cooking. I don't know that I'd go as high as 4,000 milligrams a day for preventive purposes. I might take 1,000 to 2,000 milligrams a day, in capsule form. And of course, I'd continue drinking a few cups of ginger tea a day, and I'd add even more of the herb to my cooking.

TURMERIC (CURCUMA LONGA). A relative of ginger, turmeric is a traditional ingredient in the curry dishes of Indian cuisine. The yellow pigment in

More Wisdom *from the* Garden

Nature Has Its Own COX-2s

You may have seen the advertisements for the prescription drugs celecoxib (Celebrex) and rofecoxib (Vioxx). They're the latest pharmaceutical innovation in arthritis treatment, a class of drugs called COX-2 inhibitors.

Like aspirin and other nonsteroidal anti-inflammatory drugs (NSAIDs), COX-2 inhibitors relieve pain. But they're said to lack the distressing side effects of NSAIDs: stomach upset, gastrointestinal pain and bleeding, and destruction of the digestive tract, which is sometimes fatal.

You wouldn't want to take COX-2 inhibitors preventively – they're too expensive for that. Interestingly, both ginger and turmeric contain compounds that are natural COX-2s. And these herbs are easily affordable. They deliver the latest pharmaceutical revolution in a safer, gentler package.

turmeric, curcumin, has potent anti-inflammatory and pain-relieving properties. In some studies, curcumin has been shown to be as effective an anti-inflammatory as ibuprofen and cortisone. It works like the COX-2 inhibitors celecoxib (Celebrex) and rofecoxib (Vioxx), but unlike the pharmaceuticals, it has minimal side effects.

Curcumin is available in some health food stores. Naturopaths recommend taking 400 milligrams three times a day as a treatment for osteoarthritis. I'd suggest using no more than that as a preventive.

Note If you want to make the most of the curcumin in turmeric, use the spice in combination with black pepper. Curcumin is not all that well-absorbed by the intestines. But a compound in black pepper, piperine, more than doubles curcumin levels in the bloodstream.

Dr Duke's Anti-Ageing Elixir

Joint Juice

This juice is bursting with ingredients that can help keep your joints flexible and pain-free.

WHAT YOU NEED

480 ml (16 fl oz) pineapple juice
120 ml (4 fl oz) grapefruit juice
120 ml (4 fl oz) celery juice
1–2 teaspoons turmeric
1–2 teaspoons grated fresh ginger
1–2 cardamom pods
Ground black and/or cayenne pepper
Licorice stick (optional)

WHAT TO DO

In a blender, mix the pineapple juice and grapefruit juice. Add the celery juice. Blend in the turmeric, ginger, and cardamom. Add the pepper to taste. Stir with a licorice stick (if using).

Rheumatoid Arthritis: An Immune System Gone Haywire

Doctors consider rheumatoid arthritis an autoimmune disease. For reasons that remain unclear, if you have rheumatoid arthritis, your own immune system attacks your joints, causing them to become inflamed, red, and swollen. In many cases, they also become deformed and crippled.

This disease is the most crippling form of arthritis. As I mentioned earlier, half of those who are diagnosed with the disease develop some sort of disability within 10 years.

Many people think that rheumatoid arthritis can't be prevented, that it's the product of family history or just plain bad luck. Not true. Here's what I suggest to safeguard your joints against the disease.

Stick with a plant-based Palaeolithic diet. You just don't see much rheumatoid arthritis in cultures whose traditional diets are rich in fruits, vegetables, pulses and grains and low in meat, dairy products, sugar, and junk foods. How could the typical Western meat-based diet trigger this disease? That's not clear. But some studies have suggested that people with rheumatoid arthritis are deficient in certain nutrients. Such deficiencies are much more likely with a diet of meat and junk food than with one of fruits, vegetables, and other plant foods.

A typical Western diet might also contribute to rheumatoid arthritis by causing leaky gut syndrome. When your small intestine is healthy, it allows only the nutrients that your body needs to pass into your bloodstream. But if your small intestine gets damaged by infections, food sensitivities, or drugs (including the nonsteroidal anti-inflammatory drugs often used to treat rheumatoid arthritis), it starts leaking. This allows potentially harmful substances to pass into your bloodstream – things like incompletely digested fats, proteins, and carbohydrates, plus other substances that ought to be eliminated as solid waste. When they get into your bloodstream, they can trigger joint inflammation.

One way to fix a leaky gut is to eliminate foods that are not part of the Palaeolithic diet. Finnish researchers had 20 people with rheumatoid arthritis do this, instructing them to follow a vegan diet (no meat, fish, poultry, or dairy products). Another 20 people, also with the disease, maintained their usual eating habits. Three months later, those on the vegan diet reported less pain, fewer swollen joints, and generally better health. After the study, some of the people on the vegan diet returned to their old eating habits. Guess what? Their symptoms worsened.

My Healthy Sevens eating plan isn't vegan, but it does follow the basic principles of the Palaeolithic diet. To learn more about it, see chapter 3.

Serve up some fish on occasion. In one study comparing the diets of women with and without rheumatoid arthritis, those who ate the most fish were least likely to develop the disease. This makes sense because fish, especially cold-water species such as salmon, contain oils rich in omega-3 fatty acids – and omega-3s have anti-inflammatory properties.

Even though fish isn't a plant food, it was a staple among our Palaeolithic ancestors. Eating a few servings a week seems like a good idea.

Indulge in lots of pineapple, too. Research has shown that the bromelain in pineapple can help treat rheumatoid arthritis. I don't see why it wouldn't help prevent the disease, too. Since I'm quite fond of the fruit, I'd simply eat more of it.

Supplemental Insurance against Pain

As with osteoarthritis, certain nutritional supplements and herbs may help protect your joints against rheumatoid arthritis. You might want to add some of the following to your preventive programme.

FISH OIL. If you're not especially fond of fish, you can get your omega-3 fatty acids from supplements. Andrew Weil, M.D., an alternative-medicine advocate who thinks along many of the same lines as I do, has this to say about them: 'In more than a dozen studies over the past decade, rheumatoid arthritis sufferers who took omega-3 capsules [experienced] fewer tender, swollen joints and less morning stiffness than those who didn't take them and were able to taper their use of anti-inflammatory medication.'

In one study, 66 people with rheumatoid arthritis took supplements of either corn oil or fish oil (9 grams a day) for 30 weeks. By the end of the study, only those taking the fish oil had less pain and stiffness and fewer tender, swollen joints.

Most experts suggest taking 4 to 6 grams of fish oil a day, plus one standardised capsule of borage, currant, or evening primrose oil a day, each capsule containing 70 to 240 milligrams of gamma-linolenic acid, or GLA. (Like the omega-3s, GLA is considered an essential fatty acid.) I grow all three plants – borage, currant, and evening primrose – in my Garden of Youth.

OTHER SUPPLEMENTS. Because nutritional deficiencies may play a role in rheumatoid arthritis, it doesn't hurt to take a little extra of certain vitamins and minerals. Dr Gaby offers this preventive supplement regime: 2,000 milligrams of vitamin C, 400 to 800 IU of vitamin E, 100 to 200 micrograms of selenium, 30 milligrams of zinc, and 3 milligrams of copper.

GINGER AND TURMERIC. As I mentioned earlier, ginger appears to help treat rheumatoid arthritis. So does turmeric. I see no reason why they wouldn't work as preventives, too. They're at least worth trying. I'd suggest taking 2,000 milligrams of ginger and 500 to 1,000 milligrams of turmeric a day, in capsule form. And I'd use both spices liberally in cooking.

Gout: You Can Avoid the Agony

My first experience with gout came when I was just shy of 50. I woke up one morning with the classic pain in my big toe. It hurt so much that, just like the medical books say, even the weight of a sheet was unbearable. I could hardly walk.

Gout is caused by a buildup of uric acid, a by-product of DNA metabolism. The kidneys are supposed to filter uric acid out of the blood and flush it out of the body. But in people with gout, uric acid crystals form and deposit in the joints, irritating them.

My doctor put me on colchicine, a drug that flushes the crystals from the affected joints. For me, the good news was that colchicine is derived from a herb (autumn crocus, or *Colchicum autumnale*). The bad news was that although colchicine is effective, it causes severe diarrhoea.

I had several gout attacks over the next few years. I took the colchicine, and I learned to put up with the diarrhoea that it caused.

Then my doctor urged me to take the gout-preventive drug allopurinol, one pill a day for the rest of my life. He was worried about the uric acid crystals damaging my internal organs. I was worried, too, so I took the drug for a while.

Then I came across a study suggesting that celery seed extract can lower uric acid levels. I stopped taking allopurinol and switched to four 800-milligram tablets of celery seed extract a day. It made me a believer. Whether celery seed or serendipity, I've not had one gout attack in the past 5 years. I'm now taking just two tablets a day.

Celery seed contains more than two dozen anti-inflammatory compounds. I suspect that they're the reason I haven't had any gout attacks lately.

Besides taking celery seed extract, the following strategies may help you avoid a painful encounter with gout.

Reduce your protein intake. High-protein foods such as meats, dairy products, poultry, fish, and seafood can raise your blood levels of chemicals called purines. In turn, purines elevate your uric acid levels and increase your risk of a gout attack.

Be prudent about alcohol consumption. Gout attacks often follow an evening of drinking. That's because alcohol increases uric acid production. For many people who have gout, giving up drinking ends their attacks.

Drink plenty of nonalcoholic fluids. Water, juices, teas, and other nonalcoholic fluids dilute urine and promote the excretion of uric acid.

Eat berries by the bushel. Berries contain anthocyanosides, antioxidants that have an anti-inflammatory effect. They may also help reduce uric acid levels, according to some research. Cherries and strawberries are popular folk remedies for gout.

Go easy on vitamin C and niacin. Large doses of vitamin C and niacin can raise uric acid levels. The typical multivitamin/mineral supplement doesn't contain enough of either nutrient to trigger a gout attack. But don't take more than 2,000 milligrams of vitamin C a day, and limit niacin supplementation to 35 milligrams a day.

Dr Duke's Anti-Ageing Elixir

Gout Chaser

This recipe can help you avoid a painful encounter with gout.

WHAT YOU NEED

240 ml (8 fl oz) cherry juice (the darker the better)

120 ml (4 fl oz) strawberry juice

60 ml (2 fl oz) cranberry juice

1–2 teaspoons turmeric

1–2 teaspoons grated fresh ginger

Dash of cinnamon

WHAT TO DO

Mix the cherry juice, strawberry juice, and cranberry juice. Spice up the blend with the turmeric and ginger. Add the cinnamon for flavour.

CHAPTER 16

Reliable Kidneys

Dr Duke's Anti-Ageing Elixirs

* *UTI Eradicator*
* *Stone-Stopping Sipper*

In terms of your urinary tract, your kidneys are where the action begins. They filter waste products from your blood and turn them into urine. From there, the urine travels down two narrow tubes, called ureters, and into your bladder, where it's stored. Once your bladder fills up and you get the urge to go, the urine leaves your body via the urethra.

It certainly seems like a simple enough process. But things can go wrong in your urinary tract, especially as you get older.

In this chapter, I'll focus on urinary tract infections, kidney stones, and kidney failure. I'll cover incontinence a bit later, in chapter 41.

Urinary Tract Infections: When the Going Gets Tough

You'll sometimes hear urinary tract infections (UTIs) referred to as bladder infections or cystitis. The name doesn't matter so much as the

More Wisdom *from the* Garden

Asparagus Supports Urinary Health

There's no question in my mind that asparagus has a direct effect on the urinary tract, because of the way it makes urine smell. When I eat asparagus, the odour shows up within 20 minutes. (This happens in most people, but not everyone, because of genetic variation.)

The research is scant, but asparagus has a traditional reputation as a 'farmaceutical' that helps keep the urinary tract healthy. Even Commission E, the expert panel that evaluates the safety and effectiveness of herbal medicines for the German government, endorses asparagus for the prevention and treatment of urinary tract infections and kidney stones.

I tend to agree with Commission E, because I've been so impressed by my own experience with asparagus. I think the asparagine and sterols in the plant must have some health benefit.

pain these infections cause. (Though don't confuse cystitis with cholecystitis, an inflammation of the gallbladder.)

The trouble begins when *Escherichia coli* or other bacteria that normally inhabit your anal area get into the urethra and wind up infecting your bladder. You feel a persistent urge to go to the bathroom, but when you try to relieve yourself, you are able to pass very little urine. Instead, you experience intense pain and burning, and you may notice blood in your urine.

One easy way to reduce your risk of a UTI is to change your bathroom habits. If you normally wipe from back to front, switch directions and go from front to back. This prevents bacteria in your anal area from making their way into your urethra.

Vaginal intercourse can also transport bacteria from your anal area to your urethra. To prevent this from happening, wash your anal area before intercourse, and try to urinate soon afterward. This helps flush out any germs that may have sneaked in where they don't belong.

If you're a postmenopausal woman, you may be more susceptible to UTIs. The decline in oestrogen production that occurs at menopause thins your vaginal wall and reduces natural vaginal lubrication. These changes can cause urethral irritation, especially during intercourse, and set you up for infection.

In this case, you may benefit from using a commercial vaginal lubricant. Your doctor may also recommend hormone-replacement therapy (HRT) to boost low oestrogen levels. Whether or not you should use HRT is a complicated and very personal decision. It may reduce your risk of UTIs. And it may help protect against heart disease, osteoporosis, and Alzheimer's disease. But it also increases your risk of breast cancer. You need to carefully weigh these and other benefits and risks, in consultation with your doctor.

If you and your doctor opt for HRT, I'd suggest that you consider natural phyto-oestrogens (plant oestrogens) from pulses and natural pre-oestrogen (diosgenin) from wild yams. One of the most commonly prescribed HRT drugs, Premarin, is made from the urine of pregnant mares.

Dr Duke's Anti-Ageing Elixir

UTI Eradicator

If a female family member or friend came to me in search of protection from urinary tract infections, I'd pass along this recipe.

WHAT YOU NEED

1–2 teaspoons of one of the following herbs: bilberries, blueberries, cranberries, lovage, or wintergreen

About ½ litre (1 pint) water

WHAT TO DO

In a small saucepan, add the herb of your choice to the freshly boiled water. Steep it for 10 minutes, then strain. Drink up to four cups a day.

Cranberries Aren't the Only Cure

Of course, the classic herbal approach to preventing UTIs is to drink cranberry juice. You probably won't be surprised to find out that I recommend it. Scientists used to think that cranberry juice acidified the urine, which killed the bacteria. As it turns out, cranberries work by preventing bacteria from latching onto your bladder, keeping the germs from lingering and initiating infection.

Whatever the reason, the research

shows benefit. And when you consider that cranberries are rich in anthocyanosides, which are potent antioxidants, the fruits may help more than just your urinary tract.

Cranberries certainly get the lion's share of credit for preventing UTIs. Personally, I believe that other anthocyanoside-rich fruits probably have similar benefits. Among these fruits are blueberries, raspberries, blackberries, cherries, huckleberries, whortleberries and bilberries. Enjoy all of them frequently to reduce your risk of a UTI.

If preventive approaches fail you and you get a UTI anyway, I'd start treatment by drinking lots and lots of water as well as cranberry juice or blueberry juice (which you can find in canned blueberries). I'd take the natural antibiotics garlic (up to five cloves a day) and goldenseal (in a commercial product, according to package directions). And I'd round out my herbal regime with the immune system booster echinacea (1 teaspoon of tincture in cranberry juice three or four times a day or a standardised capsule according to package directions).

If this regime doesn't work within a day or two, then and only then would I recommend starting a course of antibiotics (for which you'll need a prescription from your doctor). But I'd still advise drinking cranberry juice and taking echinacea until your symptoms have cleared. Antibiotics have their place, but I worry about increasing bacterial resistance to them, which stems from their being overprescribed. I view antibiotics as a last resort. That way, they work when you really need them.

Kidney Stones: Foods Can Stop Them from Forming

Kidney stones develop when urine has a too high concentration of urea. A waste product of protein metabolism, urea gets extracted from the blood by your kidneys. Then it's combined with water to form urine.

If there's too much urea in your urine, it causes certain other compounds, usually calcium oxalate, to form stones. If the stones get large enough, they cause excruciating pain until they pass.

Usually, the pain begins at waist level in your back, towards one side or the other, right where your kidneys sit. As the stone slowly inches its way out of your kidney and down your ureter, the pain moves from your back to your front and eventually into your groin. The pain ends when the stone finally works its way out of your ureter and into your bladder.

This entire process can take anywhere from a few minutes to 48 hours. Then as the stone finally passes from your body, you may feel some pain or burning upon urination.

Kidney stones tend to run in families. They're also more common in men than in women. But they're certainly not inevitable. These measures can help reduce your risk.

Drink more than enough fluids. Water and juices dilute your urine, discouraging kidney stones from forming. When Harvard researchers tracked beverage consumption and kidney stone risk among 81,000 female nurses for 8 years, they found that as the women's fluid intake went up, their chances of developing stones went down. Even if you get a stone, you should drink more fluids to help flush it out.

Steer clear of apple and grapefruit juice. In another Harvard study involving 45,000 male health professionals, both apple juice and grapefruit juice appeared to increase kidney stone risk. If you've already had a stone, I'd advise avoiding these beverages, as much as I love them.

Garnish your beverage with a slice of lemon. Lemon juice contains citric acid, which helps prevent the formation of calcium oxalate crystals in urine. Other good sources of citric acid include lime, pomegranate, tangerine, strawberry, purslane, potatoes, soya, and roselle, a major ingredient in Red Zinger herbal tea.

Citric acid also helps treat kidney stones. In a study at the University of California, San Francisco, researchers worked with kidney stone patients who could not tolerate conventional pharmaceuticals. The study participants were instructed to supplement their diets with 120 ml (4 fl oz) of reconstituted lemon juice a day. The treatment worked very well.

Adopt a plant-based Palaeolithic diet. Because urea is a waste product of protein metabolism, a high-protein diet featuring lots of meat and dairy products can contribute to kidney stone formation. On the other hand, a near-vegetarian, high-fibre diet – one featuring lots of fruits, vegetables, grains, and pulses – can help prevent stones.

Fibre really helps. In one study, consuming 20 grams of rice bran a day not only reduced urinary calcium but also cut the incidence of kidney stones by more than 78 per cent.

My Healthy Sevens eating plan incorporates many key principles of the Palaeolithic diet. For more details about the plan, see chapter 3.

Avoid foods that contain oxalates. Most kidney stones are composed of calcium oxalate. Many foods contain oxalates, but only a handful have been shown to raise urinary oxalate levels enough to form stones. The troublemakers include spinach, chard, rhubarb, nuts, chocolate, wheat bran, grapefruit, and strawberries. All of these are marvellous foods, but if you're prone to kidney stones, I'd suggest not eating them.

To this list, I'd add lamb's-quarter and purslane. Both of these herbs have high oxalate contents.

Dr Duke's Anti-Ageing Elixir

Stone-Stopping Sipper

If you don't have any of the herbs mentioned below, you can substitute horsetail, stinging nettle, and parsley. These also have a reputation for preventing kidney stone formation.

WHAT YOU NEED

1 teaspoon dandelion

1 teaspoon quackgrass root

1 teaspoon stoneroot

About ½ litre (1 pint) water

WHAT TO DO

In a small saucepan, add the dandelion, quackgrass, and stoneroot to the freshly boiled water. (For this tea, I prefer water in which I've cooked corn on the cob. But plain water is okay if corn is out of season.) Steep for 10 minutes, then strain. Drink up to three cups of the tea a day, refrigerating any left over for later use.

Eat more magnesium-rich foods. Magnesium slows the formation of calcium oxalate crystals in urine. Good sources of the mineral include green beans, poppy seeds, licorice, lettuce, and stinging nettle.

Take a vitamin B_6 supplement. Some studies show that vitamin B_6 helps keep kidney stones from recurring. I'd suggest taking it daily as a preventive. Follow the directions on the package.

Try the anti-stone herbs. In my Garden of Youth, I grow the following herbs, all of which help prevent and treat stones: corn silk, dandelion, quackgrass, and stoneroot.

Kidney Failure: The Problem Is Too Much Protein

In kidney failure, your kidneys become so severely fatigued that they have trouble filtering urea from your blood. It's a serious health problem, especially among people with diabetes. It's the reason why so many folks need dialysis and transplants.

The ageing process also takes a toll on your kidneys. If you're like me, you'll want to do what you can to keep these organs functioning properly. Here's what I suggest.

Adopt kidney-friendly eating habits. One way to protect your kidneys is to reduce your protein consumption and switch to a near-vegetarian Palaeolithic diet. As I mentioned earlier, your kidneys are responsible for removing protein's metabolic waste products from the blood. So if you eat a lot of protein, you make your kidneys work overtime.

Maintain a healthy blood pressure. You probably already know that high blood pressure damages your circulatory system. But you may not be aware that it also wreaks havoc on your kidneys.

You can help keep your blood pressure in check by adopting the near-vegetarian Palaeolithic diet that I've been talking about. While high-fat, high-protein meats and whole-milk dairy products raise blood pressure, low-fat, high-fibre plant foods can knock some points off your reading.

I'd also recommend eating more garlic and engaging in regular moderate exercise, both of which help control blood pressure. (For more advice on managing your blood pressure, see chapter 37.)

CHAPTER 17

Efficient Liver

Dr Duke's Anti-Ageing Elixirs

- *Savoury Liver-Saving Stew*
- *Beer Beans*
- *Love-Your-Liver Tonic*

Among the herbal liver protectors, milk thistle (*Silybum marianum*) reins supreme. Out in my Garden of Youth, this marvellous plant looks ferocious. Being a thistle, it's barbed, spiked, bristly, and very tough to harvest – even when I'm wearing long sleeves, and thick gloves.

All of my most recent crop of milk thistles flowered early last summer and died by late July, as biennials do at the end of their second season of growth. Fortunately, some of their seeds eluded the goldfinches and germinated, so I have a new crop coming in.

When my milk thistles died, I suspect they all went to heaven. After all, the herb is mentioned many times in the Bible. It also grows in many areas of my Garden of Youth. It's in the Ageing plot, because it bestows its detoxification and antioxidant benefits on the liver. It's in the Alcoholism plot, as it's the herb most likely to prevent or control the

for the
Gardener

Milk Thistle

Silybum marianum

A relative of the artichoke, milk thistle is a wonderful medicinal herb. But left untended, it can easily become a weed. Both the leaves and flowers have nasty spines, which can turn walking barefoot into an obstacle course.

Milk thistle can be an annual or a biennial, depending on where it's grown. Some seeds germinate in the fall, while others wait until spring. If you dig up the seedlings in spring, being careful not to cut the taproot, you can transplant them where you want them.

When harvesting the seeds, be sure to wear thick gloves to protect yourself from the spines. Reach into the centre of the flower, grab the peaks of the central florets with your thumb and index finger, and dig out the seeds. I harvest the seeds as early as July and continue munching on them until September. Whether green or fully ripened, they contain compounds that are good for the liver.

liver damage caused by alcohol and other drugs. And it's in the Ulcer plot, though it plays only a minor role in ulcer treatment and prevention.

But milk thistle is the star of my Liver plot. In fact, I think it's one of the most important herbs in my garden.

Milk Thistle's Many Benefits

Milk thistle grows throughout the temperate world, especially in Mediterranean climes, where it often becomes a weed. Traditional herbalists used it to treat liver problems, which led researchers to study it as a possible liver medicine. In 1968, German researchers isolated three liver-protective compounds from milk thistle seeds: silibinin, silidianin, and silicristin. Collectively, they're known as silymarin.

The tea made from steeping a few teaspoons of milk thistle seed in freshly boiled water doesn't contain enough silymarin to do the liver much good. So German botanists bred a high-silymarin variety of the herb and used it to produce a standardised extract. A 200-milligram dose of this extract contains 140 milligrams of silymarin. This dose, taken three or four times a day, is what's used in many studies of milk thistle. Even though I grow the herb, I use the standardised extract for medicinal purposes.

Milk thistle helps your liver in several ways. It binds tightly to the same receptors on liver cell membranes that allow toxins in, thus locking the toxins out. It's a powerful antioxidant, helping to protect liver cells

Dr Duke's Anti-Ageing Elixir

Savoury Liver-Saving Stew

Botanically speaking, artichokes are related to milk thistle. They have similar benefits, especially for the liver. So if you want to keep your liver healthy, I suggest eating more artichokes. Make them into a soup, if you like.

The following recipe may seem odd if you're just used to supermarket ingredients. But if you're a forager like I am, it's more inviting. I can't guarantee that you'll find it tasty, but I do.

WHAT YOU NEED

Bases cut from one or two globe artichokes
115 g (4 oz) Jerusalem artichokes
115 g (4 oz) burdock leaf stalks
115–230 g (4–8 oz) tender new shoots from chicory, dandelion, endive, and/or milk thistle
Turmeric
Hot-pepper sauce
Garlic powder
Onion powder
Salt
Ground black pepper
Milk thistle seed
Curry powder

WHAT TO DO

Bring a pan of water to the boil. Add the globe artichoke, Jerusalem artichoke, burdock, and the chicory, dandelion, endive, and/or milk thistle. Season generously with the turmeric, hot-pepper sauce, garlic powder, onion powder, salt, and black pepper. Simmer until the vegetables are tender. Garnish with milk thistle seed that's been rolled in curry powder.

growing younger naturally

She Beat Hepatitis with Milk Thistle

Back in 1998, I received the following e-mail from Lorrae Turner, who had arranged and accompanied my recent Pharmacy Ecotour to Kenya and Tanzania. Her words boosted my confidence in milk thistle as a potent liver tonic.

'Having heard you talk about milk thistle, I bought some tablets a few months ago. By a strange coincidence, my sister-in-law, Jayne, had been diagnosed with hepatitis A. Her skin and eyes were as yellow as a sunflower. A test showed that her liver was functioning at just 40 percent of its normal capacity.

'Jayne received an injection of vitamin K, then started taking my milk thistle tablets. Three weeks later, a second test showed that her liver function had improved to 82 percent.

'Her doctor couldn't believe it. He said that level of recovery usually takes months. And he had never heard of milk thistle treatment.'

from damage and supporting the repair of injured cells. It also normalises exceptionally high levels of liver enzymes.

As for silymarin, several European studies show that it speeds recovery from hepatitis. Other studies show that it helps treat cirrhosis. In one trial, 170 people – 91 with alcoholic cirrhosis – were given either a placebo (a fake pill) or 200 milligrams of milk thistle extract three times a day. Four years later, 42 per cent fewer deaths had occurred in the group taking milk thistle compared with the group taking the placebo.

Silymarin is also an effective remedy for poisoning from Amanita ('death cap') mushrooms. It works by blocking the poison's entry into liver cells. Without treatment, Amanita poisoning has a death rate of more than 50 per cent. Standard medical treatment (activated charcoal) saves many lives, but not all. Silymarin may provide the best chance of recovery. I might try both.

In one study, 60 people were given silymarin for Amanita poisoning.

None died. In another study, 189 people received standard medical care for Amanita poisoning, while another 16 were given silymarin. Among those receiving standard care, 46 died. Among those taking silymarin, none died.

Another benefit of milk thistle is that it combats liver damage caused by pharmaceuticals. Alcohol is not the only drug that can harm your liver. In large enough doses, even everyday medications such as paracetamol can cause trouble, especially if taken with alcohol.

In one laboratory study using animals, silymarin prevented liver damage from large doses of paracetamol. In other studies, silymarin has protected the liver from the effects of antibiotics, antidepressants, and antipsychotic drugs.

Milk thistle is remarkably safe. It causes no side effects in most people who use it, though a few have reported mild stomach upset or allergic reactions. If you've already been diagnosed with some sort of liver disease, you should talk with your doctor before adding milk thistle to your treatment regime.

More Herbal Allies for Your Liver

As you can tell, I'm a big fan of milk thistle. But it's not the only herb that can keep your liver functioning efficiently. Here are some others.

KUDZU (*PUERARIA MONTANA*). This weed of Asian origin has taken over my home state of Alabama and moved as far north as New York. In the Deep South, people hate kudzu, and I don't really blame them. But the vine is more than a weedy pest. Its seeds are a traditional Chinese remedy for drunkenness and alcoholism. As a bonus, they're a great source of daidzein and genistein, both of which are phyto-oestrogens (plant oestrogens).

Animal studies show that some compounds like daidzein have an effect similar to the drug disulfiram (Antabuse). They make alcohol so distasteful that people drink less and suffer less liver damage.

Kudzu also contains saponins, compounds that help protect the liver.

You can buy extracts of the herb in some health food shops. I suggest following the dosage recommendations on the label.

Dr Duke's Anti-Ageing Elixir

Beer Beans

Because so many people develop liver damage from excessive alcohol consumption, I've come up with a concoction that I call Beer Beans. (Actually, I used to call it Herbal Beer Nuts, but I got nervous about litigation from the Beer Nuts people.) It's easy to make.

WHAT YOU NEED

2 parts raw milk thistle seeds
2 parts lightly roasted kudzu vine seeds
2 parts lightly roasted broad beans
1 part soya beans
Dash of well-roasted ginkgo seeds

WHAT TO DO

Just combine the milk thistle, kudzu, and broad beans with the soyabeans. Season with the ginkgo.

BROAD BEANS (*VICIA FABA*) AND SOYA BEANS (*GLYCINE MAX*). Both varieties of beans are rich in daidzein. Broad beans also contain the anti-addictive compound L-dopa, which is converted to dopamine in your brain. Cerebral dopamine may help alleviate cravings for alcohol, nicotine, and other liver-damaging drugs.

I'd think that 115 g (4 oz) of broad beans or soya beans a day would help.

GINKGO (*GINKGO BILOBA*). This herb has long been used in the Orient to temper the effects of alcohol. The Japanese serve roasted ginkgo seeds at cocktail parties because the seeds are reputed to prevent drunkenness and hangover. Scientific studies from Japan support this use. The seeds contain an enzyme that speeds up the metabolism of alcohol.

You can buy a standardised ginkgo extract and follow the label directions for proper dosage.

CARROT (*DAUCUS CAROTA*). I've seen studies from India suggesting that carrots offer significant protection to the liver. Apparently, all their carotenoids increase the activity of liver enzymes that detoxify alcohol, drugs, and other causes of liver damage.

I'd recommend eating one or two carrot sticks a day. Enjoy them as they are or blend them into a juice.

DANDELION (*TARAXACUM OFFICINALE*). In folk medicine, dandelion is a highly esteemed liver herb. It has been used for centuries to treat jaundice, a liver ailment that turns the skin yellow. The plant's leaves and flowers contain lecithin, a compound that helps keep your liver healthy.

Like kudzu, dandelion is a hated weed. But I love it. I steam the leaves and eat them like spinach. They're bitter but tasty. And I nibble on the seeds, again, competing with the goldfinches. I even clean the root and stick it in a jar of pickle juice, after I've polished off all the pickles. In a few months, I have pickled dandelion root. Not bad.

INDIAN ALMOND (*TERMINALIA CATAPPA*). In animal studies, extracts of Indian almond have prevented chemically induced liver damage. While it isn't the easiest herb to obtain, it does grow wild along the coasts of Florida and Hawaii.

I don't know of a therapeutic dose for Indian almond. I just eat the nuts as a food.

SCHISANDRA (*SCHISANDRA CHINENSIS*). I've discussed schisandra before as a general tonic. One reason it works is that it helps protect your liver. The seeds alone contain more than 30 antioxidant and liver-protective compounds.

In studies that I've reviewed, laboratory animals were given lethal doses of various poisons that attack the liver. Some were also given schisandra. Many of them lived, while all the animals that didn't get the herb died.

You can find dried schisandra berries in some health food shops. In China, people take 1 to 7 teaspoons of the berries a day to treat hepatitis.

TAMARIND (*TAMARINDUS INDICA*). In Latin America, tamarind juice has a reputation for preventing hangover, so it's often used as a mixer with alcohol. I've tested it on occasion, and I think it helps. My

Dr Duke's Anti-Ageing Elixir

Love-Your-Liver Tonic

Here's a recipe featuring carrots, potent liver protectors in their own right.

WHAT YOU NEED

Carrots, peeled
Yellow curry powder
Dash of grapefruit or lemon juice
Dash of ground black pepper
Dash of cayenne pepper

WHAT TO DO

Throw the carrots into a blender or juicer. Add the curry powder (rich in liver-friendly turmeric) to taste. Add the grapefruit or lemon juice to make the turmeric more soluble, and the black pepper and cayenne pepper to make the turmeric more absorbable. Blend to a drinkable consistency.

opinion was strengthened by a study showing that tamarind juice helps protect the livers of animals given liver-damaging chemicals. I enjoy two glasses of the juice a day, when I can find it in Latin American markets.

LICORICE (*GLYCYRRHIZA GLABRA*). Two of the main active compounds in licorice, glycyrrhizin and glycyrrhetinic acid, help protect liver cells from damage. Animal studies from Russia show that the herb helps prevent and treat liver problems. And in Japan, doctors use licorice to treat cirrhosis and hepatitis.

Naturopaths also favour licorice as a treatment for hepatitis, based on research demonstrating the herb's effectiveness and safety. I'd use licorice if I were worried about my liver. If you want to try it, I'd recommend buying a standardised extract in a health food store and following the package directions.

BOTTLE GOURD (*LAGENARIA SICERARIA*). Scientists at the University of North Carolina School of Medicine in Chapel Hill have reported that in laboratory animals, low levels of the B vitamin choline may be associated with liver damage and increased risk of liver cancer. It's not clear whether extra choline can protect the liver, but I'd bet it probably does.

According to my database, the best source of choline is bottle gourd. Eat it like butternut or acorn squash. If you can't get hold of it see if you can plant your own. It's easy to grow.

Besides bottle gourd, almost all pulses are rich in choline. So are

More Wisdom *from the* Garden

Know Your Liver's Herbal Foes

While I'm a big supporter of herbal medicine, I should mention that quite a few herbs have been linked, at least preliminarily, to liver damage. These include alkanet, borage, butterbur, coltsfoot, comfrey, germander, liferoot, melilot, pennyroyal, and Virginia snakeroot.

They're nowhere near as poisonous as Amanita mushrooms, but over time, they can cause harm. So I caution against ingesting them regularly or in large amounts.

fenugreek leaves, shepherd's purse, and horehound.

CHINESE PEONY (*PAEONIA*, VARIOUS SPECIES). I have Chinese peony planted in my Garden of Youth. It's a perennial that dies back to the ground after the first frost, then pops up again in spring. The flowers remind me of dahlias or roses. Mine range from white to pink, but I have seen deep red ones, too.

In Europe, the seeds of Chinese peony were once ground into a spice and used to flavour ale. Mongolians brew the seeds to make a tea. The flowers are sometimes cooked as a vegetable or used to scent tea.

Animal studies show that Chinese peony safeguards the liver against chemical damage. The World Health Organisation recommends the herb for liver protection. Chinese practitioners typically prescribe between 3 and 20 grams of peony root a day.

TURMERIC (*CURCUMA LONGA*). Turmeric contains a yellow pigment called curcumin that has many medicinal uses, including as a liver protector. It's a powerful anti-inflammatory compound that can help treat hepatitis. Animal studies have shown that the damage caused by toxins that attack the liver can be minimised by turmeric or curcumin.

I like to use turmeric to season my cooking. For a more standardised dosage, I'd suggest buying a commercial curcurmin preparation and following the label directions for proper dosage.

PICRORHIZA (*PICRORHIZA KURROA*). Picroliv, an extract of picrorhiza, looks so promising as a liver protector that, as I write this, it is being tested in human trials in India. I'm betting that it will work. I don't think there's much doubt that it protects the liver. In laboratory studies, it stimulates liver metabolism and cell regeneration.

In a cursory review of Ayurvedic medicines, the National Institutes of Health Office of Alternative Medicine noted that powdered picrorhiza root is widely used in India to treat hepatitis. The research that I've seen shows that while the herb is not as beneficial as milk thistle, it's still powerful.

Picroliv is available from health food suppliers. For dosage, follow the label directions.

Lifestyle Strategies to Reduce Your Risk

The herbs mentioned above can protect your liver against all kinds of harm. But to really keep your liver healthy and functional, you may want to heed this advice, too.

Buy your mushrooms in the supermarket. Unless you really know what you're doing, don't pick wild mushrooms. Amanita mushrooms, the kind that can poison your liver, grow all over the place. Every year people die after eating wild mushrooms that they didn't recognise as death caps. Don't make the same mistake.

Keep your alcohol consumption moderate. Alcohol is the leading cause of liver disease. I must confess that my liver has not had the easiest life. I've had hepatitis, and when I lived and worked in Panama, especially in the bush, we couldn't trust the water, so we drank more alcohol than we should have.

I no longer drink immoderately. (By 'immoderately', I mean more than two 350 ml- (12 fl oz) beers, two 150 ml- (5 fl oz) glasses of wine, or two cocktails made with 45 ml (1½ oz) of 80-proof distilled spirits a day.) But sometimes I still worry about my liver, which is why I take milk thistle, especially when I'm on the road, where I'm more likely to imbibe socially.

Avoid medications unless you really need them. Drug-induced liver damage accounts for 2 to 5 per cent of the hospitalisations in the United States. But these cases get little publicity. On the other hand, if a herb puts even one person in the hospital, it makes headlines – and those headlines resurface for years. I call that a double standard.

Reduce your risk of hepatitis B and C. Hepatitis A, a food-borne illness, isn't pleasant, but it clears up and doesn't cause long-term liver damage. On the other hand, hepatitis B and C – and possibly other forms of hepatitis – can cause serious liver problems such as cirrhosis and liver cancer years after they're contracted.

Hepatitis B and C spread through sexual contact and through blood from accidental needle sticks and shared needles. Avoid unprotected sex with new partners, and stay away from syringes, except when you're getting shots from a doctor, of course.

CHAPTER 18

Menopause Management

Dr Duke's Anti-Ageing Elixir

• Full o' Phyto-oestrogens Soup

Mention menopause, and many mainstream doctors will begin extolling the virtues of hormone-replacement therapy (HRT). They make it sound so very attractive: no more hot flushes or other menopausal discomforts, and as a bonus, reduced risk of heart disease, osteoporosis, and possibly Alzheimer's disease.

The benefits are real. But so are the problems. Specifically, HRT raises the risk of breast cancer, gallbladder problems, and venous thromboembolisms (clots that block bloodflow in veins). Small wonder that menopausal American women are afraid of HRT. Only about 25 per cent of them use conventional hormone replacement.

The doctors wring their hands, pointing out that the typical woman

growing younger naturally

She Took Charge of 'The Change'

I've received literally hundreds of calls and letters from women who've attended my many lectures on natural approaches to managing menopausal discomforts. I remember one woman in particular, who heard me speak near Baltimore. She decided to try some of my recommendations, and she was so pleased with the results that she called to tell me.

I asked her to write to me about her experience, so I could share it with you. Here is her story.

'About a year ago I started missing periods and experiencing menopausal symptoms. My doctor (an open-minded family physician) took some blood and confirmed a low estrogen level. I had reached menopause.

'About that time, I heard you speak, and you mentioned plant sources of estrogen. So with my doctor's supervision, I modified my diet to include textured soy protein; plums and prunes for boron; capsules of fenugreek; more fruits and vegetables, especially crucifers and pomegranates; and an occasional cup of a "female" herbal tea. [This regimen] relieved my hot flashes.'

Later, she wrote to me again: 'Just a note to update you on my experience with plant estrogens as a way of dealing with menopause. Diet alone wasn't enough, so I resorted to the concentrated isoflavones in Nature's Herbs Phytoestrogen Power capsules (three or four a day) rather than going with synthetic estrogen plus progesterone. I'm now using wild yam cream, applied topically. I continue to eat soy burgers once a day, plus dates, broccoli, and other vegetables daily.

'All this has been enough to manage my menopausal symptoms. Thanks for your counsel in these matters.'

is more likely to develop heart disease or osteoporosis than she is to develop breast cancer. So from a cost-benefit point of view, they say, HRT is a winner. Maybe, but I don't know many women who want to take something that raises their risk of breast cancer.

Do the doctors ever recommend natural alternatives to hormone replacement? By and large, they don't. What they tout instead are the newest oestrogens, the selective oestrogen receptor modulators (SERMs). These synthetic drugs produce fewer side effects than plain old oestrogen, and they're supposedly less likely to increase the risk of breast cancer. But I predict that they'll cause some problems of their own.

Now being a man, I have only secondhand information about menopause. But I have *a lot* of information, and not just from my wife, Peggy, and our female friends. Based on what women have shared with me, I must say that this good old boy prefers the good old natural approach to menopause management. It has real benefits but without the risks of HRT.

One Expert's Approach to Menopause

People tend to think that menopause lasts a few months or maybe a year. Actually, it's a 5- to 10-year process. It begins when a woman is in her early to mid-forties, with what doctors call perimenopause. The first signs of perimenopause include changes in the menstrual cycle (heavier or shorter periods), anxiety, an inability to concentrate, memory lapses, mood swings, and sleep problems.

These changes mean that oestrogen production has begun to decline. It's the time when women can – and should – start thinking about menopause management.

For dealing with perimenopausal and menopausal discomforts, I've come to admire the approach of gynaecologist Herbert L. Jacobs, M.D., associate professor at the University of Colorado Medical Center in Denver. He was a mainstream doctor, and like most of his colleagues, he was very sceptical about alternative therapies. Then he developed an eye problem that conventional pharmaceuticals couldn't fix. But the problem cleared up after he began taking an antioxidant supplement formula.

The experience changed Dr Jacobs's clinical orientation. He used to consider himself a mechanic, trying to fix broken bodies. Now he thinks of himself as a gardener, helping people to cultivate healthy bodies.

Dr Jacobs has found that women generally have an easier time of their perimenopausal and menopausal years if they exercise regularly, control their stress levels (through meditation and deep breathing), quit smoking, and eliminate or cut back on alcohol, caffeine, and highly spicy foods. For the most part, these are sound strategies for all women, regardless of whether they're in or approaching menopause.

In addition, Dr Jacobs recommends taking certain supplements to support good health during the perimenopausal and menopausal years. His supplement plan includes antioxidant nutrients (vitamin C, vitamin E, and carotenoids such as beta-carotene) to support the immune system

for the Gardener

Black Cohosh

Cimicifuga racemosa

When I bought my farm nearly 30 years ago, black cohosh grew naturally only in partial to full shade. Now it's doing well in full sun, too – but only because I planted it there.

When it emerges from its perennial root in spring, black cohosh looks like a coiled fiddlehead fern, with a colour somewhere between black, maroon, and purple. In the fall, the tops die back, and new eyes form in the underground rhizome.

Black cohosh can be grown from seeds in cold frames or by dividing the branched rhizomes, planting the segments that have at least one eye. The plants prefer moist, fertile garden soil, but they'll survive in poorer conditions. They need a radius of 30 to 60 cm (12 to 24 in) to grow properly.

You can harvest black cohosh in autumn, after the plant has all but died back. Free the roots from the soil, wash them off, and leave them to dry.

and calcium to strengthen bones. He also suggests gamma-linolenic acid, or GLA (from evening primrose oil or borage oil) for heart disease prevention and general well-being.

To minimise hot flushes, a common problem in menopause, Dr Jacobs recommends taking black cohosh. He says that it helps about 80 per cent of the women who try it. Buy a commercial product and use it according to the package directions.

For all perimenopausal and menopausal women, Dr Jacobs advises eating soya and soya products: whole soya beans, soya milk, tofu, tempeh, and textured vegetable protein. These foods contain the isoflavones daidzein and genistein, which have a gentle oestrogen-like effect without the side effects and increased breast cancer risk of synthetic oestrogen. He prefers food sources to supplements, but if foods don't seem to help, supplements may do the trick.

To me, this seems like a good, solid menopause-management programme. Start it during your perimenopausal years, and stick with it through menopause and beyond.

Incidentally, I have black cohosh and soya growing in my Garden of Youth. The deer and groundhogs harvest most of my soya, but they've ignored the black cohosh.

Soya: Much Ado about Nothing?

If I'm allowed one quibble with Dr Jacobs's programme, it's his ringing endorsement of soya and soya products. Now, I know that a great deal has been written about how soya foods minimise menopausal discomforts, particularly hot flushes. This is true. As I mentioned earlier, soya beans contain the isoflavones daidzein and genistein. These compounds are phyto-oestrogens, or plant oestrogens. They act just like your body's own oestrogen, binding to the oestrogen receptors on cells. But chemically, they're much weaker.

Just like pharmaceutical oestrogen, phyto-oestrogens do good things for menopausal women, helping to prevent hot flushes as well as heart disease and osteoporosis. But plant oestrogens may be too weak to promote the development of breast cancer, as synthetic oestrogen does.

Dr Duke's Anti-Ageing Elixir

Full o' Phyto-oestrogens Soup

If you eat lots of fatty meats – bacon, sausage, beef, lamb, pork – you can do yourself a double-barrelled favour by replacing some of that animal fat with beans, which are top-notch sources of the isoflavones genistein and daidzein. Reducing your intake of animal foods can help prevent menopausal discomforts. Eating isoflavone-rich pulses can help even more.

You'll get plenty of genistein and daidzein by making this brimming-with-beans soup. (If you're allergic to peanuts or soya, feel free to substitute peas, kidney beans, navy beans, or string beans.)

WHAT YOU NEED

Equal parts of the following pulses: black beans, black-eyed peas, broad beans, butter beans, mung beans, peanuts, and soya beans

Olive oil

1 onion, chopped

1–5 whole cloves garlic

115 g (4 oz) diced broccoli

Hot-pepper sauce

Salt

Ground black pepper

WHAT TO DO

Put the pulses in a pot, then add twice the amount of water needed to cover. Allow to soak overnight.

In the morning, strain the beans, then put them back in the pot with fresh water. Bring to the boil, then reduce the heat and simmer until tender. Transfer the beans to a blender and purée.

Transfer the purée back to the pot. Add a little of the olive oil, plus the onions, garlic and broccoli. Bring to the boil, then reduce the heat and simmer until the vegetables are tender.

Season to taste with the hot-pepper sauce, salt, and black pepper. Allow to cool before serving.

In fact, some research suggests that phyto-oestrogens help *prevent* breast cancer. In one study, young rats that were fed isoflavones from birth to puberty were remarkably resistant to breast cancer later in life.

Increasingly, scientists believe that a big reason why Asian women have such low rates of breast cancer compared with Western women is that their traditional diet features lots of soya and tofu, as well as phyto-oestrogen-rich cabbage, bean sprouts, and wasabi (a horseradish-like condiment). Asian women also report fewer menopausal complaints than Western women, a fact that has been attributed to their traditional high-soya diet. So, yes, soya beans and soya foods can help perimenopausal and menopausal women.

Now for my quibble: the public has been led to believe that soya and soya products are the only good food sources of genistein and daidzein. This isn't true. Almost all of the beans that we eat contain the same isoflavones. In fact, quite a few varieties have even more genistein or daidzein than soya beans. Among the best sources are yellow split peas, black beans, butter beans, red kidney beans, and red lentils. Other varieties with impressive amounts of isoflavones include black-eyed peas, pinto beans, mung beans, adzuki beans and broad beans.

Here's another point to consider: allergies to soya are fairly common, and much more common than allergies to other beans (except peanuts, which, botanically, are classed as pulses). Women who are allergic may be avoiding soya without realising that they can get their isoflavones from other sources.

While I'm not disputing the value of soya, I say that we should give the other pulses their due. All of them contain phyto-oestrogens that can help ease a woman's passage through her perimenopausal and menopausal years.

Hot Flushes: A Herbal Quartet Can Douse the Flames

Of the various discomforts that women might experience during menopause, hot flushes seem to be the most bothersome. These sensations – which occur primarily in the upper body (head, neck, arms, and chest) – are characterised by intense heat, often followed by profuse sweating. They affect the majority of menopausal women, though to varying degrees. Some women experience an occasional flush every few months, while others have as many as 10 to 12 hot flushes a day.

I'll cover treatments for hot flushes later in this book, in chapter 39. In this chapter, I'll focus on prevention. But I must tell you that, as with so many other conditions, the same herbs used to treat hot flushes are also recommended as preventives.

To minimise hot flushes and general menopausal discomforts, my top four picks are black cohosh, dong quai, licorice, and chasteberry. I grow this herbal quartet in my Garden of Youth. While you can grow them, too, I suggest that you buy commercial products and use them according to the package directions.

BLACK COHOSH (*CIMICIFUGA RACEMOSA*). Although black cohosh is native to the United States, it has gained a lot more respect and study in Europe. It's excellent for both the prevention and the treatment of menopausal discomforts.

Black cohosh exerts its effects on your pituitary gland in your brain. It reduces levels of luteinising hormone, creating an oestrogen-like effect on your body.

Several studies have shown a reduction in the frequency and severity of hot flushes with doses of black cohosh equivalent to 40 milligrams of the crude herb a day. In one trial, 812 menopausal women took this dosage for 12 weeks. More than 80 per cent of the women rated the herb's effects as very good or good. Only 2 per cent reported minor side effects, such as headache and stomach upset.

DONG QUAI (*ANGELICA SINENSIS*). Also known as Chinese angelica, dong quai is a major 'women's herb' in Chinese medicine. Andrew Weil, M.D., a noted advocate of alternative therapies, says that he has seen women get good relief from menopausal discomforts when using a tincture that combines dong quai, chasteberry, and damiana. According to Dr Weil, the women take two capsules or one dropperful of tincture each day at midday, continuing until the hot flushes subside, then tapering off.

Presumably, dong quai is mildly oestrogenic, though oddly, some research says it isn't. I'm curious to see how this issue plays out. Based on my own experience as well as the experience of women I know and herbal practitioners I respect, I'm inclined to concur with the Chinese that dong quai is a good herb for the perimenopausal and menopausal years.

LICORICE (*GLYCYRRHIZA GLABRA*). Licorice is an oestrogenic herb, thanks to certain compounds it contains: estriol, formononetin, licoisoflavanone, beta-licoisoflavone, phaseollinisoflavone, and beta-sitosterol. Two licorice-tasting herbs, anise and fennel, also have some oestrogen-like effects. Both contain anethole, which is oestrogenic.

CHASTEBERRY (*VITEX AGNUS-CASTUS*). Like black cohosh, chasteberry has effects on your pituitary gland that tip the overall hormone balance in favour of oestrogen. The herb is a favourite among European herbalists, American naturopaths, and yours truly.

growing younger naturally

She Turned Down Hormones – And Turned to Herbs Instead

Sue Mustalish, a registered nurse and a good friend, told me a story about one of her clients, a 55-year-old woman who by all accounts was sailing through menopause. Then inexplicably, she began experiencing anxiety that insidiously progressed to the point where she had trouble getting out of bed some mornings. The woman was literally incapacitated by fear.

She called her gynaecologist, who hand-delivered a prescription for hormone-replacement therapy (HRT). But the woman didn't want to take hormones. She consulted Sue instead.

'I suggested a combination of chasteberry, dong quai, and black cohosh (all highly regarded herbs for menopause), plus blue vervain (a natural sedative) and *Selenicereus grandiflorus* (a cactus with tonic action),' Sue recalls. 'She began to feel relief in 48 hours.'

Vaginal Dryness: Prevent It with Wild Yams

If you're concerned about vaginal dryness, or any other perimenopausal or menopausal discomforts, you may want to try a cream made from wild yams. They contain high levels of diosgenin, which is a weak phyto-oestrogen.

I should point out that medicinal wild yams are different from the yams that you find in supermarkets next to the sweet potatoes. Supermarket yams are tasty and very nutritious, packed with lots of antioxidant carotenoids. But they don't contain the diosgenin found in medicinal wild yams.

If you opt for a yam cream, look for the words 'wild yam' or the Latin name *Dioscorea* on the label. Apply the cream according to package directions.

Making the HRT Decision

Let's return for a moment to the subject with which I began this chapter: hormone-replacement therapy. Should you or shouldn't you use HRT?

Well, that depends. If your family history has lots of heart disease and osteoporosis, but little or no breast cancer, then you and your doctor might decide to try hormone replacement. But if your family history has lots of breast cancer and little or no heart disease or osteoporosis, you may want to think twice about opting for HRT. (If you have oestrogen-receptive breast cancer, be aware that even natural phyto-oestrogens from herbs and plant foods can aggravate the condition.)

Either way, I'd urge you to consider the natural approaches that I've presented in this chapter. They're inherently good for you, and a good deal of evidence shows that they help ease your passage through menopause.

CHAPTER 19

Enhancing Men's Health

Dr Duke's Anti-Ageing Elixirs

- *Even Better Prosnut Butter*
- *Impotence-Fighting Oatmeal*

You've probably read or heard about the controversial concept of andropause, which is essentially a male version of menopause. Do men really experience 'the change', just as women do? I think so, though I know that many in the medical community are sceptical that andropause exists. I believe in it because it happened to me.

Shortly after I passed the mid-century mark, I found myself feeling oddly depressed. I would drive around aimlessly near my home, sometimes crying. I didn't sleep well, and my stomach ached. Of course, I wondered what was happening to me. Wistfully, I realised that my life was at least half over, and it hadn't turned out to be a bowl of cherries.

Other men that I know reported similar troubles around this age.

This stage of life can be marked by increased alcohol consumption to the point of abuse, loss of erection, general loss of sexual desire, or specific loss of interest in a spouse, with temptation to engage in an extramarital affair.

And all of this happens right around the time when we men are noticing our first symptoms of benign – that is, noncancerous – prostate enlargement. While women might be roused from their sleep by hot flushes, we men may get up several times a night to urinate.

The hormonal changes that drive andropause are not as well-documented as the decline in oestrogen production that occurs during menopause. But I think midlife hormonal fluctuations may affect men and women about equally. I've seen estimates that testosterone levels decline significantly in about 25 per cent of men around the age of 50. This may be a factor in some of the sexual problems that many older guys experience.

Personally, if I did go through andropause, I've got over the worst of it. I still feel blue from time to time. Only now, instead of driving around by myself and crying, I remember the words of my favourite hymn, somewhat adapted: 'I come to the garden alone, while the dew is still on the primrose.' And I head to my Garden of Youth, where I soak up some sunshine and contemplate my favourite flower, the evening primrose.

You probably know that St. John's wort is an effective herbal treatment for depression. But you may not be aware that evening primrose contains a mood-elevating compound called tryptophan. A similar compound, phenylalanine, is found in sunflower.

Of course, just looking at the lovely blooms of all three plants can make me feel better. That they contain mood-boosting substances is a bonus.

Benign Prostate Enlargement: Stop the Swelling without Surgery

As far as prostate problems go, I'm pleased to report that herbs have kept mine in check – much to my doctors' surprise. When I first became aware of prostate symptoms some years ago, the standard treatment was surgery to snip away overgrown prostate tissue and restore normal urination. But I wasn't interested in that. First of all, it's major surgery, with the usual anaesthesia risks and an extended recovery period. Second, it can leave men with erection impairment. So I said no thanks.

Meanwhile, around that time, the first pharmaceutical for prostate enlargement hit the market. Called finasteride (Proscar), it shrinks the prostate gland by interfering with an enzyme called 5-alpha-reductase, which plays a key role in the overgrowth of prostate tissue.

Proscar works, but again, I said no thanks. I knew of a herbal 5-alpha-reductase inhibitor that appealed to me more: saw palmetto (*Serenoa repens*). Most days, especially when I'm on the road and not eating as well as I should, I take either one 320-milligram capsule or two 160-milligram capsules of a standardised extract.

The doctors told me that I was crazy, that no herb could control my prostate symptoms. Well, guess what? Saw palmetto did. And it still does.

Now researchers are turning up impressive scientific evidence that saw palmetto works quite well in relieving prostate symptoms. Several European trials have demonstrated that the herb shrinks enlarged prostates, reduces nighttime bathroom runs, and helps restore normal urine flow. A few studies have even tested saw palmetto against Proscar, with good results. The herb and the drug have comparable benefits, but the herb has fewer side effects.

Saw palmetto has certainly worked for me. For the past few years, at the conclusion of my annual prostate exam, my current doctor, who is very tolerant of herbal medicine, has said, 'Just keep doing what you've been doing.' Every time I walk past the saw palmetto that grows in my Garden of Youth, I'm grateful that I didn't let the surgeons slice into my 72-year-old prostate gland.

Saw palmetto is not the only herbal 5-alpha-reductase inhibitor. Another is African wild cherry, commonly known as pygeum (*Pygeum africanum*). In one rigorous study, 263 men with symptoms of benign prostate enlargement were given either a placebo (a fake pill) or 100

Dr Duke's Anti-Ageing Elixir

Even Better Prosnut Butter

In my book *The Green Pharmacy,* I introduced a recipe for Prosnut Butter. Since then, I've continued tinkering with the ingredients and their proportions to come up with an even tastier, more prostate-friendly spread.

WHAT YOU NEED

- **8 parts each (by weight) Brazil nuts and pumpkin seeds**
- **4 parts bean paste or sprouts**
- **1 part saw palmetto (from opened capsules)**
- **Brazil nut oil or peanut oil**

WHAT TO DO

In a food processor, combine the Brazil nuts, pumpkin seeds, bean paste or sprouts (included for their genistein, which may help control prostate overgrowth), and saw palmetto. Add a little of the oil if necessary to produce a creamy texture for spreading.

Variation: sometimes I'll mix in one or more of the following ingredients, which folk herbalists have long recommended for prostate and urinary problems: cucumber seeds, watermelon seeds, sunflower seeds, peanuts, almonds, sesame seeds, soya beans, flaxseeds, walnuts, and carob powder. Experiment to get the flavour that you like best.

---

milligrams of a standardised pygeum extract every day for 60 days. Among those taking the placebo, 31 per cent reported improvement in their symptoms. Among those taking pygeum, that figure rose to 66 per cent.

Pygeum is often recommended in combination with stinging nettle because some studies have shown that the two are superior to pygeum alone in improving urinary volume. Scientists aren't sure exactly why stinging nettle helps. It may be a 5-alpha-reductase inhibitor, or it may act on other compounds in the prostate that contribute to tissue overgrowth.

Stinging nettle is safe, so I have no problem recommending it. If you want to try pygeum, stinging nettle, or both, buy a commercial preparation and take it according to the label directions.

Finally, to prevent prostate problems, don't overlook the value of making whoopie. Regular ejaculation helps keep your prostate healthy. Use it or lose it, as they say.

Prostate Cancer: Tomatoes Shift the Odds in Your Favour

Every 3 minutes, a man is newly diagnosed with prostate cancer. Every 15 minutes, a man dies of the disease – usually someone around my age.

Not so long ago, doctors had no idea how to prevent prostate cancer. But recent research has identified several effective approaches. Not surprisingly, most have a connection to the plant-based Palaeolithic diet that I've been advocating throughout this book.

As it turns out, a high intake of saturated fat is a significant risk factor for prostate cancer. The primary sources of saturated fat – meats, whole-milk dairy products, and junk foods – were virtually nonexistent in the Palaeolithic diet. You can do your prostate a huge favour by cutting back on these foods.

On the other hand, the Palaeolithic diet featured plenty of fruits and vegetables. Research has shown that fruits and veggies rich in lycopene (a member of the carotenoid family) can help protect against prostate cancer.

You can get lycopene by eating plenty of red-coloured plant foods such as watermelon, pink grapefruit, guava, and especially tomatoes. Any kind of tomato-based food can help – sauces, soups, salads, even pizza (as long as you go light on the cheese and stay away from meat toppings).

I have a cherry tomato plant in my Garden of Youth. When fruiting, it produces up to 30 plump cherry tomatoes a day. I often blend them with red peppers to make a lycopene-rich vegetable drink. It's delicious and great for my prostate.

For extra prostate protection, I'd suggest eating Brazil nuts on occasion. They're an exceptional source of cancer-preventing selenium.

Impotence: Viagra Isn't the Only Answer

Colloquially, *impotence* means that the penis has called it quits. In reality, this seldom happens. Few men experience total loss of erection. Even men with spinal cord injuries often retain some erectile function.

From an evolutionary perspective, this makes sense. The human body naturally places a high priority on safeguarding reproductive function and the sexual urges that are necessary to sustain it. So what's commonly referred to as impotence is really erection impairment or dysfunction. For purposes of this discussion, I'll use the terms interchangeably.

According to the latest studies, more than 10 million American men have some degree of impotence. But the figure is somewhat misleading, because the condition isn't all that widespread across age groups. Getting older definitely has something to do with it.

The Massachusetts Male Ageing Survey asked 1,300 men between the ages of 40 and 70 about the quality of their erections. Only 5 per cent of 40-year-olds reported severe, persistent erection impairment, while about one-third said that they experience erection difficulty from time to time. Among 70-year-olds, 15 per cent reported severe erection impairment, with another two-thirds experiencing occasional problems.

Looking at these numbers, you might conclude that impotence is an inevitable part of ageing and that every old guy could use some Viagra. I don't believe it. I do believe that a lot of 'age-related' erection troubles actually result from unhealthy habits: drinking to excess, smoking, eating too much fat, not exercising, and being overweight. Making a few lifestyle adjustments, like those that follow, just may help lower your risk of erection problems.

Drink only in moderation. Alcohol is a central nervous system depressant. It messes up the nerve function required for erection. Excessive alcohol consumption is generally recognized as one of the leading causes of erection impairment. So play it safe and limit yourself to two drinks a day (one drink is defined as 350 ml (12 fl oz) of regular beer, 150 ml (5 fl oz) of wine, or a cocktail made with 45 ml (1 fl oz) spirits).

Pack away the cigarettes. Smoking accelerates atherosclerosis, the narrowing of the arteries that causes heart disease and most strokes. It also narrows the arteries that deliver blood to your penis. When bloodflow is impaired, erections are more difficult to raise, and they feel less firm.

Replace meats with plant foods. TV commercials equate meat with manliness. In fact, the opposite is true. A diet rich in meat is also rich in fat, which accelerates atherosclerosis. If you want your erections to stay firm throughout life, stick with a low-fat diet of mostly plant foods.

My Healthy Sevens eating plan features little meat and lots of plant foods. To learn more about it, see chapter 3.

Exercise for at least 30 minutes a day. Daily physical activity improves circulation, including bloodflow into your penis. It also helps prevent obesity, another risk factor for erection impairment.

Maintain your weight within a healthy range. Carrying extra pounds strains your heart and blood vessels. Your heart has to pump harder to move blood through all the excess tissue. This elevates blood pressure, which damages your arteries, including the ones that feed your penis.

Protect yourself against diabetes. Diabetes is the disease most frequently linked to erection impairment. If blood sugar levels aren't managed very carefully, diabetes can damage your circulatory system, accelerating atherosclerosis, and your nervous system, injuring the nerves involved in erection.

More than 90 per cent of people with diabetes have type 2 (non-insulin-dependent), which more often than not results from a combination of poor diet and physical inactivity. By following my Healthy Sevens eating plan and exercising regularly, as recommended above, you may be able to avoid type 2 diabetes and the erection problems that often accompany it.

Discover the Herbal Erection Aids

A few years ago, the erectile dysfunction drug sildenafil (Viagra) took the country – and the world – by storm. If you want to take it, you need a prescription. And it's expensive. What's more, it can cause side effects, even death if it's taken in combination with nitrate medication (nitroglycerine) for heart disease.

If I needed help below the belt, I'd first try the herbal alternatives. There are several.

GINKGO (*GINKGO BILOBA*). Ginkgo improves bloodflow throughout the body, including to the penis. A few studies have concluded that the herb can help in cases of impotence caused by impaired bloodflow. Buy a commercial preparation and take it according to the label directions.

ASIAN GINSENG (*PANAX GINSENG*). A well-known Asian tonic herb, ginseng is a non-caffeine stimulant. Among the things it is said to stimulate is sexual desire and ability. Some laboratory studies involving animals suggest that these claims are more than just folklore. But I must confess that I'm including it here largely on the basis of its centuries-old healing tradition.

Ginseng is rather expensive. But if you want to try it, buy a commercial preparation and take it according to the label directions.

YOHIMBE (*PAUSINYSTALIA YOHIMBE*). Yohimbe is a West African tree with a long-standing reputation as an aphrodisiac. The research to date shows that the herb and its main alkaloid derivative, yohimbine, improve bloodflow into the penis and help treat impotence.

The FDA has approved a few prescription impotence treatments made with yohimbine but it does consider the yohimbe plant potentially toxic. So although you can buy yohimbe yourself, I

Dr Duke's Anti-Ageing Elixir

Impotence-Fighting Oatmeal

The ingredients in this recipe may help protect against erection impairment.

WHAT YOU NEED

- **1–2 teaspoons yinyanghuo leaves or 1 dropper of yinyanghuo tincture**
- **1 cup water**
- **2 standardised ginkgo capsules**
- **1 saw palmetto capsule**
- **1 serving instant porridge oats**

WHAT TO DO

Add the yinyanghuo leaves or tincture to the freshly boiled water. Allow to steep for 10 to 20 minutes. Open the ginkgo and saw palmetto capsules and pour their contents into the tea. Use the tea instead of water to make a bowl of instant porridge.

suggest consulting a qualified practitioner if you want to try it.

QUEBRACHO (*ASPIDOSPERMA QUEBRACHO-BLANCO*). Like yohimbe, quebracho, a Latin American herb, contains yohimbine. I suspect that the herb is as safe as yohimbe, though it's not as widely available. If you can find a commercial preparation, use it according to the label directions.

WILD OATS (*AVENA SATIVA*). You've probably heard people described as 'sowing their wild oats'. Wild oats are reputed to make horses – and by extension, us humans – sexually frisky.

I'm not entirely sold on wild oats. But the herb is rich in boron, a trace mineral that can substantially raise blood levels of testosterone, the hormone that stimulates the sex drive in both men and women. Look for a commercial preparation and take it according to the package directions.

YINYANGHUO (*EPIMEDIUM,* VARIOUS SPECIES). I have one of the most complete collections of yinyanghuo species in the state of Maryland. Most of the plants were imported from Asia, though a few come from Europe.

According to Chinese folklore, yinyanghuo makes goats horny (hence its common name, horny goat weed). I no longer own goats, so I can't say one way or the other. I can say that the deer on my property won't go near the herb. If you want to try it, you can buy it in tincture form. Take it according to the label directions.

Infertility: No Longer Just a Young Man's Problem

More and more older men want to have children. As a result, infertility has become an age-related issue.

Infertility is complicated. It has no quick fixes, herbal or otherwise. In general, it may respond to the same lifestyle strategies recommended for other 'male' problems: a Palaeolithic diet, regular exercise, controlled alcohol consumption, and no smoking or recreational drugs.

A few studies have found that men who are infertile might benefit from supplements of the mineral zinc. Most experts recommend taking 30 to 50 milligrams of zinc a day for infertility. You can also boost your intake by eating a variety of zinc-rich foods. Among the best sources are fish and seafood (especially oysters), eggs, all kinds of pulses, nuts and seeds (especially peanuts and pumpkin seeds), and wholegrain cereals.

Sperm are among the most delicate cells in a man's body. Anything that hurts the rest of the body harms sperm even more. Among the biggest offenders are industrial chemicals and pollutants, which can kill or deform sperm. In fact, some scientists have proposed using sperm counts to screen the safety of industrial chemicals.

If you're concerned about protecting your fertility, you'd do best to avoid pesticides, solvents, heavy metals, and any chemical that carries a warning label. You should also steer clear of xeno-oestrogens, the oestrogen-like compounds in pesticides and many plastics that tip a man's hormone balance in the female direction. You can reduce your exposure to xeno-oestrogens by buying organic produce or growing your own. And don't microwave anything in a plastic container – the xeno-oestrogens could migrate into the food.

Sperm thrive in environments that are cooler than normal body temperature. That's why the scrotum, where sperm are stored, hangs outside the male body. Anything that raises the temperature of the scrotum threatens sperm. This includes soaking in hot tubs and sitting for long periods with legs pressed together. Limit both if you wish to preserve your sperm count.

Some men develop varicose veins, or varicoceles, in their testicles. This condition has been associated with infertility, presumably because the extra blood pooling in the veins raises the temperature of the scrotum. Varicoceles can be corrected through a simple surgical procedure.

Many doctors say that varicoceles can't be prevented. But I know of a trio of herbs that can help: horse chestnut, sweet clover, and witch hazel. All three grow on my property or nearby as weeds. They're rich in flavonoids, compounds that seem to strengthen blood vessels and protect against varicose veins.

You should be able to buy any of these herbs as a commercial preparation. Take it according to the package directions.

CHAPTER 20

Mental Sharpness

Dr Duke's Anti-Ageing Elixir
* *Cerebral Choline Chowder*

Physical agility gave our Palaeolithic ancestors the edge they needed to survive. In today's world, it's mental agility that keeps us one step ahead, ready to take on whatever challenges life throws our way.

Of course, if we take care of our bodies, we're also taking care of our brains. That's because many of the strategies that protect physical health can safeguard mental health as well.

As an example, consider blood pressure. There's good research to show that having high blood pressure at midlife can set the stage for reduced mental sharpness in later years.

High cholesterol may have a similar effect. Even if you never experience a stroke or transient ischemic attack (TIA), or mini-stroke, your brain cells won't be receiving as much blood as they should, because blood can't travel freely through the arteries that have been narrowed by atherosclerotic plaques. This, too, results in a decline in mental function.

To keep your brain – and your body – healthy and vital, start with the basics of an anti-ageing lifestyle.

- *Adopt a low-fat, plant-based Palaeolithic diet (see chapter 3), which provides plenty of antioxidants and other brain-friendly nutrients.*
- *Take a multivitamin/mineral supplement for extra nutrition.*
- *Engage in regular, moderate physical activity.*
- *Don't smoke, and avoid excessive alcohol consumption.*
- *Keep stress in check.*
- *Get adequate rest.*

Beyond these fundamental strategies, preserving your mental sharpness is as simple as learning your ABCs. That's A for Alzheimer's prevention, B for brain foods, and C for central nervous system stimulants. They're the real keys to lifelong brainpower.

Forgetful? Your Medicine May Be to Blame

Most older folks take more than one pharmaceutical on a regular basis. Often these drugs can interact with one another, producing strange and unwelcome effects. And the more medications a person takes, the more likely he is to experience problems.

One of the most common symptoms of a drug interaction is mental confusion. If your thinking seems to have got fuzzy after you began using a certain combination of medications, talk with your doctor. He may be able to adjust your dosages, or even replace one medicine with another that won't affect mental function.

Another option is to replace one or more of the drugs you're taking with herbs. Of course, you should never change your dosage or discontinue a medication without first consulting your doctor. In addition, some herbs can interact with medications, leaving you right back where you started.

I've never heard of the herbs that I recommend causing confusion or loss of mental sharpness. Still, you should check in with your doctor before adding or substituting a herbal remedy in your treatment regime. For myself, I'd opt for herbs instead of pharmaceuticals whenever possible.

Alzheimer's Disease: The Cause and Cure Remain a Mystery

Experts still aren't sure what causes the memory loss and personality changes characteristic of Alzheimer's disease. But they do know that acetylcholine plays a major role. Acetylcholine is a neurotransmitter, a brain chemical that enables nerve impulses to pass from one nerve cell to another.

Most people think of the nervous system as the body's wiring. It is, but with one big difference: unlike metal wires, which are continuous filaments, nerve cells are not continuous. They don't touch each other. They have microscopic gaps between them, called synapses.

For a nerve impulse to cross a synapse, the sending cell releases a tiny amount of a neurotransmitter, often acetylcholine. The neurotransmitter allows the impulse to pass to the next nerve cell. After the impulse has jumped the synapse, the sending cell releases a tiny amount of an enzyme that cleans up the neurotransmitter, preparing the synapse for the next nerve impulse. In the case of acetylcholine, the enzyme is acetylcholinesterase – or cholinesterase for short.

Scientists have observed that people with Alzheimer's disease run low on acetylcholine, which seems to explain why their mental function declines. This observation also directed researchers to two treatment options: either help Alzheimer's patients make more acetylcholine or inhibit the action of cholinesterase, so the acetylcholine that patients have might last a little longer and let more nerve impulses through.

Both of the drugs currently approved to treat Alzheimer's disease are cholinesterase inhibitors. Named tacrine (Cognex) and donepezil (Aricept), these drugs slow the progression of the Alzheimer's but don't reverse it.

Cognex and Aricept aren't the only cholinesterase inhibitors on God's green earth. Not by a long shot. Quite a few herbs have similar effects.

Meet the Anti-Alzheimer Herbs

This brings me to Nicolette Perry, a British pharmaceutical researcher. Perry has studied herbal cholinesterase inhibition and has come up with

for the Gardener

Lemon Balm

Melissa officinalis

About 20 years ago, I bought a potted lemon balm for a dollar or so. Now I have dozens of descendants from that first plant popping up all over my garden.

A perennial, lemon balm dies back to the ground after the first hard frost, then re-emerges in March or April here in Maryland. The herb is easily started from seeds, cuttings, or root divisions. With seeds, germination takes anywhere from 1 to 6 weeks. Plant seedlings about 30 cm (12 in) apart. They may do better in partial shade than in full sun.

Feel free to clip lemon balm leaves any time. I like to use the fresh leaves when making teas. Harvest the plants about 35 days after the last frost, cutting the stems to within 7.5 cm (3 in) of the ground. If let go, they become a self-seeding weed, like so many of the aromatic mints.

If you wish, you can hang the plants in bunches to dry. But the leaves fall off quickly, losing their aroma. I prefer to dry my leaves slowly in paper bags, then pulverise them by rolling them between my thumb and finger or between my palms. A mortar and pestle will work just as well if you happen to have them handy.

a list of the herbs that do the job best. Here's her list, in descending order of potency: balm or lemon balm, lime, sage, hyssop, and rosemary.

Now I don't know of any research that proves these herbs to be as powerful as the Alzheimer's drugs or that shows they have any effect at all on Alzheimer's patients. But I think that's because the herbs haven't been studied. There are intriguing signs that they may help.

For starters, consider the anecdotal evidence provided by herbal folklore. Since ancient times, rosemary has been considered a memory herb. Students used to wear rosemary garlands when cramming for exams. And in Shakespeare's play *Hamlet*, Ophelia gives the young prince a sprig and says, 'There's rosemary, that's for remembrance.'

Consider, too, that all of the herbal cholinesterase inhibitors are very aromatic, which means they give off significant amounts of their essential oils. The small molecules that make up these fragrant compounds have a natural affinity for fatty tissue. Because of their size, the molecules just might pass right through your protective blood-brain barrier. And because of their affinity for fatty tissue, they head straight for your brain, which is fatty.

I'm not waiting for the experts to prove that herbal cholinesterase inhibitors work. I'm hedging my bets now by drinking tea made from balm, sage, hyssop, or rosemary. To make the tea, I put a teaspoon or two of herb into a cup of freshly boiled water and let it steep for maybe 5 to 10 minutes. I strain out the herbs, add a squirt of lime juice, then drink up. I'm convinced that the tea is helping to preserve my memory and protect me from Alzheimer's.

Another herb that may reduce your risk of Alzheimer's is ginkgo. It works by boosting bloodflow throughout your body, including within your brain. As bloodflow improves, brain cells get more oxygen and nutrients, which helps them resist the disease's process.

One study, published in the *Journal of the American Medical Association*, concluded that taking 120 milligrams of a standardised ginkgo extract a day can treat Alzheimer's as effectively as the approved drugs – but less expensively and with fewer side effects. As far as I know,

More Wisdom *from the* Garden

Pain Relievers May Prevent Alzheimer's

The *Journal of the American Medical Association* has reported that the latest generation of pain-relieving pharmaceuticals, called COX-2 inhibitors, may also help prevent Alzheimer's disease. If that's the case, then the herbal COX-2s may have the same effect, in proportion to their dosage and potency.

Rosemary is one of the better sources of two COX-2 compounds: oleanolic acid and ursolic acid. No wonder it has a longstanding reputation as the herb of remembrance.

Does Aluminium Cause Alzheimer's?

For years, rumours have circulated about a link between aluminium and Alzheimer's disease. Supposedly, eating food prepared in aluminium cookware or drinking beverages from aluminium cans raises your risk of Alzheimer's.

Is it true? The research to date has gone both ways. Some studies have found an association, while others have turned up nothing. My attitude is 'When in doubt, hedge your bets and be conservative.' I'd avoid aluminium cookware and beverage cans until the research shows they are undoubtedly safe.

scientists have not yet studied ginkgo as an Alzheimer's preventive, but I'm betting that it helps.

Ginkgo is the first tree that I planted in my Garden of Youth. It provides partial shade for the gazebo. I take ginkgo, but I use a commercial preparation (standardised to contain 24 per cent flavonoid glycosides). The recommended dosage on the label is 120 milligrams a day.

In addition to these herbs, one nutritional supplement has shown promise as an Alzheimer's treatment and, in my opinion, may act as a preventive, too. It's called acetyl-l-carnitine, though it's popularly known as carnitine. A few studies have shown that this nutrient slows the progression of Alzheimer's by preserving acetylcholine and other neurotransmitters. Most sources recommend taking 1 to 5 grams of carnitine a day. I've seen one study in which 300 elderly people demonstrated significant improvement in mental performance after taking 1.5 grams (1,500 milligrams) a day.

Brain Foods: Feed Your Head with Choline

Now I'd like to take a moment to gloat a little. Not too many years ago, self-described 'quackbusters' decided that they had an obligation to save unsuspecting Americans from what they had deemed medical frauds: the vitamins, minerals, and herbs being touted by people like yours truly. They announced that supplements did little more than create expensive urine (because the body excretes any amount of nutrient that it doesn't need). They insisted that there were no such things as immune system stimulants. And they scoffed at the very notion of 'brain foods'.

Scientific research has since proven that many vitamin and mineral supplements have real value in preventing and treating disease, when taken in doses higher than the RDAs. Studies have also concluded that echinacea and other herbs are, in fact, immune stimulants. And in 1998, the federal government in the USA – a bastion of quackbuster-type thinking – acknowledged the existence of brain foods by adding choline to its list of essential nutrients.

For nearly a decade, some supplement manufacturers pushed choline as an important, if not essential, dietary phytochemical. In April 1998, the US government finally realised that it should establish a daily intake for this nutrient. By then, research had suggested quite persuasively that women who take choline during pregnancy and while nursing may help their children's mental skills develop properly – and might give their kids lifelong protection against loss of mental function.

Doctors routinely advise women who are pregnant, or thinking of becoming pregnant, to supplement folic acid (a B vitamin also known as folate) as a means of safeguarding against birth defects such as spinal malformations. Supplementing choline during pregnancy and while nursing may have even longer-term benefits for a child, preventing or slowing the onset of senile dementia in later years.

Studies have found that choline is crucial to brain development. For one experiment, pregnant rats were divided into three groups. One group received no choline, another was given typical dietary amounts of the nutrient, and the third received approximately three times the typical dietary amount. For the rest of their lives, both the mothers and their offspring ate a typical rat diet. When they reached adulthood, the offspring of the mothers that had been given choline supplements demonstrated better memory and attention skills. As for the offspring of the mothers that hadn't received choline supplements, the animals showed impairment in some mental tasks.

In this experiment, prenatal choline supplementation seemed to prevent the animal equivalent of the memory decline characteristic of senile dementia. How did the choline help? Apparently, by boosting brain levels of acetylcholine, the neurotransmitter that's so important to memory and learning. As its name suggests, choline is a chemical precursor of acetylcholine.

Some studies have shown that choline supplements have little benefit for people with Alzheimer's disease. Perhaps. I'm betting that a diet featuring plenty of choline-rich foods can help prevent the disease.

The two best food sources of choline are fenugreek leaves and calabash gourd. Neither is easy to find, though I do grow both in my

---

Dr Duke's Anti-Ageing Elixir

Cerebral Choline Chowder

With the abundance of beans in this soup, you can't help getting a healthy dose of choline, a nutrient that may help protect against age-related mental decline.

WHAT YOU NEED

Any combination of the following pulses: adzuki beans, black beans, black-eyed peas, chickpeas, broad beans, peanuts, kidney beans, lentils, butter beans, mung beans, navy beans, peas, and runner beans

Barley

Any combination of the following herbs: rosemary, sage, fennel seed, savory, thyme, onion, garlic, and hot-pepper sauce

Stinging nettle leaves

WHAT TO DO

Put the pulses of your choice in a large bowl of water and allow to soak overnight.

In the morning, transfer them to a large pot of water. Add 115 g (4 oz) barley for every 230 g (8 oz) of beans. Bring the water to a boil, then reduce the heat and simmer until the beans are tender.

Transfer the beans to a food processor and mix to a suitable consistency. Add the herbs of your choice to taste.

Garnish the chowder with tender young nettle leaves, if available, before serving. Be sure to steam the leaves to get rid of their sting.

Garden of Youth. Other good sources are more readily available: barley, beans, oats, sesame seeds, and whole wheat, as well as the herbs stinging nettle, ginseng, horehound, and shepherd's purse.

Based on my family history, I don't think I'm at great risk of Alzheimer's disease. I may have obtained some protection from the choline-rich beans that my mother ate while pregnant with me. But if I were concerned about Alzheimer's, I'd make a point of eating my Cerebral Choline Chowder several times a week.

Central Nervous System Stimulants: Give Your Brain a Jolt

If you're like me and most American adults, you start every day with a dose of the world's most popular central nervous system (CNS) stimulant: caffeine. We Americans get most of our caffeine from coffee (about 100 milligrams per 180-ml/6-fl oz cup) and the rest from cola (50 to 60 milligrams per 360-ml/12-fl oz can), tea (25 milligrams per 180-ml/6-fl oz cup), and cocoa/chocolate (10 milligrams per serving).

In Asia, tea is the caffeine source of choice. Latin Americans prefer guarana and maté, also known as yerba maté. In terms of caffeine content, these herbs may rank somewhere between coffee and tea.

All of these plants are native to the tropics. I've managed to obtain coffee, tea, kola, and cocoa shrubs, which I keep potted and sheltered in my greenhouse during the winter months. I'm still looking for guarana, which is an Amazonian vine, and maté, a South American tree that's similar to holly. With all of my trips to the Amazon, you'd think I would have the plants by now. No such luck.

Caffeine isn't the only thing that these herbs have in common. They contain an array of CNS-stimulant compounds, all members of the same chemical family: the methylxanthines. Other compounds in this family include theobromine and theophylline, which are used medicinally to treat asthma. They're bronchodilators, which means they open constricted bronchial passages.

Actually, caffeine is a bronchodilator, too. If you have chest congestion from a cold or flu, or if your asthma is flaring up but you don't have your inhaler handy, a couple of cups of coffee can provide temporary relief.

Caffeine and its fellow CNS stimulants do more than relieve respiratory problems and stimulate wakefulness. Many studies have concluded that caffeine, in particular, enhances memory and the ability to concentrate. It also acts as a mild antidepressant. Since confusion is a symptom of depression, caffeine's mood-elevating effects may counter any mental lapses brought on by the blues.

Of course, caffeine has its downside. No doubt you already know that drinking too much coffee can cause insomnia, jitters, irritability, and possibly stomach upset and diarrhoea. In addition, caffeine is classically addictive. You develop a tolerance to it, so over time, you need more to obtain the desired effect. And if you suddenly stop getting your daily dose of caffeine, you're likely to suffer withdrawal symptoms: a headache that may last for several days, sluggishness, and constipation.

That said, caffeine is still a CNS stimulant, and consumed in moderation, it appears to be reasonably safe. Quite a few studies have hinted at a link between coffee and cancer, but so far, none of them has panned out. I've yet to see any research to convince me that a daily cup or two (or three) of coffee causes real harm.

I would limit my coffee consumption if I had an ulcer or some other chronic gastrointestinal condition that might be aggravated by caffeine. And nursing women should be aware that caffeine is excreted in breast milk and therefore is best avoided.

More Natural Brain-Boosters

In addition to caffeine-containing plants, a number of herbs are considered CNS stimulants. One of them is ginseng. I've been growing my own ginseng for 20 years. I've written a book about the herb, and I've attended numerous seminars on its many effects. Frankly, I haven't made up my mind as to whether ginseng can help the mind. I seldom take it, in part because the research is iffy (though the herb does contain choline), in part because ginseng is so expensive.

Of the herbal CNS stimulants, perhaps a better choice is gotu kola (not to be confused with kola). India's Ayurvedic doctors have long prescribed gotu kola as a memory enhancer. In animal experiments, the herb has improved learning capacity. And Indian research has shown that it helps build mental agility in mentally challenged children. Every time I pass the gotu kola plant in my Garden of Youth, I grab a few leaves and chew on them.

The other herbal CNS stimulants are the mints: basil, bee balm, biblical mint, hyssop, mountain mint, peppermint, rosemary, sage, spearmint, and watermint. I grow all of them in the Garden of Youth.

The mints don't deliver a jolt of caffeine. But they do contain a surprising number of compounds that have been shown to produce a mild CNS-stimulating effect – mild but noticeable, as far as I'm concerned. Among these compounds are cineole, carvone, carveol, cinnamaldehyde, chlorogenic acid, menthol, piperine, and pyrocatechol.

What's more, some research suggests that several of the compounds – notably menthol – help to preserve acetylcholine, the neurotransmitter that plays a key role in memory and learning. When I know that I'm going to be driving long distances on monotonous freeways, I'll place a few sprigs of rosemary on my dashboard to help keep me awake.

CHAPTER 21

Mellow Moods

Dr Duke's Anti-Ageing Elixirs

- *Stress-Buster Tea*
- *Tranquilli-Tea*

The sworn enemies of youth are stress, anxiety, and depression. They make young people look and feel old, and older people look and feel aged.

Because these negative emotions take a toll physically as well as mentally, keeping them in check is crucial to maintaining a sense of well-being and vitality through every stage of life. That's why I've made a point of planting so many mood-mellowing herbs in my Garden of Youth.

Stress and Anxiety: Your Immune System's Number One Enemy

Stress and anxiety are essentially two sides of the same coin. Both originate with a feeling that some aspect of your life has spun out of control. Both set the stage for a hormone imbalance by raising your blood levels of cortisone, the stress/anxiety hormone. Both trigger emotional symptoms (tension, worry, irritability, and fuzzy thinking) as well as physical symptoms (headache, neck and back pain, stomach upset, and loss of appetite). When chronic, both compromise your immune system.

In several studies, people who had been caring for spouses with Alzheimer's disease – an extremely stressful situation – showed significantly depressed immune function. This is an important finding, because as your immune system weakens, you're more vulnerable to illness. Becoming sick worsens feelings of stress and anxiety, which in turn undermine your immune system even more. It's a vicious circle.

Researchers have established stress as a contributor to an astounding array of health concerns, including angina, backache, some cancers, cataracts, colds and flu, heart attack, heart rhythm disturbances (arrhythmias), high blood pressure, high cholesterol, indigestion, insomnia, and obesity. Personally, I suspect that this list is just the tip of the iceberg. I'm convinced that stress can aggravate just about any physical or emotional problem.

Beyond 'everyday' stress and anxiety, there are the more serious anxiety disorders: phobias, obsessive-compulsive disorder, and post-traumatic stress disorder. Phobias trigger such severe anxiety that psychiatrists sometimes have trouble drawing a line between the two conditions. About 15 per cent of the general population develops an anxiety disorder that could qualify as a phobia, including simple phobia (generalised fear), claustrophobia (fear of cramped quarters), and agoraphobia (fear of going out, being in open places, or both). Agoraphobia is frequently accompanied by panic disorder, a condition characterised by severe and recurrent anxiety attacks.

The other two anxiety disorders are somewhat less common, but no less debilitating. Obsessive-compulsive disorder involves the ritualistic repetition of certain behaviours, such as hand washing. Post-traumatic stress disorder causes confusion, anxiety, and related symptoms in those who have survived emotionally catastrophic events.

People who have phobias, obsessive-compulsive disorder, or post-traumatic stress disorder should absolutely be under a doctor's (preferably a psychiatrist's) care. But even these conditions can benefit from the same herbal and lifestyle approaches routinely recommended to relieve simple stress and anxiety.

Take Steps to Protect Your Mind and Body

Many of the strategies that form the foundation of an anti-ageing lifestyle not only relieve stress and anxiety but also minimise the effects of these and related conditions on your physical and mental health. I recommend the following:

Adopt the eating habits of your ancestors. As I mentioned above, stress and anxiety impair immune function. You can bolster your body's defences by eating plenty of fruits, vegetables, grains, and beans. Plant foods supply the antioxidant nutrients that reinforce your immune system. These same foods are the cornerstone of the low-fat, high-fibre, near-vegetarian diet eaten by our Palaeolithic ancestors.

My Healthy Sevens eating plan adopts and expands on the fundamental principles of the Palaeolithic diet. To learn more about the Healthy Sevens, refer to chapter 3.

Get some supplemental support. While nutritional supplements can't compensate for a poor diet, they can provide added insurance when you're feeling stressed or anxious. You may want to take extra zinc and the antioxidant nutrients: vitamins C and E, beta-carotene, and the mineral selenium. The B vitamins are important, too, since research suggests that they're depleted by chronic stress.

Rather than taking a fistful of individual pills, perhaps your best bet is to choose one good-quality daily multivitamin/mineral supplement. Look for a formula that contains extra amounts of the antioxidants.

Reduce your caffeine intake. If you're a caffeine junkie, all that caffeine might be aggravating your feelings of stress and anxiety. Consider weaning yourself off the caffeinated beverage herbs – not just coffee but also tea, kola, maté, and guarana.

But don't quit cold turkey, or you may set yourself up for several days of caffeine withdrawal symptoms, such as headache and constipation. Instead, reduce your caffeine intake gradually. For example, mix a little decaf into your regular coffee each day for several weeks, until you're drinking all decaf. You can do the same with regular and caffeine-free cola.

Cocoa also contains caffeine, but in much smaller amounts. Still, if you're very sensitive to caffeine, you may want to consider giving up cocoa.

Limit your alcohol consumption. Alcohol is a major depressant. It also impairs immune function. Since stress has the same effects, drinking only makes matters worse. Your system doesn't need the aggravation.

More Wisdom *from the* Garden

For Stress Relief, Just Follow Your Nose

Aromatherapy, a popular offshoot of herbal medicine, uses plants' aromatic oils to enhance health. It's especially effective at inducing relaxation and short-circuiting stress.

At Memorial Sloan-Kettering Cancer Center in New York City, researchers measured the anxiety levels of people about to undergo an MRI, a diagnostic procedure that requires lying still inside a cramped, noisy, cigar-shaped chamber. Some of the patients took whiffs of heliotropin, a vanilla-like fragrance that aromatherapists consider relaxing. Compared with those who didn't inhale the oil, those who did showed a 63 per cent decline in their anxiety levels.

For stress reduction, aromatherapists recommend a variety of essential oils, including anise, basil, bay, camomile, eucalyptus, lavender, peppermint, rose, and thyme. Just place a few pieces of rock salt in a small vial, then add a few drops of the oil of your choice. (The rock salt absorbs the oil, which prevents spilling.) Cap the vial and keep it handy. Then when you need some instant relaxation, remove the cap and inhale deeply.

You can also blend one or more essential oils into a massage lotion for a soothing aromatherapy self-massage. Or add a few drops of oil to your bathwater for a calming soak. (You don't need to use a lot of essential oil to experience its effects. It's quite potent.)

Engage in regular, moderate physical activity. In my opinion, exercise is a wonderful stress and anxiety reducer. When I'm feeling tense or anxious, I go outside and dig around in my Garden of Youth, or I pedal my stationary bicycle. Something about moving my body and working up a sweat makes me feel calm and relaxed.

Practise deep breathing. Another advantage of exercise is that it forces you to breathe deeply, which promotes relaxation. But even if you're not working out, you can use deep breathing to control stress.

Sometimes when I'm driving, I do what's called a Masogi breathing exercise. I inhale through my nose and slowly exhale through my mouth, continuing for 10 to 15 minutes. I think it helps.

Experiment with meditation. Many studies have shown that meditation reduces stress and elevates mood. It also lowers blood pressure and helps control chronic pain, which is often a major source of stress and anxiety.

Of course, meditation is just one way of achieving deep relaxation. You may prefer to use biofeedback, self-hypnosis, massage, prayer, tai chi, or yoga. All of these techniques are helpful.

Relax with the Calming Herbs

A number of herbs have long-standing reputations for taking the edge off stress and anxiety. In my opinion, these work best.

CAMOMILE (*MATRICARIA RECUTITA*). Camomile contains apigenin, a compound that binds to the same cell receptors as pharmaceutical tranquillizers and has similar effects. The difference is that apigenin doesn't cause serious sedation or morning-after grogginess, nor does it pose a risk of addiction.

Another compound in camomile, bisabolol, relaxes the digestive tract. In this way, it relieves indigestion, a common physical symptom of stress.

In a Japanese study, researchers exposed experimentally stressed laboratory animals to camomile oil. Compared with a group of untreated animals, those that inhaled the oil's vapours had lower levels of stress hormones.

I have the annual variety of camomile in my garden. The plant produces small, daisylike flowers that, when crushed, give off an apple aroma. To prepare camomile tea, use 2 to 3 heaped teaspoons of the flowers per cup of freshly boiled water. Steep for 10 minutes, then strain. Allow to cool before drinking. You can also add a handful of the flowers to a hot bath and inhale the soothing scent.

VALERIAN (*VALERIANA OFFICINALIS*). Valerian root is best known as a herbal sedative. But it also has an age-old reputation for relieving stress, anxiety, and nervous tension. The herb's active compounds, called valepotriates, are both tranquillizing and sedative, depending on the dose.

For insomnia associated with stress and anxiety, the recommended dosage of valerian is one or two 470–500-milligram capsules of powdered root. Unlike some pharmaceutical sleeping pills, valerian has no life-threatening side effects, even when taken in large, sedative amounts (but see page 521 if you are planning to take it).

My valerian grows by my barn in what I call Stress-Sedative Alley, with camomile, hop, passionflower, and lavender nearby. (I'll discuss the latter three herbs in just a bit.) Valerian is an attractive perennial with little white flowers that smell bad, but not as bad as the root, which stinks.

ST. JOHN'S WORT (*HYPERICUM PERFORATUM*). St. John's wort has become

Dr Duke's Anti-Ageing Elixir

Stress-Buster Tea

This tea is made with the most palatable of the calming herbs. Blended together, they'll defuse stress and anxiety and promote sound sleep.

WHAT YOU NEED

1 teaspoon camomile flowers
1 teaspoon lavender flowers
1 teaspoon lemon balm leaves
1 teaspoon marjoram
1 spray valerian flowers
1 litre (2 pints) water

WHAT TO DO

In a large saucepan, steep the camomile, lavender, lemon balm, marjoram, and valerian to taste in the freshly boiled water. Strain out the plant material. Drink the tea hot or cool as often as needed, refrigerating any left over for later use.

famous for its antidepressant properties, but it's also able to prevent and treat stress and anxiety.

Most of the studies that examined St. John's wort as a treatment for depression used 300 milligrams of an extract containing 0.3 per cent hypericin, one the herb's active ingredients, three times a day. I'd recommend the same dosage for relieving stress or anxiety. But be patient: St. John's wort needs 4 to 6 weeks to impart its mood-elevating effects.

St. John's wort is a lovely plant that produces bright yellow flowers with purplish dots. Poetically, the dots symbolise the blood of St. John, because the plant blooms around St. John's Day, June 24th.

HOP (*HUMULUS LUPULUS*). The herb best known for giving beer a bitter taste is also a potent stress and anxiety reducer. Folktales abound of hop pickers falling asleep on the job. This comes as no surprise, since hop is a botanical relative of marijuana. It's *not* psychoactive, however.

According to research, hop's effects can range from calming to sedative, depending on the dosage. Experiment to find the right dosage for yourself. I suggest starting with a hop tea. Use ½ teaspoon of the herb per cup of freshly boiled water and steep for 10 minutes. Strain before drinking. If the tea doesn't produce the desired level of relaxation, increase the amount of herb next time around.

Hop is a vigorous, weedy climbing plant. My plant makes its home on Stress-Sedative Alley.

PASSIONFLOWER (*PASSIFLORA INCARNATA*). This herb gets its name not from passion of a romantic nature but from the Passion of Christ, the period between the Last Supper and the Crucifixion. Native peoples from the Andes to the Gulf Coast used various species of passionflower to soothe their nerves. Eventually, the herb was adopted into American herbalism.

Oddly, passionflower contains both tranquillizing compounds and stimulants. But researchers consider the herb's net effect to be tranquillizing.

In Europe, passionflower is an ingredient in many tranquillizing and sedative preparations. The herb is both non-narcotic and non-addictive. To make a pleasant-tasting tea, add 1 teaspoon of dried leaves to a cup

for the
Gardener

St. John's Wort

Hypericum perforatum

St. John's wort is a short-lived perennial that may need to be replanted every couple of years. To speed the germination of seeds, I suggest putting them in a plastic bag with some sand and refrigerating them for 2 weeks. Then press them into a flat of moist, very sandy soil.

If you live in a region with cold winters, plant the seedlings in the spring. In milder climates, plant them in the autumn. They need well-drained soil and do best in full sun, though they'll tolerate sparse shade. Place the seedlings 60 cm (24 in) apart, with 60 cm (24 in) between rows. Water regularly during their first year.

Harvest St. John's wort when the plants are in full bud and open flower. Cut off the top 25–30 cm (10 to 12 in) of each plant on a sunny morning, after the dew has dried. Tie the plants into small bundles and hang them in a dark, warm area to dry. Remove and discard the stems before using.

of freshly boiled water and steep for 10 minutes. Strain before drinking.

Passionflower is a vine that produces one of the most beautiful, complex blooms in nature. My vine spreads all over Stress-Sedative Alley.

LAVENDER (*LAVANDULA,* VARIOUS SPECIES). Lovely lavender contains compounds that bind to the same cell receptors as the Valium family of tranquillisers, suggesting that the herb has a similar effect. Lavender has a long folk tradition as a calming herb. It's a favourite among aromatherapists for stress reduction and anxiety relief.

To make a lavender tea, use 1 teaspoon of powdered herb per cup of freshly boiled water. Steep for 10 minutes, then strain and allow to cool before drinking.

My lavender plant is located on the south-facing slope of YinYang Valley. Its flower spikes are very aromatic. On a calm day, the plant is surrounded by a cloud of fragrance that can be almost overpowering.

Depression: Sadness That Accelerates Ageing

Along with stress and anxiety, depression can easily rob years from your life and life from your years. It's more than just 'the blues', that sense of disappointment when things don't work out quite as expected. It's more than the grief that follows the death of a loved one or some other devastating loss – this sort of sadness is normal, and with time, it usually subsides.

When sadness becomes permanent, when it takes the joy out of living, that's what the National Institute of Mental Health defines as depression. It's America's leading mental health problem. It's so common, in fact, that it's sometimes described as 'the common cold of mental illness'.

In any given year, 10 per cent of patients who visit their doctor are experiencing serious depression. The condition can strike at any age, but it's quite prevalent among older people. That's because compared with the younger generations, ours is more vulnerable to physical illness and more likely to experience the deaths of loved ones (spouses, relatives, and friends).

Depression itself isn't fatal. But the crushing despair it causes can drive people to commit suicide. In the United Kingdom approximately 6,300 people commit suicide each year and

Dr Duke's Anti-Ageing Elixir

Tranquilli-Tea

Feeling tense and uptight? Unwind with a cup of this tea, made with an abundance of calming herbs.

WHAT YOU NEED

1 litre (2 pints) water
Generous dash of lemon balm
Generous dash of clove
Generous dash of basil
Dash of valerian
Dash of hops
A few St. John's wort flowers
Lemon juice and peel
A natural sweetener

WHAT TO DO

Add the lemon balm, clove, basil, valerian, hops, and St. John's wort to a pan of freshly boiled water. Steep for 20 minutes, then strain. Add the lemon juice and peel, which are also tranquillizing and somewhat sedative. Sweeten if you wish. Drink a cup at a time, refrigerating any left over for later use.

More Wisdom *from the* Garden

History Supports These Calming Herbs

Herbal medicine has no shortage of natural tranquillizers. Among the herbs traditionally used for this purpose are catnip, eucalyptus, lemon balm, and skullcap. I don't discuss them here, because they've not been well-studied as preventives or treatments for stress and anxiety.

That said, all of these herbs are safe, and they make pleasant-tasting teas. Just use 1 teaspoon of the powdered herb of your choice per cup of freshly boiled water and let steep for 10 minutes. Strain before drinking.

it is estimated that more than 140,000 attempt it. The death rate from suicide equates to double the death toll of traffic accidents and twelve times the number of deaths from homicide.

These days, people who are diagnosed with depression are likely to be handed prescriptions for fluoxetine (Prozac), paroxetine (Seroxat), sertraline (Lustral), or another antidepressant. All of these pharmaceuticals are members of the same chemical family, the selective serotonin reuptake inhibitors (SSRIs). As the name suggests, these drugs change the way the brain uses serotonin, a chemical (neurotransmitter) that plays a major role in regulating mood.

Now I'm not opposed to SSRIs – they are clearly important. But these medications for fighting depression have side effects. Most common are sex problems – loss of libido in both genders, erection impairment in men, and vaginal dryness in women.

I happen to consider sexual intimacy a vital part of life, something that keeps us young. So in my mind, the benefits of SSRIs come at a high price.

For mild to moderate depression – that is, depression not severe enough to cause suicidal thoughts – I favour natural and herbal approaches over conventional drug treatment.

Lift Your Mood and Safeguard Your Health

Clinically speaking, depression and anxiety are two distinct conditions. But one is often a symptom of the other. Therefore, the lifestyle strategies that offset the effects of anxiety can do the same for depression.

If you're dealing with depression, you may benefit from the following:

Build your meals around plant foods. Depression impairs immune function even more than stress and anxiety do. So you need all the immune-boosting antioxidants that you can get. Your best sources are plant foods: fruits, vegetables, pulses, and whole grains.

Make sure your Bs are covered. University of Arizona researchers gave 14 elderly people with depression either antidepressant drugs plus a placebo or the drugs plus thiamin, riboflavin, and vitamin B_6 (10 milligrams of each per day). One month later, those who received the supplements showed greater improvement in their symptoms.

Other research has found that the B vitamin folic acid, also known as folate, produces a mood-elevating effect. According to Melvyn Werbach, M.D., a supplement expert whom I respect, even marginal deficiencies in certain B vitamins – including thiamin, riboflavin, B_6, B_{12}, and folic acid – can cause or aggravate depression.

The best food sources of the B vitamins are wholemeal breads and cereals. You can also take a supplement – 50 to 100 milligrams a day of a B-complex product that includes 25 to 300 micrograms of B_{12} and about 400 micrograms of folic acid.

Check for undiagnosed food sensitivities. Naturopath Joseph Pizzorno, N.D., cofounder and president of Bastyr University in Kenmore, Washington, describes a patient whose deep depression was triggered by a sensitivity to wheat. Such food sensitivities are fairly common.

If I were chronically depressed, I think I'd schedule an appointment with a naturopath. He could guide me through an elimination diet to identify any foods that might be affecting my mood.

Raise your spirits with coffee. While the caffeine can aggravate stress and anxiety, it also acts as a mild antidepressant. Drink as much

More Wisdom *from the* Garden

Tryptophan: Nature's Answer to Antidepressants

Some pharmaceutical antidepressants, notably the selective serotonin reuptake inhibitors (SSRIs), treat depression by altering brain levels of the neurotransmitter serotonin. You can achieve the same effect naturally by taking supplements of the amino acid tryptophan, which is a chemical precursor of serotonin.

I've been impressed by reports of tryptophan elevating mood in people with depression. Unfortunately, the amino acid got caught in the FDA's anti-supplement web.

Tryptophan is available in supplement forms. It was sold over the counter until the late 1980s, when a contaminated batch sickened a number of people and caused several deaths. When this happens to a drug, the FDA usually tells the manufacturer to add a warning to the label. But when it happened to tryptophan, the FDA banned the supplement.

Now the amino acid is available again – but only by prescription. At least it's available. If you want to try it, you'll need to ask your doctor about it. The usual dose is 1 to 2 grams three times a day, with meals.

as you can tolerate without bringing on caffeine jitters and insomnia.

Don't raise a glass of spirits. Alcohol is a powerful depressant. It's the last thing you need when you're dealing with depression.

Move your body at every opportunity. Exercise helps relieve depression in several ways. It releases endorphins, your body's own mood-elevating compounds. It reduces blood levels of cortisol, the bad-mood hormone. It helps put life in perspective. And it provides a sense of accomplishment, which raises self-esteem.

Many studies have demonstrated the positive relationship between exercise and depression. For example, at the Jean Mayer USDA Human Nutrition Research Center on Aging at Tufts University in Boston, researchers assigned 32 people over the age of 60 – all with mild to moderate depression – to one of two groups. One group enrolled in an exercise class, while the other made no lifestyle changes. After 10 weeks, the people who hadn't been working out showed no improvement in their symptoms. Among those in the exercise class, 14 of 16 felt significantly less depressed.

Which kind of physical activity can boost your mood most? Anything that you enjoy and can stick with. I potter around in my Garden of Youth and pedal my stationary cycle. You may prefer walking, square dancing, golfing, or something else. Just give it time to work: you need to commit to about a month of regular exercise before you notice any significant mood-elevating effect.

Find ways to unwind. The same relaxation therapies that defuse stress and anxiety – biofeedback, self-hypnosis, massage, prayer, tai chi, and yoga – can also ease depression. Personally, if I were mildly depressed, I'd try any of these techniques before resorting to pharmaceuticals.

I'd also try a little music therapy. I know that I get an emotional lift whenever I listen to my favourite recordings, which is fairly often.

Cultivate a support network. People who are depressed tend to withdraw from their family and friends. But at least one study has shown that maintaining these connections is essential to overcoming and even avoiding depression.

For the study, Duke University researchers tracked 506 people who had been hospitalised for heart disease, a condition that often triggers or aggravates depression. The more social contacts the patients had, the less likely they were to become depressed. Memberships in social and religious organisations had the same benefit.

Soak up some sunshine – with care. Doctors frequently use bright-light therapy to treat seasonal affective disorder, a form of depression that typically comes on in the fall and winter months. Now some research suggests this therapy can help relieve nonseasonal depression as well.

I get my daily dose of bright light by spending time in my Garden of Youth, soaking up the sunshine. Even in the winter, I'm outside in the garden, pottering around.

Of course, you have to be careful not to get too much sun, since that has health risks of its own. In general, I'd suggest avoiding sun exposure during the midday hours, when the rays are strongest. But do try to spend more time outdoors. I know that being out of doors never fails to boost my mood.

Discover the Herbal Mood-Boosters

Certain herbs act as natural antidepressants. If I were dealing with mild to moderate depression, I'd consider taking one of the following to lift my spirits.

ST. JOHN'S WORT (*HYPERICUM PERFORATUM*). Earlier I described St. John's wort as an effective preventive and treatment for stress and anxiety. The herb is also a natural SSRI. Many studies have concluded that St. John's wort relieves mild to moderate depression about as well as the pharmaceuticals.

Recently, researchers from Texas and Germany joined forces to analyse 23 studies of St. John's wort and its effects on depression. Among people who had taken placebos, 22 per cent experienced significant mood elevation. Among those who had taken St. John's wort, 55 per cent reported the same results. This figure is consistent with what's expected from pharmaceutical antidepressants. The difference is that St. John's wort has fewer side effects.

If you've been diagnosed with depression or you think you might have depression and you'd like to try St. John's wort, discuss it with your doctor first. The herb should not be taken in combination with pharmaceutical antidepressants.

GINKGO (*GINKGO BILOBA*). Ginkgo is best known for improving bloodflow through the brain, which helps minimise the effects of stroke and maybe Alzheimer's disease. The herb also normalises neurotransmitter levels in the brain, which makes it an appropriate treatment for depression.

In one study, German researchers recruited 40 elderly people with depression who had not responded well to conventional drug treatment. Half of the volunteers received a placebo, while the rest were given 80 milligrams of ginkgo three times a day. After 8 weeks, those in the placebo group showed negligible mood elevation, while those in the ginkgo group reported major benefits.

If you want to try ginkgo for yourself, I'd suggest buying one of the many commercial preparations available and taking it according to the label directions.

CHAPTER 22

Smooth Skin

Dr Duke's Anti-Ageing Elixir
• Smoothing Skin Cream

Along with grey hair, wrinkles are one of the most visible signs of ageing. They're also one of the most dreaded. That's why cosmetics companies stand to make a small fortune on 'revolutionary new formulas' that promise to erase those lines and creases and make us look years younger.

The fact is that many of these products do help. But they wouldn't be necessary if we just took a little better care of our skin, protecting it from the sun and other assorted environmental assaults. If we did that, we could easily avoid wrinkles and preserve our skin's youthful vibrancy.

Where Wrinkles Come From

In their own way, wrinkles are rather fascinating. The better we understand them, the better we can prevent and treat them.

Wrinkles result from changes in collagen, the fibrous material that's responsible for holding your skin together. Actually, collagen holds the entire human body together. It accounts for about one-third of your body's total protein and 70 per cent of the mass of connective tissue – your skin, tendons, ligaments, and so on.

In young skin, the collagen is mostly soluble, meaning that it can absorb water. It's also flexible – in other words, the strands of protein are loosely bound in the skin matrix and can move. As the collagen absorbs body fluid, it swells a little and moves a little, creating smooth, elastic, nonwrinkled skin.

In older skin, chemical changes occur to make collagen less soluble and less flexible. It no longer absorbs as much fluid, nor can it move as well. As a result, the skin loses its smoothness, and the lines and creases that we know as wrinkles begin to appear. They can show up anywhere, but they're most common in areas exposed to sunlight: your face, your neck, and the backs of your hands.

One way in which anti-wrinkle formulas, skin creams, and moisturisers work their magic is by increasing the amount of water – moisture – in your skin. While ageing collagen is less soluble than younger collagen, it's not completely insoluble. If it's exposed to concentrated fluid, it still absorbs some and swells a tad, which helps fight wrinkles.

But you won't get the same effect by holding your face under the shower spray. Plain old water can't get to where the collagen is. You need an oily carrier that can penetrate your skin. That's why commercial anti-wrinkle products contain ingredients called emollients – to deliver the water straight to the collagen. Emollients also soften your skin, enhancing its flexibility, another defence against wrinkles.

While emollients help, they can't reverse the chemical changes that rob collagen of its solubility and flexibility. These changes occur because of oxidative damage to your skin, the same kind of cellular destruction that sets the stage for so many age-related ailments, including heart disease, many cancers, Alzheimer's disease, and cataracts.

Fortunately, you can prevent oxidative damage – or at least slow it down quite considerably – by eating foods rich in antioxidants: vitamins C and E, the carotenoids (including beta-carotene), and the mineral selenium. These nutrients come almost exclusively from plant foods – the fruits, vegetables, pulses, and whole grains that were the foundation of the Palaeolithic diet. They're also the cornerstone of my Healthy Sevens eating plan. (To learn more about the Healthy Sevens, see chapter 3.)

Incidentally, you've probably noticed that many anti-wrinkle preparations are made with vitamin E derivatives. Now you know why: applied topically, some of the antioxidant penetrates into your skin to defend against cellular damage and to keep collagen soluble and flexible.

Your Personal Anti-Wrinkle Plan

Building your meals around antioxidant-rich plant foods is just one way to safeguard your skin against wrinkling. These measures can help, too.

Eat lots of dark-coloured fruits. When you're out shopping for plant foods, be sure to pick up a variety of dark-skinned fruits: blackberries, blueberries, grapes, plums, prunes, raisins, and raspberries. They get their colour from anthocyanidins, natural pigments that are also potent antioxidants. You may also be able to find concentrates of these fruits in health food shops.

Increase your antioxidant intake with a supplement. Many drugstores and health food stores now carry antioxidant formulas. While I've not seen any studies showing that these pills can erase wrinkles, I'll bet that they help with prevention.

Pack away the cigarettes. Smoking loads the blood with compounds that cause oxidative damage, which accelerates wrinkling. Just look at the face of a longtime smoker, and you'll see the results.

Protect yourself from the sun. I'll cover sunburn in greater detail a bit later in this chapter. For now, suffice it to say that sunburn is a primary cause of the skin damage that leads to wrinkling. Applying sunscreen whenever you head outdoors is a good start, but in the summer, it may not be enough. Try to stay in the shade during the midday hours, when the sun's rays are strongest. If you're out in the sun, wear a broad-brimmed hat and lightweight clothing that covers as much of your skin as possible.

During the summer months, on those days when I intend to spend more than 15 minutes working in my Garden of Youth, I always wear a broad-brimmed hat and long-sleeved shirt, and maybe long trousers. I also wear gloves much of the time. When I don't, I rub some sunscreen on my hands.

Sleep on your back. When you lie with your face smashed against a pillow night after night, year after year, it can contribute to the formation of wrinkles or worsen existing lines and creases.

Topical Tactics for Eliminating Lines

Mother Nature has developed her own line of anti-wrinkle preparations. Before you head to the cosmetics counter and shell out big bucks for a synthetic skin-smoother, you may want to try one of these herbal alternatives.

GOTU KOLA (*CENTELLA ASIATICA*). In studies, gotu kola has proven effective in strengthening collagen and other connective tissue in the skin. I suggest buying a standardised extract containing 40 per cent asiaticosides and massaging it into your skin. For best results, combine the extract with an emollient (see below). You can also take the extract internally, up to 120 milligrams a day.

I grow gotu kola in my Garden of Youth, and I often nibble on two or three of its spicy leaves. They're like little green coins hugging the soil and rocks around my pond. That's why the plant is sometimes called moneywort.

NATURAL EMOLLIENTS. There are many natural emollients, but the skin absorbs some better than others. Those that are well-absorbed include avocado oil, castor oil, coconut oil, cod liver oil, lanolin, and olive oil.

But the best emollients are cocoa butter and jojoba butter. They contain essential fatty acids, which help them penetrate the skin.

Cocoa butter is a superb moisturiser and skin softener. It is solid at room temperature but melts when you rub it into your skin, which is warmer. Jojoba has similar properties. Add gotu kola to one of these emollients, and you have a potent wrinkle-fighting cream.

You can buy cocoa butter in many health food shops. Jojoba butter isn't as widely available, but I'd suggest trying it if you can find it.

FRUIT ACIDS. You probably know fruit acids by their more common name, alpha hydroxy acids. They're derived from fruits such as grapes (tartaric acid), citrus (citric acid), and apples (malic acid). According to legend, fruits have been used since the days of Cleopatra to beautify the skin.

Fruit acids work by removing dead skin cells and hydrating living cells. Many cosmetics manufacturers put the acids in their skin-care products at concentrations of 4 to 10 per cent. Dermatologists use much higher concentrations – 30 per cent and more – to remove the dead skin cells associated with age spots and scars. But for wrinkles, such high concentrations may actually damage the skin.

If you'd like to try fruit acids on your skin, buy a commercial preparation in a health food shop and follow the package directions. Be careful not to leave the preparation on your skin longer than directed.

If I were in the Amazon, I'd get my fruit acids straight from the source by applying mashed papaya to my face. You can get fruit acids from tamarind rind as well.

Dr Duke's Anti-Ageing Elixir

Smoothing Skin Cream

A number of herbs help fight wrinkles by strengthening collagen and other connective tissue in your skin. Besides gotu kola, the anti-wrinkle arsenal includes fennel, ginkgo, horse chestnut, meadowsweet, and pineapple. I grow every one of them, even the pineapple, which is a tropical plant.

If you want to make your own anti-wrinkle cream, I recommend this basic recipe.

WHAT YOU NEED

2 horse chestnut seeds
Several fennel seeds
1 avocado, halved, pitted, and pulp scooped out

WHAT TO DO

In a food processor, grind up the horse chestnut seeds. Throw in the fennel and avocado (an emollient). I'd blend the ingredients until they're a smooth consistency. Apply the cream as often as you wish. (Never, ever take fresh horse chestnut internally. It's poisonous.)

growing younger naturally

A Herbal Trio Spared Him from Surgery

Keratoses are small, warty growths that become more common with age. Unfortunately, they sometimes turn into malignant melanomas.

When my friend Bill Thomson, former editor of *Natural Health* magazine, developed a keratosis, he took his treatment into his own hands. Here's his story.

'In 1998, a keratosis appeared on my chest. My doctor said, "Let's get rid of that, just to be safe." She wanted to either burn it or cut it out.

'Instead, I applied a small amount of fresh garlic oil, fresh aloe gel, and bloodroot tincture, all in combination. Then I covered the keratosis with the section of aloe leaf that I had taken the gel from.

'After two evenings of treatment, the keratosis withered and fell off. It has shown no signs of returning.'

Sunburn: Make Aloe Your First Line of Defence

As I mentioned earlier, sunburn damages your skin in such a way that it promotes the formation of wrinkles. So if you want to stay wrinkle-free, you should do what you can to avoid excessive sun exposure.

That said, you don't want to shun the sun completely. Some sun exposure is actually good for you. For example, your body needs to soak up rays in order to manufacture vitamin D. But it doesn't need much – just 20 minutes of sun exposure a day (on a sunny day).

So if you're going to be outside longer than that, especially during the summer months, take extra precautions. Stay in the shade as much as possible. Wear lightweight clothing that covers as much skin as possible, as well as a wide-brimmed hat, which is especially good for protecting your face and neck. And above all else, use sunscreen.

You can buy a commercial sunscreen, if you like (most experts tell you to use products with an SPF of 15 or more). But you might also consider some of the herbal skin-protectors.

At the top of my list is aloe. The creamy gel found inside the herb's leaves has a long-standing reputation as a treatment for minor burns. My wife, Peggy, keeps a potted aloe plant on our kitchen window sill. On those rare occasions when she burns herself, she cuts open a leaf and squeezes the gel onto her injured skin.

Research has shown that aloe gel is anaesthetic, anti-inflammatory, and antibiotic – all properties that can help heal minor burns. The typical dose for topical application is 1 tablespoon of gel three times a day.

While I've known for decades that aloe can treat minor burns, I never realised that it could prevent sunburn until a trip to Kenya some years ago. My guide cut off an aloe leaf and suggested that I apply the creamy yellowish gel to areas of my skin that were likely to get burned. This was the first time anyone had suggested using aloe as a sunscreen to me personally. To be scientific, I applied the gel to one arm but not the other. My guide was right: the untreated arm got burned, while the arm coated with aloe gel did not.

Aloe as a sunscreen seems to be catching on. Andrew Weil, M.D., a conventionally trained doctor who supports herbal medicine, recommends Aloe-Gator gel, an American commercial preparation with an SPF of 40 (you can get this on the Internet if you can't find it locally). In their book *Prescription for Nutritional Healing,* James Balch, M.D.,

More Wisdom *from the* Garden

Soothe Sunburned Skin from the Inside Out

Studies have shown that sunburn produces oxidative damage, the kind of cell-level devastation that's responsible for many of the diseases associated with ageing. Not surprisingly, antioxidant nutrients can help speed the healing of sunburned skin and possibly reduce the risk of wrinkling. So eat plenty of antioxidant-rich plant foods and consider taking an antioxidant supplement.

and his wife, Phyllis Balch, suggest using aloe gel for sunburn – three or four liberal applications a day to spur healing and reduce pain and scarring.

In addition to the aloe that Peggy keeps in the kitchen, I have several plants myself. I grow them in pots because they can't tolerate the Maryland winters. I leave them outdoors all summer and part of spring and autumn, then move them into the greenhouse the rest of the year.

Anyone can grow aloe. All that the plants need is light and a little water. Occasionally snipping off a leaf for medicinal purposes won't do any harm.

Herbs to Soothe Burned Skin

Among the other herbs that can prevent and treat sunburn are two members of the daisy family: camomile and calendula, or marigold. Both are anti-inflammatory and antiseptic, and both have been approved as treatments for sunburn by Commission E, the expert panel that evaluates the safety and effectiveness of herbs for the German government.

You can make a tea by adding several teaspoons of either herb to a cup of freshly boiled water and allowing it to steep for 10 minutes. Make sure that the tea has cooled off before applying it as a compress. You can use this method to prevent sunburn as well as to treat it.

Like camomile and calendula, St. John's wort is anti-inflammatory and antiseptic. It, too, may help relieve the discomfort of sunburn. You can apply the herb as a compress, following the directions above.

And let's not forget echinacea. An immune system stimulant, echinacea helps the body repair skin that's been damaged by the sun. It also contains several compounds – with names like caffeic acid, chlorogenic acid, cichoric acid, cynarin, echinacoside, and rutin – that protect collagen. You can buy a commercial echinacea extract or tincture and use it according to the label directions.

Dermatitis: Annoying at Any Age

Because your skin gets drier as you get older, you may be more vulnerable to dermatitis, an umbrella term that refers to any inflammation of the skin. I sometimes experience flare-ups in the winter months, when the air tends to be dry.

Dermatitis can also be triggered by an allergic reaction (sometimes called atopic dermatitis or eczema) or by contact with something that irritates your skin (such as poison ivy, oak, or sumac). No matter what its cause, dermatitis produces a telltale redness of your skin, often accompanied by swelling, blistering, and itching.

For atopic dermatitis, the three-star herbal remedy is also the centrepiece of my Garden of Youth: evening primrose. In studies, oral doses of evening primrose oil improved all clinical measures of atopic dermatitis, especially itchiness. The herb gets its therapeutic power from the gamma-linolenic acid (GLA) that it contains.

Personally, when I feel that I need a dose of evening primrose oil, I take two capsules of a commercial product. You can also buy topical preparations containing 12.5 per cent evening primrose oil. Applied externally, these products can help heal skin made dry and scaly by atopic dermatitis.

Evening primrose oil has shown some promise in preventing atopic dermatitis as well. I've seen studies in which people applied a topical

for the Gardener

Evening Primrose

Oenothera biennis

In the fall of their second year, the tall stalks of evening primrose (a biennial) bear elongated capsules filled with small, oil-containing black seeds. You can sow these seeds directly into a sunny, well-drained area of your garden if you live in a hot climate. They may germinate within 15 to 20 days, as long as the soil temperature stays between 21°C and 29°C (70° and 85°F.)

Much like the seeds, the seedlings of evening primrose thrive in full sun to light shade and in well-drained to dry soil. They require little, if any, care. I estimate that a big, healthy evening primrose plant can produce 30 g (1 oz) or more of tiny edible seeds.

preparation to one leg but not the other. Compared with the untreated leg, the treated leg was significantly less likely to develop inflammation and itching.

Besides evening primrose oil, good sources of GLA include borage oil and currant oil. If you wish to try either of these herbs, I suggest buying a commercial product and using it according to the label directions.

I also recommend trying camomile and calendula for relief from atopic dermatitis, because of their anti-inflammatory properties. You can apply either herb as a compress, using a tea made by steeping several teaspoons of the herb in a cup of freshly boiled water for 10 minutes. Make sure that the tea has cooled before putting it on the affected skin.

I don't know of any herbal remedies for dry-skin dermatitis. For myself, I use a cream that contains aloe and vitamin E. It seems to help. If it didn't, I'd try oral doses of vitamin E – 400 IU a day – based on an anecdotal report that appeared in the prestigious British medical journal *The Lancet* a few years ago. It seems that a physician who had begun taking vitamin E supplements to reduce his risk of heart disease found that the supplements also cleared up his severe dry-skin dermatitis. I might also treat my dry skin with a good natural emollient, like avocado oil.

CHAPTER 23

Healthy Teeth *and* Gums

Dr Duke's Anti-Ageing Elixirs

- *Basic Dental Brew*
- *Homemade Herbal Mouthwash*
- *Good-for-Your-Gums Rinse*

Among youngsters, tooth decay remains a major health issue. Even though the addition of fluoride to community water supplies reduced the rate of cavities substantially, as recently as a decade ago, an estimated 98 per cent of American children under the age of 16 had at least one filling. These days, dentists apply plastic sealants to youngsters' teeth to provide even greater protection against decay.

We grown-ups are lucky in that we don't have much of a problem with cavities, or dental caries. Oh, we still get them, especially when old fillings crack or otherwise wear out, allowing pesky tooth-rotting bacteria (notably *Streptococcus mutans, S. faecalis, S. salivarius*, and *S.*

sanguis) to invade areas where brushing and flossing can't reach.

As unpleasant as tooth decay is, it's not the primary dental woe among us older folks. That dubious distinction belongs to gum disease.

According to the estimates that I've read, about 75 per cent of American adults have some degree of gum disease, or gingivitis. Even more troubling, almost half of American adults don't receive annual dental exams, through which the condition could be detected and treated. And that's unfortunate, because without treatment, gum disease just gets worse and worse.

Unlike cavities, gum disease doesn't hurt. In fact, it's hardly noticeable until it becomes quite severe. But little by little, it erodes the roots of your teeth. Eventually, your teeth start to feel a little loose – but by then, it may be too late to save them.

Getting to the Root of Gum Disease

Have you ever wondered why television has so many commercials for denture-care products? It's because tens of millions of people wear dentures, having lost their teeth to gum disease.

I still have most of my teeth, though I've had so many crowns put in that I'm a walking gold mine. My older brother has all of his teeth; my younger brother, none of his. I attribute this to carbonated soft drinks. Our family couldn't afford them until I was about 8 years old, so my older brother didn't consume much soda as a kid. I drank more than he did, and my younger brother drank even more than I.

What's the connection between soda and gum disease? The bacteria that cause gum disease thrive on sugar. They're the same bacteria that cause cavities – only they're finding their way beneath the gum line to the roots of your teeth.

When you're young, your gum tissue forms a tight seal around your teeth, effectively keeping out bacteria. But over the years, this seal gradually weakens, allowing bacteria inside.

While brushing and flossing get rid of quite a lot of the bacteria, even regular dental hygiene doesn't go deep enough to clear out all of the germs. Those that linger in your mouth attack the roots of your teeth, setting the stage for problems in the future.

Dentists have a few different methods of treating gum disease. In the most minor cases, they can remove some bacteria and diseased gum tissue using just a scraper and water-rinse gun, which you may be familiar with from your dental visits. In mild to moderate cases, they may apply a gingival rinse. This involves squirting an antibiotic fluid underneath your gum line.

For moderate to severe gum disease, dentists may recommend gum reduction surgery. Both my wife, Peggy, and I have had it (but Peggy got such a serious infection the last time that she refuses to go through it again). In this procedure, which is performed under a local anaesthetic, the dentist cuts back your gums to remove the diseased tissue. A new gum line is established, and a healthy new seal may form between your teeth and gums.

While gum reduction surgery is effective, it's not pleasant. The procedure itself lasts several hours and requires a week or two of recovery. What's more, it can leave your teeth looking longer. That's not where the phrase 'long in the tooth' came from, but it fits.

Prevention Begins with Brushing and Flossing

Of course, given a choice between gum reduction surgery and tooth loss, I opted for the surgery. An even better choice is prevention.

Dentists can't say enough about the protective power of good oral hygiene. Most recommend brushing and flossing after every meal. That can be a challenge, especially if you're a grazer like I am. I know lots of folks whom I consider very health conscious, and I can't think of a single one who brushes and flosses three times a day. Since I retired, I'm better about brushing three times a day. But I admit that I'm a lackadaisical flosser.

Even so, I'd say give it your best shot. Remember, I've had gum reduction surgery – twice. Had I been more rigorous about brushing and flossing, I may have spared myself that experience.

Speaking of flossing, you've probably noticed that some brands of floss are flavoured with mint or cinnamon. When you use flavoured

More Wisdom *from the* Garden

For Healthy Teeth and Gums, Say 'Cheese'

If you're fond of cheese, here's some news that you'll love: eating as little as 15 g (½ oz) of cheese after a sugary food or sweet fruit can reduce its cavity- and gum-disease-causing potential significantly.

In Mediterranean countries such as France and Italy, people routinely end their meals with a plate of fruit and cheese. The fruit not only provides a satisfying sweetness but also gets saliva flowing, which helps cleanse the mouth of food particles that contribute to tooth decay and gum disease.

I often top off meals with a crisp apple and a slice of mature cheese. For extra insurance, I try to brush and floss afterwards.

floss, you get a little taste of the mint or cinnamon oil that's embedded in the string. But the oil isn't there just to refresh your breath. It's also powerfully antimicrobial.

The aromatic oils in herbs such as mint and cinnamon protect the plants against assault by microorganisms. When added to floss, these oils help kill the bacteria that cause gum disease. So when you're shopping for floss, I highly recommend buying the flavoured kind.

The Dynamic Duo of Dental Health

Mint and cinnamon are tasty antibacterials. But they're not the only herbs – or even the most potent herbs – for stamping out gum-disease-causing bacteria. To take care of your teeth and gums, I'd recommend tea and bloodroot.

TEA (*CAMELLIA SINENSIS*). The shrub known as tea is available in two forms: *black* and *green*, terms that refer to the herb's preparation. Black tea is made from fermented tea leaves. It's most popular in Europe and the United States. Asian countries favour green tea, which is made from unfermented leaves.

Tea contains antibacterial compounds called tannins and catechins.

A study by Japanese scientists – most tea research comes from Asia – has shown that both of these compounds have antibacterial synergy. In other words, they're more potent together than individually – about 100 times more potent. This finding bolsters my long-held belief that the herbal 'shotgun' is better than the pharmaceutical 'bullet', in which one compound is isolated and then developed into a drug.

Tannins aren't just antibacterial. Like other polyphenols, they help prevent the formation of dental plaque. This is the hard, sticky stuff that coats teeth and provides sustenance for bacteria.

In addition, researchers have determined that tea contains an unusually large amount of the mineral fluorine. Public health agencies routinely add fluoride to drinking water, a practice that has generated its share of controversy. But tea is nature's own fluoridation, helping to strengthen teeth against decay and calcium loss. Both green and black teas have fluorine, though the green variety may have more.

South Carolina has a number of tea plantations. That's where I get the tea plants for my Garden of Youth. I have to pot them and move them into the greenhouse over winter.

You don't have to grow your own tea. You can buy both the black and green varieties in tea bag form in supermarkets and health food shops.

Incidentally, tea is not the only plant rich in tannins and catechins. These gum-disease-fighting compounds are widely dispersed throughout the plant kingdom. (Any plant that's astringent –

Dr Duke's Anti-Ageing **Elixir**

Basic Dental Brew

By themselves, black and green teas contain an astonishing array of compounds that protect your teeth and gums. This recipe pairs tea with two other dental herbs: thyme and licorice.

WHAT YOU NEED

1 tea bag
1 cup water
Thyme
Powdered licorice root (optional)

WHAT TO DO

Just brew yourself a cup of tea. Add a pinch or two of thyme for an antiseptic boost. Sweeten, if desired, with powdered licorice root, an antibacterial.

raspberry leaf, for example – contains tannins.) Since my Healthy Sevens eating plan is plant-based, I bet that it could help keep teeth and gums healthy. (To learn more about the Healthy Sevens, see chapter 3.)

BLOODROOT (*SANGUINARIA OFFICINALIS*). Bloodroot gets its name from the red juice in its roots. The herb is also the source of sanguinarine, a powerful anti-plaque compound. Many rigorous studies have shown that sanguinarine fights tooth decay and gum disease. This is why the compound is the active ingredient in some over-the-counter plaque-fighting mouthwashes.

I have a special fondness for bloodroot because it grows all over the place around here. It has certainly made itself at home in YinYang Valley. Bloodroot was used by the Native Americans of this area, who introduced it to the colonists. According to one local legend, Indian maidens adorned their faces with bloodroot's red juice to make themselves attractive to Captain John Smith and his troops. Another story suggests that Indian warriors used bloodroot paint on their bodies to frighten their enemies during combat.

I have no idea if these tales are true. But I know for a fact that bloodroot is an important herb for oral hygiene. The Native Americans chewed the root for dental health. I've experimented with that myself, but I wouldn't recommend it. It's a lot easier to use a commercial preparation.

Herbs That Keep You Smiling Bright

Besides tea and bloodroot, several other herbs have properties that are good for your teeth and gums. You may want to add some of the following to your personal dental-care regime.

EUCALYPTUS (*EUCALYPTUS GLOBULUS*). Eucalyptus leaves are very aromatic, which suggests that they're filled with antibacterial compounds. In one study, a tincture of eucalyptus effectively killed strains of bacteria involved in the development of cavities and gum disease.

Whenever I visit Australia, I chew young eucalyptus leaves both for dental hygiene and to prevent bad breath. Back home, I steep a handful of crushed leaves in about a ½ litre (1 pint) or so of cheap vodka and

250 ml (½ pint) of water for a few weeks, then strain out the plant material and use the resulting tincture as a mouthwash.

LICORICE (*GLYCYRRHIZA GLABRA*). In addition to the antibacterial sweetener glycyrrhizin, licorice contains the synergizer indole, which can boost the cavity-preventing power of compounds in other herbs.

As an example, consider tea, with its antibacterial polyphenols. The indole in licorice (along with other compounds called sesquiterpene hydrocarbons) increases the bacteria-fighting power of the polyphenols in tea more than a hundredfold. So add just a pinch or two of powdered licorice root to your tea, and you'll do your teeth and gums a major service.

NEEM (*AZADIRACHTA INDICA*). Millions of Africans and Asian Indians use sticks from the neem tree as 'tooth twigs' to massage their gums and prevent gum disease. There's lots of anecdotal evidence to support this practice. I believe that it works.

The neem tree contains natural antibacterial and pesticide compounds so potent that organic gardeners use them to control pests, and neem is used to treat a huge variety of medical conditions in Africa and India. I've yet to see neem 'tooth twigs' for sale outside India. But as the herb gains popularity, I suspect that the sticks will turn up in Western health food shops.

Dr Duke's Anti-Ageing Elixir

Homemade Herbal Mouthwash

Why buy a commercial mouthwash when you can whip up your own? This recipe blends the potent antiseptic properties of thyme and wild bergamot with the antibacterial compounds of eucalyptus.

WHAT YOU NEED

1 tablespoon thyme
1 tablespoon wild bergamot
2 tablespoons eucalyptus
1 tablespoon wintergreen
Vodka
Powdered licorice root or any natural sweetener (optional)

WHAT TO DO

Place the thyme, wild bergamot, eucalyptus, and wintergreen in a jar. Add enough cheap vodka to cover the plant material, then enough water to dilute the vodka by 50 per cent. Let this mixture steep in a cool, dark place for a week or so before straining out the herbs. Add the sweetener if you wish. Use as you would any mouthwash.

PANAMA HAT PALM (*CARLUDOVICA PALMATA*). During my workshops in Central and South America, I show my students how to use the plentiful fibres of the Panama hat palm – the same fibres that are woven into those marvellous Panama hats – as cheap, disposable dental floss. The hats are quite durable. I had one that lasted through 10 years of wear and tear. But as dental floss, the fibres are good for only one cleaning.

The Panama hat palm grows all over the place in the Amazon, so the fibres are never in short supply there. The plant can survive in frost-free conditions. As far as I know, its 'floss' isn't yet readily available.

THYME (*THYMUS VULGARIS*). You've certainly heard of Listerine antiseptic mouthwash. Guess where it gets its antiseptic properties? From thyme oil – or more precisely, from thymol, the major constituent of the oil.

You can rinse with Listerine, knowing that you're using a partially herbal product. Or you can make a strong thyme tea and rinse with that. Just put a big handful of thyme leaves into 1 litre (2 pints) of freshly boiled water. Steep for 20 minutes, then strain. Allow the tea to cool before refrigerating. To use it as a rinse, take a half-mouthful or so and swish it around, then spit it out or swallow it. Repeat after every meal and before bed.

You can also make a tincture by soaking a handful of thyme leaves

Dr Duke's Anti-Ageing Elixir

Good-for-Your-Gums Rinse

Most commercial mouthwashes advertise their antiseptic properties. You can make your own germ-killing rinse with this recipe.

WHAT YOU NEED

4 tablespoons wild bergamot
2 tablespoons rosemary
1 tablespoon thyme
1 tablespoon sage
Vodka

WHAT TO DO

Place the wild bergamot, rosemary, thyme, and sage in a jar. Add enough cheap vodka to cover the plant material, then enough water to dilute the vodka by 50 per cent. Allow to steep at least overnight. Strain out the plant material before using the remaining tincture as a rinse.

in ½ litre (1 pint) of vodka for a week. Strain out the plant material and store the rest. As needed, take a half-mouthful of the tincture, swish it around, and spit it out.

WILD BERGAMOT (*MONARDA FISTULOSA*). Wild bergamot is well-endowed with antiseptic, cavity- and gum-disease-fighting compounds – most notably, geraniol. The herb is also rich in thymol. You can use wild bergamot just like thyme, preparing it as a tea or tincture and rinsing with it as necessary.

FIG (*FICUS CARICA*) AND MORA (*CHOLORPHORA TINCTORIA*). Fig fruits might contribute to dental problems because they're so sweet and sticky. But fig sap or fig latex, the milky white juice that flows from broken stems or leaves, has been used around the world for dental hygiene, primarily

for the
Gardener

Thyme
Thymus vulgaris

There are literally dozens of kinds of thyme – cinnamon-scented, lemon-scented, and nutmeg-scented, to name just a few. The same basic growing instructions apply to all.

A perennial, thyme becomes most aromatic in rather poor, rocky soil. The herb can be propagated from seeds, seedlings, or subdivisions. If you choose seeds, plant them in rows 45–90 cm (18 to 36 in) apart, covered by 0.6 cm (¼ in) of finely pulverised soil. They should germinate in 2 to 3 weeks. If you choose seedlings, plant them 15–60 cm (6 to 24 in) apart in rows 90 cm (36 in) apart.

Established plants can be subdivided by root division, cuttings, or layering (in which an aerial shoot is nicked with a knife, then the nicked section is weighted down below ground level – perhaps with a rock – to take root). Experts whom I respect say that root division works best. Plants should be subdivided every 2 to 3 years, so they don't become woody.

To harvest thyme for medicinal purposes, either strip the leaves from the living plants or cut off the plants and tie them into bundles. Whichever method you choose, let the herb dry before using it. You can also incorporate the flowering tops into cooking.

in tooth extractions. The latex contains enzymes that help dissolve tooth roots, making teeth easier to extract.

I had the chance to test a substance similar to fig latex, when my dentist recommended the removal of a rotting back tooth that had lost its crown. At the time, I was about to embark on a trip to the Peruvian Amazon, so I decided to postpone the procedure until I returned home.

I'd heard that the milky white latex of the mora tree, a rainforest relative of the fig, could make teeth fall out – or at least loosen them. Three times a day, my shaman friend, Antonio, cut the bark of the tree just enough to allow the latex to ooze out. I dutifully applied the latex with a cotton swab. It was tasteless and caused no pain. I felt like I was coating my soon-to-be-gone tooth with rubber.

I repeated the treatments three times a day for 5 days. The Peruvians said that wouldn't be long enough to make the tooth fall out, and it wasn't. My tooth stayed put. But when I returned home and paid a visit to my dentist, the extraction went much better than any I'd had before – thanks, I believe, to the mora latex that I'd applied.

Fig latex has a similar reputation in many cultures around the world. The same is true of fig's close botanical relative, mulberry. You can obtain the latex from potted figs. If you're a herbal experimenter like I am and you're told that you need a tooth extraction, you might try using the latex beforehand. But be aware that some people have allergic reactions to fig latex, just like rubber latex.

CHAPTER 24

Sensible Weight

Dr Duke's Anti-Ageing Elixirs

- *SerotoNut Spread*
- *Lean, Mean Bran Muffins*

I spend a good deal of my time teaching (and learning) about the Amazon's unparalleled wealth of medicinal herbs through workshops sponsored by the Amazon Center for Environmental Education and Research (ACEER). ACEER is a struggling nonprofit organisation, and from time to time, I've pondered various ways of raising funds for it.

One idea that keeps running through my mind is an on-site weight-loss clinic: Dr Duke's Lose-Weight-in-a-Week Peruvian Amazon Retreat. Don't laugh. I'm convinced that participants could slim down successfully on my programme.

All the experts seem to agree that the only surefire way to take off and keep off extra pounds is to eat healthily (fewer calories, less fat, and more fibre) and to exercise regularly. The trouble is, that doesn't appeal to most people. They change their diets too much (perhaps by severely restricting calories or focusing on a single food), then stick with it for only a short period of time. And exercise? Maybe . . . for a little while.

At Dr Duke's Lose-Weight-in-a-Week Peruvian Amazon Retreat, participants would immerse themselves in the basics of lasting weight loss. We'd eat a plant-based Palaeolithic diet, with plenty of veggies, fruits, and especially pulses. All of these foods are low in fat, high in fibre, and filling.

We'd also eat lots of walnuts and a variety of seeds. These foods aren't usually included in weight-loss programmes, because they're considered fattening. But not in my programme. In fact, some research suggests that walnuts help take off pounds (more on this later). As a bonus, their vitamin E protects against heart attack, a major risk for those who are overweight.

As for seeds, many varieties are rich in the amino acid tryptophan, a precursor to the brain chemical (neurotransmitter) serotonin. Serotonin is an antidepressant. Since people tend to overeat when they're depressed or anxious, eating seeds may help lift their spirits and prevent weight gain.

In my programme, we'll season just about everything with chilli powder or hot-pepper sauce. Chilli pepper is thermogenic – in other words, it increases the rate at which your body burns calories. That's why it makes you sweat: those burning calories create extra heat. We'll also drink coffee and teas made with Chinese ephedra (ma huang) and guarana (an Amazon native). They're thermogenic, too.

Of course, Dr Duke's Lose-Weight-in-a-Week Peruvian Amazon Retreat will feature physical activity, and lots of it. We'll go on vigorous hikes through the rainforest during the day, and we'll dance to mariachi music at night. For anyone who flags, we'll have plenty of thermogenic caffeinated beverages handy.

I predict that 80 per cent of the participants in my programme would lose 2.25 kg (5 lb), and that 10 per cent would shed even more. For the 10 per cent who lost less than that, I'd offer a second week at half-price. And everyone gets to spend a marvellous week in the Amazon, learning all about native herbs while they're slimming down. So who wants to sign up?

Seriously, I just might do this. There's certainly no shortage of people who want to lose weight, including yours truly.

Obesity: A Growing Epidemic

A World Health Organisation report published in 1996 stated that 'Overweight is widely considered to be associated with increased morbidity and mortality.' It is estimated that for every 10 per cent that a person is above their 'normal' weight, they have an increased mortality risk of 15 per cent. The prevalence of obesity is rising to epidemic proportions globally. In Europe 10–20 per cent of men are obese and 10–25 per cent of women; in Japan obesity in men has doubled since 1982 and in America an estimated one third of the population are seriously overweight..

Many of these people want to lose weight just to look better, but they also have sound medical reasons to shed the flab. Carrying extra weight raises the risk of an astonishing array of health problems, including several types of cancer, heart attack, heart failure, stroke, high blood pressure, high cholesterol, diabetes, arthritis, gallstones, and thyroid disease. These and other weight-related ailments cause untold misery and add billions to a nation's health-care costs.

Overweight and obesity are by no means limited to the elderly. But, in general, the older you get, the heavier you get. The main reason is that we tend to become more sedentary with age. Less exercise means fewer calories burned up through physical activity and more calories left over to add unwanted weight.

What's more, because you're getting less exercise, your basal metabolic rate slows down. The phrase *basal metabolic rate* refers to how fast you burn calories while you're at rest. When you work out, you raise your basal metabolic rate. It stays high for several hours afterwards, burning extra calories even while you're not active. But when you're sedentary, your basal metabolic rate stays slow. Calories don't burn off as quickly and are more likely to turn into fat.

Carrying extra weight doesn't just make you more vulnerable to disease. It also takes years off your life. You've probably read or heard about laboratory studies in which animals fed reduced-calorie diets live significantly longer than animals fed 'normal' diets. The implication of this finding is clear: fight fat, and you fight old age and early death.

Ideally, you should start with those pre-emptive measures early in life. But you're never too old to slim down and stay young. You don't even have to lose much to make a difference in your health and longevity. Many studies have shown that successfully maintaining a 5 per cent reduction in body weight – that's 5 kg (11 lb) for a 100 kg (15½ stone) person – can significantly lower the risk for most obesity-related conditions.

Unfortunately, many – perhaps most – people who lose weight end up regaining it within a few years. They set themselves up for failure by drastically changing their eating habits, to the point of letting themselves go hungry, and by not increasing their physical activity. As soon as they go back to their old eating habits – and invariably, they do – the pounds creep back on.

For real, lasting weight loss, you need to engage in regular exercise, and you need to make small but permanent changes in your food choices and eating style. If I ever launch Dr Duke's Lose-Weight-in-a-Week Peruvian Amazon Retreat, I'm going to emphasise that my programme is *not* a 'spa' or a 'fat farm'. It's a model that teaches participants how to live their lives every day and, in the process, helps them achieve and maintain a healthy weight.

Exercise: You Can't Slim Down Without It

Shortly before I began writing this chapter, I spent some time on my stationary bike, pedalling the 10 miles or so necessary to burn off the calories from a small dish of ice cream, the dessert to my dinner of vegetarian bean soup and a green salad. Usually, I read while I ride, a habit that I'd recommend to all the bookworms out there. It's healthier than sitting in a chair to do my reading.

I decided to talk about exercise first to stress how important it is to weight loss. To take off and keep off pounds, you *must* work out. Unfortunately, not many people do. They believe that they can control their weight through dieting alone. But they can't.

Staying active helps you control your weight in several ways. First, you burn more calories while you're on the move. Second, you burn more calories while you're at rest, because exercise raises your basal metabolic rate. Third, you raise your level of endorphins, the body's own feel-good compounds. Endorphins elevate your mood and reduce hunger pangs. That's why I often exercise when I'm hungry: it tends to curb my appetite.

According to conventional wisdom, you have to work out vigorously for long periods of time in order to see any difference in your waistline. In other words, you have to become a slave to exercise. That's not true at all. The research bears it out.

For one study, researchers at Stanford University recruited 56 women, all overweight and sedentary. Half of the women participated in a 40-minute workout every day, while the rest did four 10-minute workouts daily. After 20 weeks, the women in both groups lost about the same amount of weight. But those engaging in 10-minute workouts were more successful in sticking with their fitness routines.

The point is that you don't have to commit the better part of your day to exercise. You just have to find ways to increase your level of physical activity. Brief bursts may be just as effective as one continuous workout.

Conventional wisdom also says that in order to slim down, you must engage in activities that are boring or unpleasant or hard on the knees, especially older knees, which may be affected by arthritis. Jogging unquestionably aggravated my knees. Sometimes they hurt so badly that I could barely get into or out of my car. Once I quit jogging (and all other high-impact aerobic activities), my knee problems went away.

So forget the notion that only heart-pounding, joint-jarring activities can help you lose weight. Plain old walking is as good for slimming down as any other form of exercise. It's usually the best choice for older folks like me, because the risk of injury is lower than with many other fitness regimes. According to James Rippe, M.D., a cardiologist at the University of Massachusetts Medical Center in Worcester, walking a mile burns as many calories as running the same distance.

I suggest walking briskly for 40 to 60 minutes a day, either all at once or in shorter spurts. That's what I do. I can walk a good distance in just a few laps around YinYang Valley. All the work that I do in my Garden of Youth is good exercise, too.

Fibre: Nature's Best Appetite Suppressant

Of course, exercising regularly is just part of the weight-loss equation. You need to eat healthily, too.

Most weight-loss experts advocate a low-fat, low-calorie eating plan. That's good advice, and I won't argue with it. But I will give it a slightly different spin. I recommend building meals and snacks around what I call gut stuffers.

Gut stuffers are foods that fill you up. By creating a sense of fullness, they leave you feeling satisfied. In this way, they prevent you from overeating.

Gut stuffers are mostly bulky, high-fibre foods. Fibre is the non-nutritional component of a plant. Botanically speaking, it forms the cell walls that establish a plant's structure.

Fibre contains no vitamins or minerals, but it's as necessary as any essential nutrient. It keeps the digestive tract working properly. It helps prevent constipation, diabetes, heart disease, and colon cancer. (Even though one much-publicised study found that a high-fibre diet doesn't protect against colon cancer, an entire body of research has proven otherwise.) And it supports weight loss and maintenance.

Meats and other high-fat, low-fibre foods fill you up if you eat enough of them. But by the time you feel satisfied, you've packed away a whole lot of calories. On the other hand, gut stuffers fill you up with a comparatively small number of calories. And they don't sit as heavily in your stomach as fatty foods do, so you're less likely to lie down for a postmeal snooze and more likely to step out for a walk. (In addition to all of its weight-loss benefits, walking promotes good digestion.)

Incorporating the gut stuffers into your eating plan isn't difficult. Start your day with some fruit and a whole grain cereal or bread item. For lunch, have a salad, a hearty vegetable soup, or both. Include a salad and a vegetable side dish with your dinner, followed by more fruit for dessert.

If you fill up on the gut stuffers and exercise regularly, you can afford to cheat occasionally, as I did with my dish of ice cream. And you won't have to let your belt out a notch either.

The Best of the Gut Stuffers

Almost any plant food qualifies as a gut stuffer. But I do have my favourites, which I'll share with you here. One is actually considered a supplement. And another isn't a plant food at all, though it's found in all plants – often in very large amounts. (It's water.)

PSYLLIUM (*PLANTAGO OVATA*). Want to experience the weight-loss benefits of the gut stuffers in supplement form? Take psyllium.

Psyllium is the seed of a plant that's a relative of plantain (*Plantago major*). Psyllium is rich in a special kind of gut-stuffing fibre called mucilage, which expands to many times its dry size when immersed in the liquid that fills the digestive tract.

In one study, researchers gave a group of people who qualified as obese either a placebo (a fake pill) or psyllium (20 grams, about 5 tablespoons, in a tall glass of water 3 hours before meals). Those who received the psyllium felt full sooner and wound up consuming significantly less fat than those who received the placebo.

In a separate study, this one from Italy, a group of women considered obese were placed on a low-fat, low-calorie diet. Some of the women were also given psyllium (3 grams, about 2 teaspoons, in a glass of water 30 minutes before meals). Those who took the psyllium lost significantly more weight than those who followed the diet alone.

Other research has shown that taking psyllium supplements before meals helps treat several conditions associated with obesity, including high cholesterol, diabetes, and heart disease. If you want to try psyllium, I suggest buying a commercial product and using it according to the label directions.

PULSES. Pulses are great gut stuffers. Besides being high in fibre, they're very low in fat and high in protein, which makes them an excellent substitute for meat. If you're trying to reduce your meat consumption, whether for weight control or disease prevention, add some bean dishes to your recipe repertoire.

I have all sorts of pulses in my Garden of Youth, including black beans, butter beans, kidney beans, navy beans, and string beans. They're fairly easy to grow if you want to try planting them yourself.

In cooking, beans are quite versatile. They're wonderful in soups. I like to make a big container of bean or bean-vegetable soup and store it in the fridge. That way, I can have a healthy, filling lunch or dinner without going to a lot of trouble, other than reheating.

I also enjoy bean dips and spreads, which go wonderfully on breads, crisps, and biscuits (low-fat or fat-free, of course). If you're a fan of ethnic cuisine, you may like to try your hand at preparing Mexican

More Wisdom *from the* Garden

Chocolate Substitute Has Slimming Powers

Are you familiar with carob? Most Americans aren't. It happens to be one of my favourite beans.

Carob often appears as a chocolate substitute in health foods. But it's much more than a Mediterranean alternative to Amazonian cocoa. When researchers added carob gum to animal feed for 2 to 6 weeks, the animals that ate it lost more weight than those given carob-free feed.

Like other beans, carob is a fibre-rich gut stuffer. It also lowers cholesterol and helps control type 2 (non-insulin-dependent) diabetes and heart disease.

I've used carob primarily as a chocolate substitute in fondue and similar foods. You may want to try it in soups and other recipes that call for beans. Just use it sparingly, since its flavour can overpower other ingredients. Carob powder is available in most health food stores.

dishes, in which beans are a staple ingredient. If you prefer Italian fare, try substituting beans for the mince in lasagne.

WEED GREENS. Chickweed (*Stellaria media*) and other weed greens have a long-standing reputation in folk medicine as herbal 'slimmers'. I'm not sure why they have that reputation, but the older I get, the more I seem to trust herbal folklore.

I recommend tossing together a salad of gut-stuffing edible weeds such as chickweed, dandelion, stinging nettle, plantain, and purslane – whatever is available. Then instead of using salad dressing, top your greens with hot-pepper sauce and lemon juice. You'll have a tasty, though rather bitter alternative to conventional salads and vegetable side dishes. Plus, if you have a lawn full of dandelions, you'll be able to do something with them other than curse their presence.

WATER. It's not a plant food, but H_2O is nonetheless a very effective gut stuffer. Nutrition experts recommend drinking at least eight 240-ml (8-fl oz) glasses a day, just to stay hydrated. But there's another good reason to follow this advice: water tends to fill you up, so you eat less.

Many people say that they feel hungry even after they've eaten. What they perceive as hunger is more likely thirst. When you feel hungry, reach for a glass of water instead of heading for the refrigerator. You may find that water is enough.

To get your recommended eight glasses a day, I'd advise against gulping a glass at a time. It's easier if you simply keep a water bottle on hand and sip from it throughout the day. You can also alternate water with tea and juice, both of which count towards your quota.

Mood Boosters: Lift the Blues, Lose the Weight

Filling up on the gut stuffers is one way to enhance your weight-loss efforts. Another is to increase your intake of mood-boosting foods and herbs.

People who don't have weight problems tend to eat until they feel full, then stop. But people who are overweight tend to eat beyond the point of satiety, often for emotional reasons. They may feel blue or worried or anxious or stressed, and they turn to food for comfort.

Several studies have shown that enhancing mood can increase the effectiveness of weight-loss programs. This may help explain one of the more unusual findings in the scientific literature: that walnuts, a high-fat food, can help unload extra weight.

I love walnuts, so I was very intrigued when I first read about a study in which the nuts had been linked to weight control. For the study, researchers at Loma Linda University in California surveyed more than 25,000 Seventh-Day Adventists, whose religion advocates vegetarianism. Not surprisingly, the Adventists are much healthier than the typical American. Nuts are one of their few high-fat indulgences. The researchers were surprised to discover that the Adventists who ate the most walnuts were least likely to be obese.

How walnuts and their brethren might help keep people slim remains something of a mystery. Perhaps the nuts are gut stuffers that produce a feeling of fullness. But personally, I believe its their serotonin content that supports weight loss and maintenance.

Serotonin is a brain chemical (neurotransmitter) that contributes to the regulation of mood and feelings of fullness. Many antidepressant medications, most notably the selective serotonin reuptake inhibitors such as fluoxetine (Prozac), influence serotonin levels in the brain. Perhaps walnuts have the same effect.

In order to include walnuts in your weight-loss programme, you must follow an otherwise low-fat, low-calorie, plant-based diet. You can't sprinkle walnuts on a banana split and

Dr Duke's Anti-Ageing Elixir

SerotoNut Spread

You can buy all kinds of nut butters these days. This homemade version may actually enhance your weight-loss efforts. Its ingredients contain serotonin, a brain chemical that not only boosts your mood but also can regulate your appetite.

WHAT YOU NEED

A combination of walnuts and pecans
A little walnut oil

WHAT TO DO

Shell the nuts, if necessary. In a food processor, combine them with a little walnut oil until they reach a butterlike consistency. Serve with high-fibre wholemeal bread.

expect to get rid of the excess baggage. But if you're eating healthily and you want more serotonin to boost your mood, help yourself to walnuts as well as pecans – they are rich in serotonin.

You can mix the nuts to taste for munching, or grind them into recipes for breads and muffins, such as my Lean, Mean Bran Muffins (see page 284). As a bonus, these nuts are good sources of vitamin E, which helps protect against heart disease, a major health problem among those who are obese.

How Tryptophan Can Stop Overeating

You'll notice that my recipe for Lean, Mean Bran Muffins calls for sunflower seeds, evening primrose seeds, and sesame seeds. I put them in because they're tasty – but that's not the only reason. They're also rich in the amino acid tryptophan, which is a building block for serotonin. I believe that by elevating serotonin levels, the seeds can enhance mood and control overeating.

Of the three kinds of seeds, those from the evening primrose have the highest tryptophan content. In the UK, evening primrose oil is recommended as a treatment for many conditions, including obesity. I prefer the whole seed because it contains most of the tryptophan as well as a good deal of gut-stuffing fibre. When I'm out in my garden, I munch the whole seeds. I also grind them for use in cooking and baking.

Besides evening primrose seeds, sunflower seeds, and sesame seeds, good sources of tryptophan include soya beans, white mustard seeds, pumpkin seeds, and chickpeas. Among greens, the best source of tryptophan is watercress, followed by bean sprouts, spinach, asparagus, chives, mustard greens, mung beans, cauliflower, chicory, pigweed, and purslane. These foods not only help boost serotonin levels in the brain, they're also high-fibre, vitamin- and mineral-rich gut stuffers.

Aromatherapy: A 'Scents-ible' Way to Stop Cravings

Eating the right foods can help lift your spirits and promote weight loss. So can sniffing the right scents, as one expert discovered.

Duke University psychologist Susan Schiffman, Ph.D., recruited a group of people with clinical obesity who overate for emotional reasons. She instructed her volunteers to inhale apricot essential oil, which aromatherapists consider calming, while practising relaxation tech-

Dr Duke's Anti-Ageing Elixir

Lean, Mean Bran Muffins

When I mentioned these muffins in a *USA Today* interview a few years back, I was inundated with requests for the recipe. Because I never measure my ingredients, I asked a good friend of mine, nutritionist Leigh Broadhurst, Ph.D., to develop a recipe with specific ingredient amounts. It appeared in my previous book, *The Green Pharmacy*, but it remains so popular that I decided to repeat it here.

The muffins promote weight loss in two ways. First, they're rich in gut-stuffing fibre, so they fill you up but not out. Second, they're made with nuts and seeds that help raise levels of the mood-boosting brain chemical serotonin. With more serotonin, you're less likely to give in to emotion-driven food cravings – and more likely to slim down successfully.

WHAT YOU NEED

60 g (2 oz) bran flakes

60 g (2 oz) walnut pieces, sunflower seeds, or both

60 g (2 oz) raisins or dried cherries

30 g (1 oz) evening primrose seeds, ground (see note opposite)

125 g (4 oz) unbleached all-purpose flour

60 g (2 oz) old-fashioned rolled oats

75 g (2½ ounces) stone-ground cornmeal

100 g (3½ oz) sugar

1–1½ teaspoons cinnamon or mixed spice (optional)

2 teaspoons baking powder

¾ teaspoon bicarbonate of soda

½ teaspoon sea salt

1 apple or pear, chopped

240 ml (8 fl oz) low-fat or fat-free buttermilk

1 large egg

3 tablespoons cold-pressed unrefined sesame oil

Sesame seeds (optional)

niques to relieve their stress, anxiety, and depression. Over time, the people began associating the scent of apricot with feeling relaxed and less hungry.

Next, Dr Schiffman gave each of her study participants a vial of

---

WHAT TO DO

Preheat the oven to 230°C/450°F/gas mark 8. Place the rack in the centre of the oven.

Line a 12-cup muffin pan with paper muffin cups. (For best results, do not use a nonstick pan without paper liners.)

With your hands, crush the bran flakes into uniform small pieces, but not crumbs. In a small bowl, mix the bran flakes with the walnuts and/or sunflower seeds, raisins or cherries, and evening primrose seeds. Set aside.

In a large bowl, stir together the flour, oats, cornmeal, sugar, baking powder, cinnamon or mixed spice (if using), bicarbonate of soda, and salt. Add the bran flake mixture and stir together.

Place the apples or pears, buttermilk, egg, and oil in a food processor and process until the fruit is coarsely puréed. Fold the fruit mixture into the flour mixture, stirring gently to combine.

Fill the muffin cups to the top and sprinkle the tops with the sesame seeds (if using). Place the pan in the centre of the oven and immediately reduce the temperature to 190°C/ 375°F/gas mark 5. Bake for 20 to 25 minutes, or until the muffins are lightly browned and firm to the touch.

Let cool in the pan for a few minutes, then remove the muffins from the pan and place them on a rack to cool completely. Serve within 24 hours or store in an airtight container or a bag in the freezer.

Makes 12 muffins.

Note: This recipe requires that you have access to evening primrose plants. Before starting the recipe, collect some evening primrose seeds. Store them in the refrigerator and just before making the muffins, grind them in a spice mill or an electric coffee grinder. If you cannot get hold of evening primrose seeds, substitute other seeds.

Variation: Substitute 1 banana for the apple or pear.

apricot oil. She asked them to keep the vials handy and sniff the scent whenever they felt stressed and tempted to eat. According to Dr Schiffman, more than half of her volunteers were able to use the apricot oil to relax quickly and avoid overeating.

You can try Dr Schiffman's training method on your own, if you wish. Choose a relaxation technique that you find helpful when you feel stressed or depressed – perhaps meditation, yoga, or gentle stretching. While practising the technique, inhale a calming essential oil. I would recommend one of the herbal oils that aromatherapists suggest for depression: bergamot, geranium, lavender, lemon balm or rosemary. You can also use apple or peppermint essential oil, both of which are said to support weight loss. Or stick with apricot, as in the study.

Get a small vial and fill it halfway with rock salt. Add several drops of the essential oil. The salt absorbs the oil, helping to prevent spilling. Then when you feel agitated or upset, uncap the vial and take a few deep whiffs. You may be able to head off any emotion-driven cravings.

Thermogenesis Enhancers: Go for the Burn

At the beginning of the chapter, I briefly discussed the concept of thermogenesis. The term refers to the body's production of heat during metabolism. The more heat that is released by the body, the more calories are burned.

Years back, scientists theorised that combining a low-fat, low-calorie diet with thermogenesis-enhancing foods or drugs could take off more weight than following a diet alone. Many studies have proven this to be true. When people who qualify as obese add thermogenesis enhancers to their diets, they lose more weight than those who don't.

Thermogenesis enhancers don't produce miracles, but they do boost weight loss somewhat. I should mention that the pharmaceutical thermogenesis enhancers are for people who are clinically obese and enrolled in physician-supervised weight-loss programmes. They're not for people who want to lose weight because their trousers have got too tight.

In herbal medicine, the two main thermogenesis-enhancing compounds are caffeine and ephedrine. Caffeine comes from coffee, tea, cocoa, guarana, and maté; ephedrine, from Chinese ephedra.

Based on evidence from digs at Palaeolithic sites, Chinese ephedra has been used by humans for more than 50,000 years. The herb was even discovered in the highlands of Iraq, in a Neanderthal burial cave some 60,000 years old.

In the cave, archaeologists found the skeleton of a man surrounded by eight plant species, including ephedra. It wasn't there for its showy flowers, because it has none. Anthropologists speculate that ephedra was one of the world's first medicines, though the Neanderthals probably didn't use it for weight control. In those days, starvation was the major health threat, not obesity.

In the thermogenesis studies that I've seen, the typical dose of ephedrine is about 20 milligrams three times a day, before meals. That's about the amount in a Chinese ephedra tea made with 1 teaspoon of herb per cup. For caffeine, the typical dose is 200 milligrams three times

More Wisdom *from the* Garden

Eating Spicy Foods Melts Away Pounds

Caffeine and ephedrine may be the most popular and most widely researched thermogenesis enhancers, but they're not the only ones. Researchers at Oxford Polytechnic Institute in England found that hot spices are also thermogenic. When the scientists added 3 grams of hot chilli sauce and 3 grams of mustard to the diets of study participants, they discovered that the fiery condiments raised their metabolic rates an average of 25 per cent.

While the standard American diet consists of relatively bland fare, many other cultures favour hot and spicy dishes. Mexican, Korean, Indian, Thai, and Japanese cuisines are known for their fiery foods. Maybe the people of those countries know something about weight control that Americans don't.

I've also read that ginger increases metabolic rate. It's traditionally considered a hot spice, so it fits nicely with the other thermogenesis enhancers.

a day, before meals. You get about 200 milligrams from two 180 ml (6 fl oz) cups of brewed coffee.

A Word of Caution

The herbal thermogenesis enhancers are considered stimulants. So if you try one, be aware that you may experience stimulant-like side effects – most notably insomnia and tremors. Some people have also reported dizziness.

Based on the studies that I've seen, the herbal thermogenesis enhancers do not appear to elevate blood pressure, as other stimulants do. This is reassuring, because people who are obese often have high blood pressure.

Nevertheless, the potential side effects associated with taking therapeutic doses of ephedrine or caffeine for weight loss are significant enough that I recommend using medicinal amounts of the herbal thermogenesis enhancers only with professional supervision. But I remain confident that the side effects of the herbs are not as severe as those of pharmaceutical weight-loss aids.

You're undoubtedly familiar with the story of fen-phen, the combination of fenfluramine and phentermine that was banned by the FDA in America a few years ago. The FDA's action came after some people who took the two drugs to lose weight developed potentially fatal heart valve damage and blood pressure problems.

More recently, the FDA has threatened to ban or at least limit the availability of Chinese ephedra. The agency is reacting to a handful of deaths, many involving young people who took truly enormous doses of the herb as an intoxicant. In super-large amounts, the ephedrine in Chinese ephedra can cause potentially fatal heart problems.

I would never recommend using such huge doses of Chinese ephedra, nor would any reputable herbalist whom I know. When taken in the normal dose range for weight-loss thermogenesis, the herb has not produced any serious side effects. It would be a shame if people are denied the opportunity to try Chinese ephedra just because of a few instances in which the herb was used inappropriately.

CHAPTER 25

Enhancing Women's Health

Dr Duke's Anti-Ageing Elixirs

- *Borneol Cramp Cure*
- *Lemony Muscle Liniment*
- *Turn-On Tincture*

Without question, the most profound age-related change that women experience is menopause. And it's universal, affecting every woman in her fifties (though it may arrive earlier for some).

But what about the years before menopause? They're the prime time for some uniquely female health concerns. Though these problems may not be age-related, they can definitely make a woman *feel* older, hampering the youthful zest for life she used to feel. These are the ones that I'll be discussing in this chapter. (If you want more information on managing menopause and its particular problems, refer to chapters 18 and 39.)

Iron-Deficiency Anaemia: A Common Cause of Fatigue

Of the more than 90 different kinds of anaemia identified in medical dictionaries, iron-deficiency anaemia is by far the most common. I've seen estimates that some 6 per cent of the US population is iron deficient. The vast majority is women.

This makes sense, when you consider that premenopausal women lose blood every month, during their periods. Red blood cells are rich in iron. In fact, about 75 per cent of the body's supply of the mineral is found in the red blood cells.

If you become iron deficient, you can't make enough haemoglobin, the compound in red blood cells that delivers oxygen throughout your body. And if you're low on oxygen, your metabolism – your body's energy-producing mechanism – slows down. This sets the stage for the primary symptom of iron-deficiency anaemia: feeling fatigued, especially becoming tired unusually easily during exercise.

But iron-deficiency anaemia is insidious. The fatigue develops slowly, so slowly that you may not notice it. Quite often, women show no symptoms of the disease. They're surprised when it turns up in routine blood tests, perhaps as part of their annual gynaecologic exams.

Ironically, the low-fat, high-fibre Palaeolithic diet that I advocate throughout this book increases the risk of iron-deficiency anaemia. If you eat more than 35 grams of fibre a day, it may deplete your iron supply through a complex chemical process called chelation. Compared with meat eaters, vegetarians have twice the rate of iron-deficiency anaemia – partly because they eat more fibre, partly because they eat little or no meat, a good source of iron.

Overall, I still say that the Palaeolithic diet is the healthiest around. But if you're a premenopausal woman who's following the diet (or my Healthy Sevens eating plan, outlined in chapter 3), you should be aware that you need to keep an eye on your iron intake.

Despite the fibre issue, you can still get a good deal of iron from plant foods. Every herb in my Garden of Youth supplies the mineral. All plants do. According to my database, the best plant sources of iron in-

Out of the Frying Pan, Into Your Bloodstream

Do you own cast-iron cookware? If you do, it may help reduce your risk of iron-deficiency anaemia. Foods cooked in cast iron pick up some of the mineral. And your body can use it, at least according to the animal studies that I've reviewed.

clude dandelion, lamb's lettuce (*Valeriana locusta*), Cape gooseberry (Physalis), chickweed, and red clover. Other foods rich in the mineral include stinging nettle leaves, leafy vegetables, potatoes, fruits (especially pumpkin and raisins), whole grains, fish, milk, eggs, and meat.

One tasty way to manage your fibre intake is to juice plant foods, which removes the iron-depleting fibre but leaves the iron intact. Another option is to pair your iron-rich foods with something high in vitamin C, a nutrient that promotes iron absorption. Among the best sources of vitamin C are broccoli, brussels sprouts, cabbage, cauliflower, citrus fruits, turnip greens, and sweet potatoes. Or simply squeeze some lemon juice onto your iron-rich foods.

Of course, you can always get your iron from a supplement. Most experts recommend taking 20 to 30 milligrams a day, more if you're pregnant (consult your prenatal-care provider). Multivitamins with iron often provide enough of the mineral to prevent iron-deficiency anaemia.

If you already have iron-deficiency anaemia, your doctor might prescribe an iron-only supplement. For best absorption, take your supplement with a vitamin C source. Orange juice and tomato juice are good choices. Also, don't take iron at the same time as calcium. Calcium interferes with iron absorption.

And remember: keep iron supplements out of the reach of children. Not many people know this, but a toddler could die from ingesting just a few of these pills. Iron supplements are the leading cause of accidental supplement-related poisoning. So be careful with them. In fact, you should store all of your supplements where youngsters can't get them.

While we're talking about supplements, be sure that you're getting enough folic acid (also known as folate) and vitamin B_{12}. Deficiencies in either of these nutrients can cause other types of anaemia. The experts generally recommend taking 200–400 micrograms of folic acid a day, more if you have folate-deficiency anaemia. The standard recommendation for B_{12} is 1 microgram a day – again, more if you have B_{12}-related pernicious anaemia.

Menstrual Cramps: Pain Relievers Aren't the Only Answer

About half of all premenopausal women develop cramps during their menstrual periods. For most of these women, cramping causes mild to moderate abdominal pain for up to a few days each month. But an estimated 10 per cent experience severe cramps. Fortunately, they usually become less painful after women reach the age of 30. And, of course, they go away completely with the onset of menopause.

Menstrual cramps result from spasms of the uterus as it expels its blood-rich lining each month that a woman doesn't become pregnant. Certain hormones, called prostaglandins, also play a role in cramping.

If you smoke, your menstrual cramps may be quite painful. Smoking constricts the blood vessels, including those in your uterus. Impaired bloodflow in the uterus aggravates cramping.

When menstrual cramps occur, many woman run to the medicine chest for a pharmaceutical pain reliever such as ibuprofen, which happens to be the most popular. To be sure, medications can help, especially if you have severe cramping. But before you pop any pills, I'd suggest considering these natural approaches.

Cut back on nonplant foods. Red meat and dairy products boost production of the prostaglandins that aggravate cramping. For many women, simply cutting back on these foods provides considerable relief.

Practise relaxing. Menstrual cramps can cause tension and anxiety, which in turn make the pain even worse. Anything that you can do to mellow out breaks this vicious circle and may provide some relief. Choose any relaxation technique that appeals to you – perhaps walking, gardening, meditation, deep breathing, massage, or yoga.

Sniff a soothing scent. One herbal approach to relaxation is aromatherapy. Many of the essential oils in aromatic herbs serve as antidotes to stress and anxiety. They also help relieve cramping.

Kathy Keville, a herbalist and aromatherapist, recommends this blend of essential oils: 4 drops of lavender, 2 drops of marjoram, 2 drops of camomile, and 3 drops of geranium. Place the oils in a little vial half-filled with rock salt. The salt absorbs the oils, so they don't spill. Whenever you're bothered by menstrual cramps, uncap the vial and take a deep whiff.

You can also add the essential oils to body lotion, then massage the lotion into your abdomen for relief.

Calm Cramping with Herbal Muscle Relaxers

My Garden of Youth has many herbs that are said to ease menstrual cramps: black cohosh, black haw, chasteberry, dong quai, evening primrose, partridgeberry, and raspberry. Other herbs traditionally used to treat cramps include anserina, passionflower, yarrow, and yucca.

Many of these medicinal plants are well-endowed with spasmolytics, compounds that relieve muscle spasms and therefore cramping. Among the spasmolytics are alpha-bisabolol, borneol, bornyl-acetate, camphor, carvacrol, caryophyllene, limonene, linalyl-acetate, menthol, menthone, myrcene, and thymol. Herbs that have any of these compounds usually contain cineole, which helps speeds their absorption.

The nifty thing about the spasmolytics is that many of them work whether used internally or externally. So you can drink the herbs as teas, add them to baths, or both. In fact, you could make a strong tea and pour it into your bathwater. Or you can put dried herbs into a cloth bag and let the water run over it.

Of all the herbs that can help ease menstrual cramps, the following deserve special mention.

BLACK HAW (*VIBURNUM PRUNIFOLIUM*). Native American women used the bark of this woody, white-flowered shrub for gynaecological complaints. Colonial women adopted it for menstrual cramps. Most 19th-century pharmacology books listed it as a treatment for menstrual discomforts.

The bark of black haw contains at least four compounds that help relax the uterus. Two of them, aesculetin and scopoletin, also help relieve muscle spasms. Black haw (sometimes called viburnum) preparations are available in health food stores. If you buy a tincture, use it according to the label directions.

If you buy the raw bark, boil 2 teaspoons of the herb in a cup of water for 10 minutes. Allow it to steep until cool, then strain. Drink up to three cups a day during your periods.

Black haw has a very bitter taste. To make it more palatable, add lemongrass or honey, or mix the tea with juice.

RASPBERRY (*RUBUS IDAEUS*). Many women herbalists whom I respect recommend raspberry leaf tea for relieving menstrual cramps. One study showed that the herb helps relax the uterus.

Scientists still have not identified raspberry's major active compounds. But they speculate that one of the compounds may be pycnogenol, which occurs in many, if not all, woody plants. In one study, 66 to 80 per cent of women who took pycnogenol through four menstrual cycles experienced significant reductions in menstrual cramping.

Dr Duke's Anti-Ageing Elixir

Borneol Cramp Cure

Among the muscle-relaxing spasmolytic compounds, borneol is particularly potent. If you're experiencing menstrual cramps, you can get relief by drinking a tea made from one or more of the borneol-rich herbs. Cardamom is the best (and most expensive) source, followed by sage, rosemary, and mountain mint (a weed at my place).

WHAT YOU NEED

Any combination of the following herbs: cardamom, coriander, mountain mint, rosemary, sage, savory, and thyme
Lemongrass
1 cup water

WHAT TO DO

Combine the herbs of your choice. Add the lemongrass for a lemony flavour, if you wish. Put 1 teaspoon of your herb blend in the freshly boiled water. Steep for 10 minutes, then strain out the plant material. Allow to cool slightly before drinking.

Raspberry leaf is available in most health food stores. To make a tea, use 1 to 2 teaspoons of herb per cup of freshly boiled water. Steep for 10 minutes, then strain. Make sure that the tea has cooled before drinking it.

AMERICAN PARTRIDGEBERRY (*MITCHELLA REPENS*). This sparklingly beautiful evergreen herb with bright red berries grows wild in the forested area of YinYang Valley. Traditionally, it's been called squaw vine, because it was used by Native American women for gynaecological complaints, including menstrual cramps. In recent years, this name has been criticised by Native American groups, who consider it demeaning. I have some people of Indian descent in the family, so I try to be sensitive by calling the herb mitchella. The research on is a little thin. But given the number of different tribes that used the herb for the same purpose, I'm pretty much persuaded that it works.

Some women herbalists whom I respect say that the best herbal remedy for menstrual cramps is a combination of mitchella and raspberry, with or without black haw. I'd use 1 to 2 teaspoons of mitchella per cup of freshly boiled water. Steep for 10 minutes, then strain.

In the winter, I'd just munch some of mitchella's berries. They're plentiful here in Maryland, making their annual appearance in the autumn and hanging on for the next several months.

Dr Duke's Anti-Ageing Elixir

Lemony Muscle Liniment

Applied topically, this rub can soothe tense muscles and relieve menstrual cramps. All of the herbal ingredients contain spasmolytic compounds.

WHAT YOU NEED

2 parts lemongrass
2 parts lemon balm
2 parts lemon eucalyptus
2 parts lemon thyme
1 part oregano
1 part rosemary
1 part thyme
Olive oil or unscented massage oil

WHAT TO DO

In a bowl, combine the herbs. Add the oil to cover. Let it stand overnight.

The next morning, strain out the plant material. Massage the oil into your abdomen and any other areas of muscle tension. Use the oil at room temperature or slightly warmed, if you wish.

BLACK COHOSH (*CIMICIFUGA RACEMOSA*). Here's another herb that Native American women used to treat gynaecological and reproductive problems. It was adopted by White settlers and eventually became a primary ingredient in Lydia Pinkham's Vegetable Compound, one of the most popular patent medicines of the 19th century in the United States. Miss Pinkham's compound was labelled as a treatment for 'female complaints', including cramping.

Early research suggested that black cohosh contains the phyto-oestrogen (plant oestrogen) formononetin, though that finding has recently been challenged. Still, Commission E, the expert panel that evaluates the safety and effectiveness of herbs for the German government, endorses black cohosh as a treatment for menstrual cramps. If you'd like to try it, buy a tincture and follow the label directions.

Premenstrual Syndrome: Stop the Monthly Madness

For years, some doctors doubted that PMS was real. Women knew that it was, and I believed them.

Now even the gainsayers have acknowledged the existence of PMS, thanks in large part to studies by the American National Institute of Mental Health substantiating claims of premenstrual mood changes – namely, the irritability that women have always described. Other symptoms of PMS include anxiety, sadness, and distraction, as well as food cravings, bloating, breast tenderness, and weight gain. These symptoms subside shortly after menstruation begins.

I've seen estimates that 50 per cent of premenopausal women have PMS. Some 15 per cent get it pretty badly.

All of these women have normal levels of the sex hormones oestrogen and progesterone. But they're extra-sensitive to their cyclic hormonal changes. They also have unusually low premenstrual levels of endorphins, the body's naturally occurring antidepressant compounds.

For years, I've been touting evening primrose oil as the best herbal treatment for PMS symptoms. Native Americans consumed evening primrose seeds as a food. Supposedly, the women also used the seeds to

growing younger naturally

They Beat PMS with Evening Primrose

Being a man, I've never had to deal with PMS. But I've heard enough about it to know that it's a dreaded, even debilitating, condition. I've also heard lots of good things about evening primrose oil, my remedy of choice for premenstrual symptoms.

A few years back, I received a Christmas card with this note inside: 'I thought you might enjoy this picture of my supply of evening primrose oil. I take a spoonful daily and twice as much during PMS, which bothers me a lot less than it used to. Thanks again.'

Later, on an bus in Costa Rica, I happened to overhear one female pharmacist talking with another. She said that she took one evening primrose capsule a day all month until she felt her premenstrual symptoms coming on. Then she increased her dosage to four capsules a day until the start of her period. She had been doing this for several years, as had all her coworkers. 'The six of us have been working together for so long that our periods are almost synchronised,' she said. 'Can you imagine how crabby our office would be without evening primrose oil?'

Finally, during a break in one of my many herb lectures, a woman came up to me and mentioned that she had been taking evening primrose oil for 10 years. She was convinced that it had alleviated her PMS. Then she confided that she worked for the FDA, the agency that has waged a relentless campaign against claims for evening primrose – not because it's harmful, but because the FDA doesn't accept the research that led to British approval of the herb for premenstrual symptoms.

treat gynaecological complaints such as PMS.

As it turns out, evening primrose oil is a top-notch source of gamma-linolenic acid (GLA), which has been shown in studies to make women with PMS less sensitive to their premenstrual hormonal fluctuations. In the UK, evening primrose oil has been approved as a treatment for PMS. Oddly, the herb wasn't even considered by Germany's Commission E.

Around my home, evening primrose seed can be harvested for free, all winter long. I've gathered as much as half a kilo (1 lb) in a 2-hour lunch period. I like to munch on the seeds. I also chop them and add them to cornbread and muffin recipes.

But if you're not a garden grazer, as I am, I'd suggest getting your evening primrose oil in capsule form. The oil is available as a supplement, sold under the brand name Efamol. In the studies showing evening primrose oil's effectiveness against PMS, the women took 4 grams of Efamol a day for several months. Efamol is sold in health food shops.

If you want to try something other than evening primrose oil, many of the herbs that I recommended for menstrual cramps also help relieve premenstrual symptoms. You can take the same dose as for cramping, only for the entire month, increasing to two to four times the dose during the week before your period. You'll need to experiment to see what works best for you.

Tips for an Anti-PMS Lifestyle

Whichever herbs you choose, you may also want to adopt the following lifestyle strategies. They, too, can help prevent premenstrual symptoms.

Eat as the cavewomen did. Many women report that when they reduced or eliminated meats, dairy products, sugar, and salt and substituted lots of fruits, veggies, beans, and grains, their PMS improved. You may get the same results by following my Healthy Sevens eating plan.

Add a B_6 supplement. Many studies have shown that vitamin B_6 helps reduce the severity of premenstrual symptoms. In one of the studies, women were given either a placebo (a fake pill) or a B_6 supplement. Then they switched treatments. While taking the vitamin, 84 per cent reported noticeable improvement in their PMS.

Many American nutrition experts suggest starting with a supplement that provides 50 milligrams of B_6 a day, then gradually increasing to 100 milligrams a day. However, experts in the UK are more cautious and would not recommend such high doses. Be aware that high doses of vitamin B_6 have been linked to nerve damage in the extremities, a condition called peripheral neuropathy. It's remotely possible that you might experience symptoms with a dosage of 100 milligrams a day. If you notice any numbness or tingling in your fingers or toes, reduce your dosage or stop taking the supplement.

Consider extra calcium, too. Some scientific literature suggests that disturbances in calcium metabolism may contribute to PMS. The same literature says that taking 1,200 milligrams of calcium carbonate a day can significantly reduce symptoms within 3 months. It's certainly worth trying. You need calcium anyway to keep your bones strong.

Cut back on caffeine and alcohol. Many women report improvement in their premenstrual symptoms after reducing their consumption of caffeine and alcohol. Doing so may help you, too.

Increase your physical activity. As mentioned earlier, women with PMS tend to have low premenstrual levels of endorphins. Exercise triggers the production of endorphins, which can boost your mood and relieve premenstrual irritability and anxiety.

Find ways to destress. Stress aggravates irritability and anxiety. Control your stress levels, and you're likely to reduce your premenstrual moodiness. Any relaxation technique can help: biofeedback, hypnosis, massage, meditation, and yoga, among others. When I want to unwind, I potter around my garden, take walks, and play music.

Low Sexual Desire: You Can Rekindle the Flame

As women get older and their bodies' production of oestrogen and testosterone (the male sex hormone) begins to slow down, they may notice a decline in their interest in intimacy. Certain herbs, particularly those rich in phyto-oestrogens, may help recharge a flagging libido.

Any of the following could produce the desired results. All grow in my Garden of Youth.

DONG QUAI (*ANGELICA SINENSIS*). Also known as Chinese angelica, dong quai is a major women's herb in Chinese medicine. I've seen some studies showing that it is oestrogenic, though other research disputes the claim. I'm inclined to believe the findings of oestrogenic properties, because of dong quai's traditional uses among the Chinese. I suggest buying a commercial preparation and taking it according to the label directions.

Dr Duke's Anti-Ageing Elixir

Turn-On Tincture

With its potent combination of sexually stimulating herbs, this tincture just might switch on your sexual desire.

WHAT YOU NEED

1 teaspoon fresh damiana leaves
5 yinyanghuo leaves
¼ teaspoon fennel seed
½ teaspoon fenugreek seed
1 teaspoon ground ginger
½ teaspoon ginseng
120 ml (4 fl oz) vodka or 180 ml (6 fl oz) red wine

WHAT TO DO

Put all of the herbs in a jar. Add cheap vodka or red wine. Seal the jar and place it in a cool, dark spot. Let the herbs steep for 2 to 4 days. Strain out the plant material before using. Take the tincture by the dropperful.

DAMIANA (*TURNERA APHRODISIACA*). In folk medicine, damiana is a traditional aphrodisiac for women. There is some evidence that its essential oil irritates the mucous membranes, especially those in the reproductive and urinary systems. This might give women a sensation of sexual stimulation.

Over the years, I've heard so many testimonials supporting this herb that if I were a woman looking to boost my libido, I'd give it a try. Buy a commercial preparation and use it according to the package directions.

YINYANGHUO (*EPIMEDIUM*, VARIOUS SPECIES). Research in China suggests that this herb, commonly known as horny goat weed, stimulates sexual activity and sperm production in laboratory animals. It also stimulates the sensory nerves, which may play a role in sexual desire. While the herb does not appear to have oestrogenic properties, it does have some androgenic action. It's the androgens, the male sex hormones, that produce libido in both genders.

I grow quite a bit of horny goat weed in my Garden of Youth. Actually, I've toyed with the idea of bottling it up as a product called Horny GoaTea. The label would feature an old dude with a goatee, perhaps even yours truly.

To make a tea, add 1 to 2 teaspoons of the herb to a cup of freshly boiled water. Steep for 10 minutes, then strain. I'd suggest drinking a cup or two a day.

ANISE (*PIMPINELLA ANISUM*) AND FENNEL (*FOENICULUM VULGARE*). Both of these herbs are rich in anethole, an oestrogenic compound. Both also have age-old reputations as women's herbs. They're reputed to promote menstruation, facilitate childbirth, increase milk secretion, minimise menopausal symptoms, and, of course, boost libido.

Anise and fennel make pleasant-tasting teas, with a licorice flavour. Add 1 to 2 teaspoons of either herb – or a blend of both – to a cup of freshly boiled water. Steep for 10 minutes, then strain. Drink up to three cups a day.

FENUGREEK (*TRIGONELLA FOENUM-GRAECUM*). At one time, fenugreek was fed to women in Middle Eastern harems. Supposedly, the herb made the ladies more buxom. I think it might actually work.

There are also anecdotal reports of fenugreek enhancing sexual desire. This seems likely, since the herb is oestrogenic. If you can find a commercial fenugreek product, take it according to the label directions.

GINGER (*ZINGIBER OFFICINALE*). The traditional 'hot' spice, ginger is sold in Peruvian markets as a remedy for 'cold' women. My own experience suggests that ginger tea does spark sexual desire. If you'd like to try the

for the Gardener

Anise

Pimpinella anisum

True anise is a spindly, aromatic annual. The seeds are best sown in cool weather in early spring. Choose a sunny spot with tilled, well-drained soil. Cover the seeds with 3mm (⅛ inch) of soil, tamping gently. They should germinate in 1 to 2 weeks, provided the soil temperature stays around 21°C (70°F).

Thin seedlings to a 15–30 cm (6- to 12-inch) spacing. You don't have to be all that vigilant about weeding; just don't let the plants become weed-choked. Allow 3 to 4 months of growth before harvesting. Usually, the plants are pulled up after the tips of the fruits, the seeds, turn greyish green. Then they're stacked and left to dry for 4 to 5 days. The seeds should not be stored until they're dry. The leaves can be harvested fresh for use in soups and salads.

herb, you can make a tea using 1 to 2 teaspoons of freshly grated root per cup of freshly boiled water. Steep for 10 minutes, then strain and allow to cool slightly before drinking. You can also use liberal amounts of ginger in your cooking.

Speaking of hot spices . . . in the Amazon, they drink hot chocolate with Tabasco sauce to generate sexual heat.

ASIAN GINSENG (*PANAX GINSENG*). The book *Adverse Effects of Herbal Drugs* notes greater sexual responsiveness as a possible side effect of ginseng. I suppose one person's side effect is another person's benefit. To try ginseng, buy a commercial preparation and take it according to the label directions.

WILD YAM (*DIOSCOREA VILLOSA*). This is not the yam that's sold in the produce section of the supermarket. It's another species entirely.

The Chinese consider wild yam to be among the most yin, or female, of herbs. It contains compounds that are precursors to the female sex hormones. In fact, it was used to synthesize the first birth control pills.

You can find wild yam preparations in health food stores. Whatever product you choose, use it according to the label directions.

PART THREE

Fighting *the* Enemies *that* Age You

CHAPTER 26

Angina

Dr Duke's Anti-Ageing Elixirs

- *'Hearty' Hawthorn Spread*
- *Anti-Angina Juice*

Angina – in medical parlance, angina pectoris – is an ominous form of heart disease, a wake-up call that you're at high risk for a heart attack. In fact, the chest pain of angina is very similar to that of a heart attack. It's often described as squeezing, pressing, choking, or suffocating, and it may radiate up to your jaw or out to your left arm or shoulder blade.

But unlike a heart attack, angina usually occurs only when you exert yourself, such as while climbing stairs or walking briskly. The pain subsides when you stop whatever you're doing. This is what's known as stable angina.

If you have unstable angina, on the other hand, you may experience pain even while at rest. This signals a greater likelihood of an impending heart attack.

Your Body's Early-Warning System

In chapter 13, I talk at length about the risk factors and physical processes associated with the development of angina and other forms of heart disease. To give you a brief recap, heart disease occurs because of atherosclerosis, a condition in which fatty, cholesterol-rich deposits called plaques form on the walls of your arteries, including the ones that nourish your heart (the coronary arteries). These plaques narrow your arteries, reducing bloodflow and raising blood pressure. The plaques can also rupture, spilling their load of gunk into your bloodstream.

If this gunk completely blocks a coronary artery, you experience a heart attack, and an area of your heart dies. In angina, the coronary arteries don't become completely blocked. But they're so narrowed with plaques that they don't feed blood through your heart as they should. As a result, your heart runs low on food and oxygen.

While you're at rest, your heart has enough nourishment to function reasonably well. But its need for food and oxygen increases when you're active. Because blood has trouble getting through those narrowed arteries, your heart literally starves. This triggers the pain associated with stable angina.

If you have the more severe unstable angina, your heart isn't getting enough nourishment even when you're at rest. This means you're a prime candidate for a heart attack.

Angina is a major risk factor for heart attack. In fact, it's considered more predictive than any other risk factor, including family history, smoking, obesity, high cholesterol, high blood pressure, and stress.

Some heart attacks strike out of the blue. But many, perhaps most, are preceded by angina. So the condition is a peculiar sort of gift, your body's way of telling you that trouble is brewing and that you need to take action *now* to save your heart.

Many of the measures that I suggest in chapter 13 to prevent heart disease can also help control angina. Of course, if you have angina, you should be under professional care. Be sure to discuss any herbal approaches and lifestyle changes with your doctor before incorporating them into your treatment programme.

Break Those Heartbreaking Habits

For your heart's sake, the most important step that you can take is to quit smoking. I did. Smoking greatly increases your chances of having a heart attack. Once you stop, your risk drops pretty quickly.

As for alcohol, moderate consumption – a drink or two a day – may help protect against heart attack. (A drink is defined as 350 ml (12 fl oz) of regular beer, 150 ml (5 fl oz) of wine, or a cocktail made with 45 ml (1½ fl oz) of 80-proof distilled spirits.) Any more increases your risk.

Of course, if you don't drink, don't start. There are other ways that you can help your heart. If you do drink, be sensible about it.

How Low Should Your Fat Intake Go?

To prevent heart disease, I recommend steering clear of high-fat, high-cholesterol foods, especially fatty meats, fried foods, and rich desserts. This advice goes double for treating angina.

So what should you eat? No surprise here: I suggest a plant-based Palaeolithic diet, much like my Healthy Sevens plan (see chapter 3). It's naturally low in fat and cholesterol but high in heart-healthy nutrients, including the all-important antioxidants.

Depending on the seriousness of your angina, your doctor may recommend a very low fat diet, like the one developed by Dean Ornish, M.D., president and director of the Preventive Medicine Research Institute in Sausalito, California. Good studies have shown that the Ornish diet can relieve angina pain, sometimes in a matter of days. It can even reverse atherosclerosis, which neither angioplasty nor bypass surgery can do.

The Ornish diet limits calories from fat to just 10 per cent, about one-quarter of the fat in the average American diet. It completely eliminates red meat, chicken, fish, dairy products, nuts, chocolate, and coffee. But you can have all the whole grains, beans, and fresh fruits and vegetables that you want.

At Dr Ornish's Preventive Medicine Research Institute, patients learn how to adjust to this new way of eating. They also participate in activities that are good for their hearts, such as meditating, doing yoga, walking, and attending support groups. If you are interested in finding a similar programme in your area, ask your doctor.

One reason why the Ornish diet is so heart-healthy is that it has a rich supply of vitamin E. Landmark Harvard studies have shown that a high intake of vitamin E can reduce risk of heart attack by more than one-third.

Among fruits and vegetables, the best sources of vitamin E are peppers, tomatoes, currants, blueberries, peaches, plums, and rose hips.

You can get modest amounts of vitamin E from whole grains, beans, and leafy greens. I've never grown grains, but I'm big on beans. And I have bushels of purslane, a weedy but wonderful leafy green. (More on purslane a bit later.)

Vitamin E is also found in vegetable oils and nuts. Neither is permitted in the Ornish diet, but once your angina pain subsides, you might add them in prudent amounts. I enjoy nibbling on sunflower seeds, which are well-endowed with vitamin E.

The Ornish diet also contains generous amounts of magnesium. That's significant, because deficiencies in the mineral can contribute to heart disease by raising blood pressure and encouraging heart-rhythm disturbances (arrhythmias).

One highly regarded study of 25,000 Seventh-Day Adventists found that they're 40 per cent less likely to have heart attacks than the typical American. The Adventists are vegetarians, which means they eat lots of plant foods. And plant foods are rich in magnesium. The best sources of the mineral are green beans, spinach, lettuce, purslane, poppy seeds, black-eyed peas, and stinging nettle. I get my magnesium from all the green beans and purslane that I grow in my garden.

Note: Doctors sometimes use injections of magnesium to treat heart attack. Never take such large, medicinal doses on your own.

Get More of the Cardio-Nutrients

Of course, you can always get your vitamin E and magnesium in supplement form. The naturopaths whom I respect – including Joseph Pizzorno, N.D., and Alan Gaby, M.D., both of Bastyr University near

Seattle – typically recommend taking 800 IU of vitamin E a day and 750 milligrams of magnesium a day. (People with heart or kidney problems should check with their doctors before taking supplemental magnesium.)

These same experts suggest rounding out your supplement programme with l-carnitine (500 to 3,000 milligrams per day), coenzyme Q_{10} (60 to 300 milligrams per day), and vitamin C (1,000 to 3,000 milligrams per day). Carnitine prevents the accumulation of harmful fatty acids in your heart muscle, while coenzyme Q_{10} helps strengthen your heart. And vitamin C has diuretic, blood-thinning, and cholesterol-lowering properties, among other heart-healthy benefits.

Good research shows that all of these supplements help treat heart disease. If I had angina, I'd take them. If you're already using the blood thinner warfarin, talk with your doctor before taking coenzyme Q_{10}. The supplement may reduce the drug's effectiveness.

The Cream of the Heart-Herb Crop

Now we're ready to discuss my favourite angina treatments: herbs. Your best choices are hawthorn, garlic, onion, ginger, turmeric, and willow.

HAWTHORN (*CRATAEGUS MONOGYNA*). To treat heart disease and related conditions, the medical establishment routinely relies on a quartet of pharmaceuticals that's easily remembered by the abbreviation ABCD. That's *A* for ACE inhibitors and anti-aggregants, *B* for beta-blockers, *C* for calcium channel blockers, and *D* for diuretics. All of these are helpful, but they carry the unwanted baggage of serious side effects. That's why I prefer hawthorn. It delivers many of the same benefits as conventional heart medications, without causing other problems.

Hawthorn extracts improve heart function in people with angina. The herb contains both oligomeric procyanidins and flavonoids, including hyperoside, quercetin, vitexin, and vitexin rhamnoside. These compounds open (dilate) your coronary arteries by relaxing the smooth muscle tissue that lines them. This allows more blood – and more nourishment – to flow into your heart muscle. As a bonus, hawthorn lowers cholesterol.

These properties, verified by research, support hawthorn's strong

Dr Duke's Anti-Ageing Elixir

'Hearty' Hawthorn Spread

Hawthorn has many properties that can help treat angina symptoms. I recently discovered that I can blend the herb's berries into jelly within about 15 minutes. That gave me the idea for this chutney-like recipe.

WHAT YOU NEED

50 g (1¾ oz) hawthorn berries
½ onion
1 clove garlic
1 piece fresh ginger (2.5 cm/1 inch length)
Hot-pepper sauce
Turmeric
Curry powder
Water if necessary

WHAT TO DO

In a food processor, combine the hawthorn berries, onion, garlic, and ginger. Strain out the seeds. Season to taste with the hot-pepper sauce, turmeric, and curry powder. Blend to a spreadable consistency, adding water if necessary. Serve on high-fibre wholemeal bread or eat plain.

folk reputation as a heart herb. In Europe, hawthorn berry preparations have been used for generations to treat angina. They're still quite popular. Commission E, the expert panel that evaluates the safety and effectiveness of herbs for the German government, approves hawthorn for angina and several other heart ailments.

If you want to try hawthorn, I'd recommend buying a standardised extract containing 10 milligrams of flavonoids, 5 milligrams of flavones (a category of flavonoids), or 5 milligrams of oligomeric procyanidins. For dosage, follow the label directions.

Hawthorn is safe to use for extended periods of time, according to the studies that I've reviewed. Still, if you have any cardiovascular condition, you should check with your doctor before taking hawthorn. Your doctor may need to adjust your dosage of any other heart medication that you've been prescribed.

GARLIC (*ALLIUM SATIVUM*) AND ONION (A. CEPA). These ancient herbs – they're mentioned in the Bible – have longstanding reputations as treatments for angina. And no wonder: they're close botanical relatives, members of the same genus (*Allium*). Garlic is more potent, but onions also pack a punch. So do other members of the allium family, including leeks, shallots, and chives.

Garlic treats angina in several ways. It helps shrink the atherosclerotic plaques that have built up on your coronary artery walls. It lowers cholesterol and blood pressure. And it thins your blood, making it less likely to clot.

This last benefit is especially important for people with angina. Clotting factors play a key role in triggering heart attacks. By reducing the likelihood of internal blood clots, garlic goes a long way towards reducing the risk of heart attack.

It is possible for the blood to become *too* thin. Besides garlic, other blood thinners (anticoagulants) include vitamin E, aspirin, and several prescription pharmaceuticals. If you have angina, ask your doctor what you can do to reduce the likelihood of developing blood clots, then follow his recommendations. Don't take other blood thinners without your doctor's approval and supervision.

Over the years, I've grown lots of garlic, plus most of its relatives – elephant garlic, onions, leeks, chives, and shallots. They're relatively hardy plants, and oh-so-versatile in cooking. Just don't overcook them. Their medicinal properties are most potent when they're close to raw.

Besides incorporating fresh garlic into your cooking, you may want to take garlic capsules. Buy a commercial product and take it according to the label directions.

GINGER (*ZINGIBER OFFICINALE*) AND TURMERIC (*CURCUMA LONGA*). Ginger and turmeric are different herbs. But botanically speaking, they're very closely related, with very similar benefits.

Ginger and turmeric rival garlic for the number of ways in which they help people with angina. They strengthen the heart muscle. They make blood less likely to clot, reducing heart attack risk. They lower cholesterol. They contain antioxidants, which help shrink atherosclerotic plaques. And they reduce blood sugar, an important benefit for people with diabetes, who are at very high risk for angina, heart attack, and stroke.

The cardiology clinic of an Israeli hospital advises its patients with angina to take ½ teaspoon of ground ginger daily. If I had angina, I'd take at least that much. I'd also use lots of ginger and turmeric in my cooking. (Turmeric is the spice that makes curry blends look yellowish.)

In fact, you may want to invest in an Indian cookbook. Both ginger and turmeric are staple ingredients in Indian cuisine.

I'd also recommend drinking lots of ginger tea. Use 1 to 2 teaspoons of grated fresh ginger per cup of freshly boiled water. Steep for 10 minutes, then strain. Make sure that the tea has cooled before drinking.

WILLOW BARK (*SALIX*, VARIOUS SPECIES). If you have angina, the chances are that your doctor has advised you to take an aspirin a day or every other day. Aspirin is a potent blood thinner that helps prevent clots from forming in your coronary arteries. In this way, it greatly lowers your chances of suffering a heart attack.

According to the expert opinions that I've read, if everyone at risk for a heart attack – including people with angina – took aspirin regularly, it could prevent as many as 600,000 heart attacks, including 200,000 fatalities. It could also prevent 250,000 strokes caused by blocked blood vessels in the brain. At least one study has shown that aspirin reduces the risk of death among people with unstable angina.

But you don't have to rely solely on pharmaceutical aspirin. After all, it was created from plants that contain salicin, the aspirin precursor that's found in willow bark, meadowsweet, and wintergreen. With your doctor's okay, instead of taking aspirin, you might want to try willow

More Wisdom *from the* Garden

PLANT FOODS HAVE CLOT-BLOCKING POWER

You may have heard that vegetarians have a lower rate of heart attack than meat eaters. The usual explanation is that vegetarians, with their plant-based diet, have lower intakes of fat and cholesterol. That's certainly true. But here's another possibility: they may be getting protection from the aspirin-like salicylate compounds found in all plant foods. Like aspirin, the salicylates reduce the risk of blood clots that can lead to a heart attack.

Few plants contain as many salicylates as willow bark. But every plant contains some. So people who eat lots of plant foods get more of the heart-protecting compounds than those who don't.

bark tea. To make it, use 2 to 3 teaspoons of powdered bark per cup of boiling water. Simmer for 10 minutes, then strain and allow to cool. Drink up to three cups a day.

More Weapons for the Anti-Angina Arsenal

Herbal medicine boasts a number of other heart helpers. The following may be a bit less potent than the herbs mentioned above. But they're valuable nonetheless.

AMMI (*AMMI MAJUS* AND *A. VISNAGA*). Ammi, also known as bishop's weed and khella, is a Middle Eastern relative of angelica. It's not well-known in the United States, but it looks like a diminutive version of Queen Anne's lace. I tried growing ammi in my garden, but it never thrived. Eventually, I gave up. Now I'm trying to get replacement plants.

In Egypt, ammi seeds are used as a spice. Its leaves are chewed for their pleasant flavour. In 1946, one of the technicians in a medical researcher's Cairo laboratory developed a kidney stone. He treated himself with khellin, a compound extracted from ammi. It not only helped his kidney stones but also improved his angina symptoms. This prompted the medical researcher to study the effects of ammi and khellin on the heart. Both open the coronary arteries, reducing blood pressure and allowing more blood and nourishment to circulate through the heart.

In 1951, the *New England Journal of Medicine* published a report suggesting that khellin significantly improves angina symptoms. Despite this research, the compound remains on the fringes of mainstream medicine, though it is prescribed by naturopaths for angina. Commission E endorses *Ammi visnaga* fruits for mild angina symptoms.

Khellin is safe when taken as directed. As little as 30 milligrams a day can help. But the naturopaths whom I know typically suggest 250 to 300 milligrams of extract a day, standardised for 12 per cent khellin content. If I had angina, I'd try khellin. Perhaps I'd use it with hawthorn, a combination that many naturopaths recommend. Khellin may cause liver enzyme abnormalities, so it should be taken only under the care of a doctor or naturopath who can monitor your liver function.

ANGELICA (*ANGELICA ARCHANGELICA*). A member of the carrot family, angelica contains some 15 compounds that act as calcium channel blockers. My guess is that they work synergistically – in other words, their total effect is greater than the sum of their individual effects.

Calcium channel blockers are an important class of blood pressure medications. But you can get at least some of the many calcium-blocking compounds from angelica or one of its close relatives, which include carrot, celery, dill, fennel, parsley, and parsnip. Actually, this points to one possible reason why vegetarians are less likely than meat eaters to develop angina: vegetarians eat plant foods, so they're getting more of the calcium-blocking compounds in their diets.

I've grown angelica, a biennial that flowers and seeds after its second year. For a few cycles, my plants reseeded themselves. But now I have to get new starter plants. If you want to try angelica, I suggest looking for a commercial preparation and using it according to the label directions.

BILBERRY (*VACCINIUM MYRTILLUS*). You may know bilberry as European blueberry. Like American blueberry and other types of berries, bilberry gets its dark colour from pigments that contain compounds called anthocyanidins. Anthocyanidins are potent antioxidants that have several benefits for people with angina. Namely, they reduce cholesterol and blood pressure, and they make blood less likely to clot.

Now I'm not suggesting that bilberry and its relatives are as effective as pharmaceutical angina medications. But until manufacturers start studying these fruits instead of just developing more synthetic drugs, we'll never know. Each of the more promising herbal alternatives needs to be compared objectively with its pharmaceutical counterpart in order to determine which is best, in terms of safety and effectiveness.

Personally, I think that fruits with anthocyanidins are likely to be good for the heart. If I had angina, I'd eat lots of them – blueberries, blackberries, raspberries, cranberries, currants, grapes, and plums (not to mention raisins and prunes). Or you can buy bilberry in supplement form from health food shops.

KUDZU (*PUERARIA MONTANA*). This Asian vine has invaded the American South, where it's about as welcome as dandelion. But perhaps its reputation will improve, now that Chinese studies have shown that kudzu root helps treat angina. Of 71 patients given kudzu over the course of 4 to 22 weeks, 29 experienced much improvement in their symptoms, 20 showed some improvement, and 22 had little or no improvement – an overall success rate of 69 per cent.

Other research has found that kudzu helps relieve high blood pressure. In one study, 52 people with high blood pressure took a strong tea made from the herb's root in divided doses every day for 2 to 8 weeks. Seventeen of the participants (33 per cent) reported great improvement in their symptoms, while another 30 (58 per cent) experienced marked improvement. The tea used in this study was prepared with 5 teaspoons of powdered root per cup of boiling water, simmered for 10 minutes, and strained.

I've made kudzu tea, tincture, gelatin, tempura, and blended slurry – all of which need culinary help to make them palatable. Blending with

for the
Gardener

Kudzu

Pueraria montana

Throughout the South, kudzu has a reputation as a pesky plant. But I happen to like this fast-growing vine, because its roots are rich in the isoflavones daidzein and genistein. These are the same oestrogenic compounds that have made soya so popular as a treatment for menopausal discomforts as well as for osteoporosis.

I grow my own kudzu, but I take care to keep it well-contained by cutting back the branches, especially those at ground level, which may take root. I started my crop from root runners taken from plants growing wild near my place. With great effort, I pulled up some of the branches so I got a good length of root as well. If the roots have nodes, you can plant them, then transplant them to bigger pots when they're about 2 years old and well-established.

Although kudzu is viewed as a weed, it actually doesn't do well in extremely light, sandy soil or heavy, clay soil. It needs well-drained soil. One or two plants should be enough. Two well-established plants can easily produce 45 kg (100 lb) of roots.

carrot juice, celery juice, or both juices improves the flavour. But strain your kudzu; the fibres are very tough.

Kudzu grows so quickly that if you don't eat it, it just might eat you. Mine is very carefully confined to several plots in my Garden of Youth. Thanks to frequent pruning, it hasn't spread outside its boundaries.

PURSLANE (*PORTULACA OLERACEA*). Purslane 'volunteered' in my garden, so I consider it a gift from God. It's a gift to the heart as well.

The underlying cause of angina – and coronary heart disease – is oxidative damage to the coronary arteries. That's why these conditions respond to treatment with antioxidants such as vitamin E.

Well, purslane happens to be richly endowed with antioxidants – vitamin E as well as vitamin C and carotenoids. It's also the best plant source of omega-3 fatty acids, which help prevent the internal blood clots that trigger heart attack. And it's a good source of magnesium.

I prefer my purslane fresh or stir-fried, perhaps with onion, garlic, hot peppers and a little olive oil. It makes a great side dish.

Herbs with Heart-Protecting Potential

Compared with the herbs discussed above, these may not be as well-researched, but they show tremendous promise. If I had angina, I'd include them in my treatment programme.

SWEETLEAF (*SAUROPUS ANDROGYNUS*). This tropical herb won't grow in my neck of the woods. I've seen it only in Hawaii. It's a small, nondescript shrub. As its name suggests, its leaves are edible. They're quite popular as a vegetable in Asian countries, served raw in salads, steamed or fermented.

According to one report, sweetleaf contains a large amount of papaverine – about 580 milligrams per 100 grammes of fresh leaves. So 230 g (8 oz) of leaves would provide more than 1,000 milligrams of papaverine, a compound whose pharmaceutical form can be used to treat angina.

As far as I know, sweetleaf itself has never been studied as a treatment for angina. But if the report on its papaverine content is correct, the herb should definitely help. If I ever succeed in growing sweetleaf in my greenhouse, I'll steam the leaves like spinach.

This herb may be difficult to find in health food and herb shops. If you come across it, buy a commercial preparation and use it according to the package directions.

CHICORY (*CICHORIUM INTYBUS*). Dried and roasted, chicory root makes a good substitute for coffee. In some places in the American South, notably New Orleans, folks like to mix the herb *into* their coffee.

I've been on a chicory kick lately, ever since I learned that the herb is rich in inulin, a compound that helps prevent atherosclerosis and strengthens the heart. If I had angina, I'd mix chicory into my coffee. Better yet, I'd skip the coffee and just drink chicory.

If you want to try it yourself, I suggest using 1 teaspoon of powdered chicory root in a cup of freshly boiled water. Steep for 10 minutes, then strain out the powder. Cool before drinking.

EVENING PRIMROSE (*OENOTHERA BIENNIS*). Evening primrose is my favourite flower, so lovely to see in bloom in my Garden of Youth. Its oil contains gamma-linolenic acid (GLA), which reduces blood pressure and prevents the blood clots that trigger heart attack.

Most experts suggest taking 1 to 4 grams of evening primrose oil a day. If I had angina, I'd take 3 or 4 grams. I'd also combine my evening primrose oil with fish oil to gain even more heart attack protection. Both supplements are available in most health food stores.

MULAKIYA (*CORCHORUS OLITORIUS*). Mulakiya is the Arabic name for this herb. For reasons that escape me, Westerners sometimes call it Jew's mallow. In deference to Jewish people, I prefer 'edible jute'. After all, this tall, weedy annual is rather jutelike.

Mulakiya is quite rich in folate, a nutrient that's tough to get from food. On the other hand, you'd need to eat more than a ½ kilo (1 lb) of the herb a day to get the 5 milligrams of folate now recommended to treat high levels of homocysteine, which is a risk factor for heart attack.

Still, the little folate boost provided by mulakiya can't hurt, especially since the herb contains another compound, strophanthidin, that reportedly is anti-anginal.

You can eat mulakiya's leaves, shoots, and roots. Personally, I like

Dr Duke's Anti-Ageing Elixir

Anti-Angina Juice

This recipe combines the proven angina-fighting power of hawthorn with the symptom-busting potential of bromelain, an enzyme in pineapple. I grow hawthorn in the Garden of Youth, so I can pick fresh berries every fall. But dried berries, available in health food stores, work just as well.

WHAT YOU NEED

115 g (4 oz) hawthorn berries
240 ml (8 fl oz) pineapple juice
240 ml (8 fl oz) grapefruit juice
Fresh ginger, grated

WHAT TO DO

In a blender, combine the hawthorn berries, pineapple juice, and grapefruit juice. Strain. Add the ginger to taste.

the leaves steamed. If you can find a commercial preparation, use it according to the label directions.

PINEAPPLE (*ANANAS COMOSUS*). Hundreds of papers have been written on the medicinal uses of the bromelain enzymes extracted from pineapple. In one study, people with angina who took a daily dose of bromelain saw their symptoms disappear in 4 to 90 days, depending upon the seriousness of their conditions. Their symptoms returned only after they stopped taking the enzyme.

Scientists aren't sure why bromelain helps treat angina. But the enzyme is quite safe, and since the research shows that it may be beneficial, I'd take it. The typically recommended dosage is 250 to 500 milligrams three times a day, with meals. Or do what I do: eat lots of pineapple.

VALERIAN (*VALERIANA OFFICINALIS*). Valerian contains compounds called valepotriates that appear to have important therapeutic properties. According to one team of researchers, these compounds 'exhibit sedative, spasmolytic, slightly anti-anginous, and anti-arrhythmic activities that make them very suitable for treatment of nervous diseases, particularly those accompanied by functional heart disorders'.

For insomnia, the recommended dose of valerian is one or two capsules containing 470 milligrams of powdered root. I'd use the same dose for angina, but only at bedtime since valerian may cause drowsiness during the day. The herb can also cause heart palpitations in people who are sensitive to it. If you experience this side effect, stop using valerian.

CHAPTER 27

Appetite Loss

Dr Duke's Anti-Ageing Elixir
• *Appetising Appetiser*

With so many people overweight, and weight loss a modern obsession, we sometimes forget that appetite loss can be a problem. In the medical community, the condition is known as anorexia.

It's not the same as anorexia nervosa, the frightening psychological eating disorder that makes some people – overwhelmingly, young women – starve themselves. Rather, anorexia is simple appetite loss. You don't starve yourself. You just don't feel particularly hungry.

Appetite loss is most common among older folks. It might seem like a good thing if you're trying to take off some extra weight. But it's not. If you don't eat enough, your body doesn't get the nutrients it needs. Over time, it can't function properly.

This point was driven home to me by a study conducted at Johns Hopkins Medical Institutions in Baltimore. Researchers gave about 100 elderly volunteers either a placebo (a fake pill) or an off-the-shelf multivitamin/mineral formula to supplement their regular diets. Over the

Dr Duke's Anti-Ageing Elixir

Appetising Appetiser

Research has shown that a deficiency of zinc can set the stage for appetite loss. A number of plant foods supply generous amounts of the mineral. They're the key ingredients in this recipe. Eat it as an appetiser, and you may feel more hungry for the rest of your meal.

WHAT YOU NEED

Any combination of the following: asparagus, black-eyed peas, brussels sprouts, collard greens, cucumbers, endive, parsley, spinach, and string beans

Curry powder

WHAT TO DO

Toss together the zinc-rich plant foods of your choice. (I strongly recommend using spinach, which is among the best plant sources of the mineral.) Season with the curry powder, which seems to stimulate the appetite.

course of a year, the people taking the multivitamins reported fewer days of illness. Blood tests showed that they had more robust immune systems.

Of course, this study caught the attention of the supplement industry, which used it to promote their products. I don't have any problem with that. As I've discussed elsewhere in this book, moderate supplementation makes sense. But I'm convinced that part of the reason the elderly participants responded so well to the multivitamin is that they weren't eating properly to begin with. They simply didn't have the appetite to consume enough food to get all the nutrients their bodies needed. As a result, their immune systems suffered.

Food Everywhere, But No Desire to Eat

So what causes appetite loss? Often it's a symptom of an underlying health problem or a side effect of a particular drug. Interestingly, deficiencies of certain nutrients – specifically thiamin, niacin, vitamin B_{12}, and zinc – can also contribute to appetite loss. One recent clinical study found that people experiencing appetite loss ate more and gained significant weight when they took zinc supplements.

A variety of illnesses can trigger appetite loss, including cancer, digestive tract disorders, and many infectious diseases – even colds. At first, this may seem counterintuitive. You'd think that when you're sick, your body would crave more food, seeking to bolster its supply of nutrients that strengthen the immune system and help it fend off any disease-causing invaders. But that's not what happens.

The reasons for illness-related appetite loss are complex. But one way of looking at it is that when you're sick, your body has to invest so much of its energy in restoring health that it skimps on other things, like triggering a sensation of hunger. Over time, this becomes counterproductive, but in the short term, it works. From an evolutionary perspective, the fact that we're here proves it.

Appetite loss can also be triggered by a variety of medications. Stimulants are a prime example. After all, amphetamines were the original diet pills. Most of today's appetite suppressants are also stimulants. They include the herb-derived combination of caffeine (from coffee) and ephedrine (from Chinese ephedra, or ma huang) that's used in some doctor-supervised weight-loss programmes for dangerously obese people. Personally, if I experienced appetite loss, I'd cut back or even eliminate my coffee consumption to see if it helped.

Depressants also contribute to appetite loss. It's a common side effect of prescription narcotic pain relievers. But by far the chief culprit is alcohol. While one or two drinks may make you hungry, more than that can have the opposite effect. That may be why so many people with drinking problems suffer from undernourishment. If I suspected that alcohol was dampening my appetite, I'd give up drinking.

Many other medications can suppress the appetite, most notably chemotherapy drugs. When you get any prescription filled, ask about side effects, and don't be surprised if your pharmacist mentions anorexia.

Sometimes appetite loss occurs because of two other age-related changes: the gradual decline of the senses of smell and taste. Imagine that it's close to dinnertime, and you're just getting home from work. You're not feeling particularly hungry, but as you step inside the door, you immediately smell that someone has been cooking. You're enveloped in the warm aromas of food. Immediately, you become ravenous, and you can't wait to eat. As you dig in, your tastebuds dance with the flavours of the tasty meal. They also send a message to your gastrointestinal tract to release stomach acids and digestive enzymes, so they're ready when food comes their way.

As you get older, especially if you smoke, your senses of smell and taste become less sharp. That means you don't experience hunger as acutely.

Of all the taste sensations – sweet, sour, salty, bitter, and so on – it's bitter that has the strongest effect on appetite. When bitter substances meet the tastebuds near the base of your tongue, stimuli pass to special cells in your brain. In turn, they trigger the increased secretion of saliva, stomach juices, and bile – all of which enhance appetite.

According to research from the University of Washington, sensitivity to bitterness declines the most with age. Actually, this finding has an upside – namely, that bitter vegetables taste better, because they lose some of their bite. So if you hated foods such as kale and brussel sprouts as a kid, the chances are that you'll like them as you get older.

Your Body's Starving, But You're Not

Even if you don't have a problem with your appetite, your body may not absorb nutrients as it should. It could be because you're low on stomach acid, a condition called hypoacidity.

Most of what you hear about stomach acid is that too much of it causes *acid indigestion*, the TV term for heartburn. As I mention in chapter 9, heartburn is less likely to result from an overproduction of stomach acid than from a weak sphincter muscle at the top of your stomach. It allows acid to wash up into your oesophagus, which causes that familiar burning sensation.

The fact is that many people, mostly older folks, produce too little stomach acid, not too much. Without enough acid, your body can't digest food properly. So it may not be getting enough nutrients, even if you think you're eating all the right foods in the right amounts.

Mainstream doctors don't say much about hypoacidity. I suspect that they don't even consider it a problem. But naturopaths feel differently. If a naturopath suspects that you have hypoacidity, he'll likely prescribe supplements of hydrochloric acid, the main stomach acid. This not only promotes good digestion but also restores a healthy appetite.

Be aware that hydrochloric acid is very caustic. It should be taken only under the supervision of a clinician who recommends it.

Of course, with diminished sensitivity to bitterness, taste-related appetite stimulation suffers. This is where the wisdom of traditional herbal medicine comes into play.

Bitters: The Traditional Appetite Stimulants

For centuries, herbalists have prescribed bitter-herb preparations to stimulate appetite. Appropriately enough, these preparations are known as bitters. Bitters get your digestive juices flowing and your appetite growing.

Taken 20 to 30 minutes before eating, bitters stimulate the secretion of saliva, stomach acid, and bile, all of which contribute to the sensation of hunger. In one study, 200 milligrams of gentian or 25 milligrams of wormwood, both bitter herbs, significantly increased the flow of stomach acid and bile.

The Germans have ranked the bitters as follows, from most potent to least: quassia, gentian, wormwood, condurango bark, lesser centaury, devil's claw, bitter orange peel, blessed thistle, cinchona bark. Look for these herbs in bitters products sold in health food stores. The most popular ingredient in these formulas is gentian. Whichever one you choose, use it according to the label directions.

If you like, you can make your own digestive bitter tea using gentian. Commission E, the expert panel that evaluates the safety and effectiveness of herbs for the German government, reports that the bitter compounds in gentian work very well in increasing the flow of saliva and stomach acid. Studies involving stomach acid suggest that gentian might be helpful as a treatment for ulcers. To make a tea, pour freshly boiled water over 1 to 3 teaspoons of dry herb or a loose handful of fresh herb. Steep for 10 to 15 minutes, then strain. Drink up to 4 cups a day.

Wormwood is a digestive bitter that's been popular in Europe for ages. You can buy a tincture and take ½ to 1 teaspoon of tincture before eating. Just don't take more than that. In large doses, a compound in wormwood called thujone can cause problems. But in recommended doses, the herb is a safe appetite stimulant. Commission E endorses it.

Commission E also approves devil's claw as an appetite stimulant. Africans have used the herb as a digestive bitter for centuries. The commission suggests taking 1.5 grams for anorexia – unless you have an ulcer, in which case you shouldn't use the herb at all. You can buy a commercial preparation and take it according to the label directions, or make a tea using 1 to 2 teaspoons of herb per cup of freshly boiled water. Steep for 10 minutes, strain, and drink just prior to meals.

Other herbs endorsed by Commission E for appetite stimulation include dandelion root, bitter orange peel, cinnamon, coriander, fenugreek, hop, and horehound. You can make a tea from any of these using 1 to 2 teaspoons of herb per cup of freshly boiled water. Steep for 10 to 20 minutes, strain, and drink before meals. (Make sure it has cooled adequately, so you don't burn yourself.) If you opt for a tincture or fluid extract, take it according to the label directions.

Bitters help improve appetite, but they're not a quick fix. They appear to be most effective when used regularly for long periods – sometimes months or years. Note that these herbs are *not* recommended for the treatment of anorexia nervosa.

Aromatic Herbs: Enticed by Savoury Scents

Like the bitter herbs, the aromatic herbs can help enhance your appetite. Their fragrances help stimulate secretions of saliva, stomach acid, and bile. They're potent enough that even people with a diminished sense of smell can benefit from them.

Aromatherapists generally recommend sniffing one of the following essential oils: basil, caraway, camomile, coriander, fennel, garlic, ginger, juniper, lavender, lemon, nutmeg, oregano, sage, or tarragon. As an alternative, I'd try using the herbs themselves in my cooking or as teas – 1 to 2 teaspoons of herb (or herb blend) per cup of freshly boiled water, steeped for 10 minutes, then strained. The herb I'd use most is ginger, which has been found by Indian scientists to enhance appetite.

Personally, I've always found curry to be an effective appetite stimulant. If you'd rather not spend time tediously mixing herbs, try curry powder, which is a premixed blend.

CHAPTER 28

Arthritis

Dr Duke's Anti-Ageing Elixir

• *Lemony Arthritis-Ade*

In chapter 15, I offer some advice for keeping your joints flexible and pain-free as you get older. In this chapter, we'll discuss what you can do to help joints that are already hurting.

Generally, we use the word *arthritis* to describe any kind of joint pain. In fact, more than 100 conditions can produce this sort of pain, including Lyme disease, psoriasis, and various infections. This may explain why so many people are plagued by aching joints.

But for the most part, *arthritis* refers to osteoarthritis, the most common cause of chronic joint pain. Osteoarthritis affects about one person in every six, most of them women over the age of 45. The condition is characterised by stiff and painful joints, though the discomfort tends to diminish over the course of a day. Other classic symptoms include stiffness after periods of rest and pain that worsens with strenuous activity involving the affected joints.

Arthritis can also mean rheumatoid arthritis, another cause of chronic joint pain. Though not as common as osteoarthritis, rheumatoid arthritis strikes millions of people, three-quarters of whom are women. The typical symptoms of rheumatoid arthritis include pain, swelling, warmth, and tenderness in the affected joints. Often, the joints appear purplish.

With rheumatoid arthritis, the symptoms tend to come and go. People with the condition will cycle between periods of intense pain and periods of feeling all right. Over time, their joints can become deformed. Within 10 years of diagnosis, half of them will develop some sort of disability.

Compared with rheumatoid arthritis, gout isn't as potentially debilitating. But it is quite uncomfortable nonetheless. This form of arthritis largely affects men over 30. It's characterised by inflammation and often intense pain in one or more joints, usually the big toe.

Pain Relief – But at What Price?

While all three conditions have different causes and, as you'll soon see, different treatments, they also have at least one thing in common: pain. Burning, aching, gnawing pain. Pain that can impair judgement and make you crazy, desperate for relief.

That's why arthritis has always attracted medical charlatans. They know that desperate folks are often willing to shell out big bucks for 'cures' that don't really cure anything. That's why the medical profession and the Arthritis Foundation warn people with any form of arthritis not to be taken in by quack treatments, and to stick with what doctors recommend.

Now, I'm all for warnings against charlatanism. One dead giveaway is the use of the term *cure*. Based on all that I've read in the medical literature, I'm inclined to side with the experts who say that no pill can cure arthritis, rheumatoid arthritis, or gout. Anything claiming to do so is stretching the truth.

The sensational claims are usually easy to spot. But beyond them, how do you distinguish the truly helpful treatments from the hype? Honestly, sometimes I wonder who's *really* quacking their way to the bank.

Until recently, mainstream doctors relied on first-generation nonsteroidal anti-inflammatory drugs (NSAIDs) as the arthritis treatment of choice. In the United States, sales of these drugs top $1.2 billion a year. Aspirin and ibuprofen are NSAIDs, but for osteoarthritis and rheumatoid arthritis, doctors usually prescribe stronger – and more expensive – prescription versions of these pharmaceuticals.

First-generation NSAIDs are very effective at relieving the pain and inflammation of joint ailments. But this relief comes at a high price – namely, stomach distress, ulcers, and gastrointestinal bleeding. These side effects can be quite serious. I've read reliable estimates from the

The Other -*Itis*es

Medically speaking, tendinitis and bursitis don't come under the umbrella term of *arthritis*. But they are inflammatory conditions, and they are rather common among older folks (though they can affect anyone at any age). That's why I thought I'd discuss them here.

As its name suggests, tendinitis involves inflammation of one or more tendons, the tissues that connect muscle to bone. Because most tendons attach to bone around joints, tendinitis can cause joint pain.

Bursitis refers to inflamed bursae, the fluid-filled sacs that lubricate places where muscles and tendons pass over bone. As with tendons, bursae are often located around joints, which is why bursitis can produce joint pain.

Tendinitis and bursitis are so similar that sometimes even doctors can't tell which condition a patient has. It doesn't matter, really. Both are quite painful, and both respond to the same treatments.

The same herbs that relieve osteoarthritis and rheumatoid arthritis are also good for tendinitis and bursitis. Ginger and turmeric are most effective, because they're anti-inflammatory.

Another natural anti-inflammatory is bromelain, an enzyme that's found in pineapple. Naturopaths suggest taking 250 milligrams of bromelain three times a day, before meals.

Personally, if I had tendinitis or bursitis, I'd slice up some pineapple and spice it with ginger and turmeric. It's very tasty, and it makes a good side dish or dessert.

I'd also try licorice, which studies have shown to be as effective against inflammation as hydrocortisone, but without the side effects. I like using licorice sticks (the herb, not the candy) to stir my herbal teas. If I don't have time for a tea, I take one to three 300- to 500-milligram licorice capsules a day.

mid-1990s that the 68 million prescriptions for NSAIDs handed out annually in America caused some 200,000 cases of gastrointestinal bleeding, which in turn caused or contributed to 10,000 to 20,000 deaths.

First-generation NSAIDs gave people with arthritis a grim choice: joint pain or stomach pain, or worse gastrointestinal problems. It seems to me that the doctors were the ones quacking when they touted these medications, knowing that they were dangerous and that treating their side effects would cost another $500 million a year.

Now researchers have developed new, second-generation NSAIDs: the COX-2 inhibitors. These pharmaceuticals – celecoxib (Celebrex) and rofecoxib (Vioxx) are the only two as of this writing – can boast all the power of their predecessors. But they're much less likely to cause gastrointestinal side effects, at least according to the studies to date.

The COX-2 inhibitors look like real improvements over the first-generation NSAIDs. Still, I wonder about these drugs and the problems they might cause in the long run. That's why I continue to recommend natural and herbal approaches to treating joint pain.

Osteoarthritis: The Wear-and-Tear Arthritis

Of the three types of arthritis mentioned above, osteoarthritis is the one most often associated with getting older. It's sometimes described as wear-and-tear arthritis, because that's exactly what happens: the cartilage that cushions your joints deteriorates, allowing your bones to rub against each other.

Research has shown that eating foods rich in antioxidants can prevent cartilage from wearing out, which can keep osteoarthritis from getting worse. For one study, researchers at Boston University Medical Center surveyed the dietary habits of 640 older adults. The scientists determined that while antioxidants didn't protect against osteoarthritis, the people with the highest intakes of these nutrients were less likely to develop severe knee pain.

In this study, the researchers found vitamin C to be the most helpful. Compared with the people who consumed the least vitamin C, those who consumed the most were one-third as likely to develop severe osteoarthritis. Among the best food sources of vitamin C are broccoli, peppers, citrus fruits, cabbage, cauliflower, spinach, and strawberries.

This finding gives me the chance to once again extol the virtues of a plant-based Palaeolithic diet. Plant foods are the best sources of antioxidant nutrients – vitamin C, as well as vitamin E and the mineral selenium. All of these may play some role in preserving cartilage and minimising osteoarthritis pain. (My Healthy Sevens eating plan is patterned after the Palaeolithic diet, with recommendations for eating a wide variety of plant foods. To learn more about the plan, see chapter 3.)

In a separate study, the same team of researchers at Boston University Medical Center discovered that a diet high in vitamin D can significantly lower the risk of severe osteoarthritis. Your skin creates its own vitamin D when it's exposed to the sun (unless you're wearing sunscreen, which blocks synthesis of the nutrient). Foods rich in vitamin D include fortified dairy products and fatty saltwater fish such as salmon, halibut, sea bass, tuna, cod, and herring.

Supplements Keep Your Joints Jumpin'

If the antioxidants in food help to minimise osteoarthritis, do antioxidant supplements have the same effect? The research is thin, but promising.

As I've mentioned elsewhere in this book, it's prudent to take a daily multivitamin/mineral supplement, especially as you get older. Just don't fall into thinking that a multivitamin can make up for a poor diet. It can't.

In addition to a multi, you may want to consider taking the following supplements, which have shown promise as osteoarthritis treatments.

GLUCOSAMINE AND CHONDROITIN. These two nutrients gained fame a few years back as the star supplements in the book *The Arthritis Cure*, by Jason Theodosakis, M.D. Glucosamine helps repair damaged cartilage. Chondroitin draws fluid into cartilage, which increases its shock-absorbing ability. Put the two together, and you have a promising formula for relief from osteoarthritis.

I've seen some good research attesting to the power of these supplements as treatments for osteoarthritis. The data support glucosamine more than chondroitin, but one review of 13 rigorous studies – each lasting at least 4 weeks – found that the combination provides significant benefit. What's more, these supplements are safe. I've yet to see any suggestion that glucosamine or chondroitin causes any problems when taken in the recommended doses.

Unfortunately, only about half of the people who use glucosamine and chondroitin experience noticeable improvement in their osteoarthritis symptoms. So I'm inclined to agree with the experts who suggest trying these supplements for a few months. If they help, keep taking them. If not, stop.

Glucosamine and chondroitin are available wherever supplements are sold. The recommended dose of glucosamine is 500 milligrams three times a day; for chondroitin, 400 milligrams three times a day. I take both for my arthritic aches. I think they help.

SAM-E (S-ADENOSYLMETHIONINE). Pronounced 'sammy,' this new European supplement is supposed to help both osteoarthritis and depression. The

Exercise Keeps You One Step Ahead of Pain

Years ago, if you had osteoarthritis, your doctor would have advised you to go easy on the physical activity. Not anymore. In fact, one of the best treatments for osteoarthritis is regular, moderate low-impact exercise – for example, walking, gardening, swimming, or cycling.

Understandably, some days you may not feel like moving around much. But try to be as active as you can. Any activity that gently takes your joints through their full range of motion reduces pain and swelling, keeps cartilage healthy, and strengthens the supporting muscles around your joints. It also triggers the release of endorphins, your body's own pain-relieving compounds. And it helps you control your weight, which keeps your joints pain-free.

Germans have approved SAM-e for joint health based on small studies showing that it provides relief similar to first-generation NSAIDs but without the gastrointestinal side effects.

I don't claim to be an expert, but from what I've read about SAM-e, it appears to be safe when taken in recommended doses (typically 400 milligrams a day). Be aware that SAM-e is expensive. I would be inclined to try it if my current anti-arthritis regime – a combination of glucosamine and chondroitin, turmeric, and exercise – no longer worked for me.

Try the Herbal Pain-Relievers

A number of herbs have well-established reputations as treatments for osteoarthritis. Interestingly, many of them have the same pain-relieving properties as conventional pharmaceuticals. Only they tend to be cheaper and gentler, with fewer side effects. Here are my top picks from the herbal medicine chest.

WILLOW BARK (*SALIX,* VARIOUS SPECIES) AND LICORICE (*GLYCYRRHIZA GLABRA*). Instead of first-generation NSAIDs, I've always preferred the combination of willow bark, which contains salicin (the plant precursor of aspirin), and licorice, which helps prevent the ulcers and other gastrointestinal problems that salicin might cause. Of course, in its recommended doses, salicin is less likely to irritate the gastrointestinal tract than pharmaceutical NSAIDs, because it's not as potent.

The only caveat here is that in very high doses, licorice can raise blood pressure by causing fluid retention. If you have high blood pressure or congestive heart failure, talk with your doctor before you start using the herb. There's no need to panic, though. Licorice generally causes problems only when taken in doses much larger than what I recommend: one to three 300- to 500-milligram capsules a day. As for willow bark, I suggest buying a commercial preparation and taking it according to the label directions.

TURMERIC (*CURCUMA LONGA*). Those new pharmaceutical COX-2 inhibitors may prove miraculous, but I prefer the natural kind. Yes, some herbs – notably turmeric, with its curcumin – work just like the COX-2s.

Dr Duke's Anti-Ageing Elixir

Lemony Arthritis-Ade

Willow bark is the premier source of salicin, the pain-relieving precursor of aspirin. Licorice helps to offset any of salicin's potential gastrointestinal effects, though the risk of side effects is much lower than with pharmaceutical aspirin.

WHAT YOU NEED

1–2 teaspoons powdered willow bark
240 ml (8 fl oz) lemonade
Licorice stick

WHAT TO DO

In a small saucepan, add the willow bark to the lemonade. Bring it to a boil, then let it simmer for about 10 minutes. As it cools, stir it with the licorice stick. Strain out the willow bark before drinking the lemonade. Enjoy up to three cups a day.

I feel more comfortable taking turmeric than a synthetic drug because the human body has evolved to tolerate the herb. Our genes and immune systems have no experience with today's (or tomorrow's) pharmaceuticals. So who knows what problems they'll cause in the long run?

I may sound like a cranky old man here, but I wish Congress would require pharmaceutical companies testing new synthetic drugs to compare them not only with a placebo (a fake pill) but also with one or two of the more promising herbal alternatives. The manufacturers of Celebrex and Vioxx could test their products against the curcumin in turmeric to see which really does the better job of relieving osteoarthritis and rheumatoid arthritis pain. But would the companies tell us if curcumin turned out to be safer and just as effective?

Even if you take first-generation NSAIDs or COX-2 inhibitors, I recommend seasoning your food with lots of turmeric. This is the spice that gives curry blends their yellow colour. You may even want to invest in an Indian or Southeast Asian cookbook or two.

If you're not fond of spicy foods, or if you want a more consistent dose of curcumin, you can always take the compound in capsule form.

GINGER (*ZINGIBER OFFICINALE*). Ginger is a close botanical relative of turmeric. So the fact that the two herbs confer similar benefits on the joints should come as no surprise. Ginger is also a time-tested treatment for inflammation.

In one study that I've seen, researchers in Denmark encouraged 18 people with osteoarthritis and 28 with rheumatoid arthritis to take ground ginger daily. The scientists recommended a dose of 500 to 1,000 milligrams a day, but several participants took as much as 4,000 milligrams a day. After more than 2 years, about 75 per cent reported noticeable pain relief. None experienced significant side effects.

If you want, you can take ginger capsules, which are available in health food stores. Or do what I do: use ginger liberally in your cooking. You can also make ginger tea: add 1 teaspoon of fresh grated root to 1 cup of freshly boiled water, steep for 10 minutes, then strain.

STINGING NETTLE (*URTICA DIOICA*). Cultures around the world have been using nettle for centuries to relieve joint pain. What makes the herb unique is its peculiar mode of administration: self-flagellation, or urtication (from *Urtica*, the genus name for nettle). Basically, you hold some nettle in your gloved hand and flail your aching joints.

Some people say that they get as much relief from nettle stings as from conventional drugs. I've tried the herb myself, and I think that it helps reduce the pain and stiffness of osteoarthritis. The fact that it has been used for the same purpose for so long certainly suggests that it has some benefit.

for the Gardener

Stinging Nettle

Urtica dioica

If you want to raise your own stinging nettle, you need to proceed with caution. And not just because of the herb's hairs, which really sting. Left to its own devices, nettle grows very aggressively and can become a weed. I recommend consulting a local nursery for information and assistance.

In my experience, nettle prefers moist soil and tolerates full sun to partial shade. I suggest steaming or boiling the leaves for a few minutes immediately after harvesting. This takes away the sting, leaving behind tasty, vitamin-rich greens that can be eaten like spinach. I have a big plot of nettle, and I often steam the leaves as a side dish.

More Wisdom *from the* Garden

Aromatherapy Massage Eases Arthritis Pain

Many people with osteoarthritis say that massage helps relieve their joint stiffness. This healing technique may be even more beneficial when it's combined with therapeutic essential oils.

All of the following essential oils have documented pain-relieving action. Choose one or several, then mix a few drops of each into an unscented massage lotion or skin cream. Rub it vigorously into your painful joints.

Keep in mind that some people are sensitive to these oils. If you notice any irritation or rash, discontinue use.

Black pepper (*Piper nigrum*)
Clove (*Syzygium aromaticum*)
Frankincense (*Boswellia carteri*)
Ginger (*Zingiber officinale*)
Juniper (*Juniperus communis*)
Lavender, spike (*Lavandula latifolia*)
Lavender, true (*Lavandula angustifolia*)
Lemongrass (*Cymbopogon citratus*)
Marjoram, sweet (*Origanum majorana*)
Myrrh (*Commiphora molmol*)
Peppermint (*Mentha piperita*)
Rose (*Rosa damascena*)
Rosemary (*Rosmarinus officinalis*)
Verbena (*Aloysia triphylla*)

When swatted against the joints, nettle injects histamine and acetylcholine into the skin. Both of these compounds are mildly irritating, hence the 'sting' in stinging nettle. Because the body can pay attention to only so many pain signals at one time, the irritation caused by the nettle stings helps block the pain of arthritic joints. Some commercial products work in much the same way to relieve muscle soreness.

If urtication doesn't seem very appealing to you, you may want to try eating stewed nettle leaves instead. Some people claim that the leaves enhance the effectiveness of their NSAIDs. When the leaves are stewed or steamed, they lose their sting and emerge as a tasty vegetable similar to spinach.

I find edible nettle growing on the south-facing slope of my Garden of Youth all year round. I often harvest a bowlful of leaves in the morning and steam them for lunch.

If you don't have access to nettle leaves, you can do what was done in a study of 8,955 people – 7,935 with osteoarthritis, the rest with rheumatoid arthritis. These folks took a low dose of an NSAID plus about a teaspoon of a nettle tincture a day. About 80 per cent said that the combination of herb and NSAID relieved their symptoms as well as a high dose of the drug by itself did, but without the gastrointestinal side effects.

Rheumatoid Arthritis: Fish Oil Fights the Inflammation

Like osteoarthritis, rheumatoid arthritis causes joint pain. Only the pain doesn't subside with rest. It does come and go, as mentioned earlier. But when it comes, it can be quite severe.

Rheumatoid arthritis usually occurs in the small joints of your hands and feet, though it may affect other joints as well. Generally, it responds to the same treatments recommended for osteoarthritis – namely, dietary modifications, supplements, and herbs.

One notable difference is that for rheumatoid arthritis, the Palaeolithic diet may not go quite far enough. Following a low-fat, high-fibre, near-vegetarian diet should definitely improve symptoms. But in studies of the relationship between eating habits and rheumatoid arthritis, veganism appears to help the most. Vegans eat no animal products at all – no meats, no poultry, no fish, no dairy products.

Several studies have shown that a vegan diet significantly reduces rheumatoid arthritis symptoms. What's more, the symptoms tend to return when people fall off the vegan bandwagon. If I had rheumatoid arthritis, I'd be inclined to forgo the animal products and eat only plant foods – with one exception. That's fish oil.

Several studies have found that fish oil capsules (3 to 9 grams per day) help relieve rheumatoid arthritis symptoms. Fish oil contains omega-3 and omega-6 fatty acids, which are anti-inflammatory. If I had rheumatoid arthritis, I'd definitely try fish oil supplements.

One final thought on the subject: because rheumatoid arthritis pain tends to be more severe than osteoarthritis pain, people who have rheumatoid arthritis must often take large doses of NSAIDs – and suffer severe gastrointestinal consequences. Though I'm not as sold on the COX-2 inhibitors as many experts are, I would suggest that you talk with your doctor about switching from NSAIDs to COX-2s. At least they're less likely to cause gastrointestinal side effects.

Gout: Celery Seed Extract Stops the Attacks

While gout is considered a form of arthritis, it's actually quite different from osteoarthritis and rheumatoid arthritis. As I explain in chapter 15, gout results from a buildup of uric acid, a component of urine. Uric acid is supposed to be filtered out of your blood by your kidneys. But sometimes it forms crystals that get deposited in your joints, especially in your big toe. It hurts like the dickens.

I know from personal experience. As I mentioned before, I had my first gout attack just before I turned 50. My doctor at the time put me on colchicine, which relieved my pain but gave me diarrhoea. Then he switched me to allopurinol, which he told me I would have to take for the rest of my life to prevent future gout attacks.

Fortunately, I found out about celery seed extract. I had read that the extract can eliminate uric acid, so I decided to try it for myself – four 800-milligram tablets a day. That was about 5 years ago. I haven't had a gout attack since.

Besides celery seed extract, the following measures may help reduce the frequency and severity of your gout attacks. If they look familiar, that's because they also help prevent gout, as explained in chapter 15.

Partake of Palaeolithic fare. High-protein foods – mostly animal products – raise your blood level of purines. In turn, these chemicals raise your level of uric acid, which increases your risk of a gout attack.

Because it consists primarily of plant foods, the Palaeolithic diet is much lower in protein than the typical diet. So eating like your caveman ancestors may protect you from gout pain.

Of course, beans are plant foods, and they're high in protein. Should you eat them – or shouldn't you? The answer varies from one person to the next. I'm a big fan of beans, yet I haven't had a gout attack in 5 years. Other people may have problems with them. If you eat a lot of beans, you may want to try gradually reducing your consumption to see if your symptoms improve.

Rethink your drinks. Many people put an end to their gout attacks simply by giving up booze. This makes sense, since alcohol increases the production of uric acid.

Instead, try quenching your thirst with water, juices, teas, and other non-alcoholic beverages. Unlike alcohol, they dilute your urine and promote the excretion of uric acid.

Have a bowl full of berries. The anthocyanosides in berries have anti-inflammatory properties. According to some studies, these compounds also help reduce uric acid levels.

Be prudent with vitamin C and niacin. Large doses of both of these nutrients can raise uric acid levels. Most American experts recommend limiting vitamin C to 2,000 milligrams a day and niacin to 35 milligrams a day. The typical multivitamin doesn't supply enough of either nutrient to trigger a gout attack.

CHAPTER 29

Constipation

Dr Duke's Anti-Ageing Elixirs

- *Licorice-Stewed Laxative Fruits*
- *Almost-Metamucil*
- *Rhubarb Rescue Juice*

A few years ago, while I was in Peru teaching a workshop on medicinal rainforest plants for my friends at the Amazon Center for Environmental Education and Research (ACEER), one of my herbally inclined students developed a nasty case of constipation. Travel can do that to you, because it disrupts your digestive tract's usual rhythm.

It's especially hard on older folks like myself, who are dealing with balky bowels to begin with. As we age, the muscles in the colon lose some of their tone, so they can't push as forcefully as they once did. This, too, sets the stage for constipation.

Unfortunately for my student, she had forgotten to pack her cascara sagrada, a laxative herb. Actually, it's the bark of a small tree which contains anthraquinones, compounds that are responsible for stimulating the colon muscle contractions that we experience as 'the urge'.

Cascara sagrada is not the only plant with anthraquinones. Others include aloe, buckthorn, frangula, rhubarb, sea grape, and senna. I grow buckthorn in the Garden of Youth. It's even more potent a laxative than cascara. Old-time doctors would have described it as a cathartic.

Anyway, there this woman was – on the Napo River, miles from home, uncomfortably constipated and without her usual herbal remedy. She came to me and the local herbalist, my shaman friend Antonio, asking for help.

As it happened, we were standing very close to a tall senna tree. Like cascara sagrada, senna contains anthraquinones. The herb's pods and leaves have been used as laxatives since ancient times and were especially valued in the Arab world. Today, senna is recognised as one of the world's most popular and reliable laxatives.

I winked at Antonio, who proceeded to grab a handful of senna leaves, crush them, and brew a cup of senna tea for our stopped-up friend. Just a short while later, she reported dramatic relief. As a result of this and other eye-opening experiences during our workshop, she became a generous donor to the ACEER.

While I was pleased that my student got such good results with Peruvian senna, I was troubled that she even needed the herb. Unfortunately, she had already become dependent on what I call step 3 constipation treatment, the stimulant laxatives, having bypassed step 1 (diet and exercise) and step 2 (bulk-forming laxatives).

As I mention in chapter 9, even though I'm a fan of herbal medicines, I'm not all that keen on the laxative herbs. To prevent and to treat constipation, a high-fibre diet and regular exercise are always my first choice. If they don't seem to help, then I suggest trying one of the bulk-forming laxatives. The stimulant laxatives should always be a last resort.

There's Nothing Regular about Irregularity

Everyone knows what constipation feels like. But ironically, the condition is not that easily defined.

According to some doctors, if you have only one bowel movement every 2 to 3 days, you qualify as constipated. But going by the laxative commercials on television, anything less than once a day is 'irregular'.

Actually, the medical establishment has yet to develop a consensus definition for constipation. For bowel movements, the normal range of frequency runs from two or three a day to two or three a week. Constipation is more about how you feel than about how often you go. You may have difficulty going, feel uncomfortably full or bloated, and perhaps experience abdominal cramping.

Constipation is one of America's leading chronic conditions. It affects an estimated 10 per cent of Americans, including 3 per cent of the younger generation and an estimated one-third of the elderly.

What's more, some 20 per cent of Americans over the age of 60 say that they take laxatives at least once a week. Most of these laxatives contain anthraquinones, usually either cascara sagrada, the herb taken by the woman in my workshop, or senna, the herb she received from my shaman friend. I just recently read that America spends more than $20 million a year to import laxative herbs, making it the most constipated country on earth. Not an enviable distinction.

Part of the reason that constipation is so common in the United States is that the nation's population is getting older. As I mentioned earlier, the muscles that line the colon lose some of their strength with age, making constipation more likely.

But that's only a part of the reason, and a small part at that. After all, constipation is rare in many areas of Asia, Africa, and South America, even among the elderly. What keeps them regular? I'm convinced that it has something to do with diet and exercise.

Step 1: The Fitness-and-Fibre Route

As I mentioned earlier, I view diet and exercise as step 1 in treating and preventing constipation. For exercise, I recommend walking, because it's easy and accessible. I like to walk around my property every day, covering a mile or more. I also put in some mileage when I'm working in my Garden of Youth. No matter what activity you choose, it will help get things moving – and not just your arms and legs!

For diet, I suggest the Palaeolithic diet that I've been touting throughout this book. Because it's plant-based, it provides lots of fibre from fruits, vegetables, and whole grains. (Our Palaeolithic ancestors didn't have beans as we know them – but they're a good fibre source, too.)

Fibre is bulky. It fills your colon and presses against the colon wall. This pressure stimulates nerves in the area, and they alert your brain that it's time to get things moving. In turn, your brain signals the muscles surrounding your colon to start producing the wavelike contractions known as peristalsis. It's peristalsis that gives you the urge to go.

Nowadays, the gospel of fibre for preventing and treating constipation is well-established. This was not the case back in the early 1970s, when I first heard noted British medical researcher, Dr Denis Burkitt, give a colourful lecture comparing the stools of constipated Westerners with that of nonconstipated Africans.

Dr Burkitt noted that in traditional African societies with high-fibre diets, stool production averaged more than 450 g (1 lb) a day per person, with stool moving through the gastrointestinal tract in 1 to 2 days. But in industrialised cultures, with their low-fibre, meat-and-white-bread diets, stool production averaged only 115 g (4 oz) per day per person. Not only that, stools moved much more slowly through the gastrointestinal tract, typically hanging around for 3 to 5 days. Clearly, the Western diet is a one-way ticket to constipation.

At the time I heard Dr Burkitt speak, I had already adopted a high-fibre diet for myself. I must admit, I felt a little smug – and definitely not constipated. But Dr Burkitt's message was news to many of my constipated colleagues at the USDA. They demanded more proof.

So we performed a little experiment. A group of us kept food diaries and swallowed dye along with our meals. Then we collected our stools until we could no longer see the dye. My stool transit time was about 28 hours – average for someone who eats lots of fruits, vegetables, and salads. But for the meat eaters with few plant foods in their diets, the dye didn't show up for 3 weeks or longer.

My hat was off to Dr Burkitt back then, and it still is today. His

Dr Duke's Anti-Ageing Elixir

Licorice-Stewed Laxative Fruits

Raisins, dates, and figs – as well as prunes – have folk reputations as remedies for constipation. My friend, herbalist and aromatherapist Kathi Keville, sent me this recipe.

WHAT YOU NEED

3 teaspoons powdered licorice root
2 cups water
1 handful prunes
1 handful raisins
Dates
Figs

WHAT TO DO

In a large saucepan, simmer the licorice in the boiling water for 10 minutes, then strain. Add the prunes, raisins, and some dates and figs. Remove from the heat and refrigerate for a few hours or overnight. This allows the fruits to absorb the tea and plump up. Eat them cold or warmed up.

publications on the wisdom of a high-fibre diet helped introduce Western doctors to the value of nutrition in health.

Prunes Get Things Moving

Even today, not all doctors have jumped on the nutrition bandwagon. One long-time holdout was David Kessler, M.D., former commissioner of the FDA.

During Dr Kessler's tenure at the FDA, I got a call from a producer at *CBS News*. Newsman Dan Rather had just interviewed the commissioner, who had come down rather hard on herbs and nutritional supplements. The producer knew that I held the opposing view: I believed that these products could be cheap, useful, preventive, and therapeutic medicines.

So I not only defended herbs and nutritional supplements, I also criticised the FDA for its labelling requirements. At the time, the agency required manufacturers to spend tens of millions of dollars on research to substantiate label claims on their new drugs. The FDA defined a new drug as anything that it hadn't already approved – for example, prunes for constipation.

I suggested that the producer ask Dr Kessler whether he considered prunes and prune juice effective laxatives. If Dr Kessler answered no, he should be given some prunes so he could gain personal experience with their effectiveness. If he answered yes, he should be asked why his agency's regulations would not allow this well-known, time-honoured fact to be printed on the labels of prune products.

Last time I looked in my local supermarket, generic-brand prune juice cost next to nothing, making it probably the cheapest and least unpleasant laxative. It certainly was less expensive than any of the laxative herbs sold in my local herb shop, and much less expensive than any of the pharmaceutical laxatives sold in my local chemist.

The FDA says that it's interested in reducing our nation's health-care costs. I'd like to believe it. Recently, the agency has allowed more foods to carry health claims on their labels. But as far as I know, it still doesn't permit prunes and prune juice to be described as laxatives.

More Constipation-Curing Foods

Besides eating prunes and drinking prune juice, one of the easiest ways to treat constipation is to start your day with a cereal containing wheat bran. Back around the time that Dr Burkitt was changing the minds of USDA researchers about fibre, his countryman, Neil Painter, a doctor at Manor House Hospital in London, published a study in the *British Medical Journal* proving that constipation could be caused by a fibre-deficient diet and cured by increasing fibre intake.

For his study, Dr Painter recruited 70 people with chronic constipation as well as diverticular disease, a complication of constipation that causes abdominal pain. (Diverticular disease is most common in older folks.) He gave his volunteers bran-rich cereal, wholemeal bread, and plenty of high-fibre fruits and vegetables in every meal until they were able to pass one or two stools a day without straining. Dr Painter's 'treatment' cured or substantially helped 89 per cent of the study participants. The effective doses of bran ranged from 3 to 14 grams a day.

I'm a great believer in bran cereal. I often take some along for breakfast when I travel, which is about the only time I'm bothered by constipation. One bowl of bran cereal can provide 15 to 30 grams of fibre. Add raisins (or buy raisin bran), and you may get even more.

Sorbitol, a sugar found in apples, apricots, cherries, pears, and plums, also has laxative properties. It gets things moving by exerting osmotic pressure, drawing water into stools to increase bulk. Another sugar, mannitol, has the same effect.

Both sorbitol and mannitol are used as sugar substitutes in some food products. They should be listed on labels.

Step 2: The Herbal Bulk-Formers

If eating lots of fibre-rich plant foods and engaging in regular exercise don't keep you regular, then you need to move on to step 2 constipation treatment, the bulk-forming herbs. These include psyllium, fenugreek, and flaxseed, all of which grow in my Garden of Youth.

Remember what I said earlier about fibre being bulky, and about this bulk pressing on the colon wall and triggering the peristalsis that moves stool? Well, certain herbs create even more bulk than ordinary dietary fibre. That's because they contain a special kind of fibre called mucilage. Mucilage soaks up water like a sponge.

When mixed with water and digestive juices in your digestive tract, bulk-forming herbs expand to many times their original size. This adds bulk to your stool, which triggers peristalsis. Mucilage also softens stool so that it passes more comfortably with less straining. As a result, the bulk-forming herbs help prevent haemorrhoids.

Let's take a closer look at each of the bulk formers. (*Note*: While these herbs are safe for the vast majority of people, they should not be used by anyone with colitis, Crohn's disease, diverticulitis, or any condition that can cause obstruction of the gastrointestinal tract. The bulk formers can aggravate these health problems. In addition, these herbs should not be taken with antidiarrhoeals or other drugs that inhibit peristalsis.)

PSYLLIUM (*PLANTAGO OVATA*). In the United States, psyllium ranks as the most popular bulk-forming herb. Commission E, the expert panel that evaluates the safety and effectiveness of herbs for the German government, recommends 12 to 40 grams (3 to 8 tablespoons) of psyllium a day as a treatment for habitual constipation.

Perhaps your best bet is to buy a commercial laxative preparation that's pretty much all psyllium with a little sugar and flavouring. Take a few tablespoonfuls a day in water or juice around mealtimes, and you shouldn't have a problem with constipation.

Being the cantankerous oldster I am, I wouldn't use a commercial preparation even if I needed it (which I don't). Instead, I'd turn to plantain. Like psyllium, it's a *Plantago* species. And it grows in my Garden of Youth. I'd strip the husk off the plant and use the mucilage-rich seed for my homemade Practically-Psyllium. It should work just as well.

FENUGREEK (*TRIGONELLA FOENUM-GRAECUM*). This favourite bulk-former of mine occupies a place of honour in the Garden of Youth. The nice thing about fenugreek is that it has an unusual but pleasant taste, like bitter maple syrup. I like to take the herb as a tea – 1 to 2 teaspoons of seed steeped in a cup of freshly boiled water for 10 minutes. Others prefer to take capsules, which are sold in health food stores, or to grow sprouts and eat them. I even blend the seed into some of my fruit juice.

FLAXSEED (*LINUM USITATISSIMUM*). Also known as linseed, flaxseed is the bulk former most widely used in Europe. Commission E recommends 1 to 3 tablespoons of the whole or crushed seed two or three times a day as a treatment for persistent constipation. Personally, I'd take a little more, mixed into juice.

Occasionally, you hear a scary story about flaxseed containing cyanide. Some seeds do, but in minuscule amounts that won't harm you if you're taking only a few tablespoons a few times a day. But if the cyanide makes you nervous, you can always use psyllium or fenugreek instead.

Dr Duke's Anti-Ageing Elixir

Practically-Psyllium

I admit that this isn't the most flavourful concoction. But it's worth trying if you have a problem with constipation. Add lots of fibre-rich fruit to disguise the taste.

WHAT YOU NEED

115 g (4 oz) plantain seeds
Skimmed milk
Fresh fruit

WHAT TO DO

Put the seeds in a cereal bowl and top with skimmed milk. Add the fresh fruit of your choice to taste. Eat this when necessary.

Dr Duke's Anti-Ageing Elixir

Rhubarb Rescue Juice

Usually, I recommend commercial preparations of the stimulant laxatives, because they're safer than the fresh herbs. But if you really want to try something fresh, then I suggest this rhubarb recipe that I picked up from medical writer Ronald Hoffman, M.D.

Most of rhubarb's stimulating compounds, the anthraquinones, are found in the plant's roots. But the stalks contain some, as well as a whole lot of fibre. The stalks are the main ingredient in this recipe.

WHAT YOU NEED

3 stalks rhubarb

1 cup apple juice

¼ lemon, peeled

1 tablespoon honey

WHAT TO DO

In a blender or food processor, purée the rhubarb stalks (never the leaves – they're toxic) with the apple juice, lemon, and honey. Drink four cups a day until your constipation subsides.

Step 3: The Stimulant Laxatives

Now let's suppose that you've tried the high-fibre diet and exercise, and you've tried the bulk-forming herbs, but you're still stopped up. Then you need to move on to step 3, the stimulant laxatives. These herbs trigger peristalsis. Two of them, coffee and castor oil, are fairly gentle. The rest are more potent and potentially problematic.

The caffeine in coffee does more than keep you awake and alert. It gives your colon a gentle push. It doesn't work for everyone, but if I were constipated, I'd try it. The key is to drink a cup or two a day *more* than your system is already accustomed to. Also, if you're a regular coffee drinker who feels constipated, don't cut back on your consumption. One of the symptoms of caffeine withdrawal is constipation.

Castor oil is an old-time home remedy for a variety of ills. It was the bane of millions of children in the years before World War II, primarily because it tastes so bad. It may not work for many of the ailments that it was used to treat, but I believe that it can help relieve constipation. As it's metabolised by bile acids and the fat-digesting enzyme lipase, it exerts a gentle stimulant effect on the colon.

For the proper dosage of castor oil, refer to the label of the product you choose. Adults typically require 1 to 2 teaspoons to get relief in about 8 hours. Larger doses, up to a safe maximum of 6 teaspoons, may produce faster results. Remember to take castor oil on an empty stomach. And don't use it if you have gallstones or any chronic digestive condition.

The more powerful stimulant laxatives include aloe, buckthorn, cascara sagrada, frangula, rhubarb root, and senna. As explained at the start of the chapter, these herbs contain anthraquinones, compounds that stimulate strong peristalsis. Commission E endorses all of them for occasional use. The key phrase here is 'occasional use'.

Even though they're herbal, the stimulant laxatives should not be taken routinely. You can become dependent on them, until eventually, you can't go without them. I don't think any of us should get hooked on laxatives, even if they are herbal.

In general, I'd recommend using commercial preparations of the stimulant laxatives. Both senna and cascara sagrada are the active ingredients in several over-the-counter products. Look for them on labels, then use the products according to the package directions.

The main reason that I favour commercial preparations over raw herbs for treating constipation is that a number of the stimulant laxatives must age for a year or so before they're ready for use. Taken fresh, they irritate the gastrointestinal tract and may cause abdominal distress, bloody diarrhoea, and even vomiting.

The stimulant laxatives that contain anthraquinones should not be taken by women who are pregnant or nursing. The herbs can stimulate uterine contractions in expectant mothers, while the anthraquinones can get into breast milk and cause gastrointestinal problems for the babies.

For myself, the combination of a high-fibre diet and regular exercise have largely spared me from constipation and the need for powerful stimulant laxatives. This is one ailment for which lifestyle strategies should be the primary preventive and treatment. So eat lots of fibre-rich plant foods and take lots of nice long walks. Do this every day, and the chances are that constipation will become a memory.

CHAPTER 30

Corns *and* Bunions

Dr Duke's Anti-Ageing Elixirs

- *Celandine Corn Remover*
- *Hot-for-Your-Dogs Corn Paste*

I've enjoyed going barefoot all my life. I still do, in warm weather – walking around my little farm, digging my bare toes into the rich soil. Every now and then, I step on something and cut myself. When that happens, I think of my father, who never went barefoot and who told me that I shouldn't either.

But beyond its sensual pleasure, going barefoot has one rarely mentioned health benefit: it reduces the risk of corns and bunions. I don't think I've ever had either, but Dad complained about corns a good deal.

Corns: Your Body's Defence against Too Tight Shoes

Corns are extra-large, extra-hard calluses on your toes. They almost always result from tight-fitting shoes that crunch your toes, causing constant irritation. The corn is actually your body's way of protecting itself from the irritation.

Compared with men, women are much more likely to get corns, because they're much more likely to wear too small shoes in the name of fashion. In my humble opinion, fashion just isn't worth it. The easiest way to avoid corns is to wear shoes that fit, even if your feet don't look as dainty as you might like. Give your toes breathing room. And in the summertime, consider going barefoot.

Make Your Own Corn Remover

If you go to a pharmacy to buy a commercial corn remover, the chances are that you'll wind up with a product that contains salicylic acid. This mild acid is the active ingredient in most over-the-counter corn plasters. You tape the plaster over your corn, and the acid dissolves the growth within a week or two.

But salicylic acid, a chemical precursor of aspirin, is very similar to salicin, a pain-relieving compound found in willow bark. That's why you can use willow to remove corns. Moisten some powdered bark until it acquires a pasty consistency. Place a dab of the paste directly on your corn and cover it with a bandage. Apply new paste and change the bandage every few days until your corn has dissolved.

While you're treating your corn, take care to minimise contact between the willow paste and healthy skin. Salicin, being an acid, may cause irritation if left on for too long.

Most people who use willow bark to treat corns mix powdered bark with water. But if you'd like to give your paste a little extra kick, mix it with lemon juice, another mild acid.

More Herbs That Make Corns Disappear

Besides willow bark, several other herbs can help get rid of corns. Here are some of the best.

AFRICAN OR AZTEC MARIGOLD (*TAGETES ERECTA*). In one rigorous study that I reviewed, this herb showed dramatic results in clearing up corns and persistent calluses.

For the study, one group received weekly treatments with African marigold and protective felt pads. Another was given a placebo and the protective pads. A third received the herb alone, without the protective pads. After 8 weeks, the people treated with the herb plus the pads showed the most improvement: 90 per cent of their corns were gone, with 100 per cent reporting pain relief. The herb-only group recorded the second-best results, followed distantly by the placebo-pad group.

Because I've never had a corn, I've never had reason to try African

Dr Duke's
Anti-Ageing
Elixir

Celandine Corn Remover

I introduced this recipe in my book *The Green Pharmacy*. It's such a useful remedy that I thought I'd reprint it here. Its star ingredient is celandine, which contains compounds that help dissolve corns. (*Note:* Potassium chloride is a commercial salt substitute that's sold in most supermarkets.)

WHAT YOU NEED

1.4 litres (2¾ pints) water
1 teaspoon potassium chloride
115 g (4 oz) fresh celandine, chopped
240 ml (8 fl oz) glycerin

WHAT TO DO

Put the water in a medium saucepan and add the potassium chloride. Heat and stir until the potassium chloride dissolves. Remove from the heat, add the celandine, and let stand for 2 hours.

Return the pan to the heat and bring the mixture to the boil. Reduce the heat and simmer for 20 minutes.

Using a sieve, strain the liquid into a medium bowl. Discard the plant material.

Return the liquid to the pan and let it simmer until it is reduced to 360 ml (12 fl oz). Add the glycerin and continue simmering until the liquid is reduced to 480 ml (16 fl oz).

Strain the liquid, place it in a bottle, and store it in a cool place. Apply it to corns twice a day – for example, before you leave for work and before you go to bed.

marigold. But if I did, I'd make a paste using equal parts mashed-up flowers and powdered willow bark. I'd apply the paste topically, holding it in place with an adhesive bandage. I grow African marigold in my Garden of Youth, but only as an ornamental insect repellent.

CELANDINE (*CHELIDONIUM MAJUS*). This herb is famous around the world as a natural corn remover. It contains sanguinarine and chelerythrine, compounds that dissolve corns (and warts, too).

Since I've never had a corn, I've never had occasion to try celandine. But if I developed one, I'd use my Celandine Corn Remover.

PAPAYA (*CARICA PAPAYA*) AND PINEAPPLE (*ANANAS COMOSUS*). Both of these fruits have long-standing reputations as treatments for corns. This makes sense, since both plants are good sources of protein-dissolving enzymes that might help soften and eliminate corns.

For pineapple, the usual recommendation is to cut a square the size of your corn from the peel. Tape the inside of the peel to the corn overnight. The next morning, remove the peel and soak your foot in hot water for 15 to 30 minutes. If your corn is small, you may be able to remove it after just one treatment. More likely, you'll need repeat treatments, perhaps as many as a half-dozen.

For papaya, follow the same procedure. Apply a small piece of the fruit's inner peel overnight, then soak your foot the morning after. Maybe alternating between the two plants would work better than using just one. Just be careful not to tape either fruit to healthy skin overnight. Extended exposure to the fruits' enzymes might cause inflammation.

FIG (*FICUS CARICA*). Like papaya and pineapple, this herb contains protein-dissolving enzymes that might help soften and eliminate corns. In the Bible, Solomon applied the milky latex of the fig tree to his boils. I bet the treatment helped. Fig latex contains ficin, which enjoys a strong reputation for treating corns.

In order to try this treatment, you need to find a fig tree. Break off a leaf or branch and let the latex drip onto the affected area.

CALENDULA (*CALENDULA OFFICINALIS*). Calendula is most often used to treat the inflammation associated with cuts, burns, and bruises. But it's sometimes recommended for corns as well.

Dr Duke's Anti-Ageing Elixir

Hot-for-Your-Dogs Corn Paste

In this recipe, I combine the corn-dissolving properties of willow bark and fig with the pain-relieving compounds in hot pepper, ginger, and turmeric. If you like spicy foods, the paste may sound good enough to eat – but it's absolutely for topical use only.

WHAT YOU NEED

1 chilli pepper (wear plastic gloves when handling)

A piece of fresh ginger

1–2 teaspoons turmeric or curry powder

Ground black pepper

1–4 willow bark capsules

1 fig leaf (optional)

WHAT TO DO

In a food processor, combine the chilli pepper, ginger, and turmeric or curry powder to a pastelike consistency. Sprinkle with the black pepper.

Break open the willow bark capsules and pour the powder into the chilli pepper paste. Let the paste sit overnight. The next morning, blend the paste again to mix in the willow bark.

If you have access to a fig tree, break off a leaf and allow its milky latex to drip onto your corn. After the latex has soaked in, coat the corn with the chilli pepper paste. (Be careful not to let the paste come in contact with your eyes, your nose, or other sensitive areas.) Cover with a bandage. Leave on until the next day.

Reapply the fig latex and chilli pepper paste as necessary until the corn dissolves. Refrigerate the paste between uses.

Some herbalists whom I admire suggest applying a calendula salve two or three times a day to corns and calluses to soften the tissue and prevent further inflammation. You can buy these salves in most health food stores and some pharmacies. I don't need to buy a commercial preparation because this plant reseeds itself like crazy in my garden. In fact, it's threatening to become a weed.

Bunions: Your Big Toe Gets Out of Line

Bunions are another foot problem that I've been spared, thanks in part to going barefoot so much of my life. A bunion is a bone deformity in your big toe. The base of the toe protrudes outwards, forcing the rest of it to point inwards, sometimes even overlapping your other toes.

Most bunions occur because of a hereditary weakness called hallux valgus (*hallux* means 'big toe'; *valgus*, 'bowed'). Sometimes they affect people – again, mostly women – who wear shoes that are too small and narrow for their feet. The shoes end up squeezing the big toes inwards.

Bunions hurt, sometimes badly. They also cause inflammation of the joint connecting your big toe to your foot. In addition, you might notice swelling on the inside of your big toe, where a fluid-filled sac (called a bursa) sits under the hard skin.

Get Relief without Going under the Knife

To treat bunions, many doctors recommend surgery. I suggest trying these herbal approaches first and saving surgery as a last resort.

EUROPEAN MARIGOLD (*TAGETES PATULA*). This herb is different from the African marigold that I mentioned earlier. It can help reduce the size and pain of bunions.

Researchers in England had heard so many anecdotal reports of success with European marigold in the treatment of bunions that they decided to conduct their own study. They gave 121 people with bunions either a tincture of marigold leaf or a placebo. By the end of the study, those using the marigold had significantly smaller, less painful bunions.

ARNICA (*ARNICA MONTANA*). Commission E, the expert panel that evaluates the safety and effectiveness of herbs for the German government, endorses the topical application of arnica for muscle and joint complaints – which, in my opinion, could include bunions. The commission suggests making compresses of arnica tea, but I think it's probably easier and more effective to use a commercial ointment containing up to 15 per cent arnica oil.

Look for arnica ointments in health food stores and pharmacies. I just got my own arnica plant, but I'm still waiting for it to flower.

CHILLI PEPPER (*CAPSICUM*, VARIOUS SPECIES). For bunion pain, I suggest applying a pain-relieving cream made from capsaicin, the compound that gives chilli pepper its heat. Capsaicin has proven useful in treating tennis elbow, so it could conceivably help bunions.

When applied to the painful site, capsaicin depletes certain pain nerves of the brain chemical (neurotransmitter) substance P. With this chemical in short supply, your nerves don't transmit pain impulses as readily. You experience this as temporary relief.

I have chilli pepper in more than a dozen plots in my Garden of Youth. That's because capsaicin is beneficial for so many conditions.

WILLOW BARK (*SALIX*, VARIOUS SPECIES). This herb might help relieve the pain of bunions. Salicylic acid shows up in many over-the-counter bunion products, so I'm confident that the salicin in willow bark could provide similar benefit. Prepare and apply willow bark as described for corns.

GINGER (*ZINGIBER OFFICINALE*). Research has demonstrated ginger's benefit as a treatment for bunions. Indian scientists gave 56 people with joint pain 3 to 7 grams (about 2 to 4 teaspoons) of ground ginger a day. Between 3 and 30 months, more than 75 per cent of the study participants experienced varying degrees of relief. But none reported adverse effects from such large doses of ginger.

Since bunions are to some degree a joint condition, I'd try treating them with ginger. I might even take the herb for corns if I were to get one.

TURMERIC (*CURCUMA LONGA*). A close botanical relative of ginger, turmeric has many similar benefits, thanks to its active compound curcumin. Both herbs are anti-inflammatory when ingested.

For curcumin, the standard anti-inflammatory dose is 400 milligrams three times day. To get that much of the compound from turmeric, you'd have to consume a good 10 tablespoons. Instead, I'd try taking curcumin capsules, which are available in health food stores.

In addition, curcumin acts like capsaicin when applied topically. It helps relieve pain by depleting substance P. So turmeric could conceivably be useful in treating bunions. Either I'd make a paste using the turmeric from my spice rack or I'd break open a curcumin capsule and apply the contents topically.

CHAPTER 31

Diabetes

Dr Duke's Anti-Ageing Elixirs

- *Blood-Sugar-Buster Soup*
- *Beat-Diabetes Bean Soup*

About 1.4 million people in the United Kingdom have been diagnosed with diabetes and it is estimated that another million have the condition without knowing that they do. According to forecasts, the number is expected to double by the year 2010.

Diabetes is actually two diseases. They have many of the same symptoms, but different causes.

In type 1 diabetes, your pancreas stops producing the hormone insulin, which is responsible for moving your body's main fuel, blood sugar (glucose), into cells. Unless people with type 1 diabetes replace the insulin that their bodies can't make, they will die. So they must inject insulin into their bodies several times a day.

In type 2 diabetes, your pancreas continues producing insulin, but your cells aren't able use it. They become insulin resistant. Many people with type 2 diabetes take drugs that increase either the production of insulin or the cells' sensitivity to the hormone. Some of them must inject insulin as well.

Of the two kinds of diabetes, type 1 tends to get most of the attention, primarily because it's usually diagnosed in young children. But type 2 is much more common. It accounts for a whopping 90 per cent of all cases of diabetes. It's also the kind that older people get. That's why this chapter focuses on type 2.

If you're currently undergoing treatment for type 2 diabetes, I would advise you never to ignore your doctor's recommendations. That said, many mainstream doctors don't appreciate the fact that natural approaches – namely, diet, exercise, and herbs – can go a long way towards controlling type 2 diabetes. So follow your doctor's orders, but let him know that you'd like to incorporate natural approaches into your treatment programme. If you do, you might be able to reduce your dose of drugs or insulin.

Causes and Effects of High Blood Sugar

In the early stages of type 2 diabetes, your cells retain enough insulin sensitivity to function reasonably normally. But they're still insulin resistant, and they get worse as the disease progresses. This means they're getting only a fraction of the blood sugar that they actually need. The rest stays in your bloodstream, causing blood sugar levels to rise abnormally high.

As your blood sugar levels increase, all sorts of things go wrong in your body. Basically, all that extra sugar gums up your blood vessels, setting the stage for the major complications of type 2 diabetes: heart disease, stroke, eye problems (including blindness), kidney failure, nervous system impairment, and wound infections or ulcers (often requiring foot or leg amputation).

Like so many modern diseases, type 2 diabetes has been linked to poor diet and lack of exercise. This unhealthy duo also contributes to overweight – which, not surprisingly, is a major risk factor for type 2 diabetes. As body weight increases, cells become more insulin resistant. No wonder that the vast majority of people with type 2 diabetes are heavier than they should be.

Of course, the healthiest way to slim down is to eat healthfully and exercise regularly. Not coincidentally, these same strategies can help control type 2 diabetes. Losing weight makes cells less insulin resistant. So all that blood sugar goes into your cells, where it's supposed to, instead of floating around in your bloodstream and gumming up your blood vessels.

Plant Foods Stabilise Blood Sugar Levels

To lose weight *and* control type 2 diabetes, I naturally recommend a Palaeolithic diet. It's much lower in fat than the standard American or British diet, the one responsible for so many cases of diabetes. And it's plant-based, featuring lots of fruits, vegetables, pulses, and whole grains. Many studies have shown that as consumption of plant foods goes up, blood sugar comes down, thanks to all of the fibre that these foods contain.

What's more, plant foods are rich in antioxidants – vitamins C and E, the carotenoids (including beta-carotene), the mineral selenium, plus other lesser-known nutrients. They help protect against heart disease, stroke, and all of the other major diabetes complications.

Lest you think I'm alone in my praise of a Palaeolithic diet for managing type 2 diabetes, I'll share the words of my good friend and former USDA colleague C. Leigh Broadhurst, Ph.D. In her book, *Diabetes: Prevention and Cure*, she writes: 'The greater your consumption of fruits and vegetables, the lower your risk of diabetes.'

Of course, some plant foods pack more of an anti-diabetes punch than others. Checking my massive herbal database, I discovered two vegetables with a good deal of blood-sugar-lowering power: green beans and onions. The beans came as a pleasant surprise, but not the onions. They have a long tradition in Europe, the Middle East, and Asia as a diabetes treatment. According to my database, they can reduce insulin resistance by as much as 18 per cent.

I've always loved onions and green beans. Maybe that's why I've never developed diabetes, even though I could stand to lose a little

More Wisdom *from the* Garden

Supplements Fend Off Diabetes Complications

By itself, elevated blood sugar does not cause diabetes complications. But it does introduce high levels of destructive oxygen ions, called free radicals, into your bloodstream. Fortunately, much of the cell damage inflicted by free radicals can be prevented and treated with antioxidant nutrients – vitamins C and E, the mineral selenium, and carotenoids (including beta-carotene), among others.

Where do you get antioxidants? From the same plant foods that help control blood sugar – fruits, vegetables, pulses, and whole grains. Certain herbs supply generous amounts of these nutrients, too. Among the best sources are chilli pepper, grape seed, green tea, licorice, turmeric, and the mints (oregano, peppermint, rosemary, spearmint, and thyme).

In addition, I think it's a good idea for people with diabetes to take antioxidant supplements. Here's a daily regime recommended by my friend and former USDA colleague C. Leigh Broadhurst, Ph.D., in her book *Diabetes: Prevention and Cure.*

- Beta-carotene: 20,000 IU
- Selenium: 100 to 200 micrograms
- Vitamin C: 1,000 milligrams with bioflavonoids (three or four times per day)
- Vitamin E: 800 IU
- Zinc: 20 milligrams

weight. Green beans and onions is one of my favourite side dishes. I'd have it with every dinner, if only my wife, Peggy, would make it that often.

I grow green beans in the Garden of Youth. I like to eat them straight off the plant. There's nothing quite as delicious as a garden-fresh green bean. And I routinely add onions to the soups that Peggy and I make. It's a rare day when we don't have a pot of bean-vegetable soup in the refrigerator for a quick lunch, supper, or snack.

Exercise Reduces Insulin Resistance

While a Palaeolithic diet can work wonders for weight loss and diabetes management, it's that much more effective when combined with regular exercise. This two-pronged approach has the support of several good studies.

For one of these studies, UCLA researchers enrolled 652 people with type 2 diabetes in a month-long residential diet-and-exercise programme at the Pritikin Longevity Center in California. The participants followed an eating plan that was very low in fat, cholesterol, and salt but high in fruits, vegetables, pulses, and fibre – your basic Palaeolithic menu. In addition, the participants took daily walks. By the end of the month, their average blood sugar level dropped by 15 per cent. About 70 per cent of the participants were able to stop taking their diabetes medications, while another 39 per cent no longer needed insulin injections.

Other research confirms that exercise has a direct effect on type 2 diabetes. I'm especially fascinated by a study in which Japanese researchers assigned 24 people with the disease to one of two groups. One group adopted dietary changes and walked 10,000 steps (about 6½ km/4 miles) a day. The other made dietary changes only. Both groups lost weight and became less insulin

Dr Duke's Anti-Ageing Elixir

Blood-Sugar-Buster Soup

Among plant foods, green beans and onions shine for their ability to reduce insulin resistance and balance blood sugar. These veggies are easily prepared as a side dish. But if you don't like them plain, then try them in this delicious diabetes-fighting soup.

WHAT YOU NEED

½ litre (1 pint) water
4 medium onions, diced
1 tomato, diced
1 green pepper, diced
230 g (8 oz) green beans, finely chopped
1 clove garlic, diced
Rosemary
Tarragon
Cayenne pepper

WHAT TO DO

Put the water in a saucepan. Add the onion, tomato, green pepper, green beans, and garlic. Season with the rosemary, tarragon, and cayenne pepper to taste. Bring to the boil, then reduce the heat and simmer for 30 minutes. Serve hot, but not too hot.

Another Reason to Kick the Habit

Diabetes is hard on your circulatory system. Cigarettes make matters even worse, accelerating the development and progression of all diabetes complications.

For people without diabetes, smoking is slow suicide. Those who have diabetes and still smoke are putting themselves on the fast track to death.

If you have a cigarette habit, do what I did: quit. If you need help in quitting, talk to your doctor.

resistant. But comparatively, the people who were walking shed significantly more weight, and their insulin resistance and blood sugar levels dropped much lower.

Walking is a wonderful form of exercise. If I take a few circuits on the trails that ramble around my little farm, I put in about 5 km (3 miles). And that doesn't include all the to-ing and fro-ing between my house, barn, and Garden of Youth. In fact, gardening is wonderful exercise, too. If you don't have a garden, just go around the block or head to the nearest park. Or pursue another activity that you enjoy, such as cycling, swimming, or dancing.

The Best Herbs for Diabetes Control

As I said before, the combination of a Palaeolithic diet and regular exercise is the best way to lose weight permanently. By unloading that extra weight, you go a long way towards controlling type 2 diabetes. You also reduce your risk of heart disease, which kills about three-quarters of people with diabetes, compared with one-third of those who are diabetes-free. So eating healthily and exercising regularly should be your top priorities.

That said, if you want a little extra support in managing your type 2 diabetes, I urge you to explore herbal medicine. Dozens of herbs have long-standing folk reputations as diabetes treatments. They've been successful enough that scientists felt compelled to study their effects. The research has concluded that all of the following herbs lower blood sugar levels.

CINNAMON (*CINNAMOMUM VERUM*). You'll notice that cinnamon is an ingredient in my Beat-Diabetes Bean Soup on page 362. I put it in because I like its taste. But according to studies by Richard Anderson, Ph.D., also a former USDA colleague, cinnamon is by far the most potent blood-sugar reducer among those that he has studied.

Here's how Dr Broadhurst recommends using the herb: put 3 rounded tablespoons of ground cinnamon and ½ to 1 teaspoon of baking soda in a 1-litre (2-pint) preserving jar. (If you have a problem with sodium, use a smaller amount of baking soda.) Fill the jar with freshly boiled (but not boiling) water, then let it sit until cool. Strain the liquid, discarding the herb. Return to the jar, cover and refrigerate. Drink 1 cup of the tea four times a day. After 1 to 3 weeks, reduce your dosage to 1 to 2 cups a day, or as needed.

Cinnamon also comes in handy as a dessert spice. I like to put it on fruit.

FENUGREEK (*TRIGONELLA FOENUM-GRAECUM*). My Beat-Diabetes Bean Soup also contains fenugreek seed, another herb that lowers blood sugar. At the Medical College in Agra, India, researchers measured the blood sugar levels of 60 people with type 2 diabetes, then instructed them to stick with their usual lifestyles – except for one noteworthy change.

More Wisdom *from the* Garden

This Herbal Trio Keeps Blood Sugar in Line

If you're considering incorporating herbs into your diabetes-management plan, don't overlook bay, clove, and turmeric. Research by my former USDA colleague, Richard Anderson, Ph.D., has shown that all three herbs can help lower blood sugar levels. They do this by enabling your body to use its supply of insulin more efficiently.

According to Dr Anderson, you don't need a lot of these herbs to experience their benefits. As little as ⅛ teaspoon does the trick. Personally, I would use even more if it meant that I might be able to reduce my dependence on diabetes drugs or insulin injections.

Before each meal, they were to eat a bowl of soup containing almost 25 grams (1 oz) of powdered fenugreek seed. After 24 weeks, their blood sugar levels fell significantly – so did their cholesterol levels.

What makes fenugreek so effective against type 2 diabetes? It's very high in fibre – 50 to 60 per cent by weight. Fibre helps reduce blood sugar.

Dr Duke's Anti-Ageing Elixir

Beat-Diabetes Bean Soup

I intended to develop a new-and-improved version of this recipe, which originally appeared in *The Green Pharmacy* as Dia-beanie Soup. But then I began analysing the ingredients, and I realised that this hearty soup has all the right stuff to help control blood sugar and reduce the risk of diabetes complications. Why mess with a good thing?

WHAT YOU NEED

1 unpeeled onion, quartered
4 cloves unpeeled garlic
1 tin (about 455 g/1 lb) kidney beans
1 carrot, diced
115 g (4 oz) shelled uncooked peanuts
60 g (2 oz) fenugreek seeds
2 bay leaves
Cinnamon
Clove
Turmeric

WHAT TO DO

In a saucepan of water, boil the onion and the garlic, inedible skins and all. (The skins contain the most quercetin, a compound that is quite good at reducing blood sugar levels.) Let them steep in the water until cool. Then remove the inedible plant material, and chop the edible parts, and put them back in the water.

Add the kidney beans (which protect against diabetic retinopathy); carrots (a rich source of pectin, a fibre that reduces blood sugar); peanuts, with their papery covering (a good source of pycnogenol, which lowers blood sugar); and fenugreek seeds (which reduce blood sugar). Season to taste with the bay leaves, cinnamon, clove, and turmeric. Simmer for 30 minutes, remove the bay leaves, then serve.

CHICORY (*CICHORIUM INTYBUS*). Do you drink coffee? If so, I suggest adding roasted chicory root to your brew. In the American South, notably around New Orleans, many people prefer the combination of coffee and roasted chicory root to coffee by itself. Some folks just sip roasted chicory.

The reason that I recommend this herb for type 2 diabetes is that I've reviewed studies in which roasted chicory root decreased the intestinal absorption of glucose. In this way, it helps keep blood sugar levels low.

ASIAN GINSENG (*PANAX GINSENG*). While ginseng is quite versatile, its antidiabetes effects are somewhat surprising. At the University of Oulu in Finland, researchers gave 36 people with type 2 diabetes either a placebo (a fake pill) or ginseng (100 or 200 milligrams per day). Within 8 weeks, both doses of the herb significantly reduced blood sugar levels. Dr Broadhurst suggests taking two to four 200- to 500-milligram capsules of ginseng a day.

Herbal Imports with Healing Potential

While we're on the subject of herbs that lower blood sugar, I'll mention three of the more exotic: bitter melon, jackass bitters, and gurmar. They are becoming more widely available, though you may have to do some hunting to find them.

BITTER MELON (*MOMORDICA CHARANTIA*). Back in the 1960s, Indian researchers first reported on the ability of bitter melon, also known as balsam pear, to reduce blood sugar. In laboratory studies, the herb delayed the development of diabetes complications in animals. In a more recent trial involving humans, people with diabetes who consumed 60 ml (2 fl oz) of bitter melon juice a day saw their blood sugar levels decline by 54 per cent.

Like bitter melon juice, the plant's dried fruits and seeds help reduce blood sugar. To make a tea, chop about 115 g (4 oz) of the fresh fruit and boil it in 2 cups of water until it reduces by half. Drink 1 to 2 cups a day.

JACKASS BITTERS (*NEUROLAENA LOBATA*). As soon as this plant's ability to control type 2 diabetes gets some decent publicity, I believe jackass

More Wisdom *from the* Garden

Chromium Shines in Controlling Diabetes

The mineral chromium usually plays second fiddle to nutritional superstars like vitamins C and E. But it's making a name for itself in the treatment of diabetes.

In 14 of 16 studies, supplemental chromium significantly reduced blood sugar levels. The mineral works by binding very tightly to insulin, helping the hormone usher blood sugar out of the bloodstream and into cells.

Based on the research to date, the effective dosage of chromium is 200 micrograms a day. To ensure that you're getting that much, I suggest taking a supplement. You can also bolster your intake with foods. Among the best sources of chromium are onions, cabbage, carrots, lettuce, tomatoes, and beans. You can also get respectable amounts of the mineral from certain spices, including caraway, cinnamon, coriander, cumin, turmeric, cardamom, and nutmeg.

bitters will become a lot easier to find. I first became aware of the therapeutic powers of this Central American and West Indian herb in 1989, when a Florida doctor sent a sample of it to Walter Mertz, M.D., then director of the USDA Human Nutrition Research Center in Beltsville, Maryland.

One of the doctor's patients, a woman with type 2 diabetes, had picked up the herb on a trip to Trinidad. She put it in vermouth and took small sips of the concoction twice a day. Within 6 months, her blood sugar normalised. The doctor hadn't seen the herb before and wanted to know what it was.

Dr Mertz sent me the specimen, which I identified as jackass bitters. Then I went into the research literature and confirmed for the Florida doctor that the herb is indeed anti-diabetic. Animal studies have found that a tincture a little stronger than what the woman was taking – the equivalent of about a shot glass a day – significantly lowers blood sugar levels.

GURMAR (*GYMNEMA SYLVESTRE*). Like many pharmaceutical diabetes medications, gurmar stimulates insulin secretion. In one study, the herb enabled more than 20 per cent of participants to discontinue their diabetes drugs.

Native to India, gurmar is now becoming more widely available. The recommended dose is 400 milligrams of extract a day.

Diabetic Neuropathy: Chilli Pepper Takes the Edge Off Pain

As I mentioned at the start of the chapter, both type 1 and type 2 diabetes often cause complications, especially when blood sugar levels aren't managed properly. Among the most common complications is diabetic neuropathy, which involves the serious progressive degeneration of nerve function. The condition is characterised by pain, tingling, pins-and-needles sensations, and numbness in the arms, hands, and, especially, the legs and feet.

Because neuropathy causes numbness, people with diabetes who have this complication often injure their feet without realising it. This can lead to seriously infected ulcers (which I'll discuss a bit later). In addition, the combination of neuropathy and circulatory damage can cause impotence in men and loss of vaginal lubrication in women.

To relieve the symptoms of diabetic neuropathy, try chilli pepper – or more precisely, capsaicin, the compound that gives the herb its heat. Many studies have found that capsaicin creams relieve diabetic neur-opathy – so many studies, in fact, that the FDA has approved capsaicin for this condition. The compound is available in commercial preparations such as Axsain or Zecin. Use it according to the label directions.

Besides causing pain and uncomfortable sensations, diabetic neuropathy slows nerve conduction velocity – that is, the speed at which nerve impulses travel. This can impair all motor skills, such as grip strength and walking ability. The oil from evening primrose helps increase nerve conduction velocity.

In one large clinical trial, researchers scrutinised the effects of gamma-linolenic acid (GLA) from evening primrose oil on diabetic neuropathy. The scientists gave 404 people with diabetes either a vegetable oil placebo or 480 milligrams of GLA a day. This treatment lasted for a year, during which the research team tracked 28 clinical parameters, including several that measured nerve conduction velocity. Among the people taking GLA, 25 of the 28 measures improved significantly. Among those taking the placebo, 27 of the 28 measures declined.

When the trial entered its second year, all of the participants were given GLA. This time, those who had originally taken the placebo showed improvement – not deterioration – in 23 of the 28 parameters. The study participants took five or six 1,000-milligram capsules of evening primrose oil per day, which supplied a total of 480 milligrams of GLA. If I had diabetes, I'd take evening primrose oil or munch on the seeds, especially if I were experiencing the early symptoms of diabetic neuropathy.

Diabetic Retinopathy: Save Your Sight with Beans

The word *retinopathy* refers to the deterioration of the retina, the nerve-rich area in the back of the eye. Diabetic retinopathy gradually but progressively impairs vision. It's also a major cause of adult blindness.

Diabetic retinopathy occurs when blood vessels that nourish your eye become gummed up, reducing bloodflow to the retina. Your body responds to the loss of bloodflow by growing new blood vessels around the retina. But these capillaries are so weak and fragile that they leak. Their haemorrhaging worsens vision problems.

One way to minimise the damage caused by diabetic retinopathy is to stop the growth of new blood vessels. Not too long ago, I had the opportunity to discuss this issue with Judah Folkman, M.D., who has become known in scientific circles for his research into preventing the formation of blood vessels that feed cancerous tumours. Dr Folkman mentioned one compound that appears to stall the growth of these unwanted blood vessels: genistein.

Naturally, this was music to my herbal ears, since genistein is found in abundance in beans. If you've ever heard of genistein, it was probably in connection with soya beans. But almost all edible beans contain genistein. Therefore, beans might help control diabetic retinopathy.

I recommend my Beat-Diabetes Bean Soup as a potential preventive. It's made with kidney beans, which are quite rich in genistein. If you prefer, you can replace the kidney beans with black-eyed peas, broad beans, butter beans, or mung beans. All are top-notch sources of genistein.

In addition to beans, the herb bilberry may prevent and treat diabetic retinopathy. Also known as European blueberry, bilberry gets its rich blue colour from a pigment loaded with anthocyanosides. These compounds are potent antioxidants with a natural affinity for the eye.

Bilberry has a long folk history as a vision-improving herb. And several studies confirm that the berry – in the form of whole fruit or an extract – can help combat diabetic retinopathy. In one study, researchers assessed the vision of 31 people with retinopathy, 20 of whom had diabetic retinopathy. Then the study participants were treated with 400 milligrams of bilberry extract a day. All showed reduced haemorrhaging of retinal blood vessels.

If I had diabetic retinopathy, I'd take bilberry as a commercial preparation according to the label directions. The whole fruits are quite widely available, but you can probably find an extract more easily. In addition, I'd eat the following dark-coloured fruits, all of which contain anthocyanosides: blueberries, blackberries, raspberries, plums, grapes, prunes, and raisins.

Research has identified two other herbs that hold promise as treatments for diabetic retinopathy: butcher's broom and buckwheat. For one study, 60 people with type 2 diabetes and retinopathy had their vision tested. Then they were given either butcher's broom extract (two standardised tablets per day) or pressed buckwheat (six tablets per day). After 3 months, 23 per cent of those taking butcher's broom showed some reversal of retinopathy. Among those taking buckwheat, the figure was 27 per cent. Both herbs definitely appeared to increase local blood circulation within the eye.

If I had diabetes, I'd eat buckwheat, probably as buckwheat pancakes. To make them, follow a standard pancake recipe, but use buckwheat flour instead of wheat flour. As for butcher's broom, you'll have to buy a commercial preparation and use it according to the label directions.

Diabetic Ulcers: Comfrey Promotes Healing

When diabetes gums up the blood vessels, it takes a considerable toll on your body's wound-healing capabilities. People with diabetes often have cuts, scrapes, and other injuries that don't mend as they should. For those with diabetic neuropathy, wounds on the feet can be especially serious. The disease impairs sensation in the feet, so folks may not realise that they've been hurt.

If even minor wounds fester and become infected, they can turn into ulcers. Diabetic ulcers are a serious health problem. They're difficult to treat, and they may become gangrenous, leading to foot or leg amputation. In fact, a majority of limb amputations in the United States are associated with diabetes.

To heal minor wounds so they don't turn into ulcers, I recommend comfrey, which I grow in my Garden of Youth. When I was with the USDA, the father-in-law of one of my favourite secretaries developed a diabetic ulcer on one of his toes. The thing just wouldn't heal, and his doctor was starting to talk about amputation. I suggested that her father-in-law try a comfrey poultice – crushed, moistened leaves applied to the wound and held in place by a bandage.

I explained to my secretary that when topically applied, comfrey has an amazing ability to spur healing. I once experienced this myself. I had a wound that refused to mend. I began applying comfrey, and within 4 days, the wound was gone. So my secretary told her father-in-law to try comfrey. He did, and he saved his toe from amputation.

I should caution that comfrey is for external use only. The herb contains pyrrolizidine alkaloids, which have been linked to liver damage. For this reason, it should not be ingested. But it can be applied topically to wounds. It gets its wound-healing ability from allantoin, another compound that promotes new cell growth.

If you can't find comfrey, don't despair. Many other plants contain allantoin, including bearberry, beetroot, borage, cherry, clover, coffee, corn cockle, datura, horse chestnut, gloriosa, jack-in-the-pulpit, kohlrabi, lupine, pea, plantain, rape, rice, tea, and wheat.

Diabetic Microangiopathy: A Trio of Treatments Can Help

The word *microangiopathy* refers to impairment of the smallest blood vessels, the capillaries. Diabetic microangiopathy sets the stage for complications such as neuropathy, retinopathy, and ulcers. It's also associated with peripheral vascular disease, heart disease, and chronic venous insufficiency (impaired bloodflow), conditions for which people with diabetes are at very high risk.

To treat diabetic microangiopathy, I recommend bilberry. In a 6-year study of 568 people with chronic venous insufficiency, the herb significantly improved blood circulation. As a bonus, it reduced fluid retention (oedema) and varicose veins. The antioxidants in bilberry did the trick. The study used a dosage of 400 milligrams a day, which is what I'd take if I had the condition.

Another herb with potential benefits for diabetic microangiopathy is horse chestnut. In a study, 240 people with chronic venous insufficiency received one of three treatments: a placebo, compression stockings (the standard medical treatment), or horse chestnut (50 milligrams of aescin, the active ingredient, in a standardised extract twice a day). After 12 weeks, the participants had their lower legs measured for oedema. Those who were taking horse chestnut showed about the same degree of improvement as those who were wearing compression stockings. Both treatments were significantly more effective than the placebo.

Personally, if I had diabetes, I'd wear compression stockings, and I'd take horse chestnut (as a commercial preparation, following the label directions) and bilberry. Between the three treatments, they just might improve circulation in my legs and protect me from chronic venous insufficiency.

CHAPTER 32

Diverticulitis

Dr Duke's Anti-Ageing Elixirs

- *Regularity Bran*
- *Divert-Diverticulitis Tea*

Diverticula are tiny pouches that develop along the wall of your descending colon, located in your lower left abdomen. Many people get these pouches but never experience any symptoms. They have what's known as diverticulosis.

Sometimes, though, tiny food particles – such as the sesame seeds and poppy seeds added to breads – find their way into the diverticula. As a result, the pouches become inflamed and quite painful. This is *diverticulitis*, a condition that typically strikes older folks but usually starts much earlier in life.

While localised abdominal pain is the classic symptom of diverticulitis, it's not the only symptom. The condition can also cause cramping, constipation, diarrhoea, nausea, vomiting, fever, and blood-tinged stool.

Diverticulosis is very common. It affects an estimated 10 per cent of Americans over 40 and half of Americans over 60 – more women than men, for reasons that remain unclear. The situation is very similar in Europe. Even if you have the condition, you may never know it, because it seldom produces symptoms. That's the case for most people with the disease.

But for an unfortunate 10 per cent of those over 60, diverticulosis advances to diverticulitis, with all the accompanying symptoms. Diverticulitis can be quite severe. It sends some 200,000 Americans to the hospital every year.

For years, doctors instructed their patients with diverticulitis to give their digestive tracts a rest by laying off roughage, which can irritate it. In other words, eat a low-fibre diet practically devoid of plant foods.

Now if you have diverticulitis, it makes sense to avoid small seeds. After all, they can find their way into your diverticula and trigger painful inflammation. But the standard medical advice to follow a low-fibre diet was just plain wrong. You treat diverticulitis by *increasing* your fibre intake. That means eating lots of plant foods – fruits, vegetables, pulses, and whole grains.

Fibre Is the Best Medicine

If you were to root around in old medical journals as I do, you'd find that diverticulitis was virtually unheard of in this country until the late 19th century. Not coincidentally, that's when low-fibre factory-milled flour, refined sugar, and red meat became staples of the American diet. Today, diverticulitis remains rare in countries where the standard diets supply lots of fibre. In the United States, the disease is virtually nonexistent among vegetarians, who naturally have high fibre intakes.

The evidence supporting a high-fibre diet as a treatment for diverticulitis had been available to any doctor willing to do the research. But very few were. Then in the mid-1970s, a British doctor, Neil Painter, all but proved that diverticulosis and diverticulitis occur because of a fibre-deficient diet.

Dr Painter conducted a study in which he put some 70 older people with diverticulitis on a diet filled with bran cereals, wholemeal bread, and fruits and vegetables. Of the study participants, 89 per cent reported

Dr Duke's Anti-Ageing Elixir

Regularity Bran

When researchers instructed 70 people with diverticulitis to eat 12 to 14 grams of wheat bran a day, 62 reported a reduction in their symptoms. That's convincing enough for me. If I had diverticulitis, I'd try wheat bran – perhaps using this recipe, which also features two top-notch digestion-soothing herbs.

WHAT YOU NEED

1 handful slippery elm bark
2 handfuls fresh peppermint
Honey
15 g (½oz) wheat bran flakes

WHAT TO DO

Put the slippery elm and peppermint in a saucepan and add water to cover. Bring to the boil. Remove the pan from the heat and strain out the herbs. Add enough honey to the remaining liquid to achieve a syruplike consistency. Mix the syrup with the bran flakes to taste, refrigerating any left over for later use.

improvement in their symptoms.

More recently, Harvard researchers analysed dietary information collected from 48,000 middle-aged males participating in the ongoing Health Professionals' Study. The scientists compared the diets of 385 men who developed diverticulitis with the diets of a similar number of men who were disease-free. The conclusion: those with diverticulitis ate half as much fibre as those who didn't. The most protective forms of fibre came from fruits, vegetables, and beans.

These days, most doctors have come around to the wisdom of a fibre-rich, plant-based diet as a treatment for diverticulitis. So for the most part, I no longer cringe when people who have the disease share their doctors' recommendations with me.

Preventing Constipation Is Crucial

As I said earlier, diverticulitis is most common among older folks. But it starts much earlier in life, with chronic constipation – also the result of a low-fibre diet. Chapters 9 and 29 offer a number of strategies for preventing and treating constipation. If you keep yourself regular, you greatly reduce your risk of developing diverticulosis or diverticulitis.

The primary strategy for relieving constipation is the same as for diverticulitis: eat a high-fibre diet. Regular exercise also helps: when you're active, your colon does a better job of moving things along, so to speak. And if you smoke, I suggest that you quit. Besides causing heart disease and lung cancer, smoking messes up your digestive tract.

Beyond these basic lifestyle strategies, a couple of herbs can help keep you regular: psyllium and flaxseed.

PSYLLIUM (*PLANTAGO OVATA*). Powdered psyllium is rich in a special type of fibre called mucilage, which expands considerably when exposed to water and digestive juices. As it expands, it adds bulk to stool, which in turn stimulates the colon. Mucilage also softens stool, making it easier to pass.

If you want to try psyllium, I suggest taking a commercial laxative preparation that's essentially psyllium, with colouring and flavouring added. Use according to the package directions – and be sure to drink plenty of water, too. It needs water to work.

FLAXSEED (*LINUM USITATISSIMUM*). Like psyllium, powdered flaxseed is rich in mucilage. It works the same, too. I'd suggest taking 1 to 3 tablespoons two or three times a day, with lots of water.

Herbs Ease Pain and Inflammation

If you already have diverticulitis, you may want to try one of the following herbs. All soothe the digestive tract, relieve inflammation, or both.

CAMOMILE (*MATRICARIA RECUTITA*). This popular beverage herb has significant anti-inflammatory action. Since diverticulitis is an inflammatory condition, I like the idea of sipping camomile tea throughout the day. Use 2 to 3 heaped teaspoons of dried flowers per cup of freshly boiled water. Steep for 5 to 10 minutes, then strain. Drink as much as you like.

PEPPERMINT (*MENTHA PIPERITA*). Many of the culinary mints are natural digestive soothers. Naturopaths recommend enteric-coated capsules of peppermint oil as a treatment for diverticulitis. I suggest peppermint tea. Add 1 to 2 teaspoons of leaf to 1 cup of freshly boiled water, steep for 5 to 10 minutes, then strain. Drink as much as you like.

SLIPPERY ELM (*ULMUS RUBRA*). The powdered bark of this herb, prepared

for the
Gardener

Mints

Mentha, various species

The mints include the well-known peppermint and spearmint, as well as the less common biblical mint, cornmint, and watermint. All of them grow aggressively and can easily find their way out of the plots where they're planted. For this reason, I recommend keeping them in pots or in a confined area.

You can easily propagate mint. Just pinch off the top of an existing plant and put it in moist soil in a fertile, well-drained locale. It should readily root. Some people like to grow peppermint and spearmint in hanging pots in their kitchens, so they always have fresh leaves on hand for teas and spicing.

Harvest the leaves as they mature. Cut the entire plant within 5–10 inches of the ground when the first flowers appear. Most mints become woody after a few years. Dig them out and replace them with new cuttings.

as a gruel, comes highly recommended for diverticulitis. It's rich in mucilage, so it's a digestive soother and an anti-inflammatory. In addition, it contains a mild laxative compound that might help relieve constipation, the underlying cause of diverticulitis. Even the herbally conservative FDA has declared powdered slippery elm bark a safe and effective digestive aid.

Slippery elm bark gruel may not sound too appetising. But I've eaten it, and I think it's delicious. To make it, try mixing 115 g (4 oz) of powdered bark in 1 litre (2 pints) of water. Bring it to the boil, then simmer for 15 minutes, stirring occasionally. Eat 115 g (4 oz) three times a day, refrigerating any left over for later use (though it may start to gel after a while).

WILD YAM (*DIOSCOREA VILLOSA*). Many herbalists tout this herb – it's different from the yam sold in supermarkets – as a treatment for diverticulitis. I'm inclined to agree with them. I've read enough reports that wild yam can help decrease the pain and inflammation of diverticulitis.

I have wild yam in my Garden of Youth. It also grows wild down in my woods. I like my vines so much that I'd hate to uproot them. But if I had diverticulitis, that's what I'd do – dig up a whole root, shave a bit from the end, and replant the rest. Then I'd wash and chop what I'd taken and mix it in with my slippery elm bark gruel, perhaps with some extra camomile and peppermint.

DEVIL'S CLAW (*HARPAGOPHYTUM PROCUMBENS*). Some European studies that I've read have led me to believe that devil's claw, a native of Africa, would be very good for diverticulitis. The herb's root contains iridoids, bitter compounds that stimulate appetite and soothe the digestive tract.

Commission E, the expert panel that evaluates the safety and effectiveness of herbs for the German government, approves 4.5 grams (about 3 teaspoons) of devil's claw as a treatment for indigestion. I'd use the same amount for diverticulitis. I'd chop the root and simmer it in a cup or two of boiling water for 10 minutes, then strain out the plant material before drinking it. I might also try mixing the herb with camomile.

Dr Duke's Anti-Ageing Elixir

Divert-Diverticulitis Tea

When diverticulitis symptoms flare up, this tea can bring relief. It's made with several digestion-soothing herbs, plus fibre-rich flaxseed (to prevent constipation).

WHAT YOU NEED

1 part slippery elm bark
1 part wild yam root, finely shaved
1 part powdered flaxseed
2 parts fresh peppermint
A natural sweetener (optional)

WHAT TO DO

In a saucepan, combine the slippery elm, wild yam, flaxseed, and peppermint. Add water to cover and bring to the boil. Strain out the plant material and sweeten the tea, if you wish. Sip ½ cup, cool or reheated, three times a day until symptoms subside.

CHAPTER 33

Dry Skin *and* Dermatitis

Dr Duke's Anti-Ageing Elixirs

- *Ditch-the-Itch Astringent*
- *Dual-Action Dermatitis Tonic*

After 40 long years of controversy and criticism, mainstream doctors are finally discovering the therapeutic value of vitamin and mineral supplements. For proof of this collective change of heart, you need look no further than the American doctors' trade publication, the *Journal of the American Medical Association*. A 1959 issue of the journal featured an article that declared: 'There is little acceptable scientific basis for using vitamin E.' By 1994, the journal had changed its tune: 'Vitamin and mineral supplements have entered the ranks of bona fide science.'

In fact, some experts are now suggesting that vitamin E supplementation become mandatory, based on a study by Pracon, a hospital-outcomes analysis firm based in Reston, Virginia. Pracon calculated that widespread vitamin E consumption could reduce America's collective hospital bill by $7.7 billion a year, mostly through the prevention of heart attacks.

I suspect that vitamin E supplementation could also reduce our nation's collective misery from dry skin and dermatitis. I get itchy, scaly, dry-skin dermatitis every winter, especially on my legs. The treatment that works best for me is a combination of vitamin E and aloe. I buy a cream that contains both ingredients and rub it on. If my dermatitis is really bad, I might take a capsule containing 400 IU of vitamin E as well.

When I'm in the tropics, where avocados are cheap and plentiful, I sometimes rub the fruit – a natural emollient – directly on my legs. Of course, it's quite humid in the tropics, so just being there gives me a reprieve from my symptoms after a few days.

Uncomfortable in Your Own Skin

Dry, chapped skin occurs because of a loss of the oil that normally keeps the skin supple. The typical cause is a dry environment. My house gets arid during the winter months, which is why I develop dry skin every Christmas.

Dry skin can result from overzealous bathing or showering, especially in very hot water. This washes too much oil from the skin's surface.

Often, dry skin is a symptom of dermatitis. Technically, the word *dermatitis* means skin inflammation. But the term encompasses a variety of conditions, including the following:

- *Atopic dermatitis, also known as eczema, produces itching, scaling, swelling, and sometimes blistering.*
- *Contact dermatitis – a reaction to an irritating or allergy-causing substance – is characterised by dryness, cracking, redness, and rash.*
- *In seborrhoeic dermatitis, the classic symptom is greasy yellowish scales on hairy parts of the body, face, and genitals, as well as in*

the folds along the nose, under the breasts, and elsewhere.

- *Nummular dermatitis produces distinctive coin-shaped red patches, primarily on the arms, hands, buttocks, and legs.*

Nummular dermatitis is most common in people aged 55 and older. It sure sounds like what I get every winter.

Except in cases of contact dermatitis, determining what causes dermatitis is often difficult. As with dry skin, the condition is often triggered or aggravated by exposure to a dry environment or very hot baths or showers. Stress may also contribute to flare-ups.

Lifestyle Strategies for Real Relief

If you have dry skin or dermatitis, you can start treating it by speeding up your baths or showers and turning down the temperature of the water. You should also consider investing in a humidifier for your home. Unfortunately, I can't use a humidifier. I have rooms full of botany and herbal medicine books and journals, and the increased moisture makes them mildewy.

Dry skin often responds well to moisturising lotions. But choose your product carefully. If its label lists water or alcohol among its first three or four ingredients, it may actually dry your skin. Instead, look for a moisturiser made with natural emollients, such as avocado oil, coconut oil, lanolin, and olive oil.

Actually, the best emollients contain essential fatty acids, which help the emollients penetrate the skin. Both cocoa butter and jojoba butter have fatty acids. Both are fantastic moisturisers.

For dermatitis, make sure that you're taking steps to manage the stress in your life. Exercise is great for relieving tension and anxiety, as are meditation, yoga, and deep breathing. Find a relaxation technique that you enjoy, and practise it regularly.

You may also benefit from switching to a plant-based Palaeolithic diet. Few people realise that meats, dairy products, and other high-protein foods provoke biochemical reactions in the body that may aggravate inflammation. On the other hand, lower-protein plant foods

More Wisdom *from the* Garden

Essential Oils Soothe Irritated Skin

The healing discipline known as aromatherapy is actually an offshoot of herbal medicine. It got its start back in the 1920s, when French perfume chemist René-Maurice Gattefosse accidentally burned himself in his laboratory. He plunged his injured skin into lavender oil, the closest liquid at hand. Much to his surprise, he experienced remarkable relief.

To treat skin conditions, aromatherapists recommend several plant oils (essential oils), including benzoin, bergamot, cedarwood, camomile, geranium, jasmine, lavender, and tea tree. You can buy many of these oils in health food stores and bath and body shops. Add a few drops of the essential oil of your choice to almond oil or a skin lotion, then rub it into your skin.

Just don't ingest essential oils. They are extremely concentrated and can be toxic even in small amounts.

contain compounds that tend to reduce inflammation.

By trading in the typical Western diet for one that's more Palaeolithic, you'll eat less inflammation-promoting meats and more inflammation-fighting plant foods. This means you'll be less likely to aggravate an inflammatory condition such as dermatitis. You don't need to worry about running low on protein either. Most Westerners eat far more protein than they need.

My Healthy Sevens eating plan (see chapter 3) is based on the Palaeolithic diet, with a strong emphasis on plant foods.

Be aware that some people develop dermatitis as an allergic reaction to certain grains. If you notice swelling, itching, and other skin symptoms after eating grains such as corn and wheat, I suggest that you consult your doctor.

The Top Five Herbs for Healing Your Hide

Beyond these lifestyle approaches, many herbs help heal dry skin and dermatitis. The five best, in my opinion, are aloe, evening primrose, onion, turmeric, and witch hazel. Let's look at each one of these a bit more closely.

ALOE (*ALOE VERA*). The gel from the inside of the aloe leaf is probably best known as a home remedy for minor burns. Peggy and I keep an aloe plant in our kitchen, where household burns are most likely to occur.

Aloe gel helps heal other skin conditions as well. In fact, it has a long history and has been used as a treatment for skin problems since the time of the Pharaohs in ancient Egypt. Modern Egyptian scientists report that aloe gel is good for treating acne, dandruff, dry skin, and some types of dermatitis.

Aloe contains bradykininase, an enzyme that relieves pain and decreases redness and swelling. The herb also helps stop itching.

Keep a potted aloe plant handy in your home. Then when you need to, you can snip off a leaf, slit it open, and scoop out the gel with a small spoon or knife. Apply the gel directly to the affected skin. You can also buy aloe gel in health food shops.

EVENING PRIMROSE (*OENOTHERA BIENNIS*). Like cocoa butter and jojoba butter, evening primrose oil contains essential fatty acids. It's especially rich in gamma-linolenic acid (GLA). I've never understood why evening primrose oil is not more widely used in commercial skin-care products. According to the studies that I've reviewed, it helps moisturise skin when applied topically.

In one study, people with dry skin on both legs rubbed evening primrose oil into one but not the other. The skin of the treated leg cleared up in short order. Other research has shown that oral doses of evening primrose oil improve all symptoms of eczema, especially the most maddening one, itching.

If you want to try evening primrose oil, buy capsules in a health food store and take them according to the label directions. For topical treatment, break open the capsules and apply the contents to your skin until it shines with a thin layer of oil. Then rub in the oil.

If you can't find evening primrose oil in a health food shop, borage and currant oils are rich in GLA and should produce similar benefits. I have evening primrose planted in many places around the Garden of Youth, including the Dermatitis plot.

ONION (*ALLIUM CEPA*). How does onion juice grab you? If you can stomach it, your skin may be the better for it. The juicing process produces compounds not found in whole onions. These compounds, cepaenes and thiosulphinates, are strongly anti-inflammatory.

If you're not into onion juice, perhaps you'd rather try the skins. Brown, papery onion skins are rich in quercetin, one of nature's most potent anti-inflammatory compounds. The next time you make a vegetable or bean soup or a tomato sauce, add onion skins and let them simmer to extract some of the quercetin. Remove the onion skins before eating the dish.

I grow onions in my Garden of Youth. But I use so many in cooking that I buy quite a few as well.

TURMERIC (*CURCUMA LONGA*). A close botanical relative of ginger, turmeric is the Indian spice that gives curry blends their yellow colour. It contains a compound called curcumin that has potent anti-inflammatory action.

Traditional herbalists have used turmeric to treat all manner of inflammatory conditions: arthritis, hepatitis, bronchitis, gastroenteritis (stomach flu) – in fact, just about any *-itis* (the suffix means 'inflammation'). So it should come as no surprise that I'm recommending the herb for dermatitis.

The curcumin in turmeric has become so well-known as an anti-inflammatory that in 1995 a drug company obtained a patent on a pharmaceutical extract. Of course, the patent can't stop anyone from using the spice. It may be as good as the extract – and it's certainly a lot cheaper.

If you want to try turmeric, simply add liberal amounts of it to your cooking. By itself, it has a warm, delicate flavour that works well in soups and vegetable dishes. You can also experiment with yellow curry blends, which contain turmeric. If you're unfamiliar with these seasonings, you may want to invest in an Indian or Southeast Asian cookbook. Curry blends are staple ingredients in these cuisines.

I have several potted turmeric plants. I keep them in the garden

Dr Duke's Anti-Ageing Elixir

Ditch-the-Itch Astringent

This recipe will help some cases of dermatitis and aggravate others. The alcohol serves as a drying agent, so it's best used on skin that's 'weepy'. If your skin is already dry, I'd recommend trying something else.

WHAT YOU NEED

2 parts black walnut husks
1 part oak bark
1 part witch hazel bark
Rubbing alcohol

WHAT TO DO

In a jar, combine the black walnut, oak, and witch hazel. Add the rubbing alcohol to cover. Put on the lid and allow to steep for a week or two.

Apply with a cotton ball to the affected skin as needed, storing any left over in a dark place for later use.

through the summer, then move them into the greenhouse for the cold winter months.

WITCH HAZEL (*HAMAMELIS VIRGINIANA*). When your skin is red and inflamed, an astringent can feel cooling and soothing. Witch hazel – specifically witch hazel water, available in pharmacies – is one of the best astringents, thanks to its special compounds called tannins.

Commission E, the expert panel that evaluates the safety and effectiveness of herbs for the German government, endorses witch hazel for several kinds of dermatitis. In one study, scientists compared the anti-inflammatory effects of hydrocortisone cream, witch hazel, and camomile. The hydrocortisone came out on top, but not far ahead of witch hazel. Besides, the herb is much cheaper and does not cause the side effects that are possible with hydrocortisone.

I have witch hazel in my garden, in the Dermatitis plot. The plant also grows wild around my property. It's dear to me because it's my last flower each fall, blooming in late October and November.

More from the Herbal Medicine Chest

While the five herbs above are my top choices for treating dry skin and dermatitis, they're not the only ones that can help. These are also worth trying.

CALENDULA (*CALENDULA OFFICINALIS*). Also known as pot marigold, calendula contains an oil that's rich in lycopene, a compound that promotes healing and the growth of healthy skin cells. Commission E endorses the topical application of calendula as a treatment for dermatitis, eczema, minor burns (including sunburn), and other skin inflammations, as well as poorly healing wounds. I've never heard of the herb causing side effects or drug interactions.

The calendula in my garden is so robust that it's threatening to become a weed, but a weed that I welcome. I suggest using the crushed flowers to make a poultice. (A poultice consists of one or more herbs that have been steamed to an almost spreadable consistency, then cooled and applied topically to the affected skin, sometimes held in place by a bandage.) You can also steep the crushed flowers in olive oil for a week or two, then apply that to your skin.

CARROT (*DAUCUS CAROTA*). Vitamin A helps nourish the skin. One of the most concentrated sources of the nutrient is carrot oil. No wonder the oil is used in some cosmetics and sunscreens. It may not be easy to find, but if you can, apply it according to the label directions.

I don't grow carrots. They're so cheap at my local supermarket that I just buy them. I also have lots of wild carrot-family plants, known as cow parsley or Queen Anne's lace, around my property. They're the same species as store-bought carrots.

for the Gardener

Camomile

Matricaria recutita

Sow this annual self-seeder in spring, after the danger of frost has passed. Choose a location with sandy, well-drained soil and partial shade. Camomile blooms in about 6 weeks, and its flowers can be harvested over the course of several weeks. They retain their aroma for a while, even when dried and stored in a cool, dark place. Let some of your camomile plants go to seed for the following year's crop.

CAMOMILE (*MATRICARIA RECUTITA*). Camomile has a long-standing reputation as a treatment for skin conditions. Perhaps that's why the herb is an ingredient in so many skin-care products and cosmetics.

Research has shown that camomile oil contains several anti-inflammatory compounds, including chamazulene, a-bisabolol, and flavones such as apigenin. The herb is also bactericidal and fungicidal, especially good against yeast (*Candida albicans*) and staph bacteria (*Staphylococcus aureus*).

Commission E approves the topical application of camomile as a treatment for dermatitis, rashes, and skin irritations. Extracts of the whole flower work better than individual constituent compounds. In other words, it's better to apply a compress of camomile tea than a pharmaceutical preparation containing an isolated 'active ingredient'.

I grow camomile in my Garden of Youth. It has a pleasant apple aroma, especially when it's crushed. Most people make their camomile tea from dried flowers, but you get a stronger, tastier, more aromatic tea using fresh flowers. I feel lucky to have them handy. If I wanted to make a tea, I'd use 2 teaspoons of fresh flower heads per cup of freshly boiled water. I'd let them steep for 10 minutes, then strain them out.

CUCUMBER (*CUCUMIS SATIVUS*). If you'd like your dry, itchy skin to be cool as a cucumber, try applying thin slices of the vegetable. Cucumber has a long history of use in cosmetics and as a treatment for dermatitis, minor burns, and wrinkles. It's a lot cheaper than – and probably as effective as – commercial creams.

I grow cucumber in my Garden of Youth. In fact, I'm having better luck with it now than I when I had a vegetable garden, probably because the Garden of Youth is so well-mulched.

FLAXSEED (*LINUM USITATISSIMUM*). Crushed flaxseed (also known as linseed) is rich in a fibre called mucilage. When mixed with water, mucilage expands and takes on an oatmeal texture, which can help soothe irritated skin. Flaxseed has traditionally been used as a treatment for dry skin, eczema, and acne.

Commission E approves flaxseed poultices for boils, festering sores, and other skin ailments. The commission suggests mixing 30 g (1 oz) of crushed flaxseed into enough hot water to produce a thin gruel. Apply the gruel as a compress or poultice.

I have a beautiful ornamental flax here on my property. Much to my chagrin, it doesn't produce usable seed.

GARLIC (*ALLIUM SATIVUM*). Your family and friends might object to your smelling like garlic. But if your dermatitis is caused or complicated by a bacterial or fungal infection, you can't do better than applying a compress of strong garlic tea.

I've determined that garlic contains at least 13 bactericidal and 8 fungicidal compounds, plus 5 other compounds that help soothe dermatitis. The herb is especially effective against ringworm, athlete's foot, and jock itch. It also speeds the regeneration of skin cells, so it's good for sores, burns, and wounds.

Garlic occupies more plots in my garden than any other herb. If I had a local skin infection such as ringworm or athlete's foot, I might pulverise a few cloves and apply the mash as a paste or poultice.

LICORICE (*GLYCYRRHIZA GLABRA*). For many inflammatory skin conditions, doctors recommend hydrocortisone creams. The glycyrrhetinic acid in licorice works much like hydrocortisone, which is why studies have found that the herb can help treat dermatitis, eczema,

Dr Duke's Anti-Ageing Elixir

Dual-Action Dermatitis Tonic

This recipe uses a trio of anti-inflammatory herbs: camomile, licorice, and turmeric. You can drink it as a tea or apply it as a compress – or both.

WHAT YOU NEED

4 tablespoons camomile
1 tablespoon licorice
1 teaspoon basil
1 teaspoon rosemary
1 teaspoon turmeric or 1 tablespoon curry powder
Dash of ground black pepper
¾ litre (1½ pints) water
Lemon
A natural sweetener (optional)

WHAT TO DO

In a medium saucepan, combine the camomile, licorice, basil, rosemary, turmeric or curry powder, and black pepper. Add the water. Bring to the boil, then simmer for 10 minutes. Strain out the plant material and allow to cool. Drink one cup at a time, flavoured with the lemon and sweetener, if you wish. Refrigerate left over tonic for later use.

and even psoriasis (a skin condition characterised by red patches covered with white scales). From my review of the research, it seems that you get the best results from using licorice and hydrocortisone cream together.

I have licorice in my garden. But for my own medicinal purposes, I gravitate towards my stash of imported Turkish licorice, which is much more aromatic. I make a tea using 1 to 2 teaspoons per cup of freshly boiled water, then allow it to cool slightly before applying it as a compress.

MARSHMALLOW (*ALTHAEA OFFICINALIS*). Marshmallow root is not as spongy as the sugary confection that we toast over campfires. But like its relative, okra, the dried, powdered root becomes slimy in a soothing way when mixed with water.

Taken internally, marshmallow helps relieve coughs and sore throats. Applied externally, it's good for dermatitis, because of the anti-inflammatory compounds that it contains. In fact, marshmallow has been used as a treatment for chapped skin and dermatitis for thousands of years.

I have a few marshmallow plants in my garden, but I've yet to harvest any of their roots. If you buy the herb in a health food shop, chop the root finely and add enough freshly boiled water to make a slimy paste. Allow it to cool, then apply to the affected skin.

OAK BARK (*QUERCUS*, VARIOUS SPECIES) AND WALNUT BARK (*JUGLANS*, VARIOUS SPECIES). Like witch hazel, oak bark and walnut bark are soothing astringents. Commission E approves both as treatments for dermatitis. I suggest making a tea using 1 to 2 teaspoons of powdered bark per cup of freshly boiled water. Steep for 10 minutes, then strain out the plant material. Allow the tea to cool before applying it as a compress.

PURSLANE (*PORTULACA OLERACEA*). Purslane, one of my favourite weedy vegetables, is among the richest plant sources of vitamin E. As I mentioned at the beginning of the chapter, vitamin E helps keep the skin supple and healthy.

I love purslane. I eat it raw, stems and all, out in the field. Sometimes I boil or steam it like spinach, or pickle it. For dermatitis, you may want to mash it and apply it topically, as a poultice.

SOYA BEAN (*GLYCINE MAX*). Not too long ago, I received a letter from a man who had read my recommendation to eat soya foods for seborrhoeic dermatitis. He said that he had experienced 'very amazing effects'. I wasn't surprised.

Naturopaths report good results from treating seborrhoea and dandruff with biotin, a B vitamin. Soya is rich in biotin. I calculate that you'd have to eat only about 7 g (¼ oz) of soya beans, just a small handful, to get a therapeutic dose of the nutrient. I used to munch that much while wandering through the USDA's old soya bean fields at the Beltsville Research Center, where I spent much of my career. Maybe that's why I was never bothered by seborrhoea or dandruff.

I'm not sure how much tofu you'd have to eat to get a medical amount of biotin. But if I had a problem with seborrhoea or dandruff, I'd eat a few servings a week.

TEA TREE (*MELALEUCA*, VARIOUS SPECIES). Like garlic, tea tree oil is strongly antibacterial and antifungal. People whom I know have used tea tree oil as a treatment for dermatitis and skin infections, with excellent results.

You can buy 100 per cent tea tree oil in health food shops and some pharmacies. Apply it straight or diluted with a cotton wool ball or swab. Be aware that the oil may cause skin irritation. If it does, stop using it.

I have a few small potted tea trees growing in the garden. But they hardly compare with the giant trees that I've seen in Australia. When I bring the pots into the greenhouse over winter, they fill the air with a wonderful aroma.

WILD PANSY (*VIOLA TRICOLOR*). Commission E approves wild pansy tea for seborrhoea. Other herbalists whom I respect recommend the herb for acne, eczema, impetigo, and any itchy rash or dermatitis. The commission suggests making a tea using 1 teaspoon of herb per cup of freshly boiled water. Steep for 10 minutes, then strain out the plant material. Allow the tea to cool before applying it as a compress.

I don't need to grow wild pansy in my garden. It comes up all over my property as a weed.

CHAPTER 34

Fatigue

Dr Duke's Anti-Ageing Elixirs

- *Cineole Fatigue Fighter*
- *Antiviral Energy Booster*

According to the research that I've reviewed, if you were to ask a random 100 people in doctors' waiting rooms what prompted their visits, at least half would mention fatigue as one of their symptoms. This isn't surprising, since so many illnesses cause fatigue.

Think about the last time that you had a bad cold or the flu. Did you feel as perky as usual? Probably not. And that's understandable. After all, your body uses up a good deal of energy fighting colds, flu, and literally hundreds of other conditions. Quite often, the tremendous effort required to get healthy again doesn't leave much energy for anything else. As a result, you feel tired.

Illness-related fatigue clears up when you get better. But what if your fatigue doesn't go away? What if it stops being a symptom of some other illness and becomes the main problem?

Then you're no longer just plain tired. Then you have what's known as chronic fatigue. There are various degrees of chronic fatigue, ranging from mild and transient to so severe and persistent that it's debilitating.

If you just can't seem to regain your get-up-and-go, see your doctor. You want to rule out any underlying health problem. Once you know for sure that you're dealing with genuine fatigue, then I suggest trying some natural approaches to replenish your energy supply.

Start with a Little Lift

Personally, when I'm dragging a little and in need of a pick-me-up, but I want something milder than the caffeine in coffee, I'll brew myself a pot of herbal tea. A number of herbs contain pleasantly aromatic stimulant compounds such as carveol, carvone, cineole, cinnamaldehyde, menthol, piperine, and verbenalin.

Of these, my favourite by far is cineole. It not only enhances physical energy but also seems to boost mental alertness. In laboratory studies, cineole improved the ability of rats to find their way around mazes.

The best herbal source of cineole is cardamom, followed by eucalyptus, spearmint, rosemary, sweet wormwood (*Artemisia annua*), ginger, nutmeg, and lavender. (For a more complete listing of herbs and their cineole content, see 'Your Best Cineole

Dr Duke's Anti-Ageing Elixir

Cineole Fatigue Fighter

Cineole is a mild stimulant that provides a gentle pick-me-up without the jitters. It's found in a number of herbs, including bay, rosemary, sage, spearmint, and turmeric – all ingredients in this energising tea.

WHAT YOU NEED

Equal parts of the following herbs: bay, rosemary, sage, and spearmint

240 ml (8 fl oz) cup water

Dash of turmeric

1 piece fresh ginger

Lemon

A natural sweetener (optional)

WHAT TO DO

Combine the bay, rosemary, sage, and spearmint. Add 1 teaspoon (5 g) of the herb blend to the freshly boiled water. Add the turmeric and ginger. Steep for 10 minutes, then strain out the plant material. Make sure the tea has cooled before drinking it. Flavour with the lemon, and sweetener, if you wish.

Sources' on page 131.) I might munch some of these herbs straight from the Garden of Youth, or I might make them into a tea.

Find the Source of Your Tiredness

If the cineole-rich herbs don't give you the boost you need, then you should probably start examining your lifestyle. Something you're doing – or not doing – could be draining your energy supply. I recommend the following:

Make sure that you're getting enough sleep. Many people brag that they feel fine on 5 to 6 hours of sleep a night. That may be true. But I'd say that they are exceptions to the rule. I've read research showing that the vast majority of people need at least 7 – and preferably 8 – hours a night to feel and function their best.

If you normally get less than 7 hours of sleep, try for that much every night for at least 1 week. You may find that you feel less exhausted during your waking hours.

Scrutinize your pharmaceuticals. The last time that I checked, more than 100 common prescription and over-the-counter drugs list fatigue as a possible side effect. You might expect this from tranquillizers and sedatives. But among the biggest offenders are the antihistamines in cold and allergy formulas.

Ask your doctor or pharmacist if any drug that you take regularly might cause fatigue – or if the combination of certain drugs might do it. If so, ask your doctor whether he could change your prescription to something that doesn't leave you dragging.

Assess your drinking habits. Alcohol is a powerful depressant. Even social drinking can leave you feeling tired. If you imbibe regularly, reduce your consumption or stop completely. You may notice your energy levels soaring.

Phase in plant foods, phase out fats. Think of a time when you've made a meal of vegetable soup and a green salad or fruit salad. Now remember when you've had a fatty meal – maybe a burger, fries, and a shake. If you're like most people, you felt better on the plant-based meal than on the fatty meal, which left you ready for a nap. The reason is that fats are hard to digest, so your body has to work harder to metabolise them. That effort reduces your energy for other things.

The Palaeolithic diet is rich in easily digested plant foods – fruits, vegetables, pulses, and whole grains – but light on hard-to-digest fat sources such as meats and dairy products. It may help you feel more energised during the day. (To learn more about the Palaeolithic diet and my updated version of it, which I call the Healthy Sevens, see chapter 3.)

Use fitness to fight fatigue. When you're feeling fatigued, exercise may be the last thing on your mind. But it may be the best thing for boosting your energy. Go ahead, try it.

Moderate physical activity like walking feels invigorating. Sure, it can be tiring if you push yourself. But a pleasant walk is more likely to reduce your fatigue than aggravate it.

I do lots of walking around my farm and the Garden of Youth. Maybe that's why I no longer need a cup of coffee first thing in the morning. Not that I have anything against a few cups a day. I just don't need it to start my day anymore. (I'll say more about coffee a bit later.)

Make a point of unwinding. Like walking, practising relaxation can perk you up as it calms you down. When I say 'relaxation', I'm not talking about plopping down on the sofa with a beer. I'm referring to techniques such as meditation, yoga or tai chi, and listening to music.

For myself, I find that walking and gardening help me to unwind.

More Wisdom *from the* Garden

Pamper Yourself with an Energising Bath

Do you enjoy long soaks in hot baths? Next time, try adding a few drops of any of the following essential oils to your bathwater: bergamot, cardamom, eucalyptus, lavender, peppermint, or rosemary. Aromatherapists recommend all of these oils for relief from fatigue.

So does just being out in nature – exploring my woods, sitting by the creek. Playing my guitar is very therapeutic, too.

Don't sit on the sidelines. Instead of worrying about your fatigue, try to enjoy yourself. Don't say, 'I'll do X when I have more energy.' Get out there and do whatever it is to the best of your ability. Sure, you need energy to have fun. But quite often that's a two-way street: having fun increases energy.

For More Serious Stimulation . . .

Earlier I discussed some of the more gentle herbal stimulants. They're not the only ones good for an energy boost. The caffeine-containing herbs and Chinese ephedra (ma huang) are also stimulants. But they need to be used with care.

CAFFEINE-CONTAINING HERBS. This group of stimulants includes coffee, tea, cocoa, maté, guarana, and guayusa. Most Americans would probably prefer coffee or tea (black or green). I know I do. I'm a coffee man. I don't drink as much as I used to, but I still have a couple of cups during the day. When I need to stay energised to meet a deadline, I may have more. I also enjoy tea, and I'm quite fond of chocolate.

Commission E, the expert panel that evaluates the safety and effectiveness of herbs for the German government, recommends 3 grams (1 to 2 teaspoons) of maté a day for mental and physical fatigue.

Unfortunately, the caffeine-containing herbs can cause problems. Over time, you develop a tolerance for caffeine, and you need more to obtain the desired stimulation. But as you increase your consumption, you may experience jitters, irritability, and insomnia. My advice is to try the caffeine-containing herbs, but be mindful of how the caffeine affects you.

CHINESE EPHEDRA (*EPHEDRA SINICA*). Also known as ma huang, this herb produces caffeine-like stimulation. But in very high doses, it causes potentially fatal heart problems. The FDA has threatened to restrict access to the herb in America because it has been associated with several deaths. Most of the people died after foolishly ingesting enormous amounts of Chinese ephedra to experience an amphetamine-like high.

As I write this, Chinese ephedra is still legal in America. I'm saddened that anyone would use this or any herb irresponsibly. But I'd hate to see ephedra restricted because of these tragic incidents. When used responsibly in the recommended doses, the herb can be a valuable stimulant for people struggling with fatigue.

If you buy a commercial preparation, use it according to the package directions. Don't take more than the recommended dosage.

I grow Chinese ephedra in my Garden of Youth, but the plants are having a tough time. I can't figure out why.

Chronic Fatigue Syndrome/Myalgic Encephalomyelitis (ME): Exhaustion That Just Won't Quit

At its most severe, fatigue takes the form of chronic fatigue syndrome (also known as Myalgic Encephalomyelitis or ME). This illness is quite mysterious – and controversial. Even today, more than 10 years after it was officially recognised, some experts question whether ME really exists. (I, for one, believe that it does.)

Among those who are convinced that ME is a genuine illness, there's debate over just what ME is. Some say it's an immune disorder. Others contend that it's a variant of fibromyalgia.

Whatever ME is, it appears to affect millions of people. According to the American National Institutes of Health, the vast majority of these people are middle class, white, and female.

The symptoms of ME include profound fatigue not alleviated by sleep, along with depression, abdominal distress, headache, malaise, memory loss, mental confusion, poor concentration, pain and weakness in the joints and muscles, recurring infections, severe exhaustion after mild exertion, sore throat, fevers, and swollen lymph glands. Ironically, when people with some combination of these symptoms are run through a battery of medical tests, the results show no illness or abnormality. That's what makes ME so baffling.

Over the years, research has linked ME to chronic yeast infection, Epstein-Barr virus, herpes, mononucleosis, multiple-chemical sensitivity, or a combination of these things. The fact is, scientists have yet to pinpoint the cause.

The good news is that most people with ME do get better. The bad news is that it can be a long haul, lasting as long as several years. For some, the symptoms never subside.

Dr Duke's Anti-Ageing Elixir

Antiviral Energy Booster

If ME is caused by a virus, as some experts suggest, then it may respond well to treatment with antiviral herbs. This recipe contains a few of the better antivirals: hyssop, lemon balm, and self-heal.

WHAT YOU NEED

3 parts lemon balm leaves
2 parts peppermint leaves
2 parts rosemary leaves
2 parts hyssop leaves
1 part self-heal leaves
1 part skullcap leaves
1 licorice stick (to sweeten)

WHAT TO DO

Place the lemon balm, peppermint, rosemary, hyssop, self-heal, and skullcap in a pot and add water to cover. Bring to the boil. Allow to steep for 10 minutes, then strain. Drink a cup at a time as necessary, refrigerating any left over for later use. To sweeten, stir the tea with a licorice stick.

Possible Culprits behind ME

Fortunately for me, I've never experienced Myalgic Encephalomyelitis. If you think that you might have the condition, I suggest the following:

Have your thyroid checked. Located in your neck, your thyroid regulates your metabolism. If the gland is underactive (a condition called hypothyroidism), your entire body slows down. As a result, you feel persistently lethargic and fatigued.

Many people, especially women, have underactive thyroids and don't know it. To find out whether you have it, all you need is a simple blood test.

Doctors usually treat hypothyroidism with replacement thyroid hormone. In addition, I'd recommend drinking a tea brewed from herbs rich in rosmarinic acid, such as basil, oregano, rosemary, self-heal, and spearmint. Rosmarinic acid may raise levels of thyroid hormone when they're low, though the research is far from conclusive. Studies have shown that the compound can lower hormone levels when they're high.

Get tested for allergies and chemical sensitivities. Depending on the study, some 50 to 75 per cent of people with ME have inhalant (seasonal) allergies or sensitivities to various foods or drugs. Avoiding your trigger substances can help relieve your symptoms.

Ask your doctor about an elimination diet. If you have food sensitivities, a medically supervised elimination diet may help you break the grip of ME. One allergist at Georgetown University School of Medicine in Washington, D.C., found that about 60 per cent of his ME patients had food sensitivities, mostly to wheat, milk, and corn. Quite often, eliminating the trigger foods puts an end to the fatigue.

Establish a supplement regime. Naturopaths are big believers in supplementation for ME. I'm not quite as convinced, but if I had ME, I'd give it a try and follow a supplement regime under the supervision of a naturopath or clinical nutritionist.

I'd pay special attention to folic acid (also known as folate), a B vitamin that seems to be in short supply in most people's diets. The average American gets only 61 per cent of the American RDA, which is too low anyway. And the British and Australian RDAs are even lower. Extra zinc might also help, especially if you have white spots on your nails, which may signal a deficiency. Naturopaths often prescribe 100 milligrams a day.

Beyond the familiar vitamins and minerals, naturopathic doctors suggest 2 grams of aspartic acid a day, based on research showing that 75 per cent of people with ME improved while taking the supplement (compared with 25 per cent of those who were taking a placebo, or fake pill). So aspartic acid seems like a good idea. Food sources of the nutrient include beans, bean sprouts, and asparagus.

Herbal Treatments That May Help

Some herbs may help alleviate ME symptoms. But remember, they need time to work. That said, if I had ME, I'd consider incorporating the following into my self-care regime.

ANTIVIRAL HERBS. There's no proof that ME is a viral illness. Then again, there's no proof that it isn't. Viruses are very hard to identify. ME just might be viral, with the virus yet to be discovered.

One alternative practitioner whom I know claims that 85 per cent of his ME patients have improved while taking combinations of various antiviral herbs. Experimentally, I would try some of the better antiviral herbs: garlic, hyssop, lemon balm, purslane, and self-heal.

To use garlic, simply chew the fresh cloves. If you can't bring yourself to do that, lightly sauté the herb in cooking. You can also take garlic capsules.

For purslane, steam the leaves and eat it like spinach.

All the rest of the herbs can be taken as teas. Use a few teaspoons of herb per cup of freshly boiled water, steep for 10 minutes, then strain. You can also juice the herbs and mix the liquid into tomato or carrot juice.

ECHINACEA (*ECHINACEA,* VARIOUS SPECIES). Echinacea is my favourite immune enhancer. I'd mix it with the antiviral herbs to give them extra strength against any viruses that might contribute to ME. Or I'd buy a commercial tincture and take it according to the label directions.

ASTRAGALUS (*ASTRALAGUS MEMBRANACEUS*). Like ginseng, astragalus – also known as huang qi – has been used for centuries by the Chinese to boost energy and vitality. This makes sense to me. Research has found the herb to be an effective immune stimulant, though it's not quite as potent as echinacea. It appears to combat fatigue by fortifying the immune system against infections.

Most herbalists recommend taking 3 to 5 millilitres (½ to 1 teaspoon) of tincture three or four times a day, or two 400-milligram capsules three times a day. If I wanted to try astragalus, I'd buy a commercial preparation and use it according to the package directions.

GINSENG – ASIAN (*PANAX GINSENG*), AMERICAN (*P. QUINQUEFOLIUS*), SIBERIAN (*ELEUTHEROCOCCUS SENTICOSUS*). Personally, I'm not as much of a fan of ginseng as many other herbalists. I grow the herb in a wooded area, along a creek that runs through YinYang Valley (and I have a hard time keeping the deer away from the plants). But I'm not convinced that ginseng is as powerful an adaptogen/tonic as its advocates claim.

for the
Gardener

American Ginseng

Panax quinquefolius

At one time, American ginseng grew in the rich, deciduous hardwood forests of North America, from the Quebec and Manitoba provinces in Canada to Oklahoma, Louisiana, Alabama, and Florida. But because of overharvesting, the herb is now considered an endangered species.

You may be able to grow your own American ginseng from seeds. Be aware, though, that the process takes a great deal of time and patience. In nature, ginseng seeds usually lie dormant through two winters before sprouting. Your best bet is to look for pre-stratified seeds. Lightly press them into humus-rich, well-drained, acidic soil in full shade. Mulch with chopped, well-rotted leaves.

Plant the seedlings about 30 cm (12 inches) apart in the autumn, in the conditions described above. Mulch with 7.5–12 cm (3–4 inches) of rotted leaf material in cold areas. In spring, remove the leaf material to prevent fungal infections. Water weekly when it's dry.

The roots must develop for 4 to 6 years before they're harvested. At that point, you can carefully dig them up and quickly rinse off any dirt (water can leach out the active compounds). Dry them on screens in a warm, dark area with good air circulation. After about 3 weeks, put them in airtight glass or plastic containers. They'll keep for up to 2 years.

An adaptogen/tonic is a substance that helps your body adjust to stressful conditions, resist illness, improve performance, and overcome fatigue. Maybe ginseng does all of that. Maybe not. The research is pretty poor.

On the other hand, the Chinese and Koreans have revered ginseng as an invigorator for centuries. Today, the herb has passionate supporters all over the world. If I had ME, I'd probably give ginseng a try. It certainly wouldn't hurt.

Commission E recommends ginseng as a tonic to counteract fatigue and weakness, as a restorative for declining stamina and impaired concentration, and as an aid in convalescence. Russian cosmonauts and Olympic athletes reportedly use the herb as a general tonic, to reduce both physical and mental stress. In Germany, ginseng has been approved as a tonic to invigorate and fortify the body against fatigue and weakness.

Ginseng is not like caffeine or Chinese ephedra. It doesn't give you a quick buzz. Instead, it takes weeks or months to produce any effects, and even those are usually pretty subtle. If you want to try the herb, buy a commercial preparation and take it according to the package directions.

SCHISANDRA (*SCHISANDRA CHINENSIS*). Though it's not well-known in the West, schisandra (Chinese magnolia vine) is considered by Asians to have benefits similar to astragalus and ginseng. The research to date shows that the herb helps strengthen the heart and treat bacterial infections, a combination of benefits that probably accounts for its value in combating fatigue. The recommended dose is 3 millilitres of tincture three times a day.

LOMATIUM (*LOMATIUM*, VARIOUS SPECIES). Ayurvedic doctors recommend lomatium for ME. I find this most interesting because the American species of the herb (*Lomatium dissectum*) has been strongly recommended as a treatment for Epstein-Barr virus infection, once thought to cause ME.

American lomatium is often available through naturopaths, who can also recommend an appropriate dosage. I used to grow my own, but the rabbits wiped me out years ago.

For More Information . . .

If you've been diagnosed with ME, I'd recommend contacting the following: The ME Association, 4 Top Angel, Buckingham Industrial Estate, Buckingham, MK18 ITH. *www.meassociation.org.uk*; *enquiries@meassociation.org.uk*

CHAPTER 35

Haemorrhoids

Dr Duke's Anti-Ageing Elixir
• *Rutin-Tootin' Haemorrhoid Healer*

I always thought that the H in Preparation H stood not for 'haemorrhoids' but rather for 'hazel', as in witch hazel. After all, witch hazel is one of the best herbs around for soothing painful haemorrhoids.

Just recently, though, I found out that I was mistaken. Preparation H doesn't even contain witch hazel. But the herb is the main ingredient in other commercial haemorrhoid treatments.

For decades, Preparation H did contain live yeast cell derivatives, among other ingredients. Then the FDA in America told the manufacturer that the product had to be reformulated, because yeast cell derivatives were not effective. Where the FDA got this idea is beyond me. But the agency issued its order, and the manufacturer removed the disallowed ingredient from Preparation H, despite millions of satisfied customers.

Two experts whom I respect, Joe and Terry Graedon, authors of *The People's Pharmacy* books, say that they wish the FDA had not meddled with a perfectly fine product. According to the Graedons, they used to receive many testimonials for the old Preparation H formula – not just for haemorrhoids but also for many common ailments, including bedsores, burns, chafing, cracked fingers, itching, surgical scars, and wrinkles. The letters have all but stopped since the FDA-directed reformulation went on the market.

It's just another example of the FDA's prejudice against traditional, natural ingredients. It's such a shame.

Constipation's Uncomfortable End Result

Back to the subject at hand: haemorrhoids. They're incredibly common, affecting an estimated one-third of all adults at some time in life. For an unfortunate 10 per cent or so, haemorrhoids become chronic. They can turn sitting, walking, sneezing, laughing, and defecating into extremely painful endeavours.

Haemorrhoids (also known as piles) are essentially varicose veins. Only instead of showing up on your legs, they develop around or inside your anus. The veins in this area naturally expand during bowel movements and shrink back to normal size afterwards. But repeated straining during defecation from either constipation or hard stools can interfere with this process, causing the veins to permanently swell.

Once you have haemorrhoids, the chronic swelling weakens the anal veins. Defecation can rupture them, causing bleeding.

Like constipation, haemorrhoids become more common with age. Most older folks are less active than when they were younger, which makes them more likely to become constipated. To compound matters, the muscles of the colon wall tend to lose their tone over time, setting the stage for straining at stool.

Weight can be a factor in determining who gets haemorrhoids and who doesn't. If you're overweight, it puts pressure on your anal veins. Many women experience haemorrhoids during pregnancy, as the developing foetus puts pressure on the veins of the lower abdomen, interfering with normal blood drainage.

Thankfully, I've never had haemorrhoids, mainly because I've never been badly bothered by constipation. I attribute that to exercising regularly and eating lots of plant foods. Here's where I climb up on my soapbox to sing the praises of the plant-based Palaeolithic diet. All of the fibre in plant foods helps keep things moving. Plus, fibre keeps stool soft, so it passes easily without straining.

Unfortunately, far too many people subsist on a low-fibre, meat-and-junk-food diet. This produces small, dense, hard stools that pass slowly and with difficulty. The combination of hard stool and the straining required to pass it is a one-way ticket to haemorrhoids.

Ease the Pain and Itching Naturally

The best way to beat haemorrhoids is to not get them in the first place. The best way to do that is to avoid constipation. I'm not going to delve too deeply into constipation here, since the condition is discussed at length in chapters 9 and 29. But I will say that anyone who eats bran cereal for breakfast plus five servings of fruits and five servings of veggies over the course of each day is unlikely to experience chronic constipation.

In the rest of this chapter, I'm going to discuss herbal treatments for existing haemorrhoids. As you'll see, herbal medicine offers many options for relief.

WITCH HAZEL (*HAMAMELIS VIRGINIANA*). You can spend a lot of money on commercial preparations which are mostly witch hazel. Or you can

Dr Duke's Anti-Ageing Elixir

Rutin-Tootin' Haemorrhoid Healer

The three herbs in this tonic – violet, eucalyptus, and mulberry – are rich in a vein-strengthening compound called rutin. Together, they make a potent treatment for haemorrhoids.

WHAT YOU NEED

A few violet flowers
1–2 eucalyptus leaves
1–2 mulberry leaves
Lemon
A natural sweetener (optional)

WHAT TO DO

Place the violet flowers, eucalyptus leaves, and mulberry leaves in a blender. Cover with water, then combine. Add the lemon and sweetener to taste, then drink up.

make your own version by buying witch hazel water, a commercial extract sold in pharmacies, and applying it to your haemorrhoids with tissues or cotton wool balls.

Witch hazel is just what the herbalist ordered for haemorrhoids. The herb is rich in astringent compounds called tannins. When applied to broken or inflamed skin, tannins draw out inflammatory proteins, tightening the superficial cell layers. This is how the herb helps relieve haemorrhoid pain, swelling, and inflammation. As a bonus, it soothes and cools the anal area.

I can't think of a single reputable herbalist who doesn't recommend witch hazel for haemorrhoids. The herb is also endorsed by Commission E, the expert panel that evaluates the safety and effectiveness of herbs for the German government. Commission E suggests using suppositories containing 100 to 1,000 milligrams of leaf or bark extract, repeating treatments one to three times daily. For most people, though, it's easier to apply witch hazel water with tissues or cotton balls several times a day.

Witch hazel is safe for external use, even for pregnant women. I know of no side effects, though irritation is possible for those with sensitive skin. Just don't ingest witch hazel water. The astringent tannins that it contains can cause abdominal distress and, in large doses, possibly liver damage.

Witch hazel grows wild in the woods around my place. I've transplanted a few shrubs into several plots in my Garden of Youth. Each shrub's yellow flowers emerge in autumn, as its leaves turn yellow.

BUTCHER'S BROOM (*RUSCUS ACULEATUS*). Like witch hazel, butcher's broom has a long history of use as a treatment for haemorrhoids and varicose veins. This is no coincidence. The herb contains ruscogenin and neoruscogenin, compounds that strengthen vein walls and increase their elasticity. In this way, it keeps blood flowing properly and prevents blood from pooling, which helps protect against varicose veins, including haemorrhoids.

In addition, ruscogenin and neoruscogenin are anti-inflammatory. They help relieve the pain and swelling associated with haemorrhoids.

Commission E suggests taking 50 to 100 milligrams of ruscogenin a day, divided into three doses. This roughly translates to 1 to 2 teaspoons of powdered butcher's broom root a day. To make a tea, I'd simmer the herb in boiling water for 10 minutes, then strain out the plant material and let cool before drinking.

I grow butcher's broom. It's a tough little shrub with evergreen pointed leaves and red berries that hang on until Christmas.

HORSE CHESTNUT (*AESCULUS HIPPOCASTANUM*). Horse chestnut helps strengthen veins, thanks to a compound called aescin. Commission E endorses the herb for varicose veins. I'd expand that endorsement to include haemorrhoids.

Naturopaths recommend taking either 20 drops of liquid horse chestnut extract or 50 milligrams of aescin three times a day. But they advise pregnant women not to ingest aescin. Taken in large doses, the compound can cause a number of unpleasant gastrointestinal effects. The gastrointestinal tracts of mums-to-be tend to be quite sensitive.

If you're pregnant, look for a topical cream made with horse chestnut extract. The extract contains astringent tannins and saponins. It's also anti-inflammatory.

Never take fresh horse chestnut internally, because it's poisonous. Commercial preparations, on the other hand, are safe because they have been detoxified.

HYSSOP (*HYSSOPUS OFFICINALIS*). Hyssop contains a compound called diosmin that strengthens veins and helps prevent swelling. I've grown several different varieties of this herb: red-flowered, white-flowered, and blue-flowered. I still have the blue-flowering plant, which I frequently use in mint teas.

I'd suggest making a hyssop tea by adding 1 to 2 teaspoons of the herb to a cup of freshly boiled water. Steep for 10 minutes, then strain out the plant material. Drink up to four cups a day.

YELLOW SWEET CLOVER (*MELILOTUS OFFICINALIS*). Commission E has endorsed yellow sweet clover, also known as melilot, as a treatment for haemorrhoids. It contains coumarin, a compound that relieves swelling and inflammation. Commission E suggests a dosage of the herb that's equivalent to 3 to 30 milligrams of coumarin. This translates to 1 to 2 teaspoons of herb per cup of freshly boiled water, steeped for 10 minutes, then strained.

Be aware that some preliminary research has linked yellow sweet clover to liver damage. While more research needs to be done, I'd advise against taking the herb in amounts above the recommended dosage or for long periods of time.

I don't grow yellow sweet clover in my Garden of Youth. It's such a common weed here in Maryland that I don't have to.

PLANTAIN (*PLANTAGO MAJOR*) AND PSYLLIUM (*PLANTAGO OVATA*). This duo delivers a one-two punch against haemorrhoids. The seeds contain mucilage, a fibre that expands a great deal in the presence of water. In the gut, mucilage adds bulk to stools, helping to prevent constipation and, as a result, haemorrhoids. In fact, psyllium seed is one of the safest, gentlest herbal laxatives around.

In one study involving 51 people with haemorrhoids, 84 per cent experienced improvement in their symptoms after treatment with a psyllium preparation. They reported less pain, bleeding, and itching during defecation. If you want to try psyllium, I suggest buying Metamucil, which is mostly psyllium seed.

For external treatment of haemorrhoids, I recommend making a poultice from psyllium leaves, plantain leaves, or both. They contain allantoin, a compound that helps heal wounds. Just chew the leaves to crush, moisten, and soften them, then apply them directly to your haemorrhoids, holding them in place with a small bandage.

CAMOMILE (*MATRICARIA RECUTITA*). This is a good herb to close the chapter. It's recommended for all sorts of skin conditions because it's both anti-inflammatory and antiseptic. I think it might help treat haemorrhoids.

I suggest brewing a strong camomile tea using 3 to 4 tablespoons of flowers per cup of freshly boiled water. Steep for 10 minutes, then strain out the plant material and allow the tea to cool. You can drink it, or you can apply it directly to your haemorrhoids with cotton wool balls or a clean cloth.

I have lots of camomile growing in my garden. I love its apple scent.

CHAPTER 36

Hair Loss

Dr Duke's Anti-Ageing Elixirs

* *Dr Duke's Hair Saver Rosemary-and-Sage Shampoo*
* *Ginger Scalp Tonic*

A few years ago, I got a call from a herbalist friend of mine who was excited because she had discovered a herb that she thought would cure male pattern baldness. Such a herb might make her millions, from men (and some women) desperate to stop hair loss and regrow what's gone.

My friend was quite guarded about her miracle herb. She wouldn't mention it by name, I suppose out of fear that I might announce it to the balding men of America before she could. So I just listened to her as she explained that her secret herb prevented the synthesis of the hormone responsible for shutting down hair follicles on the head. (That hormone is dihydrotestosterone, created from the male sex hormone testosterone.)

'Really,' I replied. 'Your herb sounds like saw palmetto.'

I could hear her jaw dropping over the telephone. She was astonished that I'd identified her herb. She was even more surprised that I was familiar with saw palmetto's dihydrotestosterone-inhibiting action.

Saw Palmetto: The Best Choice for Balding

Saw palmetto (*Serenoa repens)* is best known for its ability to prevent and treat benign prostate enlargement. I take it almost daily for that purpose, though at my age, I should take it daily. So far, I've avoided prostate surgery. Why do the prostates of middle-aged and older men grow? In part because of the conversion of testosterone into dihydrotestosterone, the same mechanism involved in male pattern baldness.

The average adult head has about 100,000 hairs and loses about 100 a day. Usually, they grow back. But in male pattern baldness, the hair follicles shut down production over time. Male pattern baldness is unpredictable. Some men begin to lose their hair in their twenties, while others keep a full head of hair for a lifetime. (Actually, the term *male pattern baldness* is something of a misnomer, because the condition also affects many women, though rarely enough to be noticeable.)

Over the years, I've suggested that men concerned about male pattern baldness try saw palmetto for hair preservation. I've kept up with a few of them, and some seem to feel that their hair loss had slowed, maybe even stopped. I have saw palmetto growing in two plots of my Garden of Youth – ones devoted to prostate enlargement and balding.

A few years after the phone call from my herbalist friend, I wasn't surprised when I read that the drug finasteride (Proscar) was being formulated into a 'new' drug, Propecia, for hair loss. Like saw palmetto, finasteride is prescribed for benign prostate enlargement. Also like the herb, the pharmaceutical prevents the conversion of testosterone to dihydrotestosterone.

But unlike saw palmetto, finasteride had more than anecdotal reports to support its use for hair preservation and restoration. In one study, 1,553 balding men took finasteride or a placebo (a fake pill) for up to 12 months. Those treated with the drug showed significantly greater hair regrowth.

As far as I'm concerned, this study – and the FDA's approval of finasteride to treat balding – makes me believe in saw palmetto even more. After all, the herb and the drug have the same mechanism of action. So it's reasonable to assume that they'd have the same, or at least similar, effects in the body. Of course, the FDA still considers saw palmetto 'useless' for hair loss. I consider the FDA prejudiced against medicinal herbs.

While I grow saw palmetto in my Garden of Youth, for my own daily dose, I use a commercial standardised extract. Hair loss hasn't been a big problem for me, but I can't help thinking that all the saw palmetto I've been taking may be giving my genes a little hair-preserving boost.

If you'd like to try saw palmetto for hair preservation or restoration, I'd use the dosage recommended for prostate trouble – 160 milligrams twice a day. Several brands of commercial capsules provide that dose.

You can also whip up some of my Even Better Prosnut Butter, which is a lot like peanut butter. I developed the recipe to prevent prostate enlargement, but it might also help treat hair loss. Since the two conditions often go hand in hand for older men, Even Better Prosnut Butter might help them with both at the same time. For the recipe, see page 220.

for the Gardener

Sage

Salvia officinalis

A member of the mint family, sage is a perennial, shrubby plant that reaches about 45 cm (18 inches) in height. I recommend buying established seedlings or plants. Check at your local nursery.

Sage fares best under full sun in rich, well-drained loam, but it tolerates most garden soils. Space the plants 30–60 cm (12 to 24 inches) apart in rows 60–90 cm (24 to 36 inches) apart. Mulching with oat straw can increase your yield considerably.

Once it's established, sage requires little attention, though it may succumb to hard frosts. Harvest the plants by cutting them near the soil line, then bind them together with string or rubber bands for drying. Once the leaves become brittle, strip them off the stems and store them in airtight containers.

More Wisdom *from the* Garden

This B Vitamin May Reverse Balding

If you're experiencing hair loss, you may want to try taking supplements of the B vitamins, especially biotin. In a few studies that I've seen, when people with hair loss were given biotin to correct a deficiency of the nutrient, their hair grew back. Like saw palmetto, biotin helps prevent the conversion of testosterone to dihydrotestosterone. For adults, the recommended dose ranges from 30 to 300 micrograms.

In other research, women who were losing their hair were able to slow the process by taking B-complex supplements. This makes sense biologically because proliferating cells, such as those involved in hair growth, are high in biotin and other B vitamins.

More Herbal Hair-Restorers

Saw palmetto may be the best herb for treating hair loss, but it's not the only one. Based on what I've read in the medical literature and heard in anecdotal reports, the following show promise as treatments and are certainly worth trying.

EVENING PRIMROSE (*OENOTHERA BIENNIS*). Like saw palmetto, the oil from the seeds of evening primrose inhibits the conversion of testosterone into dihydrotestosterone. At home, I chew on a few pinches of gritty seed plucked from the plants. If I were concerned about hair loss, I'd take one 1,300-milligram capsule of a standardised extract (containing at least 130 milligrams of gamma-linolenic acid, or GLA) twice a day.

HORSE CHESTNUT (*AESCULUS HIPPOCASTANUM*). I've been especially interested in this herb ever since I reviewed a study showing that it contains compounds (aesculin, ximenynic acid, and lauric acid) that help treat hair loss – at least in animals. The formulation used in the study improved circulation through the scalp. It seems promising, but I've not seen any further research to support it.

I grow American horse chestnut (*Aesculus pavia*) in my garden. It's different from the European variety used in the study. Neither species should be ingested fresh, since both can be toxic. Instead, buy a commercial preparation and take it according to the label directions.

HORSETAIL (*EQUISETUM*, VARIOUS SPECIES). Naturopaths tout this herb as a treatment for baldness. They believe that its silicic acid promotes circulation to the scalp area. That's why I have horsetail growing next to the saw palmetto in the Baldness plot of my Garden of Youth. If you want to try horsetail, I suggest buying a commercial preparation and using it according to the label directions.

GINKGO (*GINKGO BILOBA*). Japanese scientists report that a tincture of ginkgo promoted hair regrowth in shaved mice. Personally, I'm sceptical. Millions of Europeans and an increasing number of Americans take ginkgo regularly to support recovery from stroke, treat Alzheimer's disease, and sharpen mental function. If the herb restored hair, I think we would have heard about it by now. Still, you're welcome to try ginkgo for this purpose. Buy a commercial preparation and take it ac-

for the Gardener

Rosemary

Rosmarinus officinalis

This evergreen, blue-flowered shrub is native to the rocky shorelines of the Mediterranean. A perennial, it can reach 1.8 m (6 feet) or more, especially in warm climates. It's easily started from seeds or cuttings. Of the two, I prefer cuttings because they're genetic clones of the mother plant. Seeds take at least 3 weeks to germinate, and even then only about 20 per cent germinate successfully. Plant 15-cm (6-inch) cuttings about 11 cm (4 inches) deep in moist sand.

My rosemary has done well the last two winters, which have been rather mild. If you live in an area where harsh winters are the norm, you may want to try growing rosemary indoors, in hanging pots placed near sunny windows.

Wait to harvest the herb until after the first flowering. Then you can cut the leaves as needed. Just don't take more than three-quarters of the new growth. Allow the leaves to dry slowly, until they're crumbly.

cording to the label directions.

GRAPE SEED (*VITIS VINIFERA*). Japanese researchers have also discovered that grape seed extract promotes hair growth in shaved mice. Grape seed contains powerful antioxidants. If you use the extract as part of a regime to prevent heart disease or cancer, take some pictures of your head to see if your hair thickens up. If it does, let me know.

ROSEMARY (*ROSMARINUS OFFICINALIS*) AND SAGE (*SALVIA OFFICINALIS*). Recently, a book on hair and skin care published a recipe called Dr Duke's Hair Saver Rosemary-and-Sage Shampoo. It grew out of a conversation

Dr Duke's Anti-Ageing Elixir

Dr Duke's Hair Saver Rosemary-and-Sage Shampoo

This namesake recipe appears in *The Take-Charge Beauty Book*, by Susan Hussey. Its star ingredients are rosemary and sage, both of which have long traditions as remedies for baldness. You should be able to buy all of these ingredients in a health food shop, though yucca and burdock root liquids can be hard to find.

WHAT YOU NEED

- 230 g (8 oz) peppermint Castile soap
- 2 tablespoons aloe gel
- 1 tablespoon sage oil
- 1 tablespoon rosemary oil
- 1 tablespoon yucca root liquid
- 1 tablespoon burdock root liquid
- 1 teaspoon shea butter (an African herb)
- 1 teaspoon comfrey leaf extract
- ½ teaspoon vegetable glycerin
- ½ teaspoon jojoba oil
- ¼ teaspoon grapefruit seed extract
- 4 drops liquid vitamin C
- 4 capsules amino acids with vitamin B_6
- 2 capsules biotin

WHAT TO DO

In a small bowl, blend together all of the ingredients. Pour the mixture into a bottle and store. Use it like a regular shampoo.

with the author, in which I pointed out that all of the herbs mentioned in the folk song 'Scarborough Fair' – parsley, sage, rosemary, and thyme – have well-established folk reputations for treating baldness. You can try the recipe for yourself.

You can also buy a commercial preparation called Dr Duke's Hair Saver Rosemary-and-Sage Shampoo, made with all the same ingredients in health food shops in America. Either way, I think the shampoo might help if you're also taking saw palmetto regularly.

Help for Alopecia Areata

Shortly after I learned that I had been immortalised by a shampoo, I read a fascinating study that supported rosemary as a hair restorer – not for male pattern baldness but for another form of hair loss known as alopecia areata. This mysterious condition comes on suddenly, with big clumps of hair falling out for no apparent reason.

Alopecia areata affects large numbers of people. No one knows what causes it, and mainstream medical treatments don't do it much good. Fortunately, the hair that falls out usually grows back. But until it does, the condition can be both frightening and disfiguring.

In the herbal medicine tradition, several herbs have gained reputations as hair restorers – not just rosemary and sage but also cedarwood, lavender, and thyme. Scottish dermatologists had heard anecdotal reports that four of these five, all except sage, help treat alopecia areata. So they decided to test the herbs in a controlled experiment.

The researchers gave 84 patients with alopecia areata either a placebo preparation (3 millilitres of jojoba oil and 20 millilitres of grape seed oil) or the placebo preparation plus 2 drops of thyme oil, 3 drops of lavender oil, 3 drops of rosemary oil, and 2 drops of cedarwood oil. The study participants were instructed to massage the oil blend into their scalps for 2 minutes each night, then wrap their heads in a warm towel to speed the oils' absorption. Three months later, 15 per cent of those using the placebo showed significant hair regrowth. Among those using the placebo plus the herbal oils, that figure rose to 44 per cent. None of the herbal oils produced side effects.

I grow all of these herbs in my Garden of Youth, except cedarwood. I don't feel I need to raise my own cedar, since it's so common in the woods around my place.

Herbs for Great-Looking Hair

To care for the hair that you have, one of the best strategies is brushing. A century ago, women used to brush their hair 100 strokes a night. That's a good idea, because brushing is a form of massage that improves circulation through your scalp. It also makes hair shine by distributing oil from the scalp through the strands.

Another good strategy is to dilute your shampoo. Most shampoos actually work better when they're diluted. I'm not sure why, but I think it's because people tend to spend more time massaging dilute shampoos into their scalps to work up a lather. Concentrated shampoos produce more lather and so don't require as much massaging.

You may also want to add a few herbs to your hair-care regime. These three can help keep your hair healthy.

ALOE (*ALOE VERA*). Cosmetologists believe that the gel from inside aloe's leaves conditions the scalp. Egyptian researchers have validated this theory with studies showing that aloe gel not only helps treat dandruff and seborrhoea but also may regrow hair in people with seborrhoeic baldness (hair loss accompanied by the formation of oily scales on the scalp). And for scalps exposed by thinning hair, aloe serves as a protective screen against the wind and sun. The gel can be applied directly to

More Wisdom *from the* Garden

Massage: The Naturopathic Treatment for Hair Loss

For patients with hair loss, naturopaths recommend a nightly scalp massage using one part rosemary oil and two parts almond oil. Massage improves circulation through the scalp, which may keep hair follicles from calling it quits. And rosemary oil has a well-established reputation as a folk remedy for baldness.

the scalp, though be forewarned that it's rather goopy.

I have an aloe plant in my kitchen for minor household burns. I also keep potted plants outside during the warm summer months, then move them indoors for winter.

RED SAGE (*SALVIA MILTIORRHIZA*). In Asia, red sage has a reputation as a hair restorer and hair-care helper. I can't vouch for the former claim, but the latter is supported by the fact that extracts of red sage are used in several shampoos.

So far, I've been unable to obtain red sage for my garden. But I'm still hoping.

SAFFLOWER (*CARTHAMUS TINCTORIUS*). The Chinese use safflower in hair-growth liniments, often in combination with red sage. Besides the benefit obtained just from massaging both of these herbs into the scalp, safflower is believed to help open the capillaries of the scalp, facilitating the absorption of other herbs into the hair follicles. Still, I don't grow my own safflower, because I consider it more cosmetic than medicinal.

Dr Duke's Anti-Ageing Elixir

Ginger Scalp Tonic

Egyptian researchers say that this herbal blend helps treat dandruff, seborrhoea, and maybe even balding. I've never tried it, but if I were losing my hair, I might.

WHAT YOU NEED

2 ginger roots, grated

3 tablespoons sesame oil

Dash of lemon juice

WHAT TO DO

Juice the ginger roots. Mix 1 to 2 tablespoons of the juice with the sesame oil and lemon juice. Massage the blend into your scalp, leaving it on for 15 to 30 minutes before rinsing. Repeat three times a week. Refrigerate leftover shampoo between uses.

CHAPTER 37

High Blood Pressure

Dr Duke's Anti-Ageing Elixirs

• *Veggie-Powered Blood Pressure Soup*
• *Hypertension Helper*

Millions of people have chronic high blood pressure, also known as hypertension. In America this condition affects more than half of all adults over 60 and about two-thirds of those over 70.

That's a lot of people. And their blood pressure medication costs a lot of money.

For those with severe hypertension – about half of the sufferers fall into this category – I don't know of any good alternative to medication. These folks can certainly benefit from lifestyle changes and herbal treatments. But they still need medication to manage their blood pressures. That's not the case for those with mild to moderate hypertension.

I believe that it's better to manage mild to moderate hypertension with non-drug approaches. Of course, the pharmaceutical industry doesn't agree with me. That's because medications for people who have mild to moderate hypertension bring in a great deal of money. In my opinion, it's an unnecessary expense. Most of these folks could manage their conditions just fine with lifestyle changes and herbal treatments alone.

Ditch Points with the DASH Diet

High blood pressure is a major risk factor for heart attack and stroke. In chapter 13, I outline a number of strategies for lowering your chances of heart attack and stroke. All of those measures can help prevent high blood pressure, too. In this chapter, I'm going to focus on your treatment options.

Luckily for me, I've never had to deal with high blood pressure. I suspect that my diet has a lot to do with it. It's a plant-based, high-fibre Palaeolithic diet. And I would recommend it to anyone who has high blood pressure. But in trying to win converts, I think I have my work cut out for me. After all, McDonald's spends more in 12 hours to promote its greasy burgers and fries than the National Cancer Institute spends in a year to promote its 'Strive for Five' programme, designed to coax Americans into eating at least five servings of fruits and vegetables a day.

But a Palaeolithic diet really does work. Several studies have shown that compared with meat eaters, vegetarians have lower blood pressure readings. The Palaeolithic diet is near-vegetarian.

In one study conducted at Colorado State University in Fort Collins, the researchers measured the blood pressures of 167 adults who were either meat eaters or vegetarians. One-third – 33 per cent – of the meat eaters had high blood pressure, compared with just 16 per cent of the vegetarians.

Findings like this prompted Harvard researchers to launch a study that they dubbed DASH, Dietary Approaches to Stop Hypertension. For their study, they recruited 459 people with high pressure. One group was instructed to follow what amounted to a typical American diet – high in fat, low in fibre, and few plant foods. Another group also ate a high-fat diet but with more fibre, fruits, and vegetables. A third group was put on a low-fat, near-vegetarian diet consisting of 8 to 10 servings of fruits and vegetables a day (about twice what the typical American eats), along with 7 to 8 servings of whole grains a day, and some fish and chicken.

Neither of the high-fat diets lowered blood pressure. But in just 8 weeks, the low-fat, near-vegetarian diet reduced readings significantly. In fact, the results rivalled those produced by even the most effective blood pressure medications.

One reason the DASH diet works is that it's low in salt. Salt is sodium chloride. The more sodium you consume, the more water your body retains. The extra fluid raises your blood pressure.

Now salt doesn't raise blood pressure in everyone, only in those whom doctors describe as 'salt-sensitive'. But if you have high blood pressure, chances are that you are salt-sensitive. Even if you're not, reducing your salt intake is a good idea. After all, your body needs only

More Wisdom *from the* Garden

Salmon May Take Your Blood Pressure Downstream

Research has proven that a near-vegetarian diet can help rein in high blood pressure. But even the heart-healthy DASH (Dietary Approaches to Stop Hypertension) plan allows room for fish. That may be because some kinds of fish – namely, the cold-water species such as salmon – contain omega-3 fatty acids, a type of fat that's actually good for your heart.

In one study that I've reviewed, when people who were not fish eaters began having salmon once or twice a week, their blood pressure readings dropped significantly. They may have gone down even more had the salmon been prepared with heart-healthy herbs like garlic and onions.

If you don't care for salmon, you can get your omega-3 fatty acids in the form of fish oil capsules. Ask your doctor whether fish oil might help you and, if so, how much you should take.

about 2,000 milligrams of sodium a day to function properly. But many of us consume three times that amount.

The easiest way to reduce your salt intake is to give up junk foods such as corn chips and potato crisps. They're very high in salt. Read nutrition labels to find out how much sodium various foods contain, and leave the worst offenders on the supermarket shelves. And remember: the vast majority of plant foods are naturally low in sodium.

If you think that less salt means less flavour, I suggest using herbs and spices as salt substitutes. Basil, cayenne pepper, black pepper, rosemary, and other culinary seasonings make foods even more tasty while helping you reduce your salt consumption.

Lower Your Reading by Shaping Up

The DASH diet is just one element of a comprehensive self-care programme for controlling high blood pressure. Exercise is another. And it's a biggie.

Regular physical activity helps you maintain a healthy weight and manage your stress, both of which have an impact on blood pressure. But research has shown that exercise has an even more direct effect on blood pressure readings.

For one study, scientists at the Cooper Institute for Aerobics Research in Dallas recruited 56 non-exercisers with high blood pressure. Some of the people participated in a fitness programme consisting of three brisk 60-minute walks a week, while the rest remained inactive. After 16 weeks, those who didn't exercise showed no change in their blood pressure readings. Those who were walking, however, experienced significant reductions.

Personally, I get lots of exercise by walking around YinYang Valley and pottering around in my Garden of Youth. When the weather is nasty, I stay indoors and ride my stationary bike.

Beside eating healthily and exercising regularly, you can knock some points off your blood pressure reading by limiting your alcohol consumption and quitting smoking. Both habits contribute to high blood pressure. A drink or two a day is probably okay, depending on your individual circumstances. Beyond that, you could be doing your heart more harm than good. (Incidentally, a drink is defined as 350 ml (12 fl oz) of regular beer, 150 ml (5 fl oz) of wine, or a cocktail made with 45 ml (1½ fl oz) of 80-proof distilled spirits.)

Control Blood Pressure with Nature's Medicines

In a 1995 study published in the journal *Hypertension*, British scientists gave 11 people with high blood pressure either two types of blood pressure medication (an ACE inhibitor and a diuretic) or the ACE inhibitor plus several anti-hypertensive herbs. The treatments lowered blood pressure by the same amount.

I mention this finding because it suggests that in managing high blood pressure, herbs can be effective substitutes for conventional pharmaceuticals. If you are currently taking a blood pressure medication, you absolutely should continue to do so. But you may want to talk to your doctor about adding one or more of the following herbs to your treatment programme. By going natural, so to speak, you may be able to reduce the dosage of your regular medicine, if not stop taking it altogether.

GARLIC (*ALLIUM SATIVUM*). One of my all-time favourite herbs, garlic is a top-notch treatment for high blood pressure. In an analysis of eight studies using garlic to manage blood pressure, seven found the herb to have benefit. Even conservative pharmacognosist Varro Tyler, Ph.D., says, 'We now know that raw garlic can reduce hypertension, even in quantities as small as a half-ounce per week.' A half-ounce (15 g) equals about a half-dozen cloves. So a clove a day may keep high blood pressure away.

Besides eating garlic raw and using it in cooking, you can take the herb as a capsule or tincture. It not only lowers blood pressure but also reduces cholesterol. Since both conditions are risk factors for heart disease, garlic can reduce your chances for experiencing a heart attack. I grow garlic in many plots in my Garden of Youth, including the one for high blood pressure.

ONION (*ALLIUM CEPA*). A close botanical relative of garlic, onion provides similar benefits for managing blood pressure and cholesterol. It can be

Dr Duke's Anti-Ageing Elixir

Veggie-Powered Blood Pressure Soup

For treating high blood pressure, nothing beats a big bowl of this tasty soup. It's a vegetarian recipe, so it fits quite nicely into the DASH (Dietary Approaches to Stop Hypertension) diet. And its ingredients are chock-full of antioxidants and other heart-healthy nutrients.

Actually, when I make this soup myself, I just use whatever vegetables I have on hand. If you're concerned about your blood pressure, you should definitely include lots of garlic, onions, and celery.

WHAT YOU NEED

Whole garlic
Onions, chopped
Celery, chopped
Maitake mushrooms, sliced
Purslane, shredded
Kaffir potatoes, wedged

WHAT TO DO

In a big saucepan, combine the garlic, onions, celery, maitake mushrooms, purslane, and kaffir potatoes in proportions to taste. Add water to cover. Bring to a boil, then reduce the heat to low. Simmer for 10 minutes, or until the vegetables are tender. Remove from the heat and allow to cool. Store the soup in your refrigerator and reheat it by the bowl for a hearty, heart-healthy meal.

---

taken in various ways. You could go with 2 to 3 tablespoons of onion oil a day, a dosage that in one study produced significant improvement in two-thirds of people with moderately high pressure. Or you could lightly cook about 60 g (2 oz) of fresh onion or 30 g (1 oz) of dried.

Over the years, I've grown many varieties of onion. I prefer the sweet varieties for taste, the hotter ones for medicine.

CELERY (*APIUM GRAVEOLENS*). In one study, eating as few as four celery stalks a day lowered blood pressure in some people. This finding should come as no surprise to Chinese herbalists, who have long recommended

for the
Gardener

Celery

Apium graveolens, var. *dulce*

Celery is considered an annual, but it may grow year-round in mild climates. Soak the seeds overnight to speed germination. Sow them in trays, then put them where they'll get at least 5 hours of sun a day.

Once the seedlings are 7.5–15 cm (3 to 6 inches) tall, they're ready to be transplanted outside. Choose a location with well-watered, richly organic soil. Space the seedlings 15–30 cm (6 to 12 inches) apart. You can keep planting seedlings until 19 weeks before the first expected harvest, so you have a continuous supply of celery. You can also get a second harvest by cutting off the stalks at ground level rather than pulling up the plants roots and all. Make sure you have enough plants so that you can let some go to seed for the following year.

celery seed and stalks as treatments for high blood pressure.

MAITAKE MUSHROOM (*GRIFOLA FRONDOSA*). This tasty Asian fungus has been shown to lower blood pressure in animals. It also helps control diabetes. In many folks, diabetes and high blood pressure go hand in hand.

You can buy maitake mushrooms in some health food shops and Asian markets as well as online. Use them as you would any mushroom.

HAWTHORN (*CRATAEGUS MONOGYNA*). One of the best herbal medicines for heart health is hawthorn. It's *the* herb for treating congestive heart failure and angina. It's also good for high blood pressure.

Hawthorn contains natural compounds that act like the four main classes of high blood pressure medication: ACE inhibitors, beta-blockers, calcium antagonists, and diuretics. The herb reduces blood pressure by opening up your blood vessels – in particular, the coronary arteries that supply blood to your heart. But because it's natural, hawthorn costs less and has fewer side effects than the pharmaceuticals.

In addition, the herb's leaves, flowers, and berries are rich in flavonoids and other antioxidants. These nutrients strengthen your heart, improve bloodflow through your heart, and lower blood pressure.

In late fall, when my hawthorn is producing berries, I often munch 10 to 12 a day. They're about 6 mm (¼ inch) in diameter and mostly seed (which I don't eat). They taste like a cross between an apple and rose hips. I often juice them. The juice sets to make a kind of hawthorn jelly.

If you have a hawthorn tree, steep a handful of berries, flowers, or both in enough freshly boiled water to cover for 10 to 15 minutes. Strain out the plant material before drinking. You can also make a tea using 1 teaspoon of finely chopped dried leaf per cup or two of boiled water. Steep for 15 minutes, then strain. Feel free to drink three to four cups a day.

Hawthorn is available in commercial preparations as well. Use these products according to their label directions.

DILL (*ANETHUM GRAVEOLENS*). This herb does more than flavour pickles. Dill seeds contain an oil that's a diuretic. Pharmaceutical diuretics are among the safest medications for treating high blood pressure. They help your body eliminate fluid, which reduces blood volume. This means less pressure in your arteries – and a lower blood pressure reading.

I grow my own dill and prefer it fresh. But when it's out of season, I use the dried herb that's in my spice rack. Sometimes I enjoy dill tea for breakfast, made with 1 to 3 teaspoons of crushed seed steeped in 1 cup of freshly boiled water for 10 minutes, then strained. I also use the herb to flavour a good many dishes.

Be aware that dill contains a large amount of sodium. If you've been following a sodium-restricted diet, this herb is not for you.

LEMON (*CITRUS LIMON*). Do you use lemon juice in cooking or add it to teas? If you have high blood pressure, you might try replacing the juice with finely grated lemon peel. The peel contains flavonoids (especially 5,6-di-c-glucosylapigenin) with proven power to lower blood pressure. Alas, I don't have a lemon tree in my garden. But I do like to grate lemon peel and add it to the heart-healthy hawthorn smoothies that I make every autumn when my hawthorn berries are ripe (see the recipe on page 422).

EVENING PRIMROSE (*OENOTHERA BIENNIS*). The oil from the seeds of my

Dr Duke's Anti-Ageing Elixir

Hypertension Helper

Hawthorn berries are great for lowering blood pressure. They also make a delicious smoothie. Here they're combined with celery seed and lemon rind for a triple-whammy blood pressure treatment.

WHAT YOU NEED

115 g (4 oz) hawthorn berries
240 ml (8 fl oz) grapefruit juice
1 teaspoon crushed celery seed
Fresh ginger, grated
Lemon peel, grated

WHAT TO DO

In a blender, combine the hawthorn berries, grapefruit juice, and celery seed. Remove the hawthorn seeds. Add the ginger and lemon peel to taste. Blend to a drinkable consistency.

favourite flower, evening primrose, lowers blood pressure. It also helps prevent the internal blood clots that trigger heart attack and most strokes. So it's a double-whammy against heart disease and stroke.

Evening primrose oil gets its medicinal benefits from an essential fatty acid called gamma-linolenic acid (GLA). It's also found in borage, currant, and hempseed oils.

Personally, I like to munch evening primrose seeds picked straight from the plant. But if I had high blood pressure, I'd buy commercial evening primrose oil capsules and take them according to the label directions.

PURSLANE (*PORTULACA OLERACEA*). Purslane leaves contain alpha-linolenic acid, an essential fatty acid that has some of the same health benefits as GLA. Around my place, purslane is easier to find wild than to plant and grow. I usually move a few specimens into my garden in spring and keep them until they die in the autumn. I eat the leaves raw in salads or cooked like spinach. Sometimes I just munch them straight off the plants.

YINYANGHUO (*EPIMEDIUM,* VARIOUS SPECIES). I'm very fond of this herb. I have several species growing in the bottom land near my creek. Yinyanghuo, also known as horny goat weed, has numerous pharmacologic effects in experimental animals, such as improving male sexual function. It does this by relaxing the arteries, making more blood available for an erection. Relaxing the arteries also reduces blood pressure.

Chinese medicine practitioners use yinyanghuo to treat high blood pressure. I think they're on to something. In the United States, the plant is grown as an ornamental.

I'm not aware of any specific dosage recommendations for yinyanghuo. But I like to nibble on the leaves, and I consider that to be safe. You may be able to find a commercial preparation in some health food shops and big herb outlets. If you do, use it according to the label directions.

DEVIL'S CLAW (*HARPAGOPHYTUM PROCUMBENS*). This herb has only recently begun to attract the attention of scientists. But the research that I've seen so far is impressive. In various animal studies, devil's claw lowers arterial blood pressure and bestows other heart-healthy benefits.

You should be able to find devil's claw in health food shops and herb outlets with large selections. The dosage recommendations usually range from 1 to 2 teaspoons of herb per cup of freshly boiled water, steeped for 10 minutes and strained. I'd suggest drinking one to two cups a day.

So far, I don't have any devil's claw in my garden. But it's definitely on my wish list.

KUDZU (*PUERARIA MONTANA*). Being a good ol' boy from Alabama, I'm acutely aware that the fast-growing Asian kudzu vine has invaded the southern states of America and become a major pest weed. I sympathise with those who toil to contain it. But in its defence, I would like to point out that kudzu is used in Chinese medicine to treat high blood pressure and heart disease.

In one study, Chinese researchers had 52 people with high blood pressure drink a strong tea made from kudzu root for 2 to 8 weeks. Seventeen of the study participants showed substantial improvement in their blood pressure readings, while another 30 experienced modest but noteworthy improvement. In a separate study, a similar kudzu preparation significantly reduced chest pain in people with angina.

The compound responsible for kudzu's heart benefits appears to be puerarin, an isoflavone with powerful antioxidant properties. At least one study has shown puerarin to be 100 times more potent than vitamin

growing younger naturally

She Wrote Her Own Blood Pressure Prescription

Sometimes the best stories about the effectiveness of herbal medicine come from people whom I've met through the classes and workshops that I teach. Just recently, a woman wrote to me about her experience with high blood pressure. Here's an excerpt from her letter:

'I saw a new allopathic M.D. several months ago. The M.D. decided that because my blood pressure was 180/80, I was about to have a stroke. She prescribed Micardis. I told her that a full dose of another medication for another problem had landed me in the emergency room. "*Full dose,*" she said. I ended up in the ER with a heart irregularity.

'She stopped the medication and told me to take vitamin C. When the Micardis was out of my system, she'd try another medication.

'Your book *The Green Pharmacy* mentions garlic and celery as the first choice for high blood pressure. I take an additional 500 milligrams of vitamin C, eat one stalk of celery, and take two Kyolic garlic capsules each day.

'Today, my blood pressure is 128/67. Pretty good for an almost-80-year-old. Thanks.'

E, which is often recommended to prevent and treat heart disease.

You can find extracts of kudzu in some health food stores. I suggest following the dosage recommendations on the label. I suspect the herb will become more widely available in this country as Americans learn more about its health benefits.

My neighbours cringed when they found out that I grow kudzu in my garden, but I keep it contained. It's tough eating without a lot of laborious processing, but the Chinese recommend consuming 4.5 to 15 grams (about 2 to 8 tablespoons) of root a day. I have been known to make kudzu smoothies, but they don't taste very good without lots of lemon and sugar.

GUAR (*CYAMOPSIS TETRAGONOLOBA*). Guar gum is a popular thickening agent in many processed foods, including soups, sauces, cheeses, and ice creams. The gum comes from the bean of the guar plant. Beans generally lower blood pressure and cholesterol, and guar is no exception. In one study that I've reviewed, guar gum reduced blood pressure by 8 per cent and cholesterol by 14 per cent.

The best way to obtain guar is to consult an Ayurvedic doctor. The dose that I've seen recommended is 15 grams a day.

KAFFIR POTATO (*COLEUS BARBATUS* OR *C. FORSKOHLII*). In India and Africa, people pickle this tuber and eat it as a vegetable. It contains large amounts of forskolin (coleonol), a compound that may become the next big blood pressure medication.

The recommended dose of forskolin for lowering blood pressure is 10 milligrams a day. You can get that much from about a teaspoon of kaffir potato. The question is: where do you get the herb? If you happen to live near an Indian market, you may be able to find it. After more than a decade of trying, I now have cuttings in the greenhouse. Stay tuned!

CHAPTER 38

High Cholesterol

Dr Duke's Anti-Ageing Elixirs

- *Pumped-with-Pectin Smoothie*
- *Good-for-Your-Heart Coleslaw*
- *Curried Cholesterol-Cutting Chutney*

Even though I don't have high cholesterol, I take great interest in all the television commercials for the cholesterol-lowering drug atorvastatin (Lipitor). The ads must be working, because prescriptions for Lipitor are ringing up to the tune of $3.6 billion a year. That's more than the gross annual income of any US-based herb company. It's more than half of the annual total of US medicinal herb sales. In other words, it's a whole lot of money.

I realise that some people with very high cholesterol may need Lipitor. But I can't help thinking that many others are taking this expensive medication unnecessarily.

For total cholesterol levels between 220 and 240, which is considered high but not super-high, I'd be willing to bet that a non-drug treatment plan consisting of nutritional strategies, exercise, and herbs would work as well as Lipitor while costing a lot less. But no one is comparing the two approaches. Pharmaceutical companies simply test new medications against old ones. Scientists who study non-drug measures typically compare people who adopt such measures with those who don't.

I wish someone, somewhere, would test drug and non-drug treatments head-to-head. I bet such research would reveal that for many people with high cholesterol, lifestyle changes would make pharmaceuticals unnecessary.

I may be a cantankerous old guy, but I'm not the only one to have this opinion. The National Cholesterol Education Program (NCEP), part of the National Institutes of Health, advises all adult Americans to reduce their total cholesterol levels to less than 200 milligrams per decilitre of blood (mg/dl) – but not with drugs. According to the NCEP, 'Lifestyle modification (diet changes, regular exercise, weight loss, and so forth) should be the primary treatment for lowering cholesterol.'

If it catches on, the NCEP's approach could go a long way towards reining in my nation's runaway health-care costs. To prove this point, I've culled the following figures from *The Healing Power of Garlic*, a book by noted herbalist Paul Bergner. They reflect the cost of extending by 1 year the lives of people with heart disease and high cholesterol, using various cholesterol treatments. (Lipitor wasn't on the market when Bergner wrote his book, but the drug falls into the same class of medicines as lovastatin, with comparable cost and effectiveness.)

- *Gemfibrozil: $108,826*
- *Cholestyramine: $92,603*
- *Colestipol: $73,406*
- *Lovastatin: $50,510*
- *Dietary advice: $2,536*
- *Garlic: $2,500*
- *Psyllium husk: $642*

You'll notice that even the cheapest drug (lovastatin) is 20 times more expensive than the most expensive lifestyle measure (dietary advice). And people wonder why this country's health-care costs keep rising.

Your Arteries under Attack

According to the NCEP, a person's total cholesterol should fall within the range of 180 to 200 mg/dl. The American nation is making progress towards that goal: the current national average for total cholesterol is between 205 and 210. But millions of people still have readings above 240, which puts them at high risk for heart attack and stroke. That's why pharmaceutical companies make so much money from their cholesterol-lowering medications.

By keeping your cholesterol within the recommended range, you can greatly reduce your chances of having a heart attack. Researchers have determined that a 1 per cent decline in total cholesterol produces a 2 per cent decline in heart attack risk. So if you cut your cholesterol by, say, 15 per cent, you reduce your heart attack risk by about one-third.

While controlling your cholesterol is a good thing, you don't want to go too low. Very low cholesterol – less than 150 mg/dl – actually increases your risk of death from certain other ailments, including liver cancer, haemorrhagic stroke, and lung disease.

If you have very high cholesterol and your doctor puts you on medication, by all means take it. But if your cholesterol is between 220 and 240, I'd recommend trying non-drug measures – nutrition strategies, exercise, and herbs – first. You can always add a low dose of a pharmaceutical later if you need to.

Plant Foods Deliver a One-Two Punch

Healthy eating habits form the foundation of any cholesterol control plan. In my opinion, the easiest way to eat healthfully is to adopt a plant-based, near-vegetarian Palaeolithic diet. It's naturally low in fat and high in fibre, a perfect combination for reducing your total cholesterol level.

Your body – or more precisely, your liver – makes some of its own cholesterol. But most of the stuff that ends up narrowing your arteries and contributing to heart attacks comes not from your liver but from foods, primarily meats and whole-milk dairy products. Not coincidentally, these foods are also high in fat. By reducing their presence in your diet, you automatically cut your fat and cholesterol intakes.

In support of this point, consider the findings of an Oxford University research team that analysed 395 studies of the effects of dietary fat and cholesterol on blood cholesterol levels. The scientists concluded that if people replaced half the meat and dairy products in their diets with plant foods and vegetable oils, their total cholesterol would decline by 10 to 15 per cent. This means that their heart attack risk would fall by 20 to 30 per cent.

Unfortunately, the wisdom of a plant-based diet is lost on many people. After all, we live in a world where McDonald's spends more in 12 hours to promote its high-fat burgers and fries than the National Cancer Institute in America spends in a year to promote its 'Strive for Five' programme, which educates people about the importance of eating at least five servings of fruits and veggies a day.

Fishing Around for Omega-3s

In terms of cholesterol control, a high-fat animal-based diet simply doesn't hold a candle to a low-fat plant-based diet. You need plant foods, and plenty of them, to keep your cholesterol low and your arteries clear. But Mother Nature has given us one exception to the minimal-animal-foods rule. It's fish, specifically, cold-water species such as salmon.

Cold-water fish are rich in omega-3 fatty acids, so-called good fats that actually cut cholesterol. The first evidence of the omega-3's heart-healthy benefits came to light back in the 1970s, in Danish studies of the people of Greenland. Their native diet is very high in fat, yet they have a remarkably low rate of heart disease. The reason? Most of the dietary fat comes from cold-water fish with an abundance of omega-3s.

Since then, a great deal of research has shown that cold-water fish can indeed lower cholesterol. For one study, researchers in Wales tracked 2,000 men with heart disease. Independent of all other risk factors, the group of men who ate two meals of fish per week had 39 per cent fewer deaths from heart disease than the men who ate no fish.

Separately, a team of Harvard researchers analysed 11 years of data from the Physicians' Health Study, an ongoing investigation of the diet, lifestyle, and health status of 20,500 middle-aged male American

More Wisdom *from the* Garden

Great Sources of Good Fat

You'd think that avocados and walnuts would be off-limits in a cholesterol-control plan. After all, both plant foods have ample supplies of fat. But it's good fat, which actually helps lower cholesterol.

Avocados are rich in monounsaturated fat, the kind found in olive oil. In one study, a group of women that followed a diet with an abundance of avocados lowered their cholesterol by 8 per cent.

Walnuts, on the other hand, contain heart-healthy linoleic acid and alpha-linolenic acid. One study found that eating about 90 g (3 oz) of walnuts a day reduced total cholesterol by 12 per cent and LDL cholesterol by 16 per cent.

Keep in mind that avocados and walnuts can help only if they're incorporated into an eating plan that's low in fat and high in fibre. If cheeseburgers and french fries are staple foods in your diet, avocados and walnuts won't do much for you. But if I were concerned about my cholesterol, I'd occasionally help myself to half an avocado garnished with chopped walnuts.

doctors. Compared with men who ate fish less than once a month, those who ate it at least once a week had half the death rate not just from heart disease but from all causes.

The American Heart Association says that it 'encourages the consumption of fish as both a good source of protein low in saturated fat and an excellent source of omega-3 fatty acids'. I wholeheartedly agree.

Edible Weapons in the Cholesterol War

If you need guidance in making the transition to a low-fat, plant-based diet (with one or two servings of fish per week), I suggest that you read through my Healthy Sevens eating plan in chapter 3. It's based on Palaeolithic principles, with a strong emphasis on plant foods.

The following plant foods have especially noteworthy cholesterol-lowering properties. By including these in as many meals as possible, you give yourself the best chance of lowering your cholesterol.

OAT BRAN. I'm sure you've heard that oat bran helps to lower cholesterol. It really works. In fact, it's been shown to reduce total cholesterol by 13 per cent in those who eat about 115 g (4 oz) a day for 3 weeks.

Oat bran contains a special kind of fibre called beta-glucan. It binds with cholesterol in your digestive tract and holds it there for elimination, so it doesn't wind up in your blood and on your artery walls.

But with all the publicity surrounding oat bran and its value in cholesterol control, one key fact has got lost: oats are not the only source of beta-glucan, or even the best. Barley contains up to three times as much of this special fibre. And studies by my former colleagues at the USDA show that rice bran, which contains less than 10 per cent of the beta-glucan in oat bran, lowers cholesterol just as much. Beans are another significant source of beta-glucan.

SOYA BEANS. Speaking of beans, soya beans and soya foods have also developed a reputation for reducing cholesterol. They're effective because of the fibre and phospholipids that they contain. (Phospholipids are considered good fats.)

An analysis of several studies, published in the *Journal of the American Medical Association*, found that consuming 30–60 g (1 to 2 oz) of soya foods (usually tofu) a day can lower cholesterol significantly. This evidence was so compelling that it even persuaded the FDA to allow foods with at least 6.25 g (¼ oz) of soya protein per serving to state on their labels that they help reduce the risk of heart disease. This should boost the sales of soya burgers and soya frankfurters.

Frankly, though, I suspect that *all* edible beans – not just soya beans – contain fibre and phospholipids. Not only that, most pulses are lower in fat than soya beans, with one exception being peanuts. So I really can't understand all the fuss over soya foods. Feel free to eat tofu and soya hot dogs, if you wish. Just keep in mind that all bean-endowed foods, from burritos to bean soups, help control cholesterol.

My wife, Peggy, and I usually keep a pot of bean-vegetable soup in our refrigerator. That way, we can have a heart-healthy meal or snack in just minutes.

Dr Duke's Anti-Ageing Elixir

Pumped-with-Pectin Smoothie

To make this recipe, use a food processor rather than a juicer. That way, you'll preserve all the pectin, the plant fibre that packs a cholesterol-lowering punch.

WHAT YOU NEED

1–2 apples, sliced
1–2 carrots, sliced
Orange peel, grated
Apple juice

WHAT TO DO

In a food processor, combine the apples, carrots, and citrus peel. Add enough apple juice to cover. Blend to a drinkable consistency.

If you're wondering why soyabeans have made headlines so many times while other beans have not, I'd say it has something to do with the fact that the soya industry financed all of those studies examining the effects of soya on cholesterol.

APPLES. Our modern scientific understanding of cholesterol has proven the wisdom of one old folk saying: 'An apple a day keeps the doctor away.' Apple pulp is rich in pectin, a plant fibre that supports cholesterol control. Pectin is also found in pears and carrots, as well as in the white stuff inside citrus peels.

ARTICHOKES. Although they don't get much attention these days as a healing food, artichokes have been used by the Egyptians for a long time to treat a variety of conditions, including heart disease. Now Egyptian researchers have validated this folk practice by identifying several cholesterol-lowering compounds in artichokes, including apigenin-7-O-glucoside, cynaroside, luteolin, and scolymoside.

How well I remember joining a group of Egyptian botanists at an outdoor cafe in the shadow of the Pyramids, savouring a big plate of artichokes, chickpeas, and aubergine. If you're eating artichokes for cholesterol control, be sure not to dip them in high-fat butter, margarine, or mayonnaise. Instead, try salsa, vinegar, or low-sodium soya sauce.

Sitosterol-containing foods.

A member of the phytosterol family, sito-sterol prevents the absorption of cholesterol into the bloodstream. In one analysis, eight of nine studies found that a diet rich in the compound reduces cholesterol significantly.

Actually, sitosterol is found in all plant foods. But some contain more of the compound than others. If I had to bring down my cholesterol, I'd make a point of eating more figs, strawberries, apricots, sesame seeds, and sunflower seeds – all top-notch sitosterol sources.

You don't need large quantities of these foods to experience their healthy effects either. I can't think of a more pleasant way to cut cholesterol than to eat a fruit salad made with the sito-sterol-rich ingredients mentioned above.

Work Out to Shape Up Your Cholesterol Profile

Adopting a plant-based diet is essential for cholesterol control. Believe it or not, so is exercise. But before I get into the cholesterol-cutting effects of regular physical activity, I must briefly explain the two different types of cholesterol: low-density lipoproteins (LDL) and high-density lipoproteins (HDL).

When high-fat, high-cholesterol foods are processed by your liver, their cholesterol gets sent out into your bloodstream attached to LDL molecules. That's why LDLs are bad: the more you have, the more cholesterol is floating around in your blood. On the other hand, HDLs are good, because these molecules remove

Dr Duke's Anti-Ageing Elixir

Good-for-Your-Heart Coleslaw

According to USDA researcher Peter D. Hoagland, Ph.D., eating two medium-size carrots or 225 g (8 oz) of chopped cabbage or onions a day can cut total cholesterol by up to 20 per cent. Why not combine these ingredients into a tasty, heart-healthy coleslaw?

WHAT YOU NEED

2 carrots, grated
1 onion, grated
225 g (8 oz) grated cabbage
½ teaspoon olive oil
Barley
Cayenne pepper
Lemon
Vinegar

WHAT TO DO

In a bowl, combine the carrots and onions with the cabbage and olive oil. Sprinkle with the barley. Season to taste with the cayenne pepper, lemon, and vinegar.

cholesterol from your bloodstream and return it to your liver for elimination. The more HDL you have, the less cholesterol is floating around your blood. That's why the National Cholesterol Education Program recommends keeping HDL above 35 and LDL below 160.

This is where exercise comes into play. While it may not reduce your total cholesterol, it does knock down LDL and build up HDL. So your cholesterol profile improves, and your risk of heart attack plummets.

Any type of exercise has this heart-healthy effect. Personally, I enjoy walking. Between taking laps around my property and working in my Garden of Youth, I put in several miles a day.

The Best Herbs for Keeping Your Arteries Clear

We've talked about nutritional strategies, and we've talked about exercise. That brings us to the third component of your cholesterol control programme: herbs.

Being plants, all herbs contain fibre, which binds to cholesterol in your gut and speeds its elimination from your body. But the following have even more potent cholesterol-lowering properties.

GARLIC (*ALLIUM SATIVUM*). For anyone who wants to prevent or treat heart disease, garlic is a godsend. It reduces blood pressure. It make blood less likely to clot, reducing the risk of heart attack (and most strokes). And of course, it lowers cholesterol. In fact, many studies have found that just a clove or two a day – or the equivalent amount of a commercial garlic supplement such as Garlicin, Kwai, or Kyolic – produces significant improvements in cholesterol profiles.

Garlic is my first-choice herb for cholesterol control. I'm convinced that if we Americans ate more of this herb, we could save billions of dollars in health-care costs by eliminating the need for cholesterol-lowering drugs, bypass surgery, and angioplasty.

If you use garlic cloves, they're more potent raw (chewed or chopped) than gently cooked. But the latter is reasonably effective. I like to blend raw garlic into carrot juice. It's quite tasty. You can also buy one of the commercial garlic supplements mentioned above and take it according to the label directions.

for the
Gardener

Garlic

Allium sativum

Garlic is grown as an annual throughout the United States. But it becomes a perennial if the bulbs are left in the ground.

Plant the bulbs about 5 cm (2 inches) deep and 15 cm (6 inches) apart in very early spring in northern climates or in autumn in the South. Choose a location with rich, loose, sandy-loamy soil and full sun. If you're planting in autumn, mulch the bulbs to keep them from heaving out of the ground with repeated freezing and thawing.

Water your garlic plants during dry spells, but stop once they start to ripen (when the leaves start to turn yellow). Cut off any flower stalks so that more of the plant's energy goes into its roots. Lift the bulbs when the leaves are nearly one-third dry and brown. Hang the bulbs to dry, like onions. Once the leaves are crumbly and the root crown is hard, the bulbs are ready to be stored in a cool, dry place.

You do need to be careful with garlic. It is a blood thinner, which makes blood less likely to clot. If you're trying to prevent heart attack, this anticoagulant action is beneficial, but only to a point. You don't want to inhibit your blood's clotting ability too much, or you may not be able to stop wounds from bleeding. So don't mix garlic with anticoagulant drugs and supplements, such as aspirin and vitamin E. And if you decide to try the herb to lower your cholesterol, be sure to tell your doctor.

I have garlic growing all over my Garden of Youth. In fact, it's so prominent that my terraced hillside could quite accurately be called the Garlic of Youth.

PSYLLIUM (*PLANTAGO OVATA*). Not familiar with psyllium? Look at commercial bulk-forming laxatives. Psyllium is the main ingredient.

Psyllium is rich in soluble fibre. Like other high-fibre foods, it helps lower cholesterol. At the University of Kentucky, researchers put 248 people with high cholesterol on the low-fat, low-cholesterol diet recommended by the American Heart Association. In addition, some of the study participants took 5 grams of psyllium twice a day. Six months later, those who followed the diet saw their average cholesterol fall by 4 per cent. Among those who combined the diet with psyllium, average cholesterol levels dropped by 10 per cent. Just as noteworthy, their LDL levels went down by 11 per cent.

I don't grow psyllium in my garden, but I do have a related *Plantago* species. Still, if I wanted to lower my cholesterol, I wouldn't fool around with my *Plantago*. I'd pick up some psyllium at the chemist or buy a psyllium product in the health food shop. I'd take 1 to 2 tablespoons three times a day at mealtimes, with plenty of water.

GINGER (*ZINGIBER OFFICINALE*). Most of the data about ginger's ability to lower cholesterol comes from animal studies. Personally, I find it persuasive. For one of these studies, laboratory animals were fed a high-fat, high-cholesterol diet. Some were also given ginger – 200 milligrams per kilogram of body weight per day. As expected, the cholesterol levels of all the animals went up. But they didn't rise nearly as much in the animals treated with ginger.

Now 200 milligrams per kilogram of body weight is a lot of ginger – about 20 g (¾ oz) for yours truly. But I'm convinced that any amount of the herb can help control cholesterol. Drink ginger tea made with 1 to 2 teaspoons of freshly grated root steeped in 1 cup of boiled water for 10 minutes. Use the herb generously in cooking. Sprinkle some on fruit.

TURMERIC (*CURCUMA LONGA*). This Indian spice gives curry blends their yellow colour. It's a close botanical relative of ginger, with similar cholesterol-cutting action.

In one study, people with high cholesterol who took a daily dose of turmeric extract containing 500 milligrams of curcuminoids, the herb's active compounds, saw their cholesterol plummet by 29 per cent. That's a remarkable decrease for any treatment, one that rivals the best (and most expensive) pharmaceutical cholesterol medication.

To take advantage of turmeric's cholesterol-reducing effects, use more of the herb in your cooking. By itself, it has a pleasantly warm flavour. In a curry blend, it has a bit more kick.

If you prefer, you can buy turmeric supplements in health food stores. Look for the words 'turmeric', 'curcuminoids', or 'curcumin' (another of the herb's active compounds) on the label. Take the supplements according to the package directions.

FENUGREEK (*TRIGONELLA FOENUM-GRAECUM*). Lately, I've been blending the seeds of this herb in my juicer. They have potent cholesterol-lowering action, thanks to fibre and compounds called saponins. One of these compounds, diosgenin, boosts the elimination of cholesterol through your digestive tract, so less gets into your bloodstream.

For one study, 60 people with type 2 (non-insulin-dependent) diabetes and elevated cholesterol followed their usual diets, with one change. They took about 30 g (1 oz) of powdered fenugreek seed, mixed into water, 15 minutes before lunch and dinner every day. After 24 weeks of treatment, their average total cholesterol level had fallen by 14 per cent, and their LDL, by 16 per cent. Any side effects were mild, with some people reporting transient diarrhoea and flatulence.

HAWTHORN (*CRATAEGUS MONOGYNA*). Hawthorn is best known as a gentle heart stimulant that helps treat congestive heart failure. But it also contains compounds that lower blood pressure and cholesterol, such as beta-sitosterol, catechin, chromium, fibre, linoleic acid, magnesium, pectin, and rutin.

I grow hawthorn on my property. In the autumn, when its fruits

Dr Duke's Anti-Ageing Elixir

Curried Cholesterol-Cutting Chutney

Individually, three of the ingredients in this recipe – hawthorn, garlic, and turmeric – have potent cholesterol-lowering powers. Together, they really pack a wallop. The chutney has a rather . . . well, unique taste. But it's a whole lot cheaper than cholesterol medication, and it causes no side effects.

WHAT YOU NEED

120 ml (4 fl oz) water
115 g (4 oz) hawthorn berries
1 clove garlic, crushed
Heavy dash of turmeric
Lemon juice

WHAT TO DO

In a food processor, combine the water and hawthorn berries to a spreadable consistency. Remove the seeds. Add the garlic, turmeric and a squeeze of the lemon for flavour. Serve on wholemeal bread or eat plain.

ripen, I like to munch them straight off the plant. But if I had high cholesterol, I'd whip up some Curried Cholesterol-Cutting Chutney.

ALFALFA (*MEDICAGO SATIVA*). A good deal of research in animals and humans has found that alfalfa helps reduce cholesterol. In one study, people with high cholesterol who took 80–160 g (3–6 oz) of alfalfa seed a day showed marked improvement in their cholesterol readings.

That is quite a large dose of alfalfa, but it may be worth trying if you have very high cholesterol. On the other hand, if you're in the mildly to moderately high range, you may get an adequate dose just by adding alfalfa sprouts to your salads.

Note: One of the compounds in alfalfa, called canavanine, has been associated with systemic lupus erythematosus, skin reactions, and gastrointestinal problems. It may also raise the risk of gout. Before taking medicinal amounts of alfalfa, you may want to check with a qualified herbal practitioner or a doctor experienced in herbal medicine.

MUKUL (*COMMIPHORA MUKUL*). If you consult a naturopath or an Ayurvedic doctor for advice on cholesterol control, you might come away with a herbal medicine called gugulipid that's extracted from the Indian mukul plant. Gugulipid is not widely known in the United States, but research in India has found that the herb compares favourably with cholesterol-cutting pharmaceuticals. I've seen studies documenting gugulipid's ability to reduce cholesterol by 14 to 27 per cent in 4 to 12 weeks, without side effects.

CAIGUA (*CYCLANTHERA PEDATA*). As a frequent visitor to the Peruvian Amazon, I have a special interest in the medicinal uses of rainforest plants. In one study, Peruvian researchers gave tablets made from dehydrated caigua fruit to a group of postmenopausal women. Over 3 months of taking six tablets a day (roughly the equivalent of one fresh caigua fruit), the women experienced significant declines in their cholesterol levels. At the beginning of the study, 75 per cent of them had high cholesterol. By the end, just 12.5 per cent did.

When I'm in Peru, I often eat caigua fruit. It is cooked like courgette and tastes similar as well. Unfortunately, if you want to try it, you'll have to join me on one of my Peruvian ecotours, since it is not readily available.

CHAPTER 39

Hot Flushes

Dr Duke's Anti-Ageing Elixirs

- *Cooling Peppermint Spritzer*
- *Temperature-Control Tonic*

Of all the physical discomforts that occur during menopause, hot flushes are probably the most bothersome. They're also the most common, affecting the majority of menopausal women.

As their name suggests, hot flushes are periods of intense flushing, usually followed by periods of intense sweating. They tend to occur in the upper body, affecting your head, neck, chest, and arms.

Hot flushes can strike during the day or at night, when they can disrupt sleep. Some women may have one flush every few months, while others may suffer through 10 to 12 a day.

Like other menopausal discomforts, hot flushes occur because of a decline in oestrogen production. Their exact cause remains somewhat obscure. The going theory is that falling oestrogen levels disrupt your body's temperature-control centre, located in the hypothalamus of your brain. This leads to the sudden sensations of heat.

Among mainstream doctors, the treatment of choice for hot flushes and other menopausal discomforts is hormone-replacement therapy (HRT). Your doctor may tell you that in addition to relieving hot flushes, HRT offers protection against heart disease, osteoporosis, and Alzheimer's disease. Unfortunately, hormone replacement also increases the risk of breast cancer. What a trade-off.

If you're interested in HRT, talk to your doctor. For some women, hormone replacement makes sense. But I feel more comfortable promoting a natural version of HRT that combines diet, exercise, and herbs. I believe that my approach provides similar benefits but without the increased risk of breast cancer.

Incidentally, if you've already read chapter 18, much of the information in this chapter may seem familiar to you. That's because the measures that prevent hot flushes also help to treat them.

Diet: There's More to the Story Than Soya

The best foods for relieving hot flushes contain phyto-oestrogens, or plant oestrogens. Phyto-oestrogens and your body's oestrogen are like slightly different master keys to the same lock: the oestrogen receptors on cells. When these receptors are occupied, your hypothalamus and pituitary gland get the message that your body has enough oestrogen. This defuses the symptoms of oestrogen deficiency, including hot flushes.

These days, probably the most highly touted source of phyto-oestrogens is soya. Scientists have observed that Asian women experience fewer hot flushes than American women, a fact that has been attributed to the large amounts of soya and tofu in the traditional Asian diet.

Like most edible pulses, soya contains specific phyto-oestrogen compounds called isoflavones. They're like a weak version of the pharmaceutical oestrogen used in HRT. The isoflavones occupy oestrogen receptors on cells, just like HRT. In this way, they help relieve hot flushes.

But because they're so much less potent than pharmaceutical oestrogen, isoflavones don't raise the risk of breast cancer as HRT does. In fact, based on the low rate of breast cancer among Asian women, it looks like phyto-oestrogens may help prevent the disease.

Armed with this information, women's health experts are urging menopausal women – indeed, all women – to eat more soya. The goal intake is 24 to 45 milligrams of isoflavones a day, the amount consumed by the average Japanese woman. You'd get 33.7 milligrams just by eating a 100-g (3½-oz) serving of tofu.

If you like tofu and other soya foods, feel free to enjoy them. They should reduce the frequency and severity of your hot flushes. But let me also pass along some important food for thought.

First, in addition to all those isoflavones, a 100-g (3½-oz) serving of tofu supplies 9 grams of fat. Now that's not anywhere near the amount of fat in a Big Mac. Still, it may be more than you want to consume.

Second, soya beans are not the only source – or even the best source – of isoflavones. These phyto-oestrogens are found in almost all edible pulses: adzuki beans, black beans, black-eyed beans, broad beans, butter beans, chick peas, kidney beans, lentils, mung beans, pinto beans, split peas, and a few others that I may have forgotten. My point is, if you eat

More Wisdom *from the* Garden

This Mineral Makes Hot Flushes Lose Their Steam

Although production of oestrogen drops off during menopause, women continue to make the hormone. Boron, a trace mineral, can support this process. In fact, one of my former colleagues at the USDA determined that women could double their blood levels of oestrogen by taking 3 milligrams of boron a day. That means fewer hot flushes.

You may not be all that familiar with boron, but it is considered an essential nutrient. If you're bothered by hot flushes, my advice is to start eating more boron-rich foods. Among the best sources are plums, quince, strawberries, peaches, cabbage, dandelion, asparagus, figs, tomatoes, broccoli, and lettuce. Ginseng also contains a decent amount of the mineral.

any of these pulses, you'll be getting plenty of isoflavones. And you'll be getting a lot less fat than you would from soya beans.

For an even bigger dose of isoflavones, help yourself to some bean sprouts. They may contain up to 10 times the amount of isoflavones in unsprouted beans. The sprouting process changes the beans chemically, enhancing their isoflavone content.

growing younger naturally

Soya and Flaxseed Stopped Her Flushes Cold

This story came to me by way of Stephanie Maxine Ross, a medical botanist who teaches first- and second-year medical students, in addition to advising clients about the medicinal uses of herbs.

'Kathleen consulted me about her fibrocystic breasts, a condition that she had been dealing with for 4 years. She was also bothered by menopausal hot flashes and night sweats.

'Kathleen's gynecologist had identified calcifications in some of her fibrocystic tissue, a possible indicator of breast cancer. The doctor recommended that she have an ultrasound exam and see a surgeon about arranging a biopsy. But Kathleen preferred to explore a natural alternative. So she met with me 3 weeks before she was scheduled to have her ultrasound.

'Since fibrocystic breasts are associated with unusually high levels of estrogen, my goal was to lower it. Kathleen's diet was already good, so I began by suggesting that she drink three to four 8-ounce glasses of soy milk a day. Soy contains estrogenic isoflavones, which compete with the body's own estrogen and reduce the amount of the hormone circulating in the bloodstream. I also suggested that Kathleen take 2 tablespoons of flaxseed oil every day. Like soy, flaxseed is estrogenic.

'After just 1 week, Kathleen reported that her night sweats and hot flashes had diminished. By the third week, they were completely gone. When she had the ultrasound to examine her calcifications, they were gone, too.

'Kathleen's gynecologist now prescribes soy milk and flaxseed oil to women in similar situations.'

Exercise: Don't Let the Sweats Stop You

When you have hot flushes, you can work up a sweat without moving a muscle. So you may not feel comfortable engaging in regular exercise. But you need to stay active, now more than ever.

Believe it or not, regular physical activity can reduce the frequency and severity of your hot flushes. It's no miracle cure, but many women say that it helps. As a bonus, it can lower your risk of heart disease, the leading cause of death among women over the age of 50.

Keep in mind, too, that certain forms of exercise – weight-bearing activities such as walking, dancing, and gardening – help preserve bone mass. In this way, they protect against osteoporosis, a major health concern for older women.

Herbs: Turn Down the Heat Naturally

Among the many herbs that can help relieve hot flushes, four rise to the top: black cohosh, chasteberry, dong quai, and licorice. All have well-established reputations as menopause treatments. Based on what I've seen, they seem to have the support of the scientific research as well.

BLACK COHOSH (*CIMICIFUGA RACEMOSA*). Native American women used black cohosh for gynaecological complaints. The herb was also a key ingredient in Lydia Pinkham's Vegetable Compound. This tonic enjoyed enormous popularity among 19th-century American women as a treatment for all manner of gynaecological conditions, including hot flushes.

Pinkham's original formula contained extracts of black cohosh, fenugreek seed, unicorn root, and a few other herbs, as well as 18 per cent alcohol. Old Lydia must have been a pretty good herbalist. Modern scientific research validates black cohosh and fenugreek (which I'll discuss a bit later) as menopause treatments.

Today, black cohosh is the key ingredient in Remifemin, a preparation that's the most popular over-the-counter medicine among German women. Based on several studies from Germany, I'm convinced that Remifemin helps relieve hot flushes.

In all of these studies, participants took either a placebo (a fake pill) or Remifemin (40 drops twice a day or two 40-milligram tablets a day

Dr Duke's Anti-Ageing Elixir

Cooling Peppermint Spritzer

When a hot flush hits, aromatherapists suggest spritzing your face and neck with an essential oil diluted in water and placed in a spray bottle. The most widely recommended oils are peppermint, lemon verbena, and rose geranium. Cheapskate that I am, I'd rather use peppermint leaf than the expensive oil. It has the same effect, so I'm told.

WHAT YOU NEED

- 2 generous handfuls fresh peppermint leaves
- 1 tablespoon anise seed
- 1 tablespoon fennel seed
- 1 tablespoon fenugreek seed
- 1 tablespoon powdered licorice root
- 10–20 drops lemon juice
- 2 litres (4 pints) spring water
- Vodka

WHAT TO DO

Combine the peppermint, anise, fennel, fenugreek, licorice, and lemon juice in the spring water. Bring to a boil, then simmer for 10 minutes. Strain out the plant material, put it in a jar, and set aside. Refrigerate the remaining tea, drinking it by the glass as needed.

Cover the plant material with cheap vodka and let steep overnight. The next morning, strain out the plant material, squeezing it to extract all of the liquid. Transfer the liquid to a spray bottle. Then whenever you feel a hot flush coming on, mist your throat area for relief.

---

for 6 to 12 weeks, depending on the study). All concluded that with Remifemin, hot flushes were fewer, briefer, and less discomforting.

In the largest of the studies, involving 629 women, 80 per cent of the participants reported significant improvement in their symptoms within a month of beginning treatment. Many experienced complete relief within 6 to 8 weeks. And Remifemin caused no significant side effects.

All of the research that I've read confirms that black cohosh is a safe and effective treatment for hot flushes. Commission E, the expert panel that evaluates the safety and effectiveness of herbs for the German government, endorses black cohosh for menopausal complaints.

How does the herb work? Experts can't seem to agree. Some say that black cohosh is oestrogenic, meaning that it acts like the hormone oestrogen. But others point out several ways in which the herb is not exactly oestrogenic. The best explanation I've seen is that black cohosh acts on the pituitary gland in your brain. It reduces levels of luteinising hormone, which has an effect similar, but not identical, to oestrogen.

But black cohosh is similar enough to oestrogen to do more than simply relieve hot flushes. An animal study from Japan found that black cohosh, like HRT, helps prevent the bone loss associated with osteoporosis. The Japanese scientists suggest that the herb 'has potential in the treatment of osteoporosis, particularly in menopausal women'. I agree.

I've done some calculations, and I've determined that the recommended daily dose of Remifemin (40 milligrams twice a day) delivers about the same amount of black cohosh as the typical dose of Lydia Pinkham's Vegetable Compound. Lydia's formula has long been off the market. But Remifemin is now available and becoming quite popular. Use it according to the label directions.

CHASTEBERRY (*VITEX AGNUS-CASTUS*). Like black cohosh, chasteberry appears to affect your pituitary gland, tipping the overall hormone balance in favour of oestrogen. Chasteberry is quite popular among European medical herbalists and American naturopaths. It's also one of my favourite herbs. Buy a commercial preparation and use it according to the label directions.

DONG QUAI (*ANGELICA SINENSIS*). Andrew Weil, M.D., a noted advocate of alternative therapies, describes dong quai as 'female ginseng'. He says that the herb does an excellent job of relieving hot flushes and other menopausal discomforts when taken in combination with chasteberry and damiana.

As with black cohosh, some experts believe that dong quai is oestrogenic, while others insist that it isn't. As a botanist, I find the controversy fascinating. It shows how much we still have to learn about herbal medicines that have been in use for centuries.

Based on what women have told me, I'm convinced that dong quai is effective for hot flushes. I suggest buying a commercial preparation and taking it according to the label directions.

LICORICE (*GLYCYRRHIZA GLABRA*). The experts agree on this one: licorice is oestrogenic, with several compounds that have oestrogenic action

---

Dr Duke's Anti-Ageing Elixir

Temperature-Control Tonic

This tasty tea combines several phyto-oestrogen-rich herbs that can help pull the plug on hot flushes.

WHAT YOU NEED

2 parts fenugreek seed
2 parts powdered licorice root
2 parts powdered broad bean
1 part powdered soya bean
1 part kudzu root
1 part red clover flowers
Aniseed
Fennel
1 litre (2 pints) water
Lemon
A natural sweetener (optional)

WHAT TO DO

In a small bowl, combine the fenugreek, licorice, broad bean, soya bean, kudzu, and red clover. (If you don't have one of these ingredients, or if you don't care for a particular herb, simply eliminate it or replace it with another phyto-oestrogen-rich herb.) Add the aniseed and fennel to taste.

This recipe works best if you brew about 1 litre (2 pints) of tea, using 1 tablespoon of the herb blend. Simmer the blend for 10 to 20 minutes, stirring it occasionally. Then strain out the plant material and add the lemon and sweetener, if you wish. Make sure that the tea has cooled before drinking.

(oestriol, formononetin, licoisoflavanone, beta-licoisoflavone, phaseollinisoflavone, and beta-sitosterol). If you want to try it, buy a commercial preparation and use it according to the label directions.

Two herbs that taste like licorice – anise and fennel – also have oestrogenic action, thanks to a compound called anethole. And like licorice, you can buy a commercial preparation of either herb and use it according to the label directions.

More Herbs That Keep You Cool

The herbs above may be the heavy hitters for relieving hot flushes. But the following also deserve a place in your treatment lineup.

POMEGRANATE (*PUNICA GRANATUM*). According to some biblical scholars, pomegranate is the 'apple' that Adam and Eve ate from the Tree of Knowledge. I don't know whether pomegranates grew in the Garden of Eden. But I do know that they grow in my Garden of Youth. I have a potted plant that I move into the greenhouse before the first frost. It's small and leafy, with leathery round fruits whose pulpy seeds make a great juice.

I recommend pomegranate for hot flushes because the fruit is the best plant source of oestrone, a form of oestrogen. By my calculations, a 100-g (3½-oz) serving of the pulp and seeds contains 1.5 milligrams of oestrone, enough to provide some relief from menopausal discomforts.

When pomegranates are out of season, you might cultivate a taste for grenadine, the sweet syrup made from the fruit. It, too, contains oestrone.

RED CLOVER (*TRIFOLIUM PRATENSE*). For more than a decade, I've been touting red clover as an oestrogenic herb that provides relief from menopausal discomforts. When 25 postmenopausal women consumed red clover seeds, soya beans, and flaxseed every day for 2 weeks, their blood levels of oestrogen rose and stayed high. As soon as they stopped using the herbs, their levels of oestrogen dropped.

If you want to try red clover, I suggest buying a commercial preparation and taking it according to the package directions. You can also

for the
Gardener

Red Clover

Trifolium pratense

Red clover is extremely common. In fact, it's so easy to find that I've never attempted to cultivate it. Once in a while, I'll transplant a specimen from the pasture to the garden for display as one of the best sources of oestrogenic isoflavones.

If you'd like to grow red clover, it's usually treated as a biennial or a short-lived perennial. Its sowing time depends on the climate and elevation. Check with your local nursery.

Harvest red clover at its first flowering. Plants that bloom late may have fungal infections. To make teas, you can use the flower heads either fresh or dried. If you dry them, store them in an airtight container away from direct sunlight.

make yourself a tea using 1 to 2 teaspoons of flowers per cup of freshly boiled water. Steep for 10 minutes, then strain out the plant material before drinking.

EVENING PRIMROSE (*OENOTHERA BIENNIS*). The oil of my favourite flower contains gamma-linolenic acid (GLA), which is known for relieving premenstrual syndrome and menstrual cramps. Many women report that evening primrose oil reduces their menopausal discomforts as well.

Now at least one good study concluded that evening primrose oil does nothing for menopause. But since so many women have said that it works, I'm inclined to believe them. Besides, evening primrose oil helps protect against heart disease. After menopause, a woman's risk for heart disease skyrockets.

If you want to try evening primrose oil, I recommend using it according to the label directions.

FENUGREEK (*TRIGONELLA FOENUM-GRAECUM*). This herb contains diosgenin, a compound that often serves as the 'starter material' for natural progesterone. Topical applications of natural progesterone are said to prevent not only hot flushes but also uterine fibroids, menstrual cramps, and cervical dysplasia.

Dosage recommendations for fenugreek range from 3–90 g (0.1–3 oz) of seeds or sprouts a day. I'd suggest sticking with the intermediate doses. Try grinding up the seeds or sprouts and adding them to soups or teas. The herb has a maple flavour.

KUDZU (*PUERARIA MONTANA*). Despite its nasty reputation as a rampaging weed, I think kudzu shows great promise as a natural alternative to HRT. It contains more daidzen and genistein – both isoflavones – than soya.

I've yet to come across any dosage recommendations for kudzu that are specific to hot flushes. I suggest adding the leaves to soups, pasta sauces, and other dishes. But if you grow your own kudzu, like I do, don't tell your neighbours. They'll worry about it spreading to their properties. It won't, as long as you keep it contained.

CHAPTER 40

Impotence

Dr Duke's Anti-Ageing Elixir

• Erection-Enhancing Beans

Ever since sildenafil (Viagra) won government approval a few years back, it has become the mainstream treatment for impotence. Just pop the pill, and a half-hour later – with or without the help of a brief penile massage – you're ready for some lovin'.

While Viagra's upside (so to speak) has received lots of media attention, its downside has not. The drug can cause a potentially fatal interaction in men taking nitrate medications for heart disease – for example, nitroglycerine for angina. So far, more than 70 men aspiring to erections have wound up in their graves instead, all because they unwittingly took two drugs that don't mix.

When you consider that heart disease raises the risk of impotence, you realise that the men who shouldn't be using Viagra are often the ones who want it most. This can only set the stage for tragedy.

Of course, Viagra isn't the only mainstream treatment for impotence. A few pharmaceuticals derived from the herb yohimbe help raise an erection. So do injections of the plant alkaloid papaverine, as well as vacuum devices, cylinders that are placed over the penis and pumped to temporarily draw blood into the organ. Penile implants are another treatment option, but they've largely fallen by the wayside since the introduction of Viagra.

Origins in the Body and Mind

The fact that Viagra is so popular hints at just how widespread impotence has become in globally. By various estimates, millions of men experience erection impairment at least occasionally. (I prefer the terms *erection impairment* and *erectile dysfunction* because both are more accurate than impotence. The latter means complete loss of erection, which is rare. For the purposes of this discussion, I'll use the terms interchangeably.)

Not so long ago, doctors and psychologists agreed that impotence was 90 per cent psychological and only 10 per cent physical. Now they've basically reversed those proportions. Impotence has many, many physical causes.

At the top of the list is atherosclerosis, the arterial narrowing that causes heart disease and most strokes. According to a report from the 1993 National Institutes of Health Consensus Conference Panel on Impotence, 'Atherosclerosis of the penile artery is the primary cause of impotence in nearly half the men over the age of 50 who have erectile dysfunction.' Even though the report is 10 years old, the panel's statement still holds true today.

Erection depends on extra bloodflow into the penis. If the penile arteries are narrowed by cholesterol-rich atherosclerotic plaques, bloodflow into the organ is limited. This is why smoking and diabetes are considered risk factors for impotence: both accelerate atherosclerosis.

Another common culprit behind erection impairment is alcohol consumption. Often guys will have a drink or two to get themselves 'in the mood'. In fact, alcohol has the opposite effect. As Shakespeare's Macbeth so eloquently stated, 'It provokes the desire, but it takes away the performance.'

In order for an erection to occur, the nervous system has to signal the penile arteries to relax, open up, and accept extra blood. Alcohol is a central nervous system depressant. Depressant medications, such as narcotics, have similar sexual side effects.

Severe fatigue – from exertion, illness, or medication – can contribute to erection impairment. After all, your body uses energy to raise and maintain an erection.

A deficiency of the male sex hormone testosterone can also contribute to impotence. Testosterone fuels the sex drive and plays a key role in the erection process. A deficiency in this hormone is not all that common. But if you're having difficulty getting or maintaining an erection, you may want to get tested.

On the psychological side, emotional stress – whether it's related to job pressures, financial worries, or marital woes – can easily deflate an erection. If you're having some personal or professional crisis, don't expect your penis to jump to attention.

For Treatment, First Things First

Because erection impairment can result from some underlying health problem, I urge you to begin your treatment by scheduling a complete physical exam with your doctor. Be sure that it includes a blood analysis of your testosterone level and a screening for diabetes. (Many people have diabetes without even realising it.)

Also, if you're taking any medication, ask your doctor whether it could produce impotence as a side effect. If so, ask whether you could switch to something else.

Once your doctor rules out a medical condition or drug side effect, your next step is to start making some lifestyle adjustments. I recommend the following:

- *If you smoke, stop.*
- *Limit alcohol to one or two drinks a day. (A drink is defined as 350 ml/12 fl oz of regular beer, 150 ml/5 fl oz of wine, or a cocktail made with 45 ml/1½ fl oz of 80-proof distilled spirits).*

- *Eat fewer meats and other animal products, instead building your meals around plant foods. A plant-based diet is naturally low in fat, which helps keep your arteries – including those that feed the penis – from clogging up. (My Healthy Sevens eating plan features plenty of plant foods. To learn more about it, see chapter 3.)*
- *Exercise every day, for at least 30 minutes. Regular physical activity helps keep your arteries healthy and functioning properly.*
- *Unload any excess weight. Being overweight raises your blood pressure, which injures your arteries, including the ones in your penis.*
- *Consider getting psychotherapy or marital counselling to help cope with any emotional stress that you're experiencing.*

These strategies alone may be enough to restore a healthy erection. If you're still having difficulty getting and maintaining an erection, you may want to add some herbs to your self-care programme.

Herbs That Enhance Erectile Function

Now, I don't know of any herb that can miraculously restore a lost erection. But several herbs can help resolve erection trouble. And many others show promise as treatments.

YOHIMBE (*PAUSINYSTALIA YOHIMBE*). Africans treasured the bark of this native tree as an erection strengthener. European explorers took the herb back to their homeland, where it developed a reputation as an aphrodisiac. It remained a popular sex stimulant in folk medicine for centuries.

Then in the 1980s, researchers determined that yohimbe contains a compound called yohimbine that opens the penile arteries, improving bloodflow into the penis. In studies, the herb benefited 46 per cent of men with impotence from psychological causes and 43 per cent of men with impotence from physical causes. These results are only a little better than what would be expected from a placebo treatment (around 33 per cent). But they were good enough for the American FDA to approve several prescription yohimbine-based medications.

Of course, once the FDA had given its blessing to these drugs, a chorus of critics began saying that the agency had erred, that yohimbine didn't work. The issue was finally put to rest in 1998, when researchers analysed all of the scientifically rigorous trials examining yohimbine as a treatment for impotence. The scientists concluded that the herb provides significant relief.

Yohimbine-based medications were available years before Viagra. Why didn't they get the same hype? I don't know. Maybe their side effects had something to do with it. Yohimbine-based drugs can cause headache, anxiety, elevated heart rate and blood pressure, flushing, hallucinations, and in men who are manic-depressive, manic episodes. Of course, Viagra can also produce side effects, even death in men taking nitrate medications.

If you're interested in trying a yohimbine-based medication, talk to your doctor. You can also find yohimbe bark extract in some health food and herb shops, but it shouldn't be taken without the guidance of a qualified practitioner.

I hope to have yohimbe in my Garden of Youth eventually. It's a woody shrub that can grow to be a small tree. But so far, I've not been able to get seeds or a cutting for planting.

QUEBRACHO (*ASPIDOSPERMA QUEBRACHO-BLANCO*). The word *quebracho* means 'axe breaker'. It's used to describe wood so hard as to be capable of damaging an axe. It also refers to one of the most widely endorsed sex stimulants in South America.

Like yohimbe, quebracho contains yohimbine. While the herb is generally regarded as safe, it is not readily available. If you can locate a commercial preparation, use it according to the label directions. And let me know where you found it.

GINSENG – ASIAN (*PANAX GINSENG*), AMERICAN (*P. QUINQUEFOLIUS*), SIBERIAN (*ELEUTHEROCOCCUS SENTICOSUS*). In Asia, ginseng is revered as a sex stimulant and a treatment for impotence. Testimonials abound, but the scientific research is surprisingly scant.

I recently learned of the work of C. Norman Gillis, Ph.D., a Yale University professor whose laboratory has studied Ginsana, a commer-

for the Gardener

Siberian Ginseng

Eleutherococcus senticosus

Be forewarned: Siberian ginseng is very difficult to grow. Its seeds germinate sporadically, over several years. I recommend using clay pots, half-buried in a shaded area of your garden and filled with good loam. Barely push the seeds into the soil, then cover them with a 2.5-cm (1-inch) layer of organic compost or peat moss. Cover the pots with a sheet of glass to protect the seeds and support germination.

Seedlings of Siberian ginseng should spend their first year in a protected nursery bed. They're ready to be transplanted when they're about 15 cm (6 inches) tall. The plants prefer cool conditions, with partial shade and plenty of water.

After 4 to 5 years of growth, the stolons (horizontal underground stems) of Siberian ginseng are ready for harvesting. Dig a trench next to the plant, so you can remove the stolons while leaving the rest of the plant intact. Rinse the stolons in water and shave off the bark with a knife. Dry the stolons in a warm, airy spot, then store them in airtight containers away from light.

cial ginseng preparation (standardised to contain 4 per cent ginsenosides). Dr Gillis reports that in animals, the herb increases brain levels of several brain chemicals, including serotonin, dopamine, and norepinephrine. He speculates that these effects may enhance the synthesis of nitric oxide, a compound that relaxes the spongy erectile tissues in the penis. This allows extra blood into the penis, raising an erection.

I confess to continued scepticism about ginseng as a sex stimulant. Still, I respect the herb's long history of use as a treatment for impotence. I grow the Asian and American species, as well as the Siberian genus, just in case the Chinese are correct about the herb making old men like me into young bucks again.

My ginseng plants are in the forest down by the creek. The deer love them, so protecting them is an ongoing battle. Lately, I've taken to surrounding each plant with sharp stakes. It seems to work.

GINKGO (*GINKGO BILOBA*). In giving us the world's most famous sex stimulant, ginseng, the Asians seem to have overlooked a herb that may be even more effective against impotence. If you're familiar with ginkgo, you probably know that it improves bloodflow through your brain, which is why it may be used as a treatment for stroke and Alzheimer's disease. But ginkgo improves bloodflow throughout your body, including into your penis.

In one study, 60 men with impotence caused by arterial atherosclerosis took 60 milligrams of ginkgo biloba extract twice a day. Within 6 months, 50 per cent had regained their potency. Another study used an even higher dosage – 80 milligrams of extract three times a day. It produced even better results, with 78 per cent reporting restored erections.

Ginkgo has also been shown to reverse impotence caused by the selective serotonin reuptake inhibitors. Perhaps the best-known member of this family of antidepressants is fluoxetine (Prozac).

I grow ginkgo in my Garden of Youth. Actually, it was the first tree that I planted, hoping that it would shade the gazebo from the summer afternoon sun. It has lovely, delicate, twin-lobed green leaves that turn a striking golden yellow in autumn, then fall almost all at once.

ASHWAGANDHA (*WITHANIA SOMNIFERA*). Ayurvedic herbalists regard ashwagandha as Indian ginseng, with similar sexual effects. From India to Africa, the root is used as a traditional tonic for male infertility and impotency. A few studies suggest that ashwagandha has some benefit. One involved a group of men in their fifties. Over the course of a year, they showed increased red blood cell counts and reduced cholesterol, and they claimed to enjoy improved sexual function.

I grow ashwagandha in my Garden of Youth. For erection impairment, the usual recommended dose is 2 to 5 grams of dried root, but it is best to start with a 1- to 2-gram daily dose until the individual is assessed for any reaction.

COCOA (*THEOBROMA CACAO*). Cocoa butter contains compounds related to aminophylline, which was an ingredient in a topical cream that helped treat erection impairment in one study.

For the study, 36 men with impotence were given an active cream and a placebo cream, which they applied during alternating weeks. Twenty-one of the men reported full erection and satisfactory intercourse while using the aminophylline cream. Interestingly, the treatment was more effective for impotence from psychological causes than for impotence from physical causes.

Aminophylline works by helping to open blood vessels. I have no idea where to obtain the cream used in the study, but cocoa butter is widely available. Try applying it as part of a penile massage.

GARLIC (*ALLIUM SATIVUM*). In ancient Egypt, garlic in wine was considered an aphrodisiac and a treatment for erection problems. I say go easy on the wine but load up on the garlic. It reduces blood pressure and cholesterol, which may help improve bloodflow into your penis. In addition, extracts of garlic increase the production of nitric oxide, which plays a role in raising and maintaining an erection.

Of course, garlic breath might put off your partner. But if you both eat lots of the herb, maybe neither of you will notice.

WILD OATS (*AVENA SATIVA*). Wild oats have an age-old reputation for making horses sexually frisky. That's why the herb is sometimes added

More Wisdom *from the* Garden

Pump Up Potency with Pumpkin

It has been said that the way to a man's heart is through his stomach. Apparently, the way to a man's penis is through his nose. And the most exciting scent of all is pumpkin pie. At least that's the finding of Alan Hirsch, M.D., director of the Smell and Taste Research Foundation in Chicago, in his study of aromas and sexual arousal. While pumpkin pie came out on top, the scent of baked cinnamon buns also got a rise out of men who sniffed it.

If you have trouble raising an erection, you may want to try scenting your bedroom with pumpkin or cinnamon potpourri or candles. You can buy these products in department stores and bath and beauty shops.

Dr Duke's Anti-Ageing Elixir

Erection-Enhancing Beans

I once read that the Roman poet Cicero considered broad beans an aphrodisiac. As it turns out, the beans are a good source of L-dopa, the treatment of choice for Parkinson's disease. Men who take L-dopa sometimes develop chronic erections, a condition known as priapism.

WHAT YOU NEED

170–230 g (6–8 oz) tinned broad beans, with liquid
230 g (8 oz) diced tomatoes
115 g (4 oz) diced celery
115 g (4 oz) diced onions
Garlic, chopped
Ground ginger
Hot-pepper sauce

WHAT TO DO

In a saucepan, combine the beans, tomatoes, celery, and onions. Add a little water. Bring to the boil, then reduce the heat and simmer for 15 minutes. Sprinkle with the garlic and season with the ginger and hot-pepper sauce before serving.

to formulas for impotence and increased libido.

Experience with animals suggests that wild oats may indeed keep men healthy and fertile, like racehorses. The herb is said to be most potent when its seeds are milky, before they harden and are rolled into oatmeal.

Testimonials abound about the sexual benefits of wild oats. I grow oats in my garden, but I can't swear that they do much more than lower cholesterol. Of course, that can enhance arterial bloodflow, which may explain how the herb contributes to an erection.

YINYANGHUO (*EPIMEDIUM*, VARIOUS SPECIES). In animal studies, cured preparations of this herb, also known as horny goat weed, have improved male sexual function. I grow several varieties of the herb in the bottom land by the creek. I munch the leaves straight from the plants. They're not cured, though. Maybe that's why I haven't noticed any effect. Or maybe I'm just not eating enough.

MUIRA PUAMA (*PTYCHOPETALUM OLACOIDES*). A native of the Amazon, muira puama appears to help restore libido and treat impotence. The herb is a nervous system stimulant, so it might help raise an erection.

In one study, 262 men took 1 to

More Wisdom *from the* Garden

Herbal Stimulants Jump-Start Your Sex Life

Because fatigue can deflate an erection and sap the libido, it should come as no surprise that the stimulant herbs have been used for centuries to enhance sex drive and performance. These herbs fall into two basic categories: those with caffeine (coffee, tea, maté, guarana, guayusa, kola, and cocoa), and those with ephedrine (Chinese ephedra, or ma huang).

Of the herbs containing caffeine, South American guarana has the sexiest reputation. A cup of tea made with this herb may contain more than twice as much caffeine as a cup of brewed coffee. Brazilians love soft drinks made with guarana and swear that the herb is an erection-boosting aphrodisiac.

As for Chinese ephedra, I wouldn't recommend using it as an aphrodisiac. It has become too controversial – though personally, I think it's safe, as long as it's taken as recommended.

2.5 grams of muira puama extract every day for 2 weeks. Of those with impotence, 51 per cent reported an improvement in erectile function. Among those with flagging libido, 62 per cent noticed an increase in sexual energy.

Muira puama is available from a few of the major herb companies. If you're able to find a commercial preparation, use it according to the label directions.

OX EYE OR OJO DE BUEY (*MUCUNA*, VARIOUS SPECIES). Years ago, while I was working in Panama, I heard that the seeds of the ox eye plant help raise an erection. I was sceptical. Then I learned that ox eye seeds contain L-dopa, one of the drugs of choice for treating Parkinson's disease. Among the side effects of L-dopa is priapism (chronic erection).

In one study, scientists found that an oral dose of 1 gram of pulverised ox eye seeds in water per kilogram of body weight hastened sexual arousal and prolonged sexual activity in animals. I've yet to find any dosage recommendations for humans.

CHAPTER 41

Incontinence

Dr Duke's Anti-Ageing Elixir

• Intercontinental Incontinence Tea

Urinary incontinence is surprisingly common. Millions of adults are living with this condition, often in silence. Most of them are older women.

When Stanford University researchers compiled and analysed statistics on urinary incontinence, they found that 34 per cent of women over 65 and 25 per cent of younger women have the condition. By comparison, only 22 per cent of men over 65 and 5 per cent of younger men are affected by it.

Why so many women? Because they're especially vulnerable to the most common form of incontinence, called stress incontinence. In this sense, *stress* does not mean emotional anxiety. Rather, it refers to pressure on the abdomen. Anything that exerts this pressure – coughing, sneezing, laughing, even hugging – causes the release of a small amount of urine, even when there's no urge to urinate.

Stress incontinence occurs because of a weakness in the muscles that surround the urethral opening, as well as in other muscles that sit beneath the bladder on the pelvic floor. These muscles, particularly the pubococcygeus (PC), support the bladder and urethra. If they weaken, the bladder and urethra sag. So any pressure on the abdomen forces out a few drops of urine.

Several things can contribute to the weakening of a woman's pelvic muscles and set the stage for stress incontinence. Perhaps the most obvious factor is pregnancy and delivery. Motherhood doesn't automatically mean that you'll develop stress incontinence later in life. But pregnancy and delivery do weaken the pelvic floor muscles. The more children that a woman has, the greater her chances of becoming incontinent.

Another factor in stress incontinence is overweight. The extra abdominal tissue presses down on the bladder, weakening the pelvic floor muscles.

As the statistics cited earlier indicate, age plays a role in stress incontinence. Our pelvic floor muscles simply lose some of their strength as we get older. This happens in both genders, not just women.

While stress incontinence is the most common form of urinary incontinence, the condition does take other forms.

- *In urge incontinence, the person (usually a woman) feels the need to urinate, but it comes too late. The urethral muscles contract involuntarily and expel urine before the person reaches the bathroom.*
- *In overflow incontinence – the kind that men usually develop – an enlarged prostate prevents complete emptying of the bladder. After a man thinks he has finished urinating, more leaks out.*
- *In drug-related incontinence, urine leakage is a side effect of medication.*

Some people have symptoms of more than one type of incontinence. For example, a woman with stress incontinence may experience urine leakage because of a drug that she's taking.

Strategies That Stem the Flow

People with urinary incontinence tend to conceal their condition, not even seeing their doctors for advice. They're too ashamed or embarrassed to admit that they're incontinent. And that's too bad, because if they got help, they'd discover that they have many options for managing and overcoming their condition.

If you're having a problem with urinary leakage, I urge you to make the following strategies part of your self-care programme.

Toss out the cigarettes. The nicotine in cigarette smoke can irritate your bladder, aggravating any type of incontinence. So if you smoke, you have one more reason to quit.

Scrutinise your pharmaceuticals. Several blood pressure medications weaken your bladder and urethral muscles, including prazosin (Hypovase), terazosin (Hytrin), cardura (Cardura), and clonidine (Catapres). Decongestants – by themselves or as ingredients in over-the-counter cold and allergy formulas – constrict the urinary sphincter (a ringlike muscle that serves as an on/off switch for the bladder), which can cause or aggravate overflow incontinence. Antihistamines, antidepressants, narcotics, cancer chemotherapy drugs, and any drugs that cause dry mouth can interfere with the contraction of your bladder muscles and contribute to overflow incontinence. I've seen estimates that 25 per cent of prescription pharmaceuticals cause dry mouth.

For urge incontinence, check your diet for irritants. Several foods and beverages can irritate your bladder and trigger urge incontinence, most notably alcohol and caffeinated beverages (coffee, tea, and cola). For some people, even decaf coffee causes problems.

For stress incontinence, practise Kegels. Developed by urologist Arnold Kegel, M.D., these exercises strengthen your PC muscle and help you retain urine despite the abdominal pressure caused by coughing, sneezing, and laughing. Kegels really do work. Depending on the study, they improve bladder control significantly in 50 to 90 per cent of women, and completely cure stress incontinence in 25 to 50 per cent of women. As a bonus, they intensify the pleasure of orgasm.

To do Kegels, your first step is to identify your PC muscle. It's the

Strengthen Your Muscles with Tai Chi

From the research that I've seen, Chinese women are less likely to experience stress incontinence than their South African, English or Australian counterparts. Scientists say that it's because the Chinese routinely practise tai chi and qigong. Apparently, the slow, deliberate dancelike movements of these disciplines strengthen the pubococcygeus muscles, much like Kegel exercises.

Tai chi and qigong aren't nearly as popular in the United Kingdom as in China, but they are catching on. Check for classes at your local health club.

one you squeeze to stop urinating in midstream. The next time you go to the bathroom, try stopping the urine flow several times so that you can feel your PC muscle.

Then when you're not on the toilet, contract the muscle 10 times in succession. Hold each squeeze for 10 seconds, with 10 seconds rest in between. Practise the exercises four times a day for 8 weeks.

If you're not sure that you're contracting the right muscle, talk with your doctor. If you have trouble mastering Kegels, you might consider biofeedback training. In one study involving 27 women, 81 per cent reported improvement in their symptoms after eight 1-hour biofeedback sessions.

For overflow incontinence, try going twice. If you're a man with overflow incontinence, urinate until you feel that you're finished. But don't zip up. Instead, take a few deep breaths and try again. You may be able to urinate more.

For stress incontinence, choose loose-fitting clothes. Tight garments can aggravate stress incontinence by squeezing your lower abdomen. Steer clear of girdles, corsets, snug belts, and form-fitting workout wear.

Herbs That Keep You High and Dry

In conjunction with the various lifestyle strategies I have described above, the following herbs may help you gain the upper hand against urinary incontinence. They're certainly worth trying.

BLACK COHOSH (*CIMICIFUGA RACEMOSA*). Doctors often prescribe hormone-replacement therapy or oestrogen creams to women with post-menopausal stress and urge incontinence. Oestrogen increases bloodflow to the pelvic muscles, which strengthens them.

To get the same results without the potential side effects of hormone replacement, I recommend black cohosh, with its phyto-oestrogens (plant oestrogens). When used as a treatment for hot flushes, black cohosh works just like hormone replacement. I believe that the herb can help treat incontinence as well.

Herbalist Susun Weed, who specialises in women's health, recommends taking 10 to 20 drops of black cohosh tincture in water or juice once or twice a day for several weeks until symptoms of incontinence subside. I'd plant black cohosh in my Garden of Youth, but I don't have to. It grows wild in the undeveloped land around my place.

CHINESE EPHEDRA (*EPHEDRA SINENSIS*). Doctors sometimes prescribe decongestants containing pseudoephedrine as a treatment for urge incontinence. Pseudoephedrine makes the urethral muscles clamp down, which helps prevent involuntary urine flow. (As mentioned above, decongestants can aggravate overflow incontinence.)

If I had urge incontinence, I'd rather go with the original source of pseu-

Dr Duke's Anti-Ageing Elixir

Intercontinental Incontinence Tea

This is my version of Cysto Fink, a German commercial preparation that has produced excellent results in treating irritable bladder and urinary incontinence. Unfortunately, it's not yet readily available. Until it is, you can make your own.

WHAT YOU NEED

1 litre (2 pints) water
6 teaspoons hops
6 teaspoons uva-ursi
4 teaspoons ephedra
6 teaspoons sage

WHAT TO DO

In a medium saucepan containing the freshly boiled water, add the hops, uva-ursi, ephedra, and sage (which prevents excess discharge of sweat, milk, and, I believe, urine). Steep for 20 minutes, then strain out the plant material. Drink one cup three times a day.

doephedrine: Chinese ephedra (ma huang). Unfortunately, the FDA is considering restricting access to Chinese ephedra in America because of a handful of deaths – many involving people who took huge doses to experience amphetamine-like intoxication. I hope the FDA leaves the herb alone. I don't think everyone should be punished because a few people made a tragic error of judgement. We'd lose a herb that's beneficial not only for incontinence but also for allergies, asthma, bronchitis, colds, flu, and sinus infections, among several other conditions.

HOP (*HUMULUS LUPULUS*). German researchers tested a herbal preparation called Cysto Fink, made with a combination of hop, uva-ursi, and vitamin E. Of 915 people with irritable bladder and urinary incontinence, 772 reported excellent results with the treatment.

To my knowledge, Cysto Fink is not readily available. But you can make your own version at home, using my Intercontinental Incontinence Tea recipe.

CRANBERRY (*VACCINIUM SOO*). If you can't stop a little urine leakage, you can at least prevent the embarrassment of urine odour. Cranberries and cranberry juice are urinary deodorants. They're commonly served in nursing homes, where many of the residents are incontinent.

Cranberry makes urine more acidic, which prevents the bacterial fermentation that leads to odour. My advice is to drink a cup of cranberry juice with meals, or as often as you like.

CHAPTER 42

Insomnia

Dr Duke's Anti-Ageing Elixirs

- *Soothing Shut-Eye Sipper*
- *Mellow Bedtime Brew*
- *Tranquillity Cake*

Many people use the word *insomnia* to describe an inability to fall asleep. Actually, the term applies to any disruption in sleep patterns – whether it's not falling asleep, not staying asleep, or waking unusually early.

Most episodes of insomnia are infrequent and temporary, often brought on by travel (especially across time zones) or a change in routine. Sometimes sleep problems linger for a few weeks, especially in situations of severe emotional stress – perhaps an illness or death in the family, or even a positive event like moving into a new home.

While occasional or short-term insomnia usually has an identifiable cause, chronic insomnia often does not. It turns sleeping into a nightly struggle that can last for years. Not surprisingly, people with chronic insomnia experience persistent fatigue during their waking hours. They're also likely to have significantly weakened immune systems and reduced resistance to disease.

Insomnia is a major health problem. Among American adults who visit family doctors, some 10 to 15 per cent report that they have chronic insomnia. Another one-third say that they experience sleep problems more than occasionally. And as many as 10 million receive prescriptions for sedatives.

While occasional or short-term insomnia can affect anyone of any age, chronic insomnia is most common among older people. That's because our sleep patterns change over time. The older we get, the less deeply we sleep, and the more likely we are to have trouble falling (and staying) asleep.

While cases of chronic insomnia do crop up in the middle-aged population, they're far more prevalent among seniors. People over 65 make up about 12 per cent of the US population, yet they're taking 35 to 40 per cent of all prescription sleep medications.

Without question, pharmaceutical sedatives have their place. They can be quite helpful to those coping with severe emotional trauma. But I'm concerned that these drugs are overprescribed.

Like most pharmaceuticals, sedatives are not completely harmless. Some are habit-forming. All cause side effects such as agitation, confusion, daytime drowsiness, and hangover, especially when they're taken in combination with other medications – as they often are.

Personally, if I were troubled by insomnia, even the chronic kind, I'd try natural approaches before resorting to prescription pills. I'm convinced that the right combination of herbs and lifestyle strategies would deliver me to dreamland. They could work for you, too.

Live Like the Well-Rested

Many elements of your daily routine can influence your nighttime sleep habits, for better or for worse. To give yourself the best chance for sound, refreshing slumber, I suggest the following:

Watch what you eat and when. Most sleep experts say that you should avoid eating big meals within 4 hours of your bedtime. If you're hungry for a snack, steer clear of fatty foods like potato chips, cookies, and ice cream. Fats are difficult to digest, which means that they may end up keeping you awake at night.

Curb your caffeine consumption. Caffeinated beverages such as coffee, tea, cola, and cocoa are notorious sleep disrupters. Even if the caffeine doesn't give you a noticeable buzz, it can affect your sleep habits. My wife, Peggy, cannot sleep if she has coffee after 2 p.m. or a coffee liqueur after dinner.

At the very least, try to avoid consuming anything caffeinated after lunch. Instead of a post-dinner cup of coffee, make a cup of tea using a sleep-friendly herb such as camomile.

Forgo the alcoholic nightcaps. Dotors used to advise patients with sleep problems to have a drink before bedtime. Not anymore. While alcohol may help you doze off, it may also disturb your normal sleep

More Wisdom *from the* Garden

Aromatherapy Makes Sleeping Easy

A decade or so ago, I was very sceptical of aromatherapy. Not anymore. Now I believe this healing discipline to be especially useful for conditions involving the brain and central nervous system – most notably insomnia.

What has changed my mind? I've been reading the growing body of research that shows how the volatile compounds in many essential plant oils are easily absorbed by inhalation and topical application to the skin, and how these compounds affect the brain in a matter of minutes. It makes sense that they could help induce sleep.

If I were having trouble sleeping, I'd try whiffing lavender essential oil before going to bed. Or I'd go into my Garden of Youth, snip off some lavender spikes, crush them in my hands, and inhale their fresh vapours. In studies, lavender appears to work like diazepam (Valium), but without the serious side effects.

You can buy lavender essential oil in many health food stores as well as in some bath and body shops.

patterns, so you're more likely to wake up in the middle of the night and less likely to go back to sleep. Personally, I try to avoid alcoholic beverages after 7 p.m.

Fit in fitness every day. Exercise is a great way to ensure a good night's sleep. Your body prefers cycles of activity and rest. If you don't provide the activity, you may not get the rest.

In chapter 2, I suggest striving for 45 minutes of continuous exercise every day. Just don't work out within 4 hours of your bedtime – it may have the opposite effect and actually keep you awake. Try to schedule your exercise session sometime before dinner if at all possible.

My personal fitness routine consists of pottering around my Garden of Youth and walking around YinYang Valley. On cold or rainy days, I'll pedal my stationary bicycle and lift my hand weights.

Keep stress in check. Tension, worry, and emotional distress can wreak havoc on your sleep habits. If you exercise regularly, as recommended above, it should help defuse everyday stress. You may also want to practice a relaxation technique, such as meditation, biofeedback, or yoga. Personally, I like to unwind by digging in my Garden of Youth.

Establish a wind-down ritual. In order to fall asleep, you need to downshift your physical and mental gears. Adopting a nightly routine can help you make the transition and prepare for bed. Some suggestions: lock up the house; have a light bedtime snack, perhaps a glass of low-fat or fat-free milk; brush your teeth; adjust the thermostat in your bedroom; set your alarm; make a 'to do' list for the next day (provided you won't dwell on it overnight); then turn out the lights and crawl between the sheets.

Create a sleep-friendly environment. Your bedroom should support a good night's rest. Invest in a comfortable bed, with a mattress that is neither too firm nor too soft. Equip it with sheets and blankets that feel good to you. Choose comfortable sleepwear, too.

As for the room itself, try to keep it dark and quiet during the night-time hours. Thick curtains can help shield out light and noise. (Or, you can wear a sleep mask and earplugs.) Also, remember to set the thermostat so that the room temperature is neither too hot nor too cold.

Try Nature's Sleep Aids

For a little extra sleep support, you may want to try one of the following sedative herbs. (They are presented in alphabetical order.) All of them work gently and safely, with almost none of the side effects common to pharmaceutical products.

BUSH TEA (*ASPALATHUS LINEARIS*). Also known as rooibos (meaning red bush), bush tea is native to South Africa, where it's widely used to relieve digestive problems, relax the nervous system, and promote sleep. It's fairly well-endowed with caffeic acid, a sedative compound – unlike its namesake, caffeine.

I've tried getting bush tea plants for my Garden of Youth, without success. Thankfully, processed forms of the herb are becoming more available in health food shops. You can probably find it if you look. I suggest buying a commercial preparation and taking it according to the label directions.

CATNIP (*NEPETA CATARIA*). The herb that's best known for intoxicating cats also promotes sleep in us humans. It contains nepetalactone, a compound that is mildly sedative.

At one time, catnip was considered as potent a sedative as valerian – and much better tasting. In pre-Elizabethan England, catnip tea was the hot beverage of choice. In fact, when Chinese black tea was introduced to England, many people protested against it, claiming that it overstimulated those who drank it. But eventually, black tea won favour.

As valerian gained a reputation as

Dr Duke's Anti-Ageing Elixir

Soothing Shut-Eye Sipper

Made from some of nature's most potent sleep inducers, this tea is a perfect nightcap for anyone with insomnia.

WHAT YOU NEED

Any combination of the following herbs: catnip, camomile, evening primrose, lavender, lemon balm, lemon eucalyptus, lemongrass, and passionflower

1 cup water

WHAT TO DO

Combine the herbs of your choice. Add 1 to 3 teaspoons of your herb blend to the freshly boiled water. Steep for 10 minutes, then strain. Allow to cool before drinking.

the sedative herb, catnip fell from popularity. Only herbalists are aware of what a powerful sleep inducer catnip can be.

In the summer months, if I want a little herbal relaxation, I might add some of catnip's flowering tops to my antioxidant teas. (The leaves sometimes hang around through December.) Like valerian, catnip causes no morning-after hangover.

CAMOMILE (*MATRICARIA RECUTITA*). Camomile is one of my favourite herbal tranquillizers. Taken after supper, it can also help induce sleep.

Camomile contains flavonoids, compounds that bind to the same cellular receptors as diazepam (Valium). This means that the herb and the drug have similar effects, only the herb is milder and causes no morning-after grogginess.

Other compounds in camomile, called chrysin and apigenin, gently reduce muscle activity. Apigenin also helps ease anxiety.

To make a camomile tea, steep 2 to 3 heaped teaspoons of flowers in a cup of freshly boiled water for 10 minutes, then strain. Make sure that the tea has cooled slightly before drinking it.

EVENING PRIMROSE (*OENOTHERA BIENNIS*). Evening primrose is my favourite flower. It also happens to be the best plant source of tryptophan that I know of. Tryptophan is an amino acid that helps induce sleep.

While evening primrose oil is often recommended for its therapeutic powers, it doesn't have much tryptophan. Most of the amino acid comes from the plant's whole seeds. I like to sprinkle crushed evening primrose seeds, along with poppy seeds, on toast as a bedtime snack, with a glass of warm milk (another traditional sedative) as a chaser. (I'll say more about tryptophan at the end of the chapter.)

HOP (*HUMULUS LUPULUS*). The herb that gives beer its flavour is famous for inducing sleep. Farmers first noticed hop's sedative powers centuries ago, when hop pickers had trouble staying awake in the fields. Since then, the herb has been widely used as a gentle sleep aid.

Commission E, the expert panel that evaluates the safety and effectiveness of herbs for the German government, has approved hop for anxiety, restlessness, and insomnia. Research has shown that the herb's oil contains several sedative compounds, including methyl-butenol, humulone, myrcene, and caryophyllene.

To make a hop tea, try steeping 1 to 2 teaspoons of the herb in a cup of freshly boiled water for 10 minutes, then strain it. Make sure that the tea has cooled before drinking it.

LAVENDER (*LAVANDULA*, VARIOUS SPECIES). Lavender tops my list of pleasant-smelling sedative herbs. It has also won the approval of Commission E as a treatment for mood disorders such as insomnia and restlessness.

Research has demonstrated that lavender works. In one animal trial, treatment with lavender oil completely inhibited stimulation by caffeine. And in a human study, elderly nursing-home residents who had been taking Valium-type sedatives discontinued their prescriptions for 2 weeks, during which time they slept very poorly. Then they were given aromatherapy with lavender oil. The quantity and quality of their sleep returned to the levels that had been achieved with drugs, but without the side effects.

As a sedative, I would rank lavender up there with valerian. It may even be better than hop, lemon balm, or passionflower. To make a lavender tea, add 1 to 3 teaspoons of the herb's flowering spikes to 1 cup of freshly boiled water. Steep for 10 minutes, then strain. Make sure that the tea has cooled before drinking it.

LEMON BALM (*MELISSA OFFICINALIS*). A

Dr Duke's Anti-Ageing Elixir

Mellow Bedtime Brew

This soothing blend of three sedative herbs can help you get a good night's sleep.

WHAT YOU NEED

2 cups water
½ handful freshly diced lemon balm
½ handful freshly diced lavender
Lemon
A natural sweetener (optional)

WHAT TO DO

In a small saucepan, pour the freshly boiled water over the lemon balm and lavender. Steep for 10 minutes, then strain. Add the lemon and sweeten to taste. Make sure that the tea has cooled slightly before drinking.

mild tranquillizer, lemon balm can promote sleep, especially when combined with other sedative herbs. It has been approved by Commission E as a treatment for sleep problems. To make a lemon balm tea, add 1 to 3 teaspoons of leaves to 1 cup of freshly boiled water. Steep for 10 minutes, then strain. Allow the tea to cool before drinking it.

PASSIONFLOWER (*PASSIFLORA INCARNATA*). My farm in Maryland is just about as far north as passionflower could grow. The plant is really invasive, sending up root shoots as much as 1.8 metres (6 feet) away from the main stem.

If I lose any sleep over the persistence of passionflower on my property, perhaps I'll drink some passionflower tea. The herb has been approved by Commission E as a treatment for mild insomnia and anxiety, based on a fair amount of animal and human research. In low doses, passionflower is a mild tranquillizer. In higher doses, it's a sedative.

For a passionflower tea that supports sound sleep, I suggest steeping 3 to 4 teaspoons of herb in a cup of freshly boiled water for 10 minutes. Strain out the herb and allow the tea to cool before drinking it. You can also buy a commercial extract and use it according to the label directions.

SOUR JUJUBE (ZIZYPHUS SPINOSA). In China, the seeds of the sour jujube are probably the most commonly used herbal treatment for insomnia and nightmares. Studies have demonstrated that the herb has sedative effects in both animals and humans. It contains quite an array of sedative compounds, including spinosin, swertisin, and zivulgarin.

Sour jujube isn't that widely available. I have the plant in my Garden of Youth, and I know of a few other places where it's grown. If you want to try it, you may be able to find it in a Chinese herb shop. The recommended sedative dose is 2 to 8 grams.

VALERIAN (*VALERIANA OFFICINALIS*). Alphabetically last, but certainly not least, is the reigning king of herbal sedatives. Valerian has been used as a sleep aid for some 1,000 years. Many studies have found the herb to be effective, though some suggest that its benefits don't kick in until it's been taken regularly for 2 to 4 weeks.

Scientists are still debating what makes valerian such a potent sedative.

Conventional wisdom attributes the herb's sleep-inducing powers to a particular class of compounds called valepotriates. But recent studies have identified other active compounds, including bornyl esters, valerenic acid, and valeranone and kessyl esters.

No matter why valerian works, the point is that it does work. It has been approved by Commission E as a treatment for insomnia. Side effects are rare but possible, with gastrointestinal distress and headache the most widely reported.

If you're interested in trying valerian, I'd advise against making a tea. It smells like very dirty, very old socks and tastes horrible. Instead, buy a commercial preparation and use it according to label directions. Even better, save valerian for the most serious bouts of insomnia and treat milder episodes with more pleasant-smelling, better-tasting herbs, such as catnip, camomile, hop, lavender, and passionflower.

Some Thoughts on Tryptophan

Earlier I mentioned evening primrose as a source of the amino acid tryptophan. In the 1970s, tryptophan developed a reputation as a safe, gentle sedative. It's a precursor of serotonin, a brain chemical (neurotransmitter) that helps induce sleep.

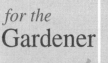

for the Gardener

Valerian

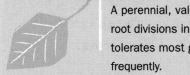

Valeriana officinalis

A perennial, valerian can be grown from seeds in spring or from root divisions in autumn. The herb prefers rich, heavy loam, but it tolerates most garden soils. It needs to be watered and weeded frequently.

If you intend to use valerian's medicinal rhizomes (the rootlike underground stems), space the plants at least 30 cm (12 inches) apart, and pinch back the tops to prevent flowering. The rhizomes are usually harvested in the autumn, before the first frost. Wash them in hot water, then store them in a cool, dry place.

According to experts in nutritional therapy, a sedative dose of tryptophan is 5 to 10 grams. Among the best-known animal sources of the amino acid are milk and turkey. Many nutritionists believe that's why drinking warm milk is a time-honoured nighttime ritual. I sometimes enjoy a glass of milk before going to bed. I'm not sure that I'd eat a turkey sandwich so late at night.

The thing is, even a tall glass of milk supplies nowhere near 5 grams of tryptophan, the amount necessary to experience sedative effects. So maybe drinking milk at bedtime is soothing for other reasons. Then again, maybe tryptophan is more potent than the experts currently realise.

Incidentally, while milk and turkey are the best-known sources of tryptophan, they're not the only sources. In fact, they're surpassed by evening primrose seeds, which have a tryptophan content of up to 16,000 parts per million. Even at this concentration, you'd have to eat close to half a kilo (1 lb) of seeds to get a sedative dose. Other relatively good sources of tryptophan include almonds, amaranth, barley, black-eyed beans, butter beans, butternuts, cabbage, chickpeas, fenugreek, kidney beans, mung beans, mustard seeds (white), oats, pistachios, poppy seeds, pumpkin seeds, sesame seeds, spinach, sunflower seeds, watercress, wheat, and drumsticks (winged beans).

Tryptophan is also available in supplement forms. It was sold over the counter until the late 1980s, when a contaminated batch sickened a

Dr Duke's Anti-Ageing Elixir

Tranquillity Cake

One of nature's better sedatives is the amino acid tryptophan. While the ingredients in this recipe can't deliver what's considered a therapeutic dose of tryptophan, they can gently nudge you towards dreamland.

WHAT YOU NEED

Recipe and ingredients for a poppy seed cake

Any combination of the following seeds: evening primrose, pumpkin, sesame, sunflower and white mustard

WHAT TO DO

Start with a basic recipe for poppy seed cake. Mix in the seeds of your choice. Eat a slice of cake ½ hour before bedtime with a glass of warm milk (also a source of tryptophan).

number of people in America and caused several deaths. In the wake of that tragic incident, the FDA banned all tryptophan supplements. The ban was lifted in 1996, but as of this writing, tryptophan remains available by prescription only.

If you want to try tryptophan supplements, talk to your doctor about them. Many sleep-disorder specialists view them as highly effective sleep aids.

CHAPTER 43

Pain

Dr Duke's Anti-Ageing Elixirs

- *Analgesic Tea*
- *Herbal COX-2 Tonic*

The worst pain that I've ever experienced resulted from a slipped disc. It hurt terribly – even more than a gout attack, which is quite agonising.

For relief, I took more prescription medications than I had ever taken in my life: pain relievers, muscle relaxants, and nonsteroidal anti-inflammatory drugs (NSAIDs). I also took more herbs than I had ever taken, in an effort to help minimise the side effects of all the medications. My regime included echinacea, to strengthen an impaired immune system; St. John's wort, to elevate my depressed mood; licorice, to prevent the gastrointestinal distress caused by NSAIDs; and milk thistle, to protect my liver.

Through a combination of drugs, herbs, acupuncture treatments, and physical therapy, my pain eventually went away. But its effects still linger: to this day, two fingers on my left hand remain slightly numb.

Nearly everyone has pain from time to time. But not everyone has chronic pain. That's the focus of this chapter.

Generally, doctors consider pain to be chronic when it persists for longer than 6 months. By comparison, acute pain – the kind associated with bumping your elbow or stubbing your toe – tends to go away almost as quickly as it comes on. It rarely has any lasting physical or psychological impact.

That's another distinguishing characteristic of chronic pain: besides its physical symptoms, it raises the risk of depression. And depression makes any pain condition more difficult to treat.

Pharmaceuticals: Relief – But at What Price?

Chronic pain is a common problem, affecting at least 10 per cent of the population. Older people are most vulnerable, because so many of them have osteoarthritis.

When treating patients with chronic pain, most doctors reach for the prescription pad. Their drugs of choice are narcotics and NSAIDs, like ibuprofen – the same pills that I took for my slipped disc.

While the old-style NSAIDs relieve pain and inflammation, they also cause gastrointestinal problems – sometimes serious ones. The newer NSAIDs, known as COX-2 inhibitors, are said to be less likely to cause gastrointestinal side effects. That's certainly an improvement. Still, even the COX-2's can cause abdominal distress. And since they've been around for only a short time, their long-term side effects are unknown.

Narcotics, the other standard treatment for chronic pain, began as herbal medicine – from the opium poppy. Today, some are synthesized in laboratories. Narcotics are very effective pain relievers. But they have potentially serious side effects, such as confusion, loss of coordination, sedation, and addiction. Of these, people tend to fear addiction the most. Addiction is possible, but among those who don't have a tendency towards substance abuse, it's actually fairly rare. In one report that I reviewed, only 7 of 25,000 people taking morphine for chronic pain became dependent on the drug. Still, the other side effects can be bad enough to discourage people from taking narcotics of any kind.

Pain Clinics: An Integrated Approach to Treatment

These days, people with chronic pain are often referred to pain clinics, special medical facilities that focus on pain as the main problem, rather than as a symptom of some other condition. Pain clinics are interesting places. The doctors prescribe medications, but they also rely on non-drug treatments, especially relaxation therapies and exercise.

Relaxation therapies are valuable because they defuse the stress caused by chronic pain. When you're tense and anxious, you hurt more – and that makes you more tense and anxious. It's a vicious circle. By reducing the stress, relaxation therapies help relieve the pain.

At pain clinics, the relaxation therapies of choice are meditation, visualisation, and biofeedback. All of these can help. For myself, I like to meditate on the beauty of nature while working in my Garden of Youth. It certainly makes me feel better.

Exercise helps control chronic pain by triggering the release of endorphins, the body's own pain-relieving, mood-elevating compounds. Many experts say – and I agree – that regular, gentle, low-impact physical activity is among the best all-around treatments for osteoarthritis, one of the leading causes of chronic pain.

Which physical activity is best? I'd cast my vote for walking. I log quite a distance almost every day just ambling around my farm. I also get a good workout in my Garden of Youth. All that walking, bending, squatting, pulling, pushing, and carrying gets my blood pumping and my endorphins flowing. As a bonus, it takes all of my major joints through their full range of motion, helping to keep them pain-free.

Herbs: Medicine without the Side Effects

Like relaxation therapies and exercise, herbal medicine plays an important role in the treatment of chronic pain. Of course, the herbal pain relievers are not always as potent as their pharmaceutical counterparts. I know of no whole herb that packs the same punch as narcotics, NSAIDs, or COX-2 inhibitors, though some come close.

On the other hand, most herbal pain relievers are not addictive and are much less likely to cause side effects. If I had chronic pain, I would try one of the following:

WILLOW BARK (*SALIX*, VARIOUS SPECIES). Willow bark contains salicin, the plant precursor of aspirin. A cup of willow bark tea is not as potent as two standard aspirin tablets, but it's also less likely to cause stomach upset and other side effects.

I have several willows in my Garden of Youth. If I experienced a bout of pain while travelling, I just might take pharmaceutical aspirin. But at home, I'd likely opt for the willow. I suggest buying a commercial preparation and taking it according to the label directions.

WINTERGREEN (*GAULTHERIA PROCUMBENS*). I enjoy the aroma of wintergreen, which, like willow, contains an aspirin-like compound called methyl salicylate. It also has three other pain-relieving compounds: caffeic acid, ferulic acid, and gentistic acid.

If my knee acts up – as it does on occasion – I may apply a cream containing a mixture of wintergreen and boswellin, an Ayurvedic herb (more on boswellin a bit later). You should be able to find the cream yourself, either in a health food store or from a reputable online source (such as www.herbshandshealing.com).

CHINESE ANGELICA (*ANGELICA SINENSIS*). Also known as dong quai, Chinese angelica has a well-established reputation as a treatment for gynaecological, menstrual, and menopausal complaints. In China, it's widely used as a pain reliever.

I've seen studies showing that injections of Chinese angelica extracts, particularly at acupuncture points, are very effective in relieving arthritis pain, muscle cramps, nerve pain (from pinched nerves and diabetic neuropathy), lower-back pain, and sciatica. In these studies, the treatment success rate has run as high as 90 per cent.

I'm certainly not suggesting that you inject yourself with Chinese angelica extract. If you're interested in that, you need to consult a Chinese medicine practitioner. But the volatile oils in Chinese angelica – the compounds extracted when the herb is prepared as a tea or a tincture – have some pain-relieving properties as well as some anti-inflammatory and antispasmodic activity.

If I wanted to use Chinese angelica, I'd probably buy a commercial

growing younger naturally

Wild Yam Ended 4 Years of Pain

You may know wild yam as a treatment for menopausal discomforts. The herb contains an abundance of diosgenin, which is a weak phyto-oestrogen (plant oestrogen). But it also has other compounds that help reduce inflammation. That's why I sometimes recommend wild yam as a natural pain reliever.

I recently heard from one woman, a registered nurse, who took my recommendation to heart. Here's an excerpt from her letter.

'After attending your lecture at the University of Iowa on herbal approaches to health, I decided to try wild yam. You had indicated that it has natural steroid properties, and can help with pain caused by inflammation.

'After 4 years of severe lower-back pain and sciatic discomfort without relief from megadoses of ibuprofen, I started taking the wild yam tablets. To my amazement, I experienced rapid relief.

'I continue to take a low dose of wild yam on a daily basis. My husband, who has had quite a bit of numbness and tingling in his shoulders and left arm and hand after a traumatic accident several years ago, also benefits from wild yam.

'Kudos to wild yam, and to you.'

tincture and take it according to the package directions. Or I'd buy capsules and take three of them three times a day. They're usually around 500 milligrams each.

CHILLI PEPPER (*CAPSICUM,* VARIOUS SPECIES). Red chilli pepper contains anti-inflammatory compounds and aspirin-like salicylates. But most of its pain-relieving kick – and its spicy-hot flavour – comes from a compound called capsaicin.

Capsaicin can cause pain on your tongue (or in your eye, if it finds its way there). But when rubbed into your skin at the site of pain, it blocks the transmission of pain signals through certain nerves by depleting them of substance P, a brain chemical.

Many studies have found that capsaicin helps control many types of chronic pain. In one study, 23 female patients with post-mastectomy

for the Gardener

Chilli Pepper

Capsicum, various species

You can probably grow your own chilli peppers. Sow the seeds indoors 6 to 8 weeks before the projected last frost. Barely press them into the potting soil, since they need light to germinate. You should have seedlings within 3 weeks.

Transplant the seedlings outdoors when the soil temperature has warmed to about 21°C (70°F) and the danger of frost has passed. Plant them 30 cm (12 inches) apart in rich, sandy loam. They prefer full sun, but they'll tolerate a little shade.

When harvesting chilli peppers, be sure to wear rubber gloves to avoid contact with the fruits' fiery compounds. Afterwards, wash your hands thoroughly before touching your eyes or nose. String up the peppers and hang them in a warm, dry place for several weeks. Once they're dry, you can grind them into a powder using a blender or a coffee grinder. Just be careful not to inhale the powder.

pain were treated with capsaicin. More than half of the women reported relief. In another study – this one examining the treatment of post-herpetic neuralgia, a type of nerve pain that can develop after a herpes infection – 19 of 39 people experienced relief after using a 0.025 per cent capsaicin cream for 8 weeks. A third study had 12 people with nerve pain from no apparent cause take a dose of capsaicin three times a day for several days. Six of the study participants reported complete relief, while another four experienced partial relief.

Some years ago, the FDA approved capsaicin ointments as treatments for pain. Several brands are available, such as Zostrix, which is marketed primarily for arthritis pain. Whichever product you choose, use it according to the package directions.

Of course, as a botanist, I like to stay as close to the plant as possible. This is why I grow chilli peppers in my garden.

CINNAMON (*CINNAMOMUM VERUM*). In tea or on toast, cinnamon has a warming, mildly spicy flavour. The herb also contains a number of pain-relieving compounds, including ascorbic acid, borneol, caffeic acid, camphor, eugenol, myrcene, p-cymene, and thiamin. My wife, Peggy, likes to take cinnamon for temporary relief of mild stomach pain. You can make a tea by adding 1 teaspoon of powdered cinnamon to 1 cup of freshly boiled water. Let it steep for 10 minutes, then strain out the plant material. Make sure that the tea has cooled slightly before drinking it.

BOSWELLIN/BOSWELLIA (*BOSWELLIA SERRATA*). Sometimes called Indian frankincense, boswellin is a traditional Ayurvedic remedy for arthritis and joint and muscle pain. Modern research has found that the herb contains both anti-inflammatory and pain-relieving compounds – notably boswellic acid. And animal studies have demonstrated the herb's strong pain-relieving action.

Naturopaths often recommend boswellin, and herb marketers often sell it in combination with curcumin, the anti-inflammatory compound in turmeric (more on turmeric later). If you're able to find such a product, use it according to the package directions.

MYRRH (*COMMIPHORA MOLMOOL*). Since ancient times, myrrh has played a role in perfumery, embalming, and medicine. The herb was recommended by Hippocrates, the father of medicine, as a treatment for mouth sores.

It turns out that Hippocrates was onto something. Research has confirmed that myrrh has several pain-relieving compounds, most notably curzerene and furano-eudesma-1.3-diene. These compounds bind to the same cell receptors in the brain as opiates, suggesting that myrrh has a mild opiate-like effect. In one laboratory study, animals treated with myrrh showed greater tolerance for pain than animals not given the herb.

So far, I've not been able to obtain true myrrh for my garden. But even if I had a tree, I wouldn't harvest it for medicinal purposes. Instead, I'd buy a commercial myrrh preparation and take it according to the label directions.

CLOVE (*SYZYGIUM AROMATICUM*). Clove oil is the classic toothache remedy. Even today, it remains popular among dentists. It's rich in eugenol, a potent pain-relieving compound. It also gets some painkilling punch from gallic acid, methyl salicylate, and quercetin.

If I had chronic pain, I'd add a dash of cloves to any pain-relieving tea – not only for its analgesic power but also for its very pleasant flavour.

CORIANDER (*CORIANDRUM SATIVUM*). This herb contains a number of pain-relieving compounds, including ascorbic acid, borneol, caffeic acid, camphor, chlorogenic acid, ferulic acid, myrcene, p-cymene, quercetin, scopoletin, thiamin, and tryptophan. I suggest adding a teaspoon or so to any pain-relieving tea.

I grow coriander in my garden. It's strongly aromatic, with annual white flowers.

TURMERIC (*CURCUMA LONGA*). For centuries, Ayurvedic doctors have prescribed turmeric as a treatment for pain and inflammation. American naturopaths often recommend the herb – or its pain-relieving, anti-inflammatory constituent, curcumin – for joint pain. Now even

More Wisdom *from the* Garden

Essential Oils Soothe Away Pain

Lavender oil isn't the only essential oil with pain-relieving effects. Personally, I believe that all of these oils have some analgesic and anaesthetic properties. My mother used to rub a drop or two of clove oil on my gums when I had a toothache. Rosemary oil has at least six anaesthetic compounds. In the Andes, people massage nutmeg oil into their painful joints.

Of course, I can't overlook peppermint oil, a proven pain reliever and anaesthetic. I've seen studies showing that peppermint oil rubbed into the temples produces headache relief comparable to a standard dose of paracetamol.

Whatever essential oil you choose, be sure to mix it with a carrier oil (such as vegetable oil) before applying it to the skin. This helps prevent irritation.

the pharmaceutical companies are jumping on the turmeric bandwagon. Sort of.

As I mentioned earlier, the latest innovation in pharmaceutical pain relievers is the COX-2 inhibitors, currently sold under the brand names Celebrex and Vioxx. They deliver all of the benefits of the old NSAIDs, but without the potentially serious gastrointestinal side effects.

Turmeric works because it contains natural COX-2-inhibiting compounds. In addition, the curcumin in turmeric depletes nerve endings of the brain chemical substance P, just like capsaicin does.

You can buy turmeric capsules, as well as curcumin capsules and tablets, in health food shops. The standard dose is 400 milligrams of curcumin three times day. But follow the label directions on the preparation that you buy.

For an extra dose of pain relief, use more turmeric in your cooking. This Indian spice gives curry blends their yellow colour. Experiment with some Indian recipes, going heavy on the curry blends.

GINGER (*ZINGIBER OFFICINALE*). A close botanical relative of turmeric, ginger has its own supply of COX-2-inhibiting compounds. It also shows great promise as a treatment for chronic pain.

In one study, researchers gave

Dr Duke's Anti-Ageing Elixir

Analgesic Tea

This brew delivers a potent pain-relieving punch, with no less than five ingredients that are loaded with COX-2 inhibitors and other proven analgesic compounds. Have a cup whenever you're aching for subtle, soothing relief.

WHAT YOU NEED

2 teaspoons cloves
2 teaspoons turmeric
1 teaspoon coriander
1 teaspoon cinnamon
1 piece fresh ginger
Dash of basil
1 litre (2 pints) water
Lemon
A natural sweetener (optional)

WHAT TO DO

In a pan, combine the cloves, turmeric, coriander, cinnamon, ginger, and basil. Add the water. Bring to the boil, then reduce the heat and simmer for 10 minutes. Strain out the plant material. Flavour with the lemon and sweetener, if you wish. Drink a cup at a time as needed, refrigerating any left over for reheating later on.

Dr Duke's Anti-Ageing Elixir

Herbal COX-2 Tonic

The new COX-2 inhibitors may be all the rage in pharmaceutical pain relief. But I can mix up my own COX-2-inhibiting remedy strictly from plant sources. You can, too.

WHAT YOU NEED

5 teaspoons ground ginger
5 teaspoons turmeric
Large dash of rosemary
Large dash of oregano
1–2 large glasses red wine

WHAT TO DO

Combine the ginger and turmeric, then add the rosemary and oregano. Steep the herbs in the red wine – which contains resveratrol, another COX-2 inhibitor – for up to 2 weeks. (The longer the herbs steep, the more potent the tonic becomes.) Strain out the plant material before using. Take by the dropperful, storing the leftovers in a cool, dark spot for later use.

ground ginger (3 to 7 grams, or $\frac{1}{10}$ to $\frac{1}{4}$ ounce, a day) to 28 people with rheumatoid arthritis and 18 with osteoarthritis. After treatment lasting from 3 to 30 months, more than 75 per cent of the study participants reported noticeable improvements in pain and swelling. None reported adverse effects from taking such large doses of the herb.

Health food stores sell ginger in capsule form. Take the capsules according to their label directions. In addition, use more ginger in your cooking and drink ginger tea. To make the tea, steep 1 to 2 teaspoons of freshly grated root in 1 cup of boiled water for 10 minutes. Strain out the plant material before drinking if you wish.

CALIFORNIA POPPY (*ESCHSCHOLZIA CALIFORNICA*). If I had muscle aches or fibromyalgia and I was being kept awake at night by the pain, I might try taking California poppy. It's a sedative with mild pain-relieving action. But it doesn't contain opium, like its more famous relative.

I've never used California poppy, but if I had chronic pain, I wouldn't hesitate to try it. I suggest making a tincture by placing a few ounces of the herb in a pint of vodka and letting it steep for a week or so. Take 15 to 30 drops as needed for pain.

LAVENDER (*LAVANDULA*, VARIOUS SPECIES). The pain-relieving power of lavender oil was first discovered by René-Maurice Gattefosse, a French perfume chemist, after he accidentally burned his arm while working in his laboratory. Frantic with pain, he plunged his arm into the nearest liquid, which happened to be a bowl of lavender oil. Not only did the pain subside almost immediately, but the burn healed remarkably quickly, with little scarring.

That incident led to the birth of modern aromatherapy. To this day, aromatherapists continue to use lavender essential oil as a treatment for pain. Modern research has found that the oil interacts with cell membranes to increase their volume. This closes off ion channels, inhibiting the transmission of pain impulses through nerves.

To use lavender oil, just mix a few drops into an emollient such as vegetable oil and rub it onto the skin at the site of pain. You can also mix the oil into an unscented skin cream and apply it that way. Just don't ingest lavender oil – or any essential oil, for that matter. Surprisingly small amounts, less than a teaspoon, can be toxic. For this reason, essential oils must be kept out of the reach of children.

CHAPTER 44

Prostate Problems

Dr Duke's Anti-Ageing Elixir
• *Fruit-Full Prostate Tonic*

At 72, I have yet to experience any serious problems with my prostate. It may just be good fortune, but I prefer to credit a combination of healthy living and herbs – especially saw palmetto.

But what if you've already been diagnosed with prostate enlargement or prostate cancer? You can still benefit from many of the same natural strategies that help prevent prostate trouble in the first place.

Prostate Enlargement: Giving New Meaning to 'Get-Up-and-Go'

Sometime after a man turns 40, his prostate begins to grow, the result of age-related hormonal changes. This condition, called benign prostate hyperplasia (BPH), causes urinary symptoms – trouble getting started, trouble finishing (dribbling), and – the big one – frequent nighttime wake-ups to urinate. Most men can live with getting up once or twice a night. But when BPH progresses to the point where it's causing three or four bathroom runs nightly, most men want treatment.

Traditionally, doctors performed surgery to remove the pieces of the prostate that were pinching the urine tube, or urethra. More recently, they've begun prescribing drugs, especially finasteride (Proscar). But in the studies that I've seen, certain herbs deliver the same benefits as Proscar, but without the cost and side effects. And they're definitely a viable alternative to surgery, with its inherent trauma and risks.

Both herbal and pharmaceutical treatments work by interfering with the action of 5-alpha-reductase, an enzyme that triggers the conversion of testosterone into dihydrotestosterone. This hormone is responsible for the overgrowth of prostate tissue that's characteristic of BPH.

Herbs That Pamper Your Prostate

If you've already read chapter 19, you know that saw palmetto is my herb of choice for preventing and treating prostate enlargement. I know that it works, from personal experience. But other herbs are good for the prostate, too. Here are the ones that I recommend.

SAW PALMETTO (*SERENOA REPENS*). Saw palmetto is a small palm tree native to Southeast America. Florida's Seminole Indians ate the tree's seeds as food. The seeds contain beta-sitosterol as well as other plant sterols (phytosterols), all of which are potent 5-alpha-reductase inhibitors.

Dozens of European studies have found saw palmetto to be an effective treatment for BPH. One of the most impressive trials, conducted at 87 urology clinics in nine European countries, tested a standard European saw palmetto extract (Permixon, a French preparation) head-to-head against the pharmaceutical 5-alpha-reductase inhibitor Proscar. The researchers gave the 1,098 study participants either 160 milligrams of the herb twice a day or 5 milligrams of the drug a day (the standard dose). After 26 weeks, both treatments showed about equal effectiveness, with Proscar decreasing BPH symptoms by 39 per cent, and saw palmetto, by 37 per cent. Urine flow improved in 30 per cent of the men taking the drug, compared with 25 per cent of the men taking the herb.

But saw palmetto caused fewer side effects such as erection impairment and loss of libido.

Of course, in the United States, mainstream doctors are much more likely to recommend Proscar or surgery than saw palmetto to their patients with BPH. My friend Rob McCaleb of the Herb Research Foundation did some very interesting cost calculations for the various BPH treatments. Surgery has a price tag of more than $5,000, while Proscar and another pharmaceutical, Hytrin, run at about $650 a year. By comparison, saw palmetto comes in at about $255 a year.

While public officials and consumer advocates rally around the high cost of health care, most doctors are reluctant to make a very cheap, very effective herb their treatment of choice for BPH. So the nation continues to spend billions of dollars a year on one of its most common health problems. It's such a shame.

From what I've read in the medical literature, you need only 40 to 60 milligrams of sitosterols per day to experience saw palmetto's prostate benefits. I'd wager that you could get that much just by eating my Even Better Prosnut Butter (see recipe on page 220). Still, you should see your doctor for proper diagnosis before beginning self-treatment with saw palmetto.

PYGEUM (*PYGEUM AFRICANUM*). Also known as African wild cherry, pygeum is a 5-alpha-reductase inhibitor, like saw palmetto. In one study, researchers gave 263 men with BPH either a placebo (a fake pill) or 100 milligrams of a standardised pygeum extract a day. After 60 days, 31 per cent of the men in the placebo group reported improvement in their symptoms, compared with 66 per cent of the men in the herb group.

To treat BPH, the standard dosage of pygeum is 50 milligrams of a bark extract twice a day. But I suggest buying a commercial preparation and taking it according to the label directions.

STINGING NETTLE (*URTICA DIOICA*). Herbalists often recommend taking the herb pygeum in combination with stinging nettle. This is because some studies have shown that for improving urine flow, the two herbs together work better than pygeum alone. Stinging nettle appears to help by inhibiting certain enzymes involved in the overgrowth of prostate tissue.

Two rigorous clinical trials and eight other observational studies confirm stinging nettle's effectiveness, leading to its endorsement by Commission E, the expert panel that evaluates the safety and effectiveness of herbs for the German government. If you want to try stinging nettle, I suggest buying a commercial preparation and using it according to the label directions.

EVENING PRIMROSE (*OENOTHERA BIENNIS*). Evening primrose has a reputation as a 'women's herb'. After all, its oil helps relieve premenstrual syndrome, menstrual cramps, and even menopausal discomforts. But according to at least one study that I've reviewed, evening primrose oil shows promise as a treatment for BPH. That's because it's rich in gamma-linolenic acid (GLA), which is a 5-alpha-reductase inhibitor.

A number of evening primrose oil products are on the market. Choose one standardised to GLA and take it according to the label directions.

KUDZU (*PUERARIA MONTANA*). A plant is considered a weed when it grows where it's not wanted. As I like to say, 'If you need a weed, it ain't a weed anymore.' This certainly applies to kudzu, an Asian vine that has invaded the southern United States and become a major pest plant in many states.

But although kudzu is running roughshod over my native Alabama, I don't condemn it as a weed. On the contrary, I think it's a valuable medicinal herb. It contains high levels of genistein, a potent 5-alpha-reductase inhibitor.

If you can find kudzu as a commercial preparation, take it according to the label directions. If you live in an area where kudzu grows wild, you may want to harvest some leaves and add them to juice blends.

STARGRASS (*HYPOXIS ROOPERI*). Like saw palmetto, stargrass is a good source of beta-sitosterol. In Germany, stargrass is often combined with saw palmetto, stinging nettle, and pumpkin seeds as a treatment for BPH.

Stargrass is not that easy to find. If you come across it, check the label. It should contain 40 to 60 milligrams of beta-sitosterol, the effective amount.

Foods That Keep the Swelling in Check

To boost the effectiveness of your herbal prostate protection regime, I recommend eating more pulses and pumpkin seeds. Both foods contain compounds that have proven themselves quite effective in relieving BPH symptoms.

PUMPKIN SEEDS (*CUCURBITA PEPO*). The people of Bulgaria, Turkey, and the Ukraine have traditionally used pumpkin seeds to prevent and treat BPH. The standard 'dosage' is a handful of seeds a day throughout adulthood.

The fatty oil in pumpkin seeds is a diuretic, which prompted some herb critics to assert that the increased urine flow brought on by the seeds has nothing to do with the shrinkage of overgrown prostate tissue. But pumpkin seeds also contain cucurbitacins, chemicals that appear to be 5-alpha-reductase inhibitors. As a bonus, the seeds are rich in zinc, a mineral that's crucial to the male reproductive system. Naturopaths often recommend zinc supplements as part of a comprehensive BPH treatment programme.

Commission E approves pumpkin seeds (10 grams of ground seed or the equivalent) to relieve the urinary symptoms associated with BPH. Around Halloween, I often roast pumpkin seeds and munch them. I also buy them when I can. The seeds are an ingredient in my Even Better Prosnut Butter (see page 220).

PULSES. Almost all edible pulses contain genistein, a compound that's best known as a phyto-oestrogen (plant oestrogen). It's also a 5-alpha-reductase inhibitor, so it can help control BPH symptoms.

I'm quite fond of pulses, and I eat lots of them – in soups, salads, and other dishes. But I must admit that I've made a point of staying off the soya bean bandwagon. In recent years, soya has received a lot of attention because of its many health benefits, most notably its ability to lower cholesterol and minimise menopausal hot flushes. It owes its reputation, at least in part, to the genistein that it contains.

What bothers me is that all of the studies involving soya were financed by the soya industry. They neglected to point out that probably all edible pulses bestow the same health benefits. In fact, many pulses have even more genistein than soya beans. Among the best sources are black beans, lima beans, kidney beans, and lentils.

Prostate Cancer: More Common Than Guys Realise

While prostate enlargement is uncomfortable and bothersome, it's seldom as serious as prostate cancer. This is the second most commonly diagnosed cancer in the UK – the lifetime risk of being diagnosed with it is 1 in 14.

The rate of prostate cancer is rising, but no one really knows why. Some experts blame an unhealthy lifestyle, characterised by a diet high in saturated fat and a lack of exercise. Others point to screening for cancer-related prostate-specific antigen, which has enabled unusually early detection of the disease. Both factors probably play roles, though the incidence of prostate cancer was increasing dramatically even before the measurement of prostate-specific antigen was possible.

More Wisdom *from the* Garden

Prostate Protection Straight from the Rainforest

I've always enjoyed Brazil nuts. As a result of my work in the Amazon, I eat even more of the nuts than I used to, and I urge others to do the same. The harvesting of Brazil nuts helps preserve my beloved rainforest.

In 1997, epidemiologists reported that 200 micrograms of selenium a day could protect against the three cancers that I'm most likely to get: colon cancer (because my father and two of his brothers died from it), lung cancer (because I smoked three packs of cigarettes a day for more than 30 years), and prostate cancer (because I'm a 72-year-old male).

One of the best sources of selenium is – you guessed it – Brazil nuts. I figure that three average-size Brazil nuts deliver the 200 micrograms of selenium that might save me from the cancers for which I'm at greatest risk.

Bolster Treatment with Dietary Changes

If you've been diagnosed with prostate cancer, you absolutely should be receiving professional medical care. In consultation with your doctor, you may want to incorporate some of the following nutritional strategies into your treatment programme.

Cut back on saturated fat. In animal studies, a diet high in saturated fat – the kind of fat found in meats and dairy products – appears to promote the growth of prostate cancer. American and British men eat a lot more saturated fat than Japanese men do. Not surprisingly, they are nine times more likely to die from prostate cancer.

Scientists have not yet determined whether saturated fat is solely at fault or whether the pesticides that accumulate in animal fat contribute to prostate cancer. I suspect that both factors are involved.

Replace animal products with plant foods. Besides being naturally low in saturated fat, plant foods – particularly fruits and vegetables – are richly endowed with cancer-fighting antioxidant nutrients. My Healthy Sevens eating plan features an abundance of plant foods. To learn more about it, see chapter 3.

Put tomatoes at the top of your shopping list. When Harvard researcher Edward Giovannucci analysed health data collected from thousands of middle-aged men, he found that compared with those who seldom ate tomatoes or tomato products, those who ate tomatoes in some form 4 to 7 times a

Dr Duke's Anti-Ageing Elixir

Fruit-Full Prostate Tonic

Tomatoes may be the best source of lycopene. But they don't have a monopoly on the cancer-fighting nutrient. In fact, it's found in many red fruits, including the watermelon and pink grapefruit in this recipe.

WHAT YOU NEED

2 parts watermelon chunks

1 part pink grapefruit sections

WHAT TO DO

In a blender, liquify the watermelon and pink grapefruit, along with a few seeds from each. For some reason, the lycopene is better absorbed when accompanied by the seed oil. Drink one cup at a time, refrigerating any left over for later use.

week were 20 per cent less likely to develop prostate cancer. Men who ate tomatoes 8 to 20 times a week had 45 per cent less chance of getting the disease.

Corroborating evidence comes from a major study of Seventh-Day Adventists, whose religion advocates vegetarianism. The more tomatoes and tomato products the Adventist men consumed, the lower their risk of prostate cancer.

Tomatoes contain lycopene, a carotenoid (in the same family as beta-carotene) that appears to protect against prostate cancer. Any form of tomato can help – fresh or tinned, in sauces and in soups. Even the sauce on pizza is good for you, as long as you go easy on the meat toppings, which are high in saturated fat.

For a two-barrelled attack on prostate cancer, I suggest making a sandwich with my Even Better Prosnut Butter (see recipe on page 220) and washing it down with a glass of tomato juice. For myself, I like to munch cherry tomatoes right off the vine. Last summer, my lone cherry tomato plant produced at least 30 fruits a day. That's lots of fresh, delicious cherry tomatoes for me, and lots of lycopene for my prostate.

Become a bean connoisseur. Prostate cancer is usually treated surgically. But it can also be treated with female sex hormones. The problem with this approach is feminisation – primarily enlarged breasts and fat deposits on the hips, plus possibly a higher-pitched voice.

Recently, Finnish researchers tried a natural version of hormone therapy, using phyto-oestrogens from soya. The researchers implanted human prostate cancer cells under the skin of mice. Then some of the animals were fed a soya-based diet, while the others ate their usual food. After 10 weeks, the tumours in the mice treated with soya were only half as large as the tumours in the untreated mice. What's more, the tumours were significantly less likely to have spread.

I find this study exciting for two reasons and disappointing for one. On the plus side, if these results can be replicated in humans, the phyto-oestrogens in soya are much less potent than the oestrogen used in conventional hormone therapy, which means that the treatment is less likely to cause feminisation. As a bonus, one of the phyto-oestrogens, genistein, can help fight cancer by preventing the growth of new blood vessels to nourish tumours.

On the downside, the study focused solely on soya beans, when in fact almost every edible bean contains phyto-oestrogens, including genistein. I eat all kinds of beans, and I suggest that any man who wants to fight prostate cancer do the same.

Create a Lifestyle That Supports Prostate Health

To round out your treatment programme, I recommend the following lifestyle strategies. They've been shown to prevent prostate cancer, so I suspect that they'll help beat the disease as well.

Get plenty of exercise. It's true: regular exercise can protect against prostate cancer. I saw one study suggesting that walking 10 miles a week significantly lowers a man's risk of the disease. I like this finding, because I put in at least 10 miles a week – if not more – just taking laps around my farm and working in my Garden of Youth.

If you drink, do so in moderation. Moderate alcohol consumption – defined as no more than two drinks a day – has no apparent impact on prostate cancer. But the more you imbibe, the more likely you are to get the disease. Heavy drinkers – those who down more than seven drinks a day – are twice as likely to be diagnosed with prostate cancer as light drinkers are. (A drink is defined as 360 ml/12 fl oz of regular beer, 150 ml/5 fl oz of wine, or a cocktail made with 45 ml/1½ fl oz of 80-proof distilled spirits.)

If you smoke, quit. Smoking makes you more likely to get prostate cancer – and more likely to die from the disease. Among men who smoke up to a pack a day, the risk of death from prostate cancer rises by 21 per cent. Among those who smoke more than that, the risk jumps by 45 per cent.

CHAPTER 45

Vaginitis *and* Vaginal Dryness

Dr Duke's Anti-Ageing Elixirs

- *Outwit-Trich Wash*
- *Antiseptic Anti-Vaginitis Wash*

Vaginitis and vaginal dryness are two different conditions and usually unrelated. But sometimes treatments for the former – both herbal and pharmaceutical – can set the stage for the latter. That's why I've decided to discuss both here.

Vaginitis: One Name, Many Ailments

Vaginitis is an umbrella term for several conditions that involve the inflammation of the mucosal lining of the vagina. They include yeast infection (candidiasis), bacterial vaginosis, and trichomoniasis.

By most estimates, vaginitis accounts for more than half of all gynaecological visits. Yeast infection is the most common diagnosis. Bacterial vaginosis doesn't occur as often, but if it happens to affect a pregnant woman, it can have serious consequences. The infection increases the risk of premature birth by 40 per cent. Trichomoniasis is commonly viewed as a sexually transmitted disease, though it can be contracted in other ways as well. While all three forms of vaginitis may seem most common in younger women, I suspect that they're quite prevalent in older women, too.

Some women recognise which form of vaginitis they have just by the symptoms they experience. Other women have difficulty distinguishing one infection from the other, because any of them can cause itching, burning, and a white, cottage cheese–like discharge.

If you suspect that you have any kind of vaginitis, your best bet is to consult a doctor for a proper diagnosis. Most likely, you'll receive a prescription for antibiotics – antifungals for yeast infection, antibacterials for bacterial vaginosis, or antiprotozoans for trichomoniasis. Some broad-spectrum antibiotic medications combat more than one infectious invader. Others are effective against one germ but do nothing to eradicate another.

Opt for the Herbal Infection-Fighters

If you're diagnosed with vaginitis, don't overlook your herbal treatment options. Some herbs actually enhance the potency of antibiotics. Others may provide sufficient relief from symptoms, making pharmaceutical treatment unnecessary.

ECHINACEA (*ECHINACEA*, VARIOUS SPECIES). In a German study, women with yeast infection were instructed to use a standard pharmaceutical antifungal medication (econazole nitrate). Some of the women were also given echinacea. Of those treated with the antifungal alone, 61 per cent had at least one recurrence of yeast infection. Of those treated with the pharmaceutical plus echinacea, only 16 per cent experienced a recurrence.

Commission E, the expert panel that evaluates the safety and effectiveness of herbs for the German government, approves echinacea as supportive treatment – meaning, as a supplement to antibiotics – for urinary tract infections. Going by the study mentioned above, I'd say that the herb is good for yeast infection as well. It contains cichoric acid, which stimulates infection-fighting white blood cells to gobble up more germs. Some herbalists recommend taking echinacea as a tincture – 1 to 2 dropperfuls in water or juice, up to five times a day. Others favour capsules, taken according to the label directions.

GARLIC (*ALLIUM SATIVUM*). Garlic is rich in antibiotic and antifungal compounds, which is why it's so effective for healing vaginitis. Women herbalists whom I know and respect often suggest wrapping a peeled clove in gauze and inserting it into the vagina overnight to treat yeast infection and bacterial vaginosis. Some also recommend soaking a tampon in a blend of fresh garlic juice and acidophilus yogurt and inserting it overnight. And they advise eating lots of fresh garlic – 12 to 20 cloves a day. As much as I love garlic, I couldn't eat that much. But I'm fairly certain it would help. Just be aware that eating this amount of garlic can cause gastric distress.

GOLDENSEAL (*HYDRASTIS CANADENSIS*). Goldenseal is a potent herbal antibiotic. It seems to work best for digestive problems such as amoebic dysentery, cholera, and giardiasis. But according to one study that I've reviewed, the antibiotic compound in goldenseal, berberine sulphate, is also effective against trichomoniasis.

To treat trichomoniasis, mainstream doctors typically prescribe metronidazole. It works, but it can cause nasty side effects, especially if you happen to drink alcohol while taking it. In my opinion, berberine, if not whole goldenseal, might be a better choice for many women with trichomoniasis.

I suggest using whole goldenseal both orally and topically. I'd brew a tea made with about 3 grams of root, letting it steep for 10 minutes before straining out the plant material. Then I'd either drink it or apply it with a clean cloth after it has cooled. You can also buy a commercial goldenseal preparation and use it according to the package directions. Many herb companies manufacture goldenseal tinctures. I've also seen goldenseal-echinacea combination products. Actually, adding echinacea to any goldenseal treatment should definitely help treat infection.

TEA TREE (*MELALEUCA*, VARIOUS SPECIES). Tea tree oil is a powerful antiseptic and antibiotic. It appears to work even better against yeast than against bacteria. Australian chemists have determined that it takes only about one-fifth as much tea tree oil to defeat yeast as to eradicate the bacteria *Staphylococcus aureus*.

More Wisdom *from the* Garden

Goldenseal

Hydrastis canadensis

After years of overharvesting, goldenseal has become an endangered species in the wild. You can grow your own from seed, but bear in mind that the roots may take up to 5 years to become mature enough to harvest.

Stratify freshly collected seeds for 3 months before sowing. (In stratification, seeds are kept in moist but not waterlogged soil, so they can continue developing without drying out.) If you plant the seeds in trays and let them stratify outdoors, you should have seedlings by spring. Allow them to grow until the autumn of their second year, then separate them and plant them 15 cm (6 inches) apart.

If you want your goldenseal crop more quickly and you don't mind paying the price, you can purchase 2-year-old dormant root divisions. Plant them 30 cm (12 inches) apart in autumn.

In order to thrive, goldenseal needs a growing environment that mimics a mixed hardwood forest: deep, rich loam; at least 70 per cent shade; and a mulch of chopped well-rotted leaves. Water occasionally to keep the soil moist but not soggy.

Harvest goldenseal roots in the autumn, when the tops die back. Save the biggest roots for replanting. Wash the rest in water and dry them on a screen in a shaded area with good air circulation. Store them in sealed plastic bags or jars. Whole roots can keep for at least 5 years.

You can also harvest goldenseal's leaves and stems in the fall, before the leaves begin to wither. Allow them to dry, then store them in plastic or glass containers.

Still, tea tree oil may prove helpful as a treatment for bacterial vaginosis. One case study reported in the British medical journal *Lancet* described a 40-year-old woman with bacterial vaginosis. After using tea tree vaginal suppositories (200 milligrams of tea tree oil in a vegetable oil base) for 5 days, she was deemed cured.

Of course, one case study isn't a whole lot for tea tree to hang its hat on. But I've heard other testimonials in support of tea tree oil for vaginitis, so I'm persuaded that it can help. Women herbalists whom I respect suggest this treatment for recurrent yeast infections: 2 to 3 drops of tea tree oil in 1 teaspoon of honey (another natural antibiotic), applied vaginally twice a day for 3 days. Take a break for 4 days, then repeat.

Another treatment option is to soak a tampon in acidophilus yogurt and 2 to 3 drops of tea tree oil, then insert it overnight. Repeat for up to 6 nights in a row.

CAMOMILE (*MATRICARIA RECUTITA*). Commission E approves camomile for several conditions that cause skin inflammation, including bacterial infections and anal and genital irritations. Certain compounds in the herb – chamazulene, alpha-bisabolol, and apigenin – are potent anti-inflammatories. No wonder many European women treat vaginitis with a camomile douche, typically made as a tea from 30–60 g (1 to 2 ounces) of camomile flowers per litre of water. I'd recommend letting the herbs

Dr Duke's Anti-Ageing Elixir

Outwit-Trich Wash

The ingredients in this recipe are among the best medicinal herbs for treating trichomoniasis. They contain a number of compounds that help combat the protozoan (*Trichomonas vaginalis*) that causes trich.

WHAT YOU NEED

Any combination of the following herbs: clary sage, cornmint, lavender, marjoram, oregano, rosemary, peppermint, sage, savory, and thyme

1 cup water

WHAT TO DO

Combine the herbs of your choice. Add 1 to 2 teaspoons of your herb blend to the freshly boiled water. Steep until cool, then strain out the plant material. Apply the tea as a compress or use it as a douche. (If you choose the latter, remember to discontinue douching as soon as your infection subsides.)

Dr Duke's Anti-Ageing Elixir

Antiseptic Anti-Vaginitis Wash

The lovely labiates, members of the mint family, are so named because most of them have two-lipped flowers. They are not only pleasantly aromatic but also antiseptic. I would recommend this wash, made with labiates, for any kind of vaginitis.

WHAT YOU NEED

Any combination of the following herbs: basil, horsemint, oregano, peppermint, savory, and thyme

1 cup water

WHAT TO DO

Combine the herbs of your choice. Add 1 to 2 teaspoons of your herb blend to the freshly boiled water. Steep until cool, then strain out the plant material. Apply as a compress or use as a douche. (If you opt for the latter, remember to stop douching as soon as your symptoms subside.)

steep overnight, to extract more of the active compounds. Strain out the plant material before using.

Use this type of douche *only* when you have vaginitis. Douching is not necessary or appropriate for routine feminine hygiene. It raises the risk of pelvic inflammatory disease, a serious infection of the reproductive organs.

CALENDULA (*CALENDULA OFFICINALIS*). The flowers of calendula have a long history as a treatment for inflammation. Certain compounds in the herb have demonstrated some antibacterial activity, especially against staphylococcus.

Naturopaths recommend washing the vulva and vagina with calendula juice. I suggest throwing some calendula flowers into a blender and processing them until they're a pastelike consistency. You can apply this paste to the vaginal area. You may also be able to find calendula salves in health food stores. Use the salve according to the label directions.

BLACK WALNUT (*JUGLANS NIGRA*). In one study, the fresh husk of black walnut destroyed the fungi that cause yeast infection better than a commonly prescribed antifungal medication. Californian herbalist/aromatherapist Kathy Keville suggests applying a tincture made from 30 g (1 ounce) each of black walnut husk, lavender flowers, valerian root, and pau d'arco, plus 10 drops of tea tree oil. Add vodka to cover, then place in a cool, dark spot to steep. After 1 to 2 weeks, the

More Wisdom *from the* Garden

A Vinegar Bath Soothes Away Symptoms

Many women herbalists, including Jeanne Rose, suggest treating vaginitis by bathing in a blend of vinegar and essential oils. Vinegar is a weak acid that makes the vaginal environment more acidic and less hospitable to the germs that cause vaginitis. The essential oils are antibiotics that help finish off the germs.

Rose suggests adding 3 cups of vinegar and 5 drops each of tea tree, lavender, and camomile essential oils to a hot bath. Sit in the water and spread your legs to allow the water to flow into your vagina. Repeat once a day for as long as symptoms persist, then discontinue treatment.

Based on some studies that I've seen, I'd suggest using a different trio of essential oils for trichomoniasis. Follow the same instructions as above, substituting 3 drops each of thyme, eucalyptus, and rosemary oils for tea tree, lavender, and camomile.

tincture is ready for use. You can apply it externally as needed, perhaps dabbing it on with a cotton wool ball.

Vaginal Dryness: Common When Oestrogen Runs Low

While vaginitis is brought on by an infection of one sort or another, vaginal dryness occurs because of a shortage or lack of natural vaginal lubrication. Without lubrication, your vagina can become irritated, and intercourse can be painful.

As I mentioned earlier, vaginal dryness can be triggered by various pharmaceutical and herbal treatments for vaginitis. It is also among several common signs of a dwindling supply of the female hormone oestrogen. (Others include absence of menstruation, cramping during menstruation, heavy periods, spotting between periods, and osteoporosis.) Low oestrogen levels often indicate the onset of menopause, which is why vaginal dryness is particularly problematic among older women. But a shortage of oestrogen and vaginal dryness can also result from smoking, strenuous physical activity (like athletic training), severe emotional stress, and nutritional deficiencies.

To treat vaginal dryness, doctors usually prescribe hormone-replacement therapy or hormonal creams. Of the two options, I'd advise using the creams.

Oral hormone replacement does indeed increase oestrogen levels and vaginal lubrication. As a bonus, it may help prevent heart attack, osteoporosis, and Alzheimer's disease. But in exchange, it increases the risk of breast cancer. It also has some unpleasant side effects, including fluid retention, breast tenderness, irritability, and weight gain. These may be as troublesome as the menopausal discomforts that hormone replacement treats.

The decision of whether or not to use hormone-replacement therapy is very individual. You need to discuss the pros and cons with your doctor, based on your own health history, symptoms, and risk factors. Personally, I favour a more natural approach to hormone replacement and vaginal dryness treatment, featuring foods and herbs that contain phyto-oestrogens (plant oestrogens).

Before You Try Hormone Replacement...

If you're bothered by vaginal dryness, you may get significant relief just by incorporating these measures into your lifestyle. They restore vaginal lubrication naturally, possibly eliminating the need for hormone replacement.

Pack your diet with phyto-oestrogens. A number of plant foods contain phyto-oestrogens, which are similar to your body's own oestrogen. They occupy the same receptors on cells, signalling the hypothalamus and the pituitary gland that your body has enough oestrogen. In this way, they help prevent vaginal dryness and other symptoms of an oestrogen shortage.

Among the best-known food sources of phyto-oestrogens are apples, beans, broccoli, brussels sprouts, cabbage, celery, nuts, and whole grains. Among the herbs, alfalfa, anise, black cohosh, dong quai, fennel, hops, licorice, and red clover have ample supplies.

Broaden your bean repertoire. Of all the plant sources of phyto-oestrogens, beans are the most misunderstood. Soya beans and foods made with them have been touted as the best sources of phyto-oestrogens. They're not. Almost all edible beans contain generous amounts of the compounds. And some have even more than soya.

Take extra vitamin E. Vaginal dryness can improve with supplementation, especially vitamin E. I've seen studies in which a daily oral dose of 400 IU helped about 50 per cent of women with vaginal dryness in about a month.

Some naturopaths suggest topical application of vitamin E as well. You can break open a capsule and apply the contents directly to your labia, or you can buy a vitamin E cream and use that.

Herbalist Jeanne Rose suggests combining vitamin E with a comfrey ointment and applying it to the labia before sex. Sounds good to me, though you may have to hunt around for a comfrey ointment.

Increase your vitamin C, too. In one study, 900 menopausal women were given 1,200 milligrams of vitamin C plus 1,200 milligrams of citrus flavonoids. Half of the women reported fewer hot flushes. I'd wager that they had less vaginal dryness as well. If you want to try vitamin C to relieve vaginal dryness, most naturopaths recommend taking 300 milligrams a day.

Try topical applications of black cohosh. As I mentioned earlier, black cohosh is an excellent source of phyto-oestrogens. In addition to taking the herb orally, you might try it as a topical ointment. It may help relieve vaginal dryness. If you can't find the ointment in a health food store, you may want to check with a herbalist.

Take steps to control stress. Emotional stress triggers the release of the hormone adrenaline, which directs blood away from the central body and into your limbs. It's all part of the fight-or-flight response, which primes your body to cope with a stressful situation either by escape or self-defence.

The release of adrenaline also channels blood away from your vagina. With less blood circulating through the vagina, there's less blood fluid (plasma) to contribute to vaginal lubrication. That's why managing stress is so important when treating vaginal dryness.

If you douche regularly, stop. I've already cautioned against douching as routine feminine hygiene. I'd especially discourage it if you have a problem with vaginal dryness. The repeated application of douche water eventually dries vaginal tissues by rinsing away beneficial lubrication.

If you smoke, stop. Smoking constricts your blood vessels, including the ones located in your vaginal wall. This accelerates vaginal atrophy and the loss of vaginal lubrication, especially after menopause. Smoking also contributes to hormonal changes that aggravate vaginal dryness.

Include sex in your treatment plan. Regular sexual intercourse helps keep your vaginal tissues toned and healthy, which in turn keeps vaginal lubrication flowing. Sex is also relaxing, which helps reduce stress and the vaginal dryness that it can cause.

CHAPTER 46

Varicose Veins

Dr Duke's Anti-Ageing Elixir
• *Vein-Ade*

Varicose veins are the twisted, spidery, bluish-purplish lines – some big, some minute – that typically develop on the calves and along the inside of the legs. Veins in other parts of the body can become varicose as well. Haemorrhoids, for example, are varicosities around the anus. And varicoceles are varicosities in a man's scrotum. For our purposes, though, we'll use the phrase varicose veins to refer to varicosities in the legs.

What Goes Down Can't Get Up

Veins near the surface of the skin in your legs become varicose when their valves stop working properly. These valves are supposed to help your leg muscles return blood to your heart, against gravity.

Any leg movement contracts your leg muscles, pushing blood up through your veins. The valves in these veins act like gates, opening to allow blood to pass, then closing to keep blood from flowing backward. But if a valve doesn't close properly, blood can pool in the vein. This stretches and twists the vein, causing it to become varicose.

Another factor that contributes to the formation of varicose veins is the overproduction of so-called lysosomal enzymes. When levels of these enzymes run high, it destroys the 'glue' that holds veins together. This allows your veins to become distorted and swollen.

Varicose veins affect a large proportion of the population, many of them women over 45. You can get them if you're younger, though, especially if they run in your family. The condition has a strong genetic component.

Besides genetics, anything that impairs the movement of blood up your legs also raises your risk of varicose veins. Sitting or standing in one place for long periods is a big factor, because your leg muscles have to move in order to push blood towards your heart. Being overweight is another big factor. The excess body tissue compresses veins, inhibiting upward bloodflow. (Mums-to-be often develop varicose veins that usually go away on their own shortly after childbirth.)

First-Choice Treatments – And the Last Resort

If you have varicose veins, you can do yourself the world of good just by getting more exercise. Any physical activity that works your leg muscles will do: walking, swimming, bicycling, dancing, and gardening, to name just a few. They help pump blood through your leg veins and towards your heart, so it can't pool and form varicosities.

If you have a job that keeps you in one position for long periods, make a point of moving around. If you stand on an assembly line, for example, try jogging in place for a few minutes every hour. If you sit at a desk, stand up and pace while you're talking on the phone.

You can also help your varicose veins by wearing support stockings. This specially designed hosiery gently squeezes your legs, so the valves inside the leg veins close more completely.

For really severe or painful varicose veins, doctors may recommend surgery to remove the affected veins. Sometimes surgery is necessary. But in my opinion, it should be a last resort. Before consenting to go under the knife, I'd want to explore all of my herbal options.

Herbs for Healthy Veins

Now herbal medicine rarely works miracles with varicosities. It probably won't make your purple lines vanish completely. But herbs can strengthen veins so they hold together better and don't become swollen and twisted. In this way, herbs provide some relief from the uncomfortable symptoms of varicose veins.

If I had varicose veins, I'd try the following:

VIOLET (*VIOLA*, VARIOUS SPECIES). *The Merck Manual* is a standard medical textbook for doctors. The seventh edition states quite clearly that the compound rutin helps strengthen veins and so may play a role in the treatment and prevention of varicosities. According to the manual, an oral dose of as little as 20 to 100 milligrams – less than $\frac{1}{300}$ of an ounce – can protect against the changes that contribute to vein problems, especially varicosities.

I find this very interesting because dried violet flowers are rich in rutin, delivering the compound at a rate of 20,000 to 230,000 parts per million. Typically, the fresh flowers provide only about 10 per cent of that amount because they contain so much water. Doing the mathematics, I figure that fresh violets supply rutin at a rate of 2,000 to 23,000 parts per million. So 100 grams of the flowers would contain between 200 and 2,300 milligrams of the compound. To get the maximum of 100 milligrams that the seventh edition of *The Merck Manual* recommends, I'd need only about 50 flowers. Other top-notch sources of rutin include pansy flowers and eucalyptus leaves.

You might have heard that eating violet flowers can make you sick. I disagree, because I've tried them myself numerous times. I grow violets in my Garden of Youth, and I enjoy munching on the blossoms. In fact, I've eaten as many as 50 flowers at lunch on several different occasions, and I've yet to experience any ill effects. The roots nauseated me, but the flowers didn't. I suppose that a person with a very sensitive stomach might get queasy. But most folks won't.

On the other hand, if you're leery of eating violet flowers 'straight', you could just as well make them into a tea. Fill a cup halfway with flowers, then fill it to the top with boiling water. Steep for 10 minutes, then strain out the plant material. Add lemon to taste, if you wish.

BUCKWHEAT (*FAGOPYRUM ESCULENTUM*). Buckwheat is another excellent source of rutin. A 100-gram serving could deliver up to 6,000 milligrams of the compound, many times more than the seventh edition of *The Merck Manual* recommends to strengthen varicose veins.

I don't grow my own buckwheat. It's not a particularly attractive plant, especially when compared with lovely violet flowers. But I have made buckwheat pancakes. I doubt there's much rutin left after the grain has been processed into flour. But I suspect there's enough to bestow vein-strengthening effects.

HORSE CHESTNUT (*AESCULUS HIPPOCASTANUM*). The seeds of the horse chestnut plant have a long history in folk medicine as a treatment for varicose veins. They contain aescin, a compound that strengthens vein walls and increases their elasticity. This helps prevent varicosities.

In one study, researchers gave 22 people with leaky veins – the kind that become varicose – either a placebo (a fake pill) or 600 milligrams of horse chestnut extract containing 50 milligrams of aescin. Three hours later, fluid leakage had increased among those who had taken the placebo. But among those who had taken the extract, fluid leakage had *decreased* by 22 per cent, indicating a strengthening of their veins.

This study is one of several that prompted Commission E, the expert panel that evaluates the safety and effectiveness of herbs for the German government, to endorse horse chestnut extract as a treatment for varicose veins. The typical dose is 50 milligrams of aescin three times a day. I grow my own horse chestnut, but if I had varicose veins, I'd buy a commercial preparation of a standardised extract and use it according to the label directions. Never take fresh horse chestnut internally, because it's poisonous. Commercial preparations, on the other hand, are safe because they have been detoxified.

ONION (*ALLIUM CEPA*). Onions are one of our best sources of quercetin, a flavonoid that has an effect on veins similar to rutin. The greatest concentration of quercetin is found in the brown papery covering that most folks throw away. If you want to extract quercetin from onions, simmer whole ones (with their brown covering) in boiling water for about ½ hour. Then strain out the onions and use the water to make soup. Remove and discard the onions' covering. Chop the onions and throw them back in the pot.

PINEAPPLE (*ANANAS COMOSUS*). The area surrounding varicose veins often becomes hard and lumpy. These lumps consist of a protein called fibrin. The walls of healthy veins contain a compound, plasminogen activator, that breaks down fibrin. But when veins become varicose, they lose plasminogen activator. This allows fibrin to get deposited in nearby tissue.

Bromelain, an enzyme in pineapple, helps break down fibrin and smooth out the lumpy skin surrounding varicose veins. It's also a potent anti-inflammatory that helps treat phlebitis, an inflammatory condition that affects leg veins. Specifically, bromelain stimulates the production of an anti-inflammatory compound (prostaglandin-E_1) while inhibiting the production of an inflammatory compound (prostaglandin-E_2).

At one time, scientists believed that bromelain didn't work when taken orally. But recently, I read that about 40 per cent of dietary bromelain is absorbed from the intestine into the bloodstream, meaning that it would reach varicosities.

Phlebitis: Inflammation under the Skin

The word *phlebitis* means inflammation of a vein. The condition usually affects leg veins near the surface of your skin – the same ones that often become varicose. In fact, if you have varicose veins, you're at risk for phlebitis.

Phlebitis usually occurs because of an infection or injury. When a vein becomes inflamed, bloodflow is disrupted, and internal clots may form (a condition called thrombophlebitis).

The symptoms of phlebitis usually include pain, itching, swelling, and tenderness in the area of the vein. You may also feel something like a hard cord under your skin. That's the inflamed vein.

Should a blood clot form, there's a chance that it could break loose and circulate around your body, eventually lodging in a spot where it could cause more serious problems. That's why doctors treat phlebitis aggressively, with antibiotics. In addition, I'd recommend herbs, the same ones that benefit varicosities, to help repair weakened veins.

You can buy supplements of bromelain. Take them according to the package directions. You can also get more of the enzyme just by eating lots of pineapple.

GRAPE SEED (*VITIS VINIFERA*) AND PEANUTS (*ARACHIS HYPOGAEA*). Both grape seed extract and the red papery covering on peanuts are well-endowed with oligomeric procyanidins, or OPCs. These compounds help hold vein tissue together, reducing the fragility and permeability that contribute to varicosities.

Even though OPCs are relative newcomers to the herbal medicine scene, they've been studied extensively. The research indicates that the compounds help strengthen veins and relieve the pain, itching, and swelling associated with varicose veins. In one study, a daily dose of 150 milligrams of OPCs reduced leg discomfort significantly.

I grow my own grapes, and I juice the seeds right along with the fruit. So I get grape juice and grape seed extract at the same time. If you want to try grape seed extract, I suggest buying a commercial preparation and using it according to the package directions. As for peanuts, buy the whole nuts, shell them, and eat the papery covering along with the nuts.

GOTU KOLA (*CENTELLA ASIATICA*). Extracts that contain gotu kola's active compounds – triterpenes, asiatic acid, madecassic acid, and asiaticoside – help strengthen veins. They've also been proven effective in treating poor circulation in the lower limbs (venous insufficiency), which contributes to varicose veins, phlebitis, and swelling of the ankles and feet.

In one study, French researchers gave 94 people with venous insufficiency a placebo or gotu kola extract (either 60 milligrams or 120 milligrams per day). Two months later, the group taking the placebo showed no change in leg swelling or discomfort. But both groups taking the herb showed improvement, with those taking the larger dose experiencing the greatest benefit.

To treat varicose veins, many naturopaths recommend taking 30 milligrams of gotu kola extract three times a day.

GINKGO (*GINKGO BILOBA*). Because ginkgo improves blood circulation throughout the body, I bet that it would help treat varicose veins. Even if you have a ginkgo tree in your yard, as I do, the active compounds (called ginkgolides) in teas made from ginkgo leaves are too dilute to be of any benefit. I suggest buying a commercial ginkgo preparation and using it according to the label directions.

HYSSOP (*HYSSOPUS OFFICINALIS*). Of the herbs that I'm familiar with, hyssop is the best source of diosmin, a compound that has effects similar to rutin. It not only strengthens veins, it also has anti-inflammatory properties, suggesting that it may be good for varicosities and phlebitis.

Hyssop can be as much as 6 per cent diosmin (dry weight). So you'd need only about 5 grams (2 teaspoons) of the herb to get the 300 milligrams of the compound considered necessary to experience vein-strengthening effects. You can prepare hyssop as a tea. Just put your 2 teaspoons of herb in a cup of freshly boiled water, let it steep for 10 minutes, then strain out the plant material. You can drink up to three cups of the tea a day.

I grow my own hyssop. It's an attractive plant, just like its relatives, the mints.

Dr Duke's Anti-Ageing Elixir

Vein-Ade

If I ever develop serious varicose veins, I'll treat them with this tonic. It contains good amounts of diosmin (from hyssop) and rutin (from eucalyptus), two of the most powerful vein-strengthening compounds.

WHAT YOU NEED

2–6 teaspoons hyssop
1 teaspoon eucalyptus
1 teaspoon grated citrus peel
1 teaspoon chopped rhubarb stalks
3 cups water
Lemon
A natural sweetener (optional)

WHAT TO DO

In a bowl or saucepan, combine the hyssop, eucalyptus, citrus peel, and rhubarb. Cover with the freshly boiled water. Steep for 10 minutes, then strain. Flavour with the lemon and sweetener, if you wish. Drink up to three cups a day, refrigerating any left over for later use.

BUTCHER'S BROOM (*RUSCUS ACULEATUS*). Butcher's broom might help sweep away varicose veins and phlebitis, thanks to the ruscogenin and neo-ruscogenin that it contains. Both of these compounds are anti-inflammatory and help strengthen veins.

Butcher's broom has a long history as a treatment for varicose veins and haemorrhoids. In one study, 40 people with venous insufficiency of the lower leg took a formula made with butcher's broom (16.5 milligrams), vitamin C (50 milligrams), and hesperidin, a compound in hyssop, rosemary, and citrus peel (75 milligrams). The study participants reported relief from leg pain, swelling, heaviness, itching, and tingling.

If you want to try butcher's broom, I suggest buying an extract standardised for ruscogenin content. The typical recommendation is 50 to 100 milligrams of ruscogenins a day, taken as three separate doses.

YELLOW SWEET CLOVER (*MELILOTUS OFFICINALIS*). Also known as melilot, yellow sweet clover is a widely dispersed leguminous weed that contains coumarin, a compound that helps strengthen veins. Ten grams (about 5 teaspoons) of dried herb delivers about 20 milligrams of coumarin. That ought to be enough to help varicose veins. I sometimes mix the dried herb into other teas; you may want to do the same.

Commission E endorses yellow sweet clover for venous insufficiency and for pain, swelling, heaviness, itching, and nighttime cramping in the legs. The commission also approves the herb for thrombophlebitis, a serious form of phlebitis characterised by the development of a blood clot.

Some preliminary research has linked yellow sweet clover to liver damage. While more research is needed, I'd advise against taking the herb in amounts above the recommended dosage or for long periods of time.

LEMON (*CITRUS LIMON*). If you brew herbal teas to treat your varicose veins, I recommend adding some grated lemon peel. Besides adding flavour, the bioflavonoids in the peel help strengthen blood vessels.

WITCH HAZEL (*HAMAMELIS VIRGINIANA*). Commission E approves the topical application of witch hazel as a treatment for haemorrhoids. Since haemorrhoids are varicosities, I suspect that the herb might benefit varicose leg veins as well.

Witch hazel is cooling and astringent, meaning that it helps draw tissue together. This action can alleviate the symptoms of varicose veins. The easiest way to use the herb is to buy commercial witch hazel water (it's sold in pharmacies) and apply it with a clean cloth.

Consumer's Guide *to* Safe Self-Care

Herbs and Their Compounds

While herbal remedies are generally safe for self-care and cause few, if any, side effects, herbalists are quick to caution that botanical medicines should be used cautiously – and knowledgeably.

First and foremost, if you are under a doctor's care for any health condition or are taking any medication, do not use any herb or alter your treatment regime without consulting your doctor. If you are pregnant, do not self-treat with any natural remedy without the consent of your obstetrician or midwife. The same applies to nursing mothers and women trying to conceive.

Some herbs may cause adverse reactions in people who are allergy-prone, have a major health condition, or are using prescription drugs. Like any medicine, herbs can also have harmful effects if they're taken for too long or in too large amounts or if they're used improperly.

The safety guidelines presented in the chart below are based on the American Herbal Products Association's *Botanical Safety Handbook* – a recognised source of herb safety information – and on the advice of experienced herbal healers. The chart is intended to help you make informed decisions when incorporating herbs into your self-care regime. It covers only the herb or herbal compounds discussed in this book for which potential side effects, interactions, or both have been identified.

The guidelines themselves apply only to adults and usually refer to internal use. Be aware that some herbs may cause a skin reaction when applied topically. If you're trying a herb topically for the first time, your best bet is to do a patch test. Apply a small amount to your skin and monitor the area for 24 hours. If you notice any redness or a rash, discontinue use.

HERB OR COMPOUND	SAFETY GUIDELINES AND POSSIBLE SIDE EFFECTS
Alfalfa	Contains a compound called canavanine that has been linked to systemic lupus erythematosus, gastrointestinal problems, and skin reactions. It may also increase the risk of gout. Before taking medicinal amounts of alfalfa, check with a qualified herbal practitioner or a doctor who is knowledgeable in herbal medicine.
Aloe	Do not apply the gel to any surgical incision; it may delay healing. Do not ingest the dried leaf gel, as it is a habit-forming laxative.
American ginseng	Should not be taken by people with high blood pressure. May cause irritability if used in combination with caffeine or other stimulants.
Angelica	Use sparingly and only for short periods of time. Increases sun sensitivity.
Arnica	Do not apply to broken or abraded skin.
Ashwagandha	Do not use in combination with barbiturates, because it may intensify their effects.
Asian ginseng	Should not be taken by people with high blood pressure. May cause irritability if used in combination with caffeine or other stimulants.
Birch bark	Do not use if you need to avoid aspirin. Birch bark's active ingredient, salicin, is related to aspirin.
Black cohosh	Do not use if you have heart disease or if you're taking medication for high blood pressure. Otherwise, do not take black cohosh for more than 6 months.
Black tea	Not recommended for excessive or long-term use because of its stimulant effects on the nervous system.
Blessed thistle	May irritate the stomach and cause vomiting if taken in large doses.
Boneset	May cause adverse reactions in those with allergies or sensitivities, especially to camomile, feverfew, ragwort or other members of the daisy family. Can cause vomiting and severe diarrhoea in large doses.
Buchu	Do not use if you have kidney disease.
California poppy	Do not use in combination with antidepressant MAO inhibitors such as phenelzine sulphate (Nardil) and tranylcypromine (Parnate) unless under medical supervision.

HERB OR COMPOUND	SAFETY GUIDELINES AND POSSIBLE SIDE EFFECTS
Camomile	In rare instances, can cause an allergic reaction when ingested. People allergic to closely related plants such as ragwort, asters, and chrysanthemums should drink the tea with caution.
Cascara sagrada	Do not use if you have any intestinal inflammation, intestinal obstruction, or abdominal pain. Otherwise, discontinue treatment after 14 days, as cascara sagrada can cause laxative dependency and diarrhoea.
Castor	Do not use castor oil internally if you have intestinal obstruction or abdominal pain. Otherwise, discontinue treatment after 10 days.
Cat's claw	Do not use if you have haemophilia. Side effects include headache, stomach ache and difficulty breathing.
Cayenne	*See* Chilli pepper
Celery seed	Therapeutic doses should be taken cautiously by those with kidney disorders. Can cause sun sensitivity. Considered safe when used as a spice.
Chasteberry	May counteract the effectiveness of birth control pills. Can elevate blood pressure. Read product labels carefully if you have high blood pressure.
Chilli pepper	Internally, may irritate the gastrointestinal tract if taken on an empty stomach. Externally, should not be used near the eyes or on injured skin.
Comfrey	For external use only. Do not apply to deep or infected wounds; it can cause the surface of the skin to mend too quickly, preventing the healing of underlying tissue.
Dandelion	If you have gallbladder disease, consult your doctor before taking dandelion root preparations. Do not use dandelion as a weight-loss aid.
Devil's claw	If you have gallstones, consult your doctor before taking. Do not use if you have gastric or duodenal ulcers.
Dill seed	Contains high levels of sodium; should not be taken by anyone who's following a sodium-restricted diet. Should also be avoided by people who are allergic or sensitive to spices, since it's likely to cause an adverse reaction.
Echinacea	Do not use if you're allergic to closely related plants such ragwort, asters, and chrysanthemums. Do not use if you have tuberculosis or an autoimmune

HERB OR COMPOUND	SAFETY GUIDELINES AND POSSIBLE SIDE EFFECTS
	condition such as lupus or multiple sclerosis, as echinacea stimulates the immune system.
Elderberry	The seeds, bark, leaves, and unripe fruit can cause vomiting or severe diarrhoea.
Ephedra	Do not take more than 8 milligrams in a single dose. Avoid ephedra products that contain caffeine, and steer clear of foods that contain caffeine while using ephedra. People who have high blood pressure, heart problems, diabetes, prostate problems, glaucoma, or thyroid disease or who are taking medication for asthma should not use ephedra at all. If you must take the herb for more than 7 days, do so only under the close supervision of a doctor who can monitor your vital signs and ephedra's effects on any medications you may be using.
Eucalyptus	Do not use if you have an inflammatory disease of the bile ducts or gastrointestinal tract or severe liver disease. May cause nausea, vomiting, and diarrhoea in doses above 4 grams a day.
Fennel	Do not use medicinally for more than 6 weeks unless under medical supervision.
Feverfew	If chewed, the fresh leaves can cause mouth sores in some people.
Flaxseed	Do not use if you have a bowel obstruction. Otherwise, take with at least 240 ml (8 fl oz) of water.
Garlic	Do not use if you are taking anticoagulants (blood thinners) or if you're about to have surgery, as garlic thins the blood and may increase bleeding. Do not use if you are taking drugs to regulate your blood sugar.
Gentian	May cause nausea and vomiting if taken in large doses. Do not use if you have high blood pressure, gastric or duodenal ulcers, or gastric irritation and inflammation.
Ginger	If you have gallstones, do not take therapeutic amounts of the dried root or powder without medical supervision. May increase bile secretion.
Ginkgo	Do not use in combination with antidepressant MAO inhibitors such as phenelzine sulphate (Nardil) or tranylcypromine (Parnate), with aspirin or other nonsteroidal anti-inflammatory medications, or with blood-thinning

HERB OR COMPOUND	SAFETY GUIDELINES AND POSSIBLE SIDE EFFECTS
	medications such as warfarin. In doses above 240 milligrams a day, the concentrated extract can cause dermatitis, diarrhoea, and vomiting.
Ginseng	Do not use if you have high blood pressure. May cause irritability if taken in combination with caffeine or other stimulants.
Goldenseal	Do not use internally if you have high blood pressure.
Guarana	Contains twice as much caffeine as coffee; can overstimulate the nervous system when used in excessive amounts for a long period of time. Can also irritate the gastrointestinal tract.
Gurmar	If you have diabetes, do not use without medical supervision. May affect blood sugar levels.
Hawthorn	If you have a cardiovascular condition, do not take hawthorn regularly for more than a few weeks without medical supervision. Your doctor may need to reduce your dosages of other medications, such as blood pressure drugs. Likewise, if you have low blood pressure caused by heart valve problems, do not take hawthorn without medical supervision.
Hop	Do not use if you're prone to depression. In rare instances, hop can cause a skin rash, so handle the fresh and dried forms carefully.
Horse chestnut	May interfere with the action of other drugs, especially blood thinners such as warfarin. May irritate the gastrointestinal tract.
Horseradish	Do not take therapeutically if you have stomach inflammation or a kidney disorder. Safe when used as a spice.
Horsetail	Do not use the tincture if you have heart or kidney problems. May cause a thiamin deficiency. Do not take the powdered extract for prolonged periods or in a dosage of more than 2 grams per day.
Kaffir potato	May intensify the effects of asthma or high blood pressure medications, with negative results. Do not use without medical supervision.
Kelp	If you have high blood pressure or heart problems, use no more than once a day. Do not use at all if you have

HERB OR COMPOUND	SAFETY GUIDELINES AND POSSIBLE SIDE EFFECTS
	hyperthyroidism. Otherwise, take with adequate liquid. Long-term treatment with kelp is not recommended.
Licorice	Do not use if you have diabetes, high blood pressure, liver or kidney disorders, or low potassium levels. Otherwise, do not use daily for more than 6 weeks; overuse can lead to water retention, high blood pressure caused by potassium loss, or impaired heart and kidney function.
Lomatium	May cause a skin rash when taken internally.
Lovage	Do not use therapeutically if you have kidney disease.
Marshmallow	If taken in combination with medications, may slow their absorption.
Meadowsweet	Do not use if you need to avoid aspirin; meadowsweet's active constituent, salicin, is related to aspirin.
Myrrh	Can cause diarrhoea and irritate the kidneys. Do not use if you have any type of uterine bleeding.
Oak bark	Do not use externally if skin is damaged.
Psyllium seed	Do not use if you have a bowel obstruction. Otherwise, take with at least 240 ml (8 fl oz) of water at least 1 hour after other medications.
Pygeum	Before using to treat an enlarged prostate, consult your doctor for proper diagnosis and monitoring.
Rhubarb	Do not use if you have an intestinal obstruction, abdominal pain of unknown origin, or any inflammatory condition of the intestines such as appendicitis, colitis, or irritable bowel syndrome. Use with caution if you have a history of kidney stones. Otherwise, discontinue treatment after 10 days.
Rosemary	In therapeutic amounts, may cause excessive menstrual bleeding. Considered safe when used as a spice.
Sage	In therapeutic amounts, can increase the sedative side effects of medications. Do not take if you're hypoglycaemic or undergoing anticonvulsant therapy. Considered safe when used as a spice.
St. John's wort	Do not use in combination with antidepressants or other prescription medication without medical supervision. May cause sun sensitivity.

HERB OR COMPOUND	SAFETY GUIDELINES AND POSSIBLE SIDE EFFECTS
Saw palmetto	Before using to treat an enlarged prostate, consult your doctor for proper diagnosis and monitoring.
Senna	Do not use if you have a bowel obstruction. Otherwise, take with at least 240 ml (8 fl oz) of water at least 1 hour after other medications.
Sorrel	Do not use without medical supervision if you have a history of kidney stones. Sorrel contains oxalates and tannins that may adversely affect this condition.
Stinging nettle	May aggravate allergy symptoms in people who have them. Take only one dose a day for the first few days.
Turmeric	Do not use therapeutically if you have excessive stomach acid, ulcers, gallstones, or a bile duct obstruction.
Uva-ursi	Do not use for more than 2 weeks without medical supervision. Do not use at all if you have kidney disease, because uva-ursi contains compounds called tannins that may cause further kidney damage. Tannins can also irritate the stomach. Do not take uva-ursi as a weight-loss aid.
Valerian	Do not use in combination with sleep-enhancing or mood-regulating medications, because it may intensify their effects. May cause heart palpitations and nervousness in those who are sensitive to it. If such stimulant action occurs, discontinue use.
Wild cherry bark	Do not exceed recommended dose. Not appropriate for long-term use.
Willow	Do not use if you need to avoid aspirin, especially if you are taking blood-thinning medication such as warfarin; willow's active ingredient is related to aspirin. The herb may interact with barbiturates or sedatives such as aprobarbital (Amytal) or alprazolam (Xanax), and it can cause stomach irritation when taken with alcohol.
Yohimbe	Do not use without medical supervision.

Essential Oils

Essential oils are inhaled or applied topically to the skin. With few exceptions, they're never taken internally.

Of the most common essential oils, lavender, tea tree, lemon, jasmine, and rose can be used undiluted. The rest should be diluted in a carrier base – which can be an oil (such as almond), a cream, or a gel – before being applied to the skin.

Many essential oils may cause irritation or allergic reactions in people with sensitive skin. Before applying any new oil to the skin, always do a patch test. Put a few drops on the back of your wrist. Wait for an hour or more. If any irritation or redness occurs, wash the area with cold water. In the future, use half of the amount of oil or avoid the oil altogether.

Do not use essential oils at home for serious medical problems. During pregnancy, do not use essential oils unless they're approved by your doctor. Store essential oils in dark bottles, away from light and heat and out of the reach of children and pets.

ESSENTIAL OIL	SAFETY GUIDELINES AND POSSIBLE SIDE EFFECTS
Bay	Do not use for more than 2 weeks without the guidance of a qualified practitioner. May cause lethargy and unconsciousness.
Bergamot	Except for bergapten-free products, can cause sun sensitivity. Avoid direct sunlight for duration of use.
Black pepper	Do not add more than 3 drops to bathwater. Do not use in combination with homeopathic remedies.
Clove	Do not add more than 3 drops to bathwater. Okay to apply undiluted for tooth pain. Do not use for more than 2 weeks without the guidance of a qualified practitioner because of potential toxicity.
Eucalyptus	Do not add more than 3 drops to bathwater. Do not use in combination with homeopathic remedies. Okay to apply undiluted for tooth pain. Do not use for more than 2 weeks without the guidance of a qualified practitioner.
Juniper	Do not use if you have kidney disease. Otherwise, do not use for more than 2 weeks without the guidance of a qualified practitioner because of potential toxicity.
Lemon verbena	Can cause sun sensitivity; avoid direct sunlight for duration of use.
Myrrh	Do not use for more than 2 weeks without the guidance of a qualified practitioner because of potential toxicity.
Nutmeg	Inhale with caution, as it can cause nausea. Do not use for more than 2 weeks without the guidance of a qualified practitioner because of potential toxicity.
Peppermint	Externally, do not apply near your eyes. Internally, do not use without medical supervision if you have gallbladder or liver disease. May cause stomach upset in those who are sensitive to it. Do not use in combination with homeopathic remedies.
Rosemary	Do not use if you have high blood pressure. Do not use if you have epilepsy, because of the essential oil's powerful effects on the nervous system.
Thyme	Do not use if you have high blood pressure. May irritate the skin when applied in high concentrations. If you experience an adverse reaction, dilute the essential oil with additional carrier base. Do not add more than 3 drops of the oil to bathwater.

Vitamins, Minerals, and Other Supplements

Although side effects and interactions while using vitamins, minerals, and other supplements are rare, they do occur. This guide is designed to help you use certain supplements discussed in this book safely and effectively.

The doses mentioned below are not recommendations; rather, they reflect the levels at which harmful side effects can occur. Some people may experience problems at significantly lower doses.

For best absorption and minimal stomach irritation, be sure to take your supplements with a meal. If you have a serious chronic illness that requires continual medical supervision, always consult your doctor before self-treating. Even if you're perfectly healthy, tell your doctor which supplements you're taking. This way, if you need medication for any reason, your doctor can factor in your supplements and avoid dangerous interactions. If you are pregnant, nursing, or attempting to conceive, do not take any supplement without first consulting your doctor.

SUPPLEMENT	SAFETY GUIDELINES AND POSSIBLE SIDE EFFECTS
Beta-carotene	Doses above 25,000 IU a day seem to have no benefit and should be taken only under medical supervision.
Bromelain	May cause nausea, vomiting, diarrhoea, skin rash, and heavy menstrual bleeding; may increase the risk of bleeding in people who are taking aspirin or anti-coagulants (blood thinners). Do not use bromelain if you are allergic to pineapple.
Calcium	Doses above 2,500 mg a day must be taken under medical supervision. Some natural sources of calcium, such as bonemeal and dolomite, may be contaminated with lead.
Carnitine (also known as L-carnitine or acetyl L-carnitine)	Doses above 2 g a day may cause mild diarrhoea.
Coenzyme Q_{10}	If you are taking the blood thinner warfarin, discuss supplementation with your doctor. On rare occasions, coenzyme Q_{10} may reduce warfarin's effectiveness. Supplementation should be monitored by a knowledgeable naturopath or doctor if it lasts for more than 20 days at levels of 120 mg per day or higher. Side effects are rare but may include heartburn, nausea and stomach ache. These can be prevented by taking the supplement with a meal.
Curcumin	May cause heartburn in some people.
Fish oil	Increases the duration of bleeding, possibly resulting in nosebleeds and easy bruising. May also cause upset stomach. Do not take fish oil supplements if you have a bleeding disorder or uncontrolled high blood pressure, if you are on anticoagulants (blood thinners) or use aspirin regularly, or if you're allergic to any kind of fish. Be sure to buy fish oil, not fish-liver oil (it is high in vitamins A and D and is toxic in large amounts). People with diabetes should not take fish oil because of its high fat content.
Folic acid	Doses above 1,000 mcg a day must be taken only under medical supervision. Excess folic acid can cause progressive nerve damage in people with vitamin B_{12} deficiencies. Doses as low as 400 mcg a day can mask a B_{12} deficiency.
Glucosamine	May cause upset stomach, heartburn, or diarrhoea.

SUPPLEMENT	SAFETY GUIDELINES AND POSSIBLE SIDE EFFECTS
Hydrochloric acid	Use only under the care of a qualified practitioner.
Magnesium	If you have heart or kidney problems, check with your doctor before beginning supplementation in any amount. Doses above 350 mg a day can cause diarrhoea in some people.
Niacin	Doses above 35 mg a day should be taken only under medical supervision, as they may cause flushing, itching, and other side effects.
SAM-e (*S-adenosylmethionine*)	May increase blood levels of homocysteine, a significant risk factor for cardiovascular disease.
Selenium	Doses above 200 mcg a day must be taken only under medical supervision, as they may cause hair and nail loss, dizziness, nausea, a garlic odour on the breath and skin, and a metallic taste in the mouth.
Vitamin B_6 (pyridoxine)	Doses above 100 mg a day should be taken only under medical supervision. Such large doses may cause nerve damage, resulting in a tingling sensation in the fingers and toes. Other possible side effects include pain, numbness and weakness in the limbs, depression, and fatigue.
Vitamin C	Doses above 2,000 mg a day can cause diarrhoea in some people. To help maintain levels of vitamin C throughout the day, take half of the recommended dose in the morning and half at night.
Vitamin D	Doses above 1,000 IU a day may cause headache, excessive thirst and loss of appetite. Doses above 2,000 IU (50 mcg) a day must be taken only under medical supervision, as they may cause headache, fatigue, nausea, diarrhoea, and loss of appetite.
Vitamin E	Talk with your doctor before taking amounts above 400 IU a day. One study involving low-dose vitamin E supplements showed increased risk of haemorrhagic stroke. Because vitamin E acts like a blood thinner, consult your doctor before taking supplements in any amount if you are already using aspirin or a blood-thinning medication, such as warfarin.
Zinc	Daily doses of more than 30 mg may cause nausea and vomiting. When levels of zinc are elevated, the absorption of copper can become impaired.

References

Through my years of studying medicinal plants, I've amassed quite a collection of books, which I refer to often in my research and writing. The following list is by no means complete, but it highlights some of my personal favourites. I recommend them if you want to learn more about the herbs discussed in this book or about herbal and alternative medicine in general.

Some of the references are older and may be out of print, but if you're in luck, your local library will have copies. Others are more for the professional than the layperson, depending on your level of interest. I've also included several of my own books, in case you'd like to see more of my work.

Beyond Aspirin by Thomas M. Newmark and Paul Schulick (Prescott, Ariz.: Hohm Press, 2000).

Blended Medicine: The Best Choices in Healing by Michael Castleman (Emmaus, Pa.: Rodale Inc., 1999).

CRC Handbook of Medicinal Herbs by James A. Duke (Boca Raton, Fla.: CRC Press, 1985).

Encyclopedia of Common Natural Ingredients Used in Food, Drugs, and Cosmetics, 2nd ed., by Albert Y. Leung and Steven Foster (New York: John Wiley and Sons, 1995).

A Field Guide to Medicinal Plants and Herbs of Eastern and Central North America (Peterson Field Guides) by Steven Foster and James A. Duke (Boston: Houghton Mifflin, 2000).

The Green Pharmacy by James A. Duke (Emmaus, Pa.: Rodale Inc., 1997).

The Green Pharmacy Herbal Handbook by James A. Duke

(London.: Rodale/Pan Macmillan, 2003).

Herbal Drugs and Phytopharmaceuticals, English translation, edited by Norman Grainger Bisset (Boca Raton, Fla.: CRC Press, 1994).

The Herbal Drugstore by Linda B. White and Steven Foster, et al. (Emmaus, Pa.: Rodale Inc., 2000).

Herbal Medicine: Expanded Commission E Monographs by Mark Blumenthal, Alicia Goldberg, and J. Brinckmann (Newton, Mass.: Integrative Medicine Communications, 2000).

Herbal Medicines: A Guide for Health-Care Professionals by Carol A. Newall, Linda A. Anderson, and J. D. Phillipson (London: The Pharmaceutical Press, 1996).

Herbal Prescriptions for Better Health by Donald J. Brown (Roseville, Calif.: Prima Health, 2000).

Medical Botany by Walter H. Lewis and P. F. Elvin-Lewis (New York: John Wiley and Sons, 1977).

Native American Ethnobotany by Daniel E. Moerman (Portland, Ore.: Timber Press, 1998).

The New Healing Herbs by Michael Castleman (Emmaus, Pa.: Rodale Inc., 2001).

Physicians Desk Reference for Herbal Medicines, 2nd ed., by J. Gruenwald, et al. (Montvale, N.J.: Medical Economics Company, 2000).

Potter's New Cyclopaedia of Botanical Drugs and Preparations, revised ed., by R. C. Wren (Essex: C. W. Daniel Co. Ltd., 1989).

Principles and Practice of Phytotherapy by Simon Mills and Kerry Bone (Edinburgh: Churchill Livingstone, 1999).

Rational Phytotherapy: A Physician's Guide to Herbal Medicine, 3rd ed., by Volker Schulz, Hansel Rudolf, and Varro E. Tyler (Heidelberg: Springer Verlag, 1998).

Tyler's Herbs of Choice by James E. Robbers and Varro E. Tyler (Binghamton, N.Y.: Hawthorn Herbal Press, 1999).

Resources

For additional information on herbal medicine and other alternative therapies, you may want to contact one of the following organisations:

UK

Association of General Practitioners of Natural Medicine
38 Nigel House
Portpool Lane
London ECIN 7UR
Tel: 020 7405 2781
Fax: 020 7430 1173

The Association of Natural Medicine
19a Collingwood Road
Witham
Essex CM8 2DY
Tel: 01367 502 762
www.anm.org.uk
info@naturalmedicine.fsnet.co.uk

The British Complementary Medicine Association
PO Box 5122
Bournemouth
BH8 0WG
Tel: 0845 345 5977
www.bcma.co.uk
web@bcma.co.uk

The British Naturopathic Association
Goswell House
2 Goswell Road
Street
Somerset BA16 0JG
Tel: 08707 456 984
Fax: 08707 456 985
www.naturopaths.org.uk
admin@naturopaths.org.uk

Federation of Holistic Therapists
3rd Floor, Eastleigh House
Upper Market Street
Eastleigh SO50 9FD
Tel: 023 8048 8900
Fax: 023 8048 8970
www.fht.org.uk
info@fht.org.uk

The Institute for Complementary Medicine
ICM PO Box 194
London SE16 7QZ
Tel: 020 7237 5165
Fax: 020 7237 5175
www.icmedicine.co.uk
icm@icmedicine.co.uk

International Federation of Aromatherapists
182 Chiswick High Road
London W4 1PP
Tel: 020 8742 2605
www.ifaroma.org
office@ifaroma.org

National Institute of Medical Herbalists
56 Longbrook Street
Exeter
Devon EX4 6Ah
Tel: 01392 426 022
Fax: 01392 498 963
www.nimh.org.uk
nimh@exeteruk.freeserve.co.uk

Natural Medicines Society
PO Box 205
Hampton
Middlesex
TW12 3WP
Tel: 0870 2404784
www.the-nms.org.uk
enquiries@the-nms.org.uk

Register of Chinese Herbal Medicine
PO Box 400
Wembley
Middlesex HA9 9NZ
www.rchm.co.uk

AUSTRALIA

The Australian Complementary Health Association
247 Flinders Lane
Melbourne
Victoria 3000
Tel: 03 9650 5327
Fax: 03 9650 8404
www.diversity.org.au
diversity@diversity.org.au

Australian Natural Therapists Association Ltd
PO Box 856
Caloundra
QLD 4551
Tel: 07 5491 9850
Fax: 07 5491 5679
www.anta.com.au

Australian Naturopathic Practitioners Association
1st Floor
609 Camberwell Road
Camberwell, 3124
Tel: 03 9889 0334
Fax: 03 9889 0334
www.anpa.asn.au
admin@anpa.asn.au

National Herbalists Association of Australia
13 Breillat Street
Annandale
NSW 2038
Tel: 02 9555 8885
Fax: 02 9555 8884
www.nhaa.org.au
nhaa@nhaa.org.au

NEW ZEALAND

New Zealand Association of Medical Herbalists
PO Box 15313
Tauranga
www.nzamh.org.nz

New Zealand Charter of Health Practitioners Inc.
Private Box 302
305 North Harbour
Auckland
Tel: 649 414 5501
Fax: 649 414 5503
www.healthcharter.org.nz
email@healthcharter.co.nz

NZ Society of Naturopaths Inc
PO Box 90–170
Auckland Central Post Office
Auckland
www.naturopath.org.nz

SUPPLIERS OF HERBAL PRODUCTS

UK

Biocare Limited
Lakeside
180 Lifford Lane
Kings Norton
Birmingham B30 NU
Tel: 0121 433 3727
Fax: 0121 433 3879
www.biocare.co.uk
biocare@biocare.co.uk

Essential Oils Direct
PO Box 161
Oldham
OL2 6FA
Tel: 0161 633 3952
Fax: 0161 652 9693
www.essentialoilsdirect.co.uk
eodteam@essentialoilsdirect.co.uk

Greenhill Direct
11 The Paddocks
Totnes Industrial Park
Totnes
Devon T19 5XT
Tel: 01803 868 733
Fax: 01803 864 948
www.greenlife.co.uk
enquiries@greenlife.co.uk

Health4All Limited
2 Meadoway
Steeple Claydon
Buckingham
MK18 2PA
Tel: 01494 792 789
Freephone (within UK):
0800 028 1421
Fax: 0196 738 260
www.health4all.co.uk
info@health4all.co.uk

The Herbal Factory
Unit 22/26
Addington Business Centre
Vulcan Way
Croydon
Tel: 01689 843 733
Freephone (within UK):
080 800 43722
Fax: 01689 843 701
www.herbal-factory.mcmail.com
hvitamed@aol.com

Herbs Hands Healing
Station Warehouse
Station Road
Pulham Market
Norfolk IP214XF
Tel (Local rate in UK):
01379 608 201/
0845 345 3727
www.herbshandshealing.co.uk
info@herbshandshealing.co.uk

AUSTRALIA

Hillside Herbal Products
110 Cradoc Hill Road
Cadoc
TAS 7109
Australia
Tel: 03 6266 3790
Fax: 03 6266 3890
www.hillsideherbal.com.au
herbal@hillsideherbal.com.au

Father Nature's Pharmacy Database

Back in 1978, while working for the United States Department of Agriculture (USDA), I started what has become known as the USDA Phytochemical Database. I prefer to call it Father Nature's Pharmacy Database. Currently, it contains information on the medicinal compounds that have been identified in some 3,000 medicinal plants. Of course, that's just a fraction of the 250,000 plant species known worldwide. As scientists expand their study of the therapeutic properties of herbs and foods, the database will continue to grow.

Even though I'm retired, I continue to collect information for the database, and the USDA occasionally updates it. These days, I compile most of my data from the $3,000 worth of journals that I receive each year. I focus my searches on the most promising herbs and foods, though so many exist that I just barely keep up.

I've input much of the database information myself, using my own three-fingered typing. But I've had lots of help over the years, and I want to recognise the people who have contributed to the database's success: Judi DuCellier, who was my secretary when the database launched; Kay Wain, who helped collect the early ethnobotany entries; Stephen Beckstrom-Sternberg, Sue Mustalish, R.N., and Leigh Broadhurst, who developed many of the search queries; Mary Jo Bogenschutz-Godwin, who currently manages the database; and Allan Stoner, Jimmie Mowder, and Ed Bird, who update it.

I'm told that the database draws up to 80 percent of the visitors to the USDA website. I invite you to check it out as well. If you have access to the Internet, go to www.ars-grin.gov/duke. You can search by plant, by ethnobotanical use, or by medicinal compound (chemical). You can also link in to other databases and websites, or send an e-mail to me. I welcome your suggestions and comments.

Index

Underlined page references indicate boxed text and tables.
Bold references indicate illustrations.

A

D

E

F

H

I

Q

R

S

Z

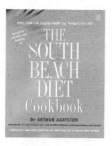

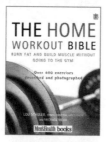

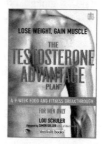

NOTES

NOTES

NOTES

NOTES

NOTES

NOTES

NOTES

NOTES

NOTES

NOTES

NOTES

NOTES

NOTES

NOTES

NOTES

NOTES